WHITE HOUSE STUDIES

# PRESIDENTS AND WAR

# WHITE HOUSE STUDIES

Additional books in this series can be found on Nova's website under the Series tab.

Additional E-books in this series can be found on Nova's website under the E-books tab.

WHITE HOUSE STUDIES

# PRESIDENTS AND WAR

ANTHONY J. EKSTEROWICZ
AND
GLENN P. HASTEDT
EDITORS

Nova Science Publishers, Inc.
*New York*

For permission to use material from this book please contact us:
Telephone 631-231-7269; Fax 631-231-8175
Web Site: http://www.novapublishers.com



**LIBRARY OF CONGRESS CATALOGING-IN-PUBLICATION DATA**
Presidents and war / editors, Anthony J. Eksterowicz and Glenn P. Hastedt.
p. cm.
Includes bibliographical references.
ISBN 978-1-61668-917-9 (hardcover)
1. Presidents--United States--History. 2. War and emergency
powers--United States--History. 3. United States--History, Military. I.
Eksterowicz, Anthony J. II. Hastedt, Glenn P., 1950-
JK558.P745 2010
342.73'062--dc22
2010016727

*Published by Nova Science Publishers, Inc. † New York*

*The authors would like to dedicate this work to the late Professor Harold M. Barger of Trinity University in San Antonio, Texas. His friendship and encouragement over the years was much appreciated. He was the consumate gentleman and scholar, well traveled and sophisticated. We will miss him dearly.*

# CONTENTS

# ACKNOWLEDGEMENTS

The authors wish to thank the editorial department at Nova Science Publishers for their help and support on this project. We especially would like to thank Ms. Donna Dennis for her tireless efforts in bringing this work to successful completion.

# INTRODUCTION

One of the key issues facing our republic in this century is the exerscise of presidential war powers. The constitutional structure which gives the Congress responsibility for dedclaring war is being challenged and some would argue usurped by a succession of modern, aggressive commander-in-chief presidents.The authors in this volume examine many aspects of this problem and place it in historical context. Both pre and post modern presidents are subject to their analytical insights. One thing is clear, a return to the original constitutional order will take an enormous effort on the part of our leaders and their people. However, without such an effort the fate of the republic would indeed seem bleak.

*Ryan Staude* begins by detailing President Washington's efforts to build and maintain a professional army. Washington faced objections from Congress to this initiative. The Congress demanded a citizen-soldier type of army. The executive/legislative struggle, at its heart, was one concerning which branch of government would control such a force. In the end, Washington's views were triumphant. This victory has had tremendous implications for executive/legislative relations until today. Now a president had at his disposal a professional fighting force that was bound to grow and multiply.

*Craig L. Symonds* examines President Jefferson's problem with the Barbary Pirates. He notes that this was America's first war against terrorism. It triggered a national debate over how best to deal with this problem. As such it was America's first policy discussion concerning counter-terrorism.

*Eksterowicz and Hastedt* attempt to define the difference between wars of choice and wars of necessity and place them on a continuum. They then examine President Madison and the War of 1812 and President George W. Bush and the Iraq War to ascertain the effect of wars of choice on presidential legacies. They find that the more presidents engage in wars of choice the more trouble there will be for their legacy absent other redeeming accomplishments.

Much has been said about Lincolon's fitness to serve as commander-in-chief and his rather minimal military experiences prior to his presidency. However, as *Frank J. Williams* notes Lincoln's wartime presidency benefited in many ways from his military service, regardless of its length.

President George W. Bush touched off a national debate concerning the use of military commissions after the 9/11 attacks. *Joseph R. Thysell, Jr.* explores President Lincoln's use of military commissions and their effect upon the law and constitution.

*Jeffrey Bloodworth* assesses the impact of the Spanish American War on the principle of American isolationism. He challenges the notion that the nineteenth century was strong on American isolationism. He argues that this period may be more properly characterized as "individual internationalism" and "governmental detachment." In fact, international humanitarianism began in the American midwest. It was present in President McKinley's desires to go to war with Spain. It was also on the rise in the nineteenth century.

*Brent Strathman* examines the role of presidential military advisors. He notes that the president sets the tone for his/her advisors. A president tries to avoid bias and inject the foreign policymaking system with trust. The president's management of trust has an enormous impact upon his advisors and the decision making system. Strathman uses a case study of the Spanish American War to illustrate his points.

As the United States became a more influential actor in international relations at the dawn of the twentieth century, there was a change in the nation's foreign policy regime. *Tom Lansford* traces the development of the new political regime that accompanied the increased American presence on the world stage during the administration of Theodore Roosevelt. His essay begins with an examination of the role and influence of domestic political regimes. It then focuses on the role of Roosevelt in foreign policy regime construction and the broader implications of presidential power on foreign policy.

With the terrorist attacks of September 11, 2001, some analysts characterized the United States as entering upon an entirely new situation in foreign and defense policy, with supposedly unprecedented implications for the presidency or the U.S. Navy. But as *George H. Quester* notes, there are some close analogs in the past debates about whether the United States should invest in a powerful navy, especially with the American 1917 entry into World War I, preceded by a 1916 decision to build a navy second to none.

*David T. Leary* notes the importance of Franklin D. Roosevelt's first trip to the West Coast in April of 1914. Major stops included Los Angeles, San Diego, San Francisco and Seattle. The things FDR said and did along the way provide insights into his future presidency. This is especially the case with Mexico and his belief in the importance of naval bases.

*John Schussler* argues that because the Soviet Union along with North Korea were aggressors in precipitating the Korean War, President Truman was able to conduct the Cold War honestly and with public and congressional support. This is largely due to the fact that the United States absorbed the first blow. This analysis sheds new light on the war of choice or necessity continuum as it applies to Korea.

*Nicole Anslover* examines the role of continuity in the decisions that Lyndon Johnson made with respect to Vietnam. The author demonstrates that Johnson was well aware of the need for continuity in policy and documents the lengths that President Johnson would go to achieve it. He was influenced by public opinion in favor of such continuity. His own insecurities and the advice from his advisors also influenced him to seek what some might consider the safety of continuity.

*Lawrence J. McAndrews* explores the interesting relationship between President Johnson and Pope Paul VI concerning Vietnam War policy. The author discusses the splits within the Catholic Church that confronted the Pope in his attempts to reach peace. On the other hand, President Johnson sought refuge within the Church from a complicated and complex world that would eventually overwhelm both of them.

*Bernd Kaussler* examines President Reagan's role in the Iran/Iraq War of the 1980s. He finds that President Reagan was affected by a deep mistrust of and hostility to the past Iranian hostage regime. His support of Iraq and the actual involvement of U.S. forces against Iran is a testament to this fact. Kaussler also assesses the diplomatic impact of this policy to the current environment in the area.

*Martin S. Sheffer* argues for the use of prerogative power by the president during a dire emergency. However this power is limited by the actual emergency itself. The exercise of extraordinary power ends when the level of the emergency sufficiently lessens or other governmental institutions become capable of resuming power. Sheffer then considers the "Authorization for Use of Military Force" in the Bush Administration and its impact upon executive/congressional relations.

*James K. Oliver* reviews the contemporary war powers relationship between the president and Congress. He considers the recommendations of the National War Powers Commission in this light. His analysis focuses on the post Cold War era of presidential primacy and how this challenges Madison's notions of constitutionalism. He assesses the question of Madisonian relevance in contemporary times.

The authors close this anthology with *President Barack Obama's* Afghanistan address at the U.S. Military Academy at West Point. President Obama campaigned on the necessity of fighting and winning the war in Afghanistan. Only time will tell if his surge will accomplish U.S. objectives.

In: Presidents and War
Editors: A. Eksterowicz and G. Hastedt, pp. 1-15
ISBN 978-1-61668-917-9


*Chapter 1*

# FORGING THE EAGLE'S SWORD: PRESIDENT WASHINGTON, THE CONGRESS AND THE ARMY

***Ryan Staude***

## INTRODUCTION

From 1784 to 1798 the American army never numbered more than 3,000 men. In theory it was a professional army, but in practice it was nothing more than a frontier constabulary. However, in the first half of the 1790s the army was at the center of a debate between President George Washington and Congress. The contest centered on which branch of government would exercise greater control over the nation's military policy. The resolution to the debate set the precedent for future civilian control over the military, and more importantly, it decided how the army would be used to pacify the natives in the Northwest Territory.

This essay examines the struggle between the executive and legislative branches over control of military policy in the early republic. American victory in the Revolutionary war confirmed the nation's independence, but whereas Americans once looked to London for guidance on issues of defense, the questions of protection and national self-defense now had to be answered within the country. Old prejudices against a professional army insinuated themselves into the national dialogue about a military establishment. Equally vociferous were the proponents of a standing, albeit very small, army. During the Confederation period (1783-1787), the Congress put together a patchwork solution to keep peace on the frontier. Satisfactory to very few people, the issue of national defense was one of the many items which propelled politicians and elites to call for a new constitutional convention in 1787 [1].

The Constitution provided that the president was the commander-in-chief of the military, but Congress controlled the purse. This idea needed to be translated into reality during George Washington's first presidential administration. The crucible for the debate was the Northwest Indian Wars of the early 1790s. As Americans streamed into the Ohio territory, they encountered hostile Shawnee, Miami, and Wabash Indians. Washington favored using a professional force to subdue the natives, while Congress argued that a militia was more suitable to the task. This was an important debate from which Washington did not shrink. The president held his ground because he witnessed the Continental Congress's inefficacy during the Revolutionary war, and while he agreed with the principle of civilian rule, he thought it better if that rule were exercised within a clear chain-of-command with the president at the top. In addition to the implications over executive/legislative control of the military, the resolution had practical ramifications for the settlement of the frontier. Washington's firm decision that military policy and strategy fell into the provenance of the executive branch established the model which all subsequent wartime presidents (and Congresses) have followed.

## THE CONFEDERATION YEARS

As there was no executive branch in the Articles of Confederation, the question was not who controlled the army, but whether there would be a professional army at all. Upon George Washington's resignation as commander-in-chief, and the subsequent discharging of most of the Continental army, the new nation was left with a paucity of soldiers. For most of the summer of 1784, the American army consisted of 80 soldiers under ranking officer Captain John Doughty at West Point, New York [2].

It was by no means clear what type of force would protect the nation after the Revolution. Congressman Alexander Hamilton of New York chaired a committee charged with gathering information. Writing to General Washington in April 1783, Hamilton asked the general's opinion on what type of post-war military structure "...may best be adapted...with the principles of our governments"[3]. Washington asked several of his officers for their opinions, and after compiling their ideas, composed his "Sentiments on a Peace Establishment"[4]. In the letter, Washington made four recommendations for the nation's military establishment: (1) a regular army of 2,631 officers and men to "awe the Indians, protect our Trade, prevent the encroachment of our Neighbours of Canada and the Florida's, and guard us at least from surprises; Also for security of our Magazines"[5]. (2) a "well-organized militia" to augment the army in times of war; (3) the establishment of three general deposits to hold munitions and supplies; and, (4) the Congress should establish military academies to "keep alive and diffuse the knowledge of the Military Art..."[6]. However, even the "sunshine of the General's [Washington's] name" could not overwhelm the traditional American fear of standing armies as a danger to liberty [7].

The Congress debated Hamilton's plan, to no resolution, for much of the summer and autumn of 1783. After Virginia's cession of its western lands in early 1784, the need for a military establishment became even more imperative. The Congress recognized the need for "some [frontier] garrisons...to be maintained...at the expense of the United States"[8]. With Hamilton and his allies still clamoring for a professional army, Massachusetts Congressman Elbridge Gerry rose to deliver an impassioned speech against standing armies on May 26. The spokesperson for the anti-army side, Gerry personified the republican fear of classical standing armies as dangers to liberty. Charging Hamilton and the Nationalists, those who favored a stronger central government, with trying to empower the national government at the expense of the states Gerry waxed melodramatically, "...standing armies in time of peace are inconsistent with the principles of republican governments, dangerous to the liberties of a free people, and generally converted into destructive engines for establishing despotism." The fiery rhetoric fulfilled its mission as, a week after the speech, Congress, behind a solid bloc of the New England states, voted to disband the last remaining regiment of the Continental army stationed at West Point. The following day, June 3, Congress "recommended" that four states recruit 700 soldiers from their militia for one year's service on the frontier. The legislature adjourned not having resolved the basic issues surrounding the place of the peace establishment in the new republic; nevertheless, a peacetime army had been created [9].

Designated the First American Regiment, these 700 soldiers were tasked with the mission of patrolling the Northwest Territory: an area that encompassed 248,000 square miles, and was four times the size of England and Wales combined [10]. Pennsylvania was given the selection of the lieutenant-colonel commandant of the Regiment by dint of its furnishing the largest number of men for service. On the recommendation of its president, Thomas Mifflin, Congress appointed Josiah Harmar to the position on August 13, 1784. The Revolutionary war veteran relished the opportunity and wrote to his friend, John Dickinson, that he would give "steady attention to the duties of this appointment [and] …render every possible service to my country…"[11]. The commandant, though, was hamstrung by a number of difficulties, including poor soldiering by his troops, lack of financial support and material support from the government, and the need to report both to Congress and the to the Supreme Executive Council of Pennsylvania [12]. Harmar had barely 30 percent of his authorized force when he was ordered to move west in September 1784 [13].

The army's life on the frontier was arduous. Its main tasks were to evict white squatters from federal lands, keep peace between Indians and the whites, and provide protection for the government officials tasked with surveying the land and negotiating with the Indians. Harmar fought to keep his command intact even though the force was rife with desertion and his soldiers spent a considerable amount of time inebriated. Two years after the act of 1784, the army was still 182 soldiers short of its authorized strength [14]. Whites kept moving west, but the Congress hesitated to augment the army. As the Americans further encroached on Indian lands, the natives began to retaliate against the whites, and the army. In 1787 a Wyandot Indian hunting party kidnapped and killed a federal soldier, then proceeded to parade his scalp through various Indian villages. It was the first time the Indians had attacked the army; the significance was understood by everyone involved: by assaulting the symbol of the U.S. on the frontier, the Indians were declaring war against the United States [15]. At the close of 1787, the frontier was a powder keg ready to explode, and the officers and soldiers of the United States army were ill-equipped to deal with the impending firestorm.

## The Army and the Constitution

Historian Walter Millis wrote that the Constitution was "as much a military as a political and economic charter"[16]. The confluence of events in the mid-1780s including a slight economic depression, Shays' Rebellion in western Massachusetts, and the unrest on the frontier, forced the men gathered at Philadelphia to seriously examine the Confederation's military policies. A majority of the 55 delegates gathered in Philadelphia had been involved intimately with the Revolution either as soldiers or politicians. After watching the debacle of Massachusetts militia refusing to fire at Daniel Shays in 1786, and through their own experiences in the war, most favored the employment of regulars over militia. Even the small state advocate, William Patterson of New Jersey, in presenting his plan of government said, "there must be a small standing force to give every government weight"[17]. Only anti-standing army diehard, Elbridge Gerry, spoke against giving the government the power to raise a permanent, perhaps limitless, federal army.

The final military provisions mirrored the spirit of checks and balances that pervaded the document: the president would be commander-in-chief of the army, thereby maintaining civilian control, but Congress would be the financier. Any appropriation of money could last no longer than two years. The vital difference between the Constitution and the Articles of Confederation was the centralization of the military power in the hands of the federal government. The national government was charged with recruiting and supporting federal soldiers; also, the federal government alone held the responsibility of providing the nation with external security and internal tranquility.

The states had to ratify the document before it became the law of the land. Opponents of ratification, called anti-Federalists, were determined to defeat the Constitution, and were prepared to play the venerable standing army card to do it [18]. The anti-Federalists tied the issue of raising armies to the larger issue of the states conceding sovereignty to the newly created federal government. Writing in the New York Journal, fiery anti-Federalist Robert Yates proclaimed,

> It might be here shown, that the power in the federal legislature, to raise and support armies at pleasure, as well in peace as in war, and their controul over the militia, tend, not only to a consolidation of the government, but the destruction of liberty [19].

Elbridge Gerry was joined by prominent statesmen like Patrick Henry of Virginia in his denunciation of the Constitution's military clauses. The new government, according to the latter, was a "government of force," and the standing armies clause was the "genius of despotism expressly" [20]. The Federalists, though, won the debate over ratification; partly because they tied the central government's authority to control the military with the continued survival of the republic. Indeed, the Federalists opined that "the establishment of a militarily independent national government was essential for the survival of republican institutions in America" [21]. In the Ohio wilderness, Lt. Colonel Harmar followed with rapt attention the events unfolding back east. Upon hearing of the Constitution's acceptance, Harmar wrote to a subordinate with the hopes that the "wheels of government will now be soon in motion," and that a "proper force" would be raised to chastise the Indians [22].

## The Harmar Campaign of 1790

Even before he was officially elected as president, Americans were already turning to George Washington for his advice concerning frontier unrest. Harry Innes wrote to Washington in December 1788 informing him of a possible British conspiracy involving the Indians in the Ohio territory. Not knowing to whom he should turn, Innes sent his letter to Washington because "whatever tends to disturb the peace" of the United States would surely "distress and injure" Washington's "tranquility and repose"[23]. Less than two weeks after he was inaugurated on April 30, 1789, Washington received a letter from Arthur Campbell on the best method of dealing with the Indians, stating that regular troops (and not militia) were needed to "foment divisions and play off the interests, and view of one Tribe against that of another..."[24].

Frontier warfare escalated significantly in 1789. "Murders, scalpings, the stealing of horses and even of livestock, and the most dreaded fate of all, Indian captivity, were prevalent throughout the entire frontier" [25]. Westerners pleaded with the president for assistance [26]. For pragmatic reasons, the country's lack of funds, and the paucity of soldiers, Washington initially favored a peaceful approach to dealing with the Indians. However, even though peace was to be preferred, the new president warned the territorial governor, Arthur St. Clair, that the "national dignity" may demand war [27]. As 1789 drew to a close, the situation began to deteriorate faster than ever before. St. Clair wrote Washington, "The constant hostilities between the Indians who live upon the river Wabash and the people of Kentucky must necessarily be attended," but should force be required, the "handful of troops, sir, that are scattered in the country, though they may afford protection to some settlements, can not possibly act offensively by themselves." Appearing to be at the end of his tether, St. Clair asked the president for instructions. In his response Washington still hoped to avoid war because it would jeopardize "the security of the frontier inhabitants, the security of the troops, and the national dignity." "But," he added,

> If, after manifesting clearly to the Indians the dispositions of the General Government for the preservation of peace, and the extension of a just protection to the said Indians, they should continue their incursions, the United States will be constrained to punish them with severity [28].

Washington concluded his letter by instructing St. Clair to send an emissary to the Wabash Indians to inform them of the government's intentions, and to gauge the tribes' attitudes [29].

The president delivered his first annual address to Congress on January 8, 1790. He had been in office for approximately nine months, and the Indian hostilities continued to be one of the most pressing problems confronting the nation. In consultation with his Secretary of War, Henry Knox, and St. Clair, Washington had decided on negotiations to try and stem the violence. While some Indians would negotiate with the government, many of the hostiles (with British support) refused to yield. Mindful of America's small military, Washington began his first State of the Union address with a frank discussion of the nation's need for a stronger military. Arguing that the common defense merited the Congress's "particular regard," President Washington asserted that "To be prepared for war [was] one of the most effectual means of preserving peace." Immediately after calling for a stronger army, the president advanced the idea that the time may soon approach where the nation would be required to "punish aggressors" on the frontier if the peace initiatives failed.

Initially, the House of Representatives gave the president wide latitude to conduct diplomacy, and military operations against the Indians. In its response to the president's address, the House lamented that the "pacific arrangements pursued with regard to certain hostile tribes of Indians, have not been attended with that success which we had reason to expect from them." Essentially giving the president carte blanche to deal with the problem, the House went on to say that they would not "hesitate to concur in such further measures as may best obviate any ill effects which might be apprehended from the failure of those negotiations "[30]. The House's willingness to approve of Washington's conduct stems from two sources. First, the House was engaged in two particularly thorny issues: the question of the location of the permanent national capital, and the assumption of the state debts advocated by Secretary of the Treasury Alexander Hamilton. Indeed, since the beginning of the national government, the Congress had dealt with other issues leaving Indian affairs totally to the president's purview. The Congress did not hesitate to take up the question of the frontiers, but "Hitherto it has been necessarily excluded by subjects of prior necessity" [31]. Second, the legislature intimately trusted the president's judgment because he had more "than common knowledge of western and Indian affairs..." [32]. These two factors allowed Washington to formulate military policy with almost no recourse to the legislative branch.

What the Congress did not know was that they had already given Washington the authority to start an Indian war. In September 1789, Washington transmitted a letter from St. Clair to the Congress detailing the escalating troubles on the frontier. In his covering letter he asked the Congress for permission to call forth the militia to "embrace the cases apprehended by the Governor of the Western Territory." The Congress, in complying with the request, laid the groundwork for the administration's first attempt to defeat the Indians [33].

The expedition, however, was a failure. Knox, St. Clair, and Harmar planned a two-pronged attack against the Indians. Lt. Colonel Harmar would march from Ft. Washington (present-day Cincinnati) with 300 regulars and 1,200 militia to the Miami Indian villages at Kekionga. Meanwhile, Major John F. Hamtramck would move up the Wabash River from Fort Knox with 100 regulars and 300 militia to attack the Indians at Vermillion, thereby diverting attention from Harmar's column [34]. The plan was put into action in late September 1790. Hamtramck's column never reached Vermillion as the Kentucky militia threatened to desert and the major returned to Ft. Knox rather than risk mutiny. Harmar fared no better. He did raze some Indian villages, but on two separate occasions, Indians routed detachments from his main force. Claiming victory, Harmar trekked back to Ft. Washington. Though, St. Clair and Harmar sent official reports back to the administration at Philadelphia claiming that the Indians' "headquarters of inequity" had been destroyed, the rumors and letters from westerners convinced Washington otherwise [35]. Washington hesitated to make any official report to Congress, in mid-November he wrote Knox that his "...forebodings with respect to the expedition against the Wabash Indians are of disappointment; and a disgraceful termination under the conduct of B. Genl. Harmar." His worst fears had been realized – the campaign had produced nothing but "expence without honor or profit"[36].

## Defeat and Despair: The St. Clair Campaign of 1791

The New Year did not alleviate the problems on the frontier. In January, Washington's old comrade from the Revolutionary war, Rufus Putnam, wrote him from the Marietta settlement in the Ohio territory. The recent victories over Harmar had emboldened the Indians, and Putnam feared a general uprising once spring reached the wilderness. "...the war, which was partial before the campaign of last year, is, in all probability become general...We are in the utmost danger of being swallowed up" [37]. Secretary Knox admitted that Harmar's expedition had been a failure, and the nation faced an increasingly hostile enemy. Knox presented the president with an even greater fear that, "their [the Indians] own opinion of success, and the number of trophies they possess, will probably not only encourage them to a continuance of hostilities, but may be a means of their obtaining considerable assistance from the neighbouring tribes" [38]. The specter of a united Indian resistance, the discontent of the western settlers, and the need to redeem the national honor pushed Washington to call for another campaign.

Together Knox and Washington decided to ask Congress for an increased professional military establishment. The two men believed that the poor performance of the militia was to blame for Harmar's defeat; therefore they determined to use more regular soldiers in the 1791 campaign. Both realized that Congress would scrutinize more closely their handling of military policy, and that cries from western constituents for a greater reliance on militia would reach the ears of pliant representatives. Virginians and Kentuckians advocated using militia and not regulars for fighting because "militia officers and privates having their all at stake, and well accustomed to rifles, and the Indian mode of warfare are preferable to the best regular troops, armed with muskets" [39]. Some Congressmen also began to question the administration's motives in conducting the war. The most vociferous of these opponents was Senator William Maclay. He made known to all who would listen that the war was "undertaken without the shadow of authority from Congress," and that Congress, instead of "begging our own servants to spare the effusion of human blood," should initiate a line of inquiry into the executive's conduct of the war [40].

Maclay's calls, however, were in vain, as the president and Secretary of War were able to devise a solution which they thought would placate the Congress and meet their needs for a stronger, federal army. Washington furthered the ideas of using levies, short-term volunteers that would fall under federal control. This was a compromise between having to use militia and enlarging the regular army. Levies would fall under federal supervision and discipline, but would be dismissed at the expiration of their enlistment terms. Washington was confident that a corps of levies combined with a strengthened regular army could quell any Indian resistance.

Accordingly, Knox officially submitted the administration's plan to the Congress. Since the current army was "utterly inadequate" for disciplining the Indians, Knox proposed a three-step plan,

> First – That the situation of the frontiers requires an additional defensive protection, at least until offensive measures shall be put into operation – The plan of a regiment of rangers is therefore submitted.
>
> Secondly – That the peculiar situation of the frontiers requires the augmentation of one regiment of regular troops to consist of nine hundred and twelve non commissioned Officers and privates.
>
> Third – That another expedition which shall effectually dispose the Wabash and other hostile Indians to peace, seems indispensable [41].

Knox's letter contained the troop numbers he and Washington thought would be enough to overwhelm the Indians: 1,200 regular soldiers, 500 rangers, and 1,300 levies. The government, Knox concluded, must "regulate events instead of being regulated by them"[42].

As in the previous year, Congress complied with the administration's request, but they did not pass the authorization until March 3, 1791 – the last day of the First Congress. An additional regiment of 912 non-commissioned officers and privates was to be raised, and the Congress also gave the president authority to "engage a body of militia to serve as Cavalry," and "a Corps, not exceeding two thousand non-commissioned officers, privates and musicians...under the denomination of Levies..."[43].

Satisfied with their new establishment, Washington and Knox put their plans in motion. While the new and enlarged federal army was being recruited, the two men authorized Brigadier General Charles Scott of the Kentucky militia to fulfill the "ranger" component of the mission. As Knox told Scott, quick, penetrating raids would carry "the war into the enemy's country, [and] prevent in a great degree their invading the frontiers" [44]. After directing Scott to begin his raids, Knox consulted with the newly commissioned Major General Arthur St. Clair, and his second-in-command Brigadier General Richard Butler. The army, under St. Clair, would march north to the Maumee Valley (the same destination of Harmar's campaign) building a chain of forts along the way. When the army reached the Miami villages it was to draw the enemy into battle, and, afterwards, establish a permanent post on the site of the towns [45]. President Washington wrote that the post "was the primary object of the campaign," after building it, "every thing else would be easy." One of Harmar's most trusted subordinates shared the President's ideas, "The Indians can never be subdued by just going into their towns and burning their houses and corn, and returning the next day, for it is no hardship to an Indian to live without..." In order for the government to be able to dictate terms, "respectable garrisons in the most important parts of their country," must be established [46]. As St. Clair was preparing his army he was to send out peace offerings to the hostile Indians, and as such President Washington composed a message to the Indians stating that a war with the United States would mean "absolute destruction to you, your women and your children"[47].

A variety of delays kept St. Clair and his force in the vicinity of Ft. Washington until mid-September. He began his campaign with 2,000 regular soldiers (including levies) and 400 militia. Stopping at various points to build forts, the first snow of the season had already fallen when the force (now numbering just under 1,400 due to desertions, illness, and garrison duty), reached the banks of the Wabash river on November 4, 1791. That morning, 1,000 natives attacked the force shortly after reveille. The resulting battle was one of the worst losses in the army's history. The Indians stormed through the camp while the regulars sought to maintain discipline amidst the fleeing militia. After trying to salvage the situation, St. Clair ordered a retreat. Lieutenant Ebenezer Denny accurately captured the mood of the fleeing soldiers when he wrote that to "Delay was death." The Indians' lack of discipline had compelled them to stop fighting and begin plundering the American camp. This hesitation allowed the survivors to make their way back to the relative safety of Ft. Jefferson, thirty miles distant from the battlefield. When battle casualties were finally tallied it was discovered that of the 1,400 American combatants, 900 were either killed or wounded. The Indians had virtually annihilated the American army [48].

## The Eagle's Sword

As with Harmar's defeat, rumors trickled into Philadelphia before St. Clair's official report made its way to the capital. On December 4, Henry Lee wrote to Washington of the "late disaster in the west," and included a testimony from Kentuckian John Rogers of St. Clair's defeat. Newspapers began reporting rumors of the terrible loss on Monday, December

5 [49]. As with Harmar's campaign, Washington waited for official word which he received on December 9. On the following Monday he submitted the following message to both houses of the U.S. Congress,

> It is with great concern that I communicate to you the information received from Major General St. Clair, of the misfortune which as befallen the troops under his command.
>
> Although the national loss is considerable, according to the scale of the event, yet it may be repaired without great difficulty, excepting as to the brave men who have fallen on the occasion, and who are a subject of public as well as private regret.
>
> A future communication will shortly be made of all such matters as shall be necessary to enable the Legislature to judge of the future measures which it may be proper to pursue [50].

With this message, Washington launched into a protracted battle with Congress over the fate of who exerted more control over military policy. The contest lasted for most of 1792 and took the form of two issues: did the Congress have the right to investigate an executive action without looking to impeachment, and what would the next step in the campaign against the Northwest Indians look like?

## The Investigation of Major General St. Clair

On March 27, 1792, William Giles of Virginia put forward a motion in the House of Representatives which called on the president to "institute an inquiry into the causes of the late defeat of the army under the command of Major General St. Clair…" Most particularly the Congress was interested in whether the "the detentions or delays which are suggested to have attended the money, clothing, provisions, and military stores, for the use of the said army…" caused the defeat [51]. Debate quickly began over whether the House had the authority to direct the president to begin an investigation. Congressman Giles answered his critics by stating that the "House was the proper source as the immediate guardians of the public interest" [52]. In addition to the question of whether the House could ask the president to investigate a matter of the executive branch, a second issue arose: was the executive the correct person to even investigate the situation? Abraham Baldwin of Georgia was,

> Convinced the House could not proceed but by a committee of their own. Such a committee would be able to throw more light on the subject, and then the House would be able to determine how to proceed; and, if any failure had taken place on the part of the Executive officers, he should then be prepared to address the President, and to request him to take the proper steps in the case [53].

The debate continued until both motions (Giles's and Baldwin's) were put to a vote. The motion to direct the president to investigate the defeat lost by a vote of 35 to 21, but Baldwin's motion (to have the House investigate the defeat) won by a margin of 34 votes [54]. For the first time in American history, the legislative branch of the government investigated actions taken by the executive branch.

The House referred the matter to a select committee and on March 30 it subsequently asked Secretary of War Knox to submit papers relevant to the expedition for the committee's consideration. The president convened his cabinet on the following day to discuss the appropriate response to the Congress's request. In his memorandum on the meeting, Secretary of State Thomas Jefferson asserted that Washington "neither acknowledged nor denied, nor even doubted the propriety of what the house was doing" [55]. The president did feel, however, and the cabinet agreed that Congress should make their requests of the department heads *through* the president and not directly to the secretaries. Washington wanted it clear that the secretaries were members of the executive branch and answered to him *before* they answered to Congress. The fact that Washington did not have issue with the House's inquest belied the fact that he felt the executive branch had acquitted itself in the preparations for the campaign, and secondly, it revealed that he had his own problems with St. Clair's expedition. According to Jefferson, the president had always disapproved of "two lines of St. Clair's conduct." First, he had never gathered enough intelligence about the Indians, and he did not keep "his army in such a position always to be able to display them in a line behind trees in the Indian manner at any moment." A House investigation would bring the expedition's errors to light and vindicate the executive's line of conduct.

Washington's wishes, however, were not fulfilled. Indeed, though the final report does not directly blame the executive for St. Clair's defeat, there was enough veiled criticism to raise Washington's and Knox's ire. In its report of May 8, 1792, the committee gave three causes for the defeat. They first blamed the "delay in furnishing the materials and estimates" for the campaign. Second, the delays in the quartermaster's department caused a "want of provisions" on the frontier. Lastly, the "want of discipline and experience in the troops" caused the defeat. General St. Clair was exonerated for his "coolness and intrepidity." Secretary Knox objected to the report because he thought it sullied his reputation. After further consideration the committee confirmed its initial findings in February 1793 [56]. The president's personal reputation remained unscathed, but the legislature had won a victory over the executive. For the next campaign, the Congress would take a more active role in the type of force that would compose the military establishment.

## THE PRESIDENT'S WAR

While it investigated St. Clair's defeat, the Congress made ready to receive the president's next plan for the war against the Indians. Knox presented the administration's plan to Congress with the warning that the Indians' victories would make them deaf to any peace pleas; therefore, a "strong coercive force" was needed [57]. The plan called for raising the two existing regiments to their full strength, and adding three more regiments for a total troop complement of 5,168 men.

The subsequent Congressional debate mirrored the public's divided opinion over the administration's approach to the protection of the frontiers, and also the growing sentiment among congressmen that the legislature needed to exercise a greater voice in making military policy. The debate began with an excoriation of the war and the statement that it was "unjustly undertaken as it has since been unwisely and unsuccessfully conducted..." [58]. The main arguments against the bill took two lines: the first was financial, the second was tactical. The cost of this new army was a large halter around the government's neck, according to some of the legislators. The plan called for expenditures up to $1.1 million – a sum that was twice the amount budgeted for the other branches of government [59].

The real contest, though, centered on the policy aspect of the question; namely, what type of soldier was best suited to protect the frontiers? Washington firmly believed that only the discipline and numerical strength of a professionally trained army could offer hopes of victory.

Many congressmen, finally responding to their constituents' cries, urged the use of militia to solve the problem. The arguments offered in favor of citizen-soldiers centered on their experience fighting the Indians, and their trustworthiness as opposed to regular soldiers. Most agreed that regulars were fine for garrison duty, but "as to active service, the frontier militia and rangers were pronounced to be by far preferable to regular troops..."[60]. Aspersions were cast on the men who joined the regular establishment as the dregs of society. Mostly from cities, the Indians frightened these urban poor, whereas frontier militia was accustomed to the "war whoop," it did "not strike them with that degree of terror with which it inspires those men who enlist in the regular establishment"[61].

Some Congressmen questioned the administration's needs for such a large force. The "strange policy" to "raise five or six thousand men to oppose a handful of Indian banditti, whose utmost amount does not...appear to exceed twelve hundred" troubled the legislators. There was a conspiratorial mention of the "secrets of the [president's] Cabinet" as the only place where the truth was known. Just when it appeared that the naysayers would triumph, reason was restored with the plain fact that between 1783 and 1790, 1500 settlers had been killed or captured on the frontier. The militia had not been able to stem this violence, and may have, with their punitive raids, further incited it.

One need only look at the militia's performance in the Harmar and St. Clair campaigns to see that a "very trifling disaster, or a slight cause of discontent, is sufficient to make them disband and forget all subordination, so far as even to neglect the means of self-defence..."[62]. When the final vote was called, the president's plan triumphed, notwithstanding the opposition's efforts. Ten months after the bill was passed, in January 1793, the Congress again took up the question of the military establishment, this time over a motion to eliminate the three additional regiments called for in the March 1792 act. Once again, the president emerged victorious, but not before the motion was given considerable vocal support on the House floor [63].

## CONCLUSION

Washington and Knox were vindicated when their army won a smashing victory against the Indians in August 1794 at Fallen Timbers in the Maumee valley. The president selected Revolutionary war veteran Anthony Wayne to command the new army, and "Mad Anthony" spent two years training and disciplining his army before launching a campaign in the summer of 1794. After defeating the Indians, Wayne marched to the nearby British-held Ft. Miamis and dared the commander to stop him. Not wanting to precipitate an international incident, Wayne backed down, but his primary goal had been accomplished: in 1795 at the

Treaty of Greeneville the Indians signed over most of the present-day state of Ohio to the American government [64].

The Northwest Indian War from 1790-1794 was the first armed conflict the new American government, under the Constitution, faced. Armies were raised and employed in an aggressive manner and all understood that precedents would be set for future conflicts. The Constitution made the president commander-in-chief of the military, but gave Congress the power to declare war. Did this mean that the president could use the military at his pleasure? As commander-in-chief, was he solely responsible for the composition of the army? The Constitution was silent on these questions and it was left to the first administration to answer them. After the defeats in 1790 and 1791, the Congress felt obliged to insert itself in military matters which Washington interpreted as his purview. The administration held fast even when the cry to use militia instead of regulars arose in Congress and among the public. In addition to the practical consequences for the northwest frontier, the clash marked an important victory for the executive branch in fashioning military policy. Washington knew that public opinion demanded he use militia in some capacity, but he wanted regular soldiers to provide the backbone of the United States army. Through Congressional questioning and investigations he held his ground on the matter, and Wayne's victory at Fallen Timbers justified his tenacity. In future conflicts the Congress and president would spar over the latter's wartime powers, but never again did the legislature seriously battle the executive branch over the composition of the military, if only because Washington's firmness had made the question moot. The Constitution gave the president the power on paper to be commander-in-chief, but it was George Washington who made that authority real and tangible.

## REFERENCES


[1] The most succinct study on military policy during the Confederation is Lawrence Delbert Cress, *Citizens in Arms: The Army and the Militia in American Society to the War of 1812* (Chapel Hill: University of North Carolina Press, 1982). See also Richard H. Kohn's seminal study *Eagle and Sword: The Federalists and the Creation of the Military Establishment in America, 1783-1802* (New York: Free Press, 1975).

[2] Don Higginbotham, *The War of American Independence: Military Attitudes, Policies, and Practicies, 1763-1789* (New York: Macmillan, 1971; reprint, Boston: Northeastern University Press, 1983), 445; Russell F. Weigley, *History of the United States Army* (New York: Macmillan, 1967), 80-81; James Ripley Jacobs, The Beginning of the United States Army, 1783-1812. (Princeton: Princeton University Press, 1947)14-15.

[3] The committee also included James Madison, Samuel Osgood, James Wilson, and Oliver Ellsworth. Alexander Hamilton, *The Papers of Alexander Hamilton*, ed. Harold C. Syrett, in 27 volumes (New York: Columbia University Press, 1961-1987), III, 322.

[4] George Washington, *The Writings of George Washington*, ed. John C. Fitzpatrick, in 39 volumes (Washington, DC: Government Printing Office, 1931-1944), XXVI, 374-398. (Hereafter referred to as *Writings GW*)

[5] Ibid., 375.

[6] Ibid., 396-397.

[7] Edmund C. Burnett, ed., *Letters of Members of Continental Congress*, in 8 volumes (Washington, DC: Carnegie Printing Institute, 1921-1936), VIII, 842. (Hereafter referred to as *LMCC*).

[8] Worthington C. Ford, ed., *Journals of the Continental Congrss, 1774-1789* in 34 volumes (Washington, DC: Manuscript Division of the Library of Congress, 1904-1937), XXIV, 806-807. (Hereafter referred to as *JCC*)

[9] For Gerry's speech see *JCC*, XXVII, 433-434; for the decision to reduce the army see Ibid., 524. For the politics behind the vote see Kohn, *Eagle and Sword*, 54-60. For the resolution of June 3 see *JCC*, XXVII, 530-531.

[10] William Guthman, *March to Massacre: A History of the First Seven Years of the United States Army, 1784-1791* (New York: McGraw-Hill, 1975), vii.

[11] Alan S. Brown, "The Role of the Army in Western Settlement: Josiah Harmar's Command, 1785-1790," *Pennsylvania Magazine of History and Biography* 93 (1969), 163-164; Jonathan Heart, *The Journal of Captain Jonathan Heart*, ed. Consul Willshire Butterfield (Albany: John Munsell's Sons, 1885), 30-31.

[12] Kohn, 63.

[13] Ibid.; Brown, 164-165.

[14] For army life on the frontier see Jonathan Heart, *The Orderly Book of Captain Jonathan Heart, September 7, 1785 to May 2, 1788*, Record Group 94, National Archives; and Josiah Harmar to Jonathan Heart, April 17, June 1 1787, *Letter Book of Captain Jonathan Heart, April 17, 1787 to January 26, 1788*, Record Group 94, National Archives.

[15] Kohn, 68.

[16] Walter Millis, *Arms and Men: A Study in American Military History* (New York: G.P. Putnam's Sons, 1956), 47.

[17] Dave R. Palmer, *1794: America, Its Army, and the Birth of a Nation* (San Rafael: Presidio Press, 1994), 104-108; Max Farrand, ed., *The Records of the Federal Convention of 1787*, in 4 volumes (New Haven: Yale University Press, 1937), III, 145. (Hereafter referred to as *Records*).

[18] For Anti-Federalist ideology see Cecilia M. Kenyon, "Men of Little Faith: The Anti-Federalists on the Nature of Representative Government," *William and Mary Quarterly* 12 (1955): 8-43; Jackson Turner Main, *The Anti-Federalists: Critics of the Constitution, 1781-1788* (Chapel Hill: University of North Carolina Press, 1961), 119-186; Gordon S. Wood, *The Creation of the American Republic, 1776-1787* (Chapel Hill: University of North Carolina Press, 1969), 485-523.

[19] *New York Journal*, October 10, 1787

[20] Jonathan Elliot, ed., *The Debates in the Several State Conventions on the Adoption of the Federal Constitution*, in 5 volumes (Buffalo, NY: William S. Hein, 1891), III, 378-396. (Hereafter referred to as *Debates*).

[21] Cress, 105.

[22] *Outpost*, 100, 137

[23] George Washinton, *The Papers of George Washington: Presidential Series*, ed. W.W. Abbot, et al., 14 volumes to date (Charlottesville: University Press of Virginia, 1987-), I, 187-189. (Hereafter referred to as *Papers: GW*)

[24] Ibid., II, 253-255.

[25] Wiley Sword, *President Washington's Indian War: The Struggle for the Old Northwest, 1790-1795* (Norman: University of Oklahoma Press, 1985), 75.
[26] *Papers: GW*, II, 314-315.
[27] Ibid., III, 140-142.
[28] Arthur St. Clair, *The St. Clair Papers: The Life and Public Services of Arthur St. Clair*, ed. William Henry Smith, in 2 volumes (Cincinnati: Robert Clarke and Company, 1882), II, 123-126.
[29] Ibid.
[30] "Proceedings January 12, 1790," *Annals of Congress*, House of Representatives, 1st Congress, 1st Session, ed. Joseph Gales, Sr. (Washington, DC: Gales and Seaton, 1849), 1089 (Hereafter referred to as *Annals*)
[31] James Madison, *The Papers of James Madison*, ed. Robert Rutland, et al., 17 volumes to date (Charlottesville: University Press of Virginia, 1962-), XII, 318.
[32] Ibid.
[33] Kohn, 97-98; *Annals*, 927-928.
[34] Jacobs, 50-52
[35] *American State Papers: Indian Affairs.* 2 volumes (Washington, DC: Gales and Seaton, 1832-1834), I, 104. (Hereafter referred to as *ASP: IA*).
[36] *Papers: GW*, VI, 668.
[37] Ibid., VII, 208-209.
[38] Ibid., 262-268.
[39] Ibid., 187.
[40] William Maclay, February 17, 1791, March 1, 1791, *Papers of William Maclay*, Library of Congress
[41] Linda Grant DePauw, ed., *A Documentary History of the First Federal Congress, 1789-1791*, 14 volumes (Baltimore: Johns Hopkins University Press, 1971-1986), V, 1367-1370. (Hereafter referred to as *Documentary History*).
[42] Ibid, 1369-1371
[43] Ibid., 1302-1303
[44] *ASP: IA*, I, 130-131
[45] Ibid., 131-137.
[46] *Writings: GW*, XXXI, 449; St. Clair, II, 197.
[47] *Papers: GW*, VII, 549-551.
[48] Winthrop Sargent, "Winthrop Sargent's Diary while with General Arthur St. Clair's Expedition Against the Indians," *Ohio State Archaeological and Historical Quarterly* 33 (1924), 263.
[49] *Papers: GW*, IX, 249-250; Douglas Southall Freeman, *George Washington: A Biography*, 7 volumes (New York: Charles Scribner & Sons, 1948-1957), VI, 336.
[50] *Annals*, 2nd Congress, 1st Session, 48.
[51] Ibid., 490.
[52] Ibid.
[53] Ibid., 492
[54] Ibid., 493-494
[55] *Papers: GW*, X, 169.
[56] *American State Papers: Military Affairs.* 7 volumes ( Washington, DC: Gales and Seaton, 1832-1861), I, 36-39, 41-44 (Hereafter referred to as *ASP: MA*).

[57] *ASP: IA*, I, 197-198

[58] *Annals*, 2nd Congress, 1st Session, 337.

[59] Ibid., 763.

[60] Ibid., 339.

[61] Ibid., 341.

[62] Ibid., 343, 347.

[63] See Ibid., 773-802 for the debate.

[64] For the Battle of Fallen Timbers see Paul David Nelson, *Anthony Wayne: Soldier of the Early Republic* (Bloomington: Indiana University Press, 1985), 264-266; for the Treaty of Greeneville see *ASP: IA*, I, 577-583.

In: Presidents and War
Editors: A. Eksterowicz and G. Hastedt, pp. 17-28
ISBN 978-1-61668-917-9


*Chapter 2*

# "A SQUADRON OF OBSERVATION": THOMAS JEFFERSON AND AMERICA'S FIRST WAR AGAINST TERRORISM

*Craig L. Symonds*

## INTRODUCTION

An on-line poll conducted in January 2003 invited Americans to share their views about the best way to handle the pending crisis with Iraq's Saddam Hussein. The results were mixed, and betrayed some of the uncertainty and diffidence with which Americans approached the looming conflict. The greatest number (though at 29% far less than a majority) favored war, and another 22 percent favored exile for Saddam Hussein, though they did not specify how that might be achieved. Some 19 percent thought (or perhaps hoped) that an internal coup might take care of the problem; another 19 percent wanted to allow the diplomats to negotiate a settlement; and 11 percent wanted the United States simply to leave Iraq alone. Fundamentally, the options came down to the application of military force, relying on diplomacy, or bowing out completely, and Americans were obviously divided about which of those options was most desirable [1].

The United States confronted similar options in 1785, barely two years into its national existence, when an armed vessel flying the flag of the North African city-state of Algiers stopped and boarded the American schooner *Maria* on the high seas. The Algerines (as the residents of Algiers were known in the Eighteenth Century) declared the *Maria* to be a prize, stripped the American prisoners naked, and locked them in the hold. When the captured vessel reached Algiers, the American men were sold into slavery at public auction and the one woman on board was shipped off to Constantinople to be a concubine in a Turkish harem. As if to demonstrate that this was not an isolated incident, the Algerines struck again only days later, seizing the American ship *Dauphine* of Philadelphia, treating its crew similarly. One can only imagine what the governmental response would be to such outrages today. In 1785, however, the U.S. Confederation government was hamstrung not only by its lack of defined powers, but also by an embarrassed public treasury. In consequence, the seizure of the *Maria* and the *Dauphine* initiated a lengthy policy struggle inside the U.S. government about how best to handle this assault on American citizens and American interests. Over the next two decades, U.S. policy makers were deeply conflicted and sharply divided about how to respond [2].

The rulers of the small city-states of North Africa – Algiers, Tunis, and Tripoli – had no particular political objective in targeting American vessels. Unlike the leaders of al Qaeda, they did not object to American policy, or for the most part have any notion of what that policy was. These were equal-opportunity pirates who attacked unarmed vessels from any western (that is, non-Muslim) nation that did not pay an annual tribute. Today such behavior would very likely be labeled "state-sponsored terrorism." Terror, however, was not the objective; the Barbary System was no more and no less than organized brigandage. When the ruler of a city state determined that there were profits to be had, he simply declared war on one or more of the Western maritime powers, often signaled in melodramatic fashion by sending a team to chop down the flagpole at the embassy of the target nation. No *causus belli* was deemed necessary in such cases because the Muslims claimed sovereignty over the whole Mediterranean, and argued that any transit of that sea by other nations took place only at their sufferance, a claim similar to Muammar Qaddafi's assertion of Libyan sovereignty over the Gulf of Sidra in 1986. Though the Muslim rulers of Algiers, Tunis, and Tripoli justified their piracy on the grounds that, after all, westerners were "infidels" and therefore fair game for true believers, their actual motive was pecuniary. They did it for the money.

## The Argument for Paying off the Pirates

A modern reader might wonder why the maritime powers of Europe did not simply put an end to this nonsense by sending a fleet to smash the impertinent upstarts. After all, the "navies" of these North African states were not particularly impressive. The largest of them, that of Algiers, consisted of four frigates, an equal number of lateen-rigged xebecs with fewer than 24 guns each, and a handful of gunboats. Surely it would require no great effort on the part of Britain or France to shatter this small fleet and end the Barbary system. The explanation for European tolerance of this maritime robbery is two-fold. First, it was generally cheaper to buy protection in the form of tribute payments than it was to carry on a lengthy war, even if the outcome was certain; and second, some nations (Britain in particular) found it useful for the Barbary States to maintain their system of brigandage in order to discourage maritime competition from others [3].

By the time the Barbary corsairs turned their attention to the infant United States in the 1780s, this tribute system was already more than a century old. The British had begun making regular payments to Algiers and Tunis as part of a ransom agreement in the mid-Seventeenth Century. At the time, England was wracked by civil war and focused on internal considerations; the government had few military assets to devote to a war against the city-states of North Africa, and even less interest. Wars, after all, were expensive. As a result, the tribute policy begun by Charles I in 1642 was continued by Cromwell and then by the Restoration kings up through the time of the American Revolution, by which time the British were shelling out the equivalent of a quarter million dollars in tribute payments each year. The amount of tribute paid varied form state to state. Spain paid the most, a total of $1.2

million per year. In part, this was because the Muslims of North Africa recalled and resented Spain's lengthy war against Islam. Smaller European nations paid smaller amounts: the Danes and the Swedes paid the least, about $20,000 per year.

Paying tribute was America's first instinct as well. Lacking a navy, or indeed any kind of organized military at all, there was not much that the Confederation government in the United States could do in response to North African piracy other than pay the price demanded or suffer the consequences. Even if the wherewithal could be found to carry on a war against these brigands, such a war would be open ended. Contemporaries understood that it would not be enough to defeat the Barbary States. To ensure that they did not simply renew their old habits once the American warships departed, it would be necessary for the United States to maintain a naval force in the Mediterranean indefinitely. In other words, though most Americans were confident that they could win a war with Algiers, they shrunk from the open-ended commitment to maintaining the ensuing "peace." In 1785, most Americans concluded that it was better and cheaper to pay the tribute as a kind of maritime insurance policy than to embark upon a potentially endless – and endlessly expensive – war with the states of North Africa.

After the seizure of the *Maria*, Richard O'Brien, the U.S. Consul at Algiers, urged the government to settle at once. Familiar as he was with the Barbary System, he argued that "The United States should use every means to obtain a peace with the Barbary States," and he especially feared the negative effect that any attempt to fight back would have on U.S. relations with the North African states. "It is bad policy," he wrote in June of 1786, "to use any threats or make any parade with cruisers [warships] if we intend suing for a peace." The key to a satisfactory settlement was to pay a ransom like everybody else. "Money is the God of Algiers," he wrote [4].

The Confederation government was willing enough to pay. The question was how much would it cost? The Congress authorized a payment of $200 per citizen to ransom the Americans captured on board the *Maria* and the *Dauphine*, but the Dey of Algiers demanded more: $1,200 per person. Somewhat reluctantly, Congress approved the larger amount – but the Dey then demanded more than twice as much: $3000 per person. From the start, the issue was not whether to pay or to fight, but rather how much the United States was willing to pay. While dickering continued over the price, some 50 Americans languished in captivity. O'Brien, who saw the prisoners on a regular basis, urged Congress to act quickly. He reported in the spring of 1787 that in addition to being put to hard labor on public projects, the American hostages were subject to "the pest" (as he called the plague), so that in his view it was unlikely they would last very long. By 1787, one had died; five more would perish over the next three years [5].

## The Application of Limited Naval Force

One man who disagreed with the policy of paying ransom was Thomas Jefferson, who at the time was the American ambassador to France. Jefferson is remembered in American history as the champion of small government, and therefore an opponent of both a standing army and a sea-going navy. And, to be sure, Jefferson did oppose the idea of building the kind of navy that might be noticed by the great powers of Europe and therefore pull the United

States into the game of great-power politics. Building a large standing navy, he believed, would very likely make the young nation a pawn in Europe's nearly–interminable wars. On the other hand, Jefferson also had a strong practical streak (witness the several inventions on display at Monticello), and it seemed to him that in this particular case, the application of naval power was the most practical solution to the problem of North African piracy. In a famous letter to John Adams, he laid out his argument for opposing the Barbary System with force. Though he couched his arguments in the language of offended national honor, the core of his position was that over the long haul it would be both cheaper and more certain to produce a good result to build and maintain a small navy than it would be to continue making annual tribute payments [6].

Jefferson conducted what a latter day systems analyst would call a cost-benefit calculation. He first determined the precise strength of the Barbary navies that the United States would have to confront in a war against Mediterranean piracy. Based on the information he was able to collect, he calculated that a U.S. "fleet" mounting a total of about 150 guns would be sufficient to compel even the most powerful of the Barbary states to grant the United States a favorable treaty. In making this calculation, Jefferson amortized the expense of a 150-gun fleet over the presumed life of the ships, and concluded that the annual cost of building and maintaining a navy would be less than the annual tribute payments demanded by the Barbary States. In addition, Jefferson argued, tribute payments were subject to revision at the whim of the North Africans (as the continued increase in ransom demands demonstrated), whereas building and maintaining a fleet was a fixed cost (or so he assumed, though subsequent events would prove otherwise). And finally, he insisted that the maintenance cost of a navy could be reduced even more if, when the vessels were not in use, they were laid up in dockyards to await the next emergency. In this respect, Jefferson envisioned a U.S. Navy that would be more or less the national equivalent of the musket that frontier settlers kept above the fireplace: an instrument ready to hand when emergencies arose [7].

In his reply to this missive, John Adams made it clear that he saw the problem much differently. Philosophically, Federalists like Adams were advocates of a stronger and more assertive national government, one that could (and in their view, should) play an important role in world events and which would therefore maintain a strong national navy as well as a standing army. But Adams and his fellow Federalists envisioned a navy of a quite different sort than the one proposed by Jefferson. In order to influence world events, Adams wrote, the United States would need a navy composed of several dozen two-deck ships of the line, not the musket-over-the-mantelpiece navy advocated by Jefferson. Besides, while Adams readily conceded that the United States should build a navy "whether to be applied to the Algerines or not," in this particular case he doubted that Congress could be convinced to support a naval force. Demonstrating that he knew his fellow citizens well, Adams asserted that Americans did not have the stomach (or the pocketbook) to fight an extended overseas war with a determined enemy. "We ought not to fight them," Adams wrote, "unless we determine to fight them forever," and an open-ended overseas conflict, he wrote, "is too rugged for our people to bear"[8].

Adams was proved correct in his suspicion that Congress would not support the construction of a naval force in 1786; the congressional response to the Barbary threat was to negotiate a treaty, one that included tribute payments. But the issue did not go away. The event that triggered a reconsideration of American policy toward North Africa was Portugal's decision to sign a peace treaty with Algiers in order to join the anti-French coalition sponsored by Britain at the outset of the Wars of the French Revolution. Until 1793, Portugal's small navy served as the cork in the Mediterranean bottle: Portuguese warships patrolling the Straits of Gibraltar had kept the North African corsairs within the confines of the Mediterranean Sea. With their adherence to the coalition against France, however, the Portuguese had bigger fish to fry, and they pulled their navy out of the strait. Almost at once, a large Algerine force of four frigates, three xebecs, and a brig-of-war sailed through the strait to attack American merchant ships in the Atlantic. No fewer than 11 U.S. vessels were taken by these Algerine cruisers within only a few weeks. This dramatically strengthened the hand of the ruling Bey of Algiers, Ali Hassan, because with each capture, Algiers gained another score or so of American hostages. In addition to combating terror, the United States also faced a hostage crisis [9].

This time, however, the policy debate in the United States took on a different tone. For one thing, the nation had a new government. The ratification of the Constitution in 1788-89 had established a stronger central government, and with the Barbary powers in mind, the new president, George Washington, had warned legislators in December of 1791 that "If we desire to avoid insult, we must be able to repel it; if we desire to secure peace . . . it must be known at all times that we are ready for war" [10]. In consequence, instead of dickering over the price per head that the United States might pay to have its hostages released, Congress addressed the crisis in 1793 by debating a resolution declaring that "a naval force, adequate to the protection of the commerce of the United States against the Algerine corsairs, ought to be provided" [11].

Apart from Indian hostilities on the western frontier, this was America's first attempt to combat a non-Western assault on American interests. Of course, the context was dramatically different from America's modern campaign against terror. Far from being the world's greatest superpower attracting foes because of its perceived influence or heavy-handedness, the United States in 1794 was a fledgling nation, itself buffeted by the powerful gusts of wind generated by the mighty blows that Britain and France aimed at one another. Nor was ideology a factor. Though Americans suspected the British of brokering the Portuguese-Algerine Treaty in order to weaken competition from American merchants, Algiers did not target U.S. interests because of its support for one side or the other in the ongoing war (in fact, the U.S. took special care to be as neutral as possible in that conflict). It was simply a matter of opportunity. Nor was religion a factor except insofar as the North African city-states used it as a justification for their piracy.

On the other hand, economic interests were a factor; indeed, they were the dominant factor. A hundred U.S. ships a year sailed from America to the Mediterranean, and they carried upwards of 20,000 tons of rice, dried fish, and wheat annually, returning with cargoes of citrus fruit, olive oil, and occasionally, Turkish opium. The protection of this trade was clearly as important to American policy makers as the health and safety of the growing number of American hostages held in Algiers. (Oil, of course, was not a factor, for at the turn of the Nineteenth Century oil was a commodity that as yet had no perceived value on the world market.)

Still, the options with which American policy makers wrestled in 1793 were not significantly different from those facing modern policy makers: 1) they could negotiate with their tormentors and seek an agreement based on mutually acceptable terms (that is, paying tribute, while dickering over the amount); or 2) they could confront the perpetrators with armed force. And as alternatives within that second option, they could confront their enemy independently or as part of a coalition.

Back in 1786, Jefferson had toyed with the idea of constructing a Franco-American alliance to suppress the Algerine corsairs – Jefferson had always been a Francophile, and in his mind a stronger Franco-American relationship was a worthy end in itself. But most of his fellow citizens were opposed to such an alliance, and once the French Revolution turned Europe into a theater of war – a war that would last, with only short interruptions, for some 22 years – it became clear that an alliance with France would drag the United States into a European war. Wary of such involvement, the government renounced the treaty it had signed with France in 1778. By 1793, it was evident to Jefferson that if the United States opted to use force to solve the problem of the Barbary pirates, it would have to do so unassisted.

Even after the Algerines renewed their attacks on U.S. trade that year, not all Americans agreed that the application of force was necessary or even desirable. The debate that took place in Congress in 1793-1794 over the proposal to build six frigates for the purpose of suppressing North African piracy exposed a deep cleavage in American attitudes about constructing and maintaining a navy, and by extension, about the role that the United States should play in world affairs.

The congressional debate that took place in 1793-1794 focused not so much on whether it was proper to build a navy at all as it did on the question of that navy's ultimate purpose. Jefferson's supporters, who wanted the six frigates strictly for the current emergency, were suspicious that Federalists who backed the motion did so only to gain a foot in the door for the subsequent development of a standing naval force that would make the United States a player in the game of great power politics – a goal Jeffersonians abhorred. Nor were their suspicions groundless. One of the bill's floor leaders, William Laughton Smith of South Carolina, declared openly that he supported the bill principally because it was proper that the nation should become a naval power – the sooner the better. "Whatever gentlemen may think," he announced, "it was probable that we should at some time become a naval power; and even with the most distant prospect of that, it would show economy to prepare for it" [12].

Most of the bill's supporters, however, denied that this was their objective. They asserted that the six warships proposed in the pending legislation were needed only for the immediate emergency and not as part of any long-term scheme to make the United States a naval power. Denying that the construction of a large standing navy was their goal, they poked fun at those who accused them of such ambitions. Somewhat disingenuously, Uriah Tracy of Connecticut declared that it was "a sorry compliment to the good sense of the United States . . . to say that if we build six ships this year, we much never stop until we built two hundred." This curious debate led Federalists who opposed the use of force in the Mediterranean to support the bill, while Republicans who favored the use of force (in this limited instance) tried to keep the number of ships limited so that their mission would also be limited. Many found it confusing if not absurd. James Madison reported to Jefferson that "the vague idea of protecting trade when it needs it, misleads the interested who are weak, and the weak who are not interested" [13].

Whatever the motives of the bill's backers, the final wording of the proposal declared flatly that the measure was motivated solely by "the depredations committed by the Algerine corsairs." Suspicious Jeffersonians included language specifying that "if a peace shall take place between the United States and the Regency of Algiers" the construction of the ships would stop, that funding would cease, and that "no farther [sic.] proceeding be had under this act" [14].

The bill became law on March 27, 1794, and for all practical purposes, it marked the beginning of both a U.S. Navy and of an American policy to confront overseas assaults against American interests with force. But it bore the potential to become even more: by authorizing a standing navy, even one so small and focused on so specific an object, the bill was a major step toward re-defining the role that America would play in the world.

## Influencing World Events through Naval Power

The passage of the 1794 Naval Act did not end the crisis with Algiers, nor the debate over how to deal with it. Two years later the United States and the Dey of Algiers, Ali Hassan, struck a deal. Hassan agreed to release the 119 U.S. hostages he held in exchange for a one-time payment of $620,000 and an annual tribute of another $21,000. It was a far cry from "victory," but it was a deal that U.S. negotiators felt they could accept, and a price they could pay [15].

Or perhaps not. The United States had trouble raising the money; American credit was so poor that U.S. officials could not turn their bills of credit into cash – and Ali Hassan was a strictly cash negotiator. Hassan agreed to wait for his money, but only after America pledged itself to sweeten the deal by promising him, in addition to the ransom already negotiated, a brand new 36-gun frigate in exchange for the 119 hostages. Thus nearly two centuries before Ronald Reagan, the United States agreed to its first arms-for-hostages exchange.

It was hardly a diplomatic triumph, but it was peace, and according to the "Peace Establishment Act," all work on the six U.S. frigates was now to cease. The Federalist advocates of an active, internationalist United States were disappointed by these developments. Their disappointment stemmed not so much from a concern that American honor had somehow been compromised – they did not object in principle to paying the tribute – but rather from a conviction that other international disputes would surely arise eventually, and it seemed to them only common sense to anticipate such problems now by building a standing navy. Besides, they argued, so much had already been spent on building the six frigates: most of the timber had been acquired, the plans had been drafted, and the keels had been laid. To abandon all that now was simply wasteful.

Opponents found it hard to defend the deal with Algiers, but they repeated their concerns about a standing naval force. They asserted that it would somehow drag the United States into European squabbles. They claimed that it would necessitate a new bureaucracy including: "A Marine Department, something like a War Department" [16]. Proponents did not deny it, but they insisted that such a bureaucracy was both desirable and inevitable. With remarkable prescience, John Swanwick of Pennsylvania predicted that "whenever an equal number of years has passed over this country to that which passed between the reign of Queen Elizabeth and George 3rd [a period of 147 years], America will doubtless be found to possess naval strength equal to that possessed by any other power whatever." Adding those 147 years to 1796 makes 1943 the year that Swanwick prophesied that America would emerge as the greatest naval power on earth [17].

By now the issue had metamorphosed from "Should the United States use force or diplomacy in dealing with the Barbary powers?" into "Should the United States aspire to become a great power in order to influence world events?" Navalists in Congress wanted to complete the six frigates not so much because they feared that the Algerines would recant the recent agreement as because they wanted a standing American Navy to serve as a tool of power politics. Though six frigates were not particularly impressive when measured against the gigantic fleets of Britain and France, they were at least a start, and navalists offered up visions of a small U.S. Navy that could tilt the world balance of power to its favor. If the United States only had a navy, Samuel Smith of Maryland declared, it would be possible to tell the European nations "we will throw our weight into the opposite scale if you continue to insult and injure us." [18].

Opponents of a standing navy were horrified by such a vision. They cited the danger of being drawn into the ongoing world war in Europe; they cited the great expense of building and maintaining a navy; they cited the threat to democratic processes posed by creating a standing military force with its own hierarchy and self-interest. They objected that the ships had no immediate utility. "The expense was certain," one declared, "and the advantages doubtful" [19].

Such arguments won the day. Navalists failed to convince Congress to complete all six frigates; the best they were able to do was gain an authorization to complete three of the six, and moreover, even those three were to be kept out of service to await a future emergency much like Jefferson's musket-over-the-mantelpiece navy.

In March 1801, Thomas Jefferson became the third president of the United States after a confusing and controversial election that had to go to the House of Representatives after the vote in the Electoral College ended in a tie. At last Jefferson was in a position to direct American foreign and defense policy. By then the navy that he inherited from his old friend and rival John Adams consisted of 13 frigates. It had grown from the original three to nearly 50 warships during the Quasi War with France, and was then reduced to a baker's dozen by the Peace Establishment Act passed just before Jefferson took office. That act stipulated that of the 13 frigates, only six were to be kept on active duty; the rest were to be placed in storage (what a later generation would call "mothballed") to await a future crisis. This was precisely the kind of navy-in-waiting that Jefferson had long advocated. As far as he was concerned, a 13 ship navy was just the right size: large enough to get the job done in the Mediterranean where the North African city states continued to cause trouble, but not so large as to pose a realistic threat to the major powers of Europe, still locked in their interminable death struggle [20].

Moreover, Jefferson knew exactly what he wanted to do with his small navy. With only six ships in active service, he would divide this force into two squadrons, sending one to the Mediterranean to act as a restraining influence on the Barbary States, and keeping the other at home. After six months, the two squadrons would rotate. In this way, the United States could maintain what Jefferson called "a squadron of observation" on duty full time in the Mediterranean. In effect, this was the origin of what is now the U.S. Sixth Fleet: a standing American naval force on guard in the Mediterranean to enforce American policy and protect American interests.

It did not take long for this policy to be tested. When Commodore Richard Dale arrived in the Mediterranean with the first such "squadron of observation," he discovered that the bashaw of Tripoli, a wily political survivor named Yusuf Karamanli, had already decided to nullify the existing treaty with the United States and resume hostilities with an eye to renegotiating a new and more profitable arrangement. Jefferson's policy of distancing the nation from European entanglements while applying force to the Barbary corsairs would now be put to the test [21].

Jefferson's use of naval force during his first term was consistent with his longstanding opposition to navalist ambitions and to his pragmatic roots. His object was the specific and narrow goal of defending American commerce in the Mediterranean from the corsairs of North Africa, and the means he employed were proportionate to that end. It is worth noting that the force he dispatched – three frigates and a sloop of war – mounted a total of 130 guns, very nearly the size of the force he had proposed back in 1785. At the same time, Jefferson was careful not to conduct the war in a way that would involve the United States in any aspect of the ongoing war in Europe. Jefferson's use of naval force was thus both limited and specific; his fear of wider entanglement remained a key aspect of his naval policy [22].

The American war against Tripoli progressed haltingly. Dale proved a disappointment as a wartime commander, as did his successor, Richard Valentine Morris. Not until the arrival of Edward Preble in 1803 did the small U.S. squadron find both leadership and success in its first overseas military adventure. At first it seemed that Preble, too, was doomed to failure. Just before he arrived, his principal subordinate, Captain William Bainbridge, ran the U.S. frigate *Philadelphia* aground on Kailusa Reef outside Tripoli Harbor. Unable to re-float his vessel, Bainbridge ordered the crew to toss the ship's guns over the side in an effort to lighten ship. Alas, the *Philadelphia* remained hard aground, and now it was also defenseless. The Tripolitans soon captured it as a prize, and though the ship itself was subsequently burned in a daring raid led by Lieutenant Stephen Decatur, Yusuf Karamanli had gained an invaluable bargaining chip: more than 300 American prisoners of war, including Bainbridge.

In spite of this disaster, Preble soon imposed a full-time blockade on Tripoli Harbor, and conducted several daring raids into the harbor (including Decatur's). Eventually, he also agreed (though with some initial reluctance) to cooperate with a scheme concocted by William Eaton, the American consul in Tunis, to engineer a plot designed to bring about a coup d'etat inside Tripoli. To unseat Karamanli, Eaton recruited Yusuf's older brother Hamet, then living in Egypt, and convinced him to claim the throne. Backed by a rag tag Arab army bolstered by a company of nine U.S. Marines, Hamet began a quixotic march across North Africa aimed at toppling Yusuf from power. Just as American policy makers in the early Twenty-first Century hoped that Saddam Hussein's own people would overthrow him once it became clear that the United States would provide aid and support for such a venture, so to did American policy makers in the early Nineteenth Century hope to engineer a "regime change" in Tripoli.

Then as now, not all Americans believed that a regime change was a good idea. Tobias Lear, the chief American negotiator, thought that Hamet, once on the throne, was likely to be worse than Yusuf, for Hamet was more mercurial and therefore less reliable. Even William Bainbridge, languishing as a POW in the bashaw's castle, was skeptical. Secretly he wrote from his prison (using invisible ink made from lemon juice) to urge Lear not to allow the United States to get involved in "such an impolitic & extraordinary measure" [23].

## ACCEPTING SUCCESS OR PURSUING VICTORY?

The war lasted most of five years, though the active phase occupied little more than two. In the end, American success was marked not by a military victory, but by another negotiated settlement. Yusuf was pragmatic enough to recognize that prolonging the war indefinitely was not in his best interest. The lengthy American blockade was having a disastrous effect on Tripoli's economy and therefore on his own popularity, and the Arab-American army, with his brother Hamet in tow, was coming closer. Yusuf's determination to remain in power trumped his reluctance to give in to American demands. He decided to seek a deal.

By now, the American naval commanders of the Mediterranean Squadron believed that victory was close, and they wanted to fight it out to a final conclusion. But Lear was practical enough to appreciate that a complete victory – which would necessitate the conquest of Tripoli, the release of the American prisoners, and the elimination of Yusuf Karamanli – was sure to be costly if not, in fact, impossible. Yusuf had warned John Rodgers, who now commanded the blockading squadron, that if U.S. forces tried to seize the city, he would take the American hostages and flee inland to a fortress in the desert from which he would continue his defiance [24].

Lear concluded that it was more realistic to accept a quick settlement than to press for a final and complete victory. His minimum goals were (1) the release of the American POWs, and (2) an end to the tribute system. As for a "regime change," Lear decided that as long as Yusuf was reasonable in his demands, he could stay on as bashaw. To him, a chastised Yusuf was better for future U.S. interests than his unpredictable brother who, after all, might not be able to consolidate power in Tripoli. Hamet, Lear concluded, was disposable. Lear agreed to pay a token sum for the release of the POWs if Yusuf would drop his demands for an annual tribute.

Yusuf was willing. He asked for a one-time fee of $200,000 for the American hostages. Lear offered $60,000, and after some blustering, Yusuf agreed. As for Hamet, now that he was no longer needed, the Americans dropped him. He was given $200 for his trouble and cut loose. Few second-guessed the decision. This American *volte face* angered only William Eaton, who had recruited Hamet and organized the overland expedition designed to bring about a regime change. Eaton conceived of his mission as one that involved American honor as well as American interests, and he felt that Lear's decision to abandon Hamet was dishonorable. In a passionate letter to Congress, he declared that "honor recoils" from such perfidy. His anguished complaint, however, fell on deaf ears. With the war over, most Americans, including Jefferson, were willing to accept the terms [25].

## CONCLUSION

There was a postscript to the American success at Tripoli. A decade later in 1815 as America's second war with Britain was winding down, the Dey of Algiers tried to renew the Barbary System, and once again corsairs from North Africa struck at American trade in the Mediterranean. The U.S. response was swift. President Madison sent not one but two squadrons to the Mediterranean to uphold American maritime rights. Stephen Decatur, in command of the first squadron, captured the flagship of the Algerine Navy en route to Algiers and this gave him decisive leverage in negotiating an end to the tribute system with Algiers as well as with Tripoli. A year later an English squadron put a final end to the Barbary System by pounding Algiers into submission, and in 1830 France made it a colony.

In the end, the United States used a variety of tools to bring about a satisfactory solution to the crisis in the first half decade of the nineteenth century. After several attempts to purchase a peace, policy makers eventually concluded that such negotiations were unreliable as well as dishonorable. But the application of naval force also proved of limited utility. It was only the combination of military pressure, political isolation, and financial inducement that led to the re-establishment of peace. Though Yusuf Karamanli remained bashaw in Tripoli, the American hostages came home, and U.S. trade returned to the Mediterranean. Jefferson's decision to focus U.S. naval power on a specific and obtainable objective, as well as his determination to keep the United States out of the broader and more dangerous European war, were important elements in securing this success. Though William Eaton felt that the United States acted ignobly by dumping Hamet Karamanli, and John Rodgers was disappointed not to be allowed a final assault on the citadel at Tripoli, Tobias Lear was willing to accept a success rather than insist on victory. That success came at a modest cost whereas a commitment to victory would have prolonged the war indefinitely with no certainty of a satisfactory outcome.

## REFERENCES


[1] Poll figures from AmericaOnLine, accessed 20 January 2003.

[2] The trauma of the American crew aboard the *Maria* is contained in James Leander Cathcart, *The Captives: Eleven Years in Algiers* (LaPorte, IN: J.B. Cathcart, 1899).

[3] The Barbary system is described in Gardner Allen, *Our Navy and the Barbary Corsairs* (Boston: Houghton Mifflin, 1905); Glenn Tucker, *Dawn Like Thunder: The Barbary Wars and the Birth of the U.S. Navy* (Indianapolis, IN: Bobbs-Merrill, 1963); and A.B.C. Whipple, *To the Shores of Tripoli: The Birth of the U.S. Navy and Marines* (New York: William Morrow, 1991).

[4] Richard O'Brien to Thomas Jefferson, June 8, 1786, *Naval Documents Related to the United States Wars with the Barbary Powers*, Dudley Knox, ed. (Washington: Government Printing Office, 1939-1955), vol. I, p. 3. Hereafter cited as *NDBW*; all references are to volume I.

[5] O'Brien Report dated April 28, 1787, and Jefferson's letters to Congress dated December 28 and December 30, all in *NDBW*, pp. 18-26.

[6] See, for example, Jefferson to Adams, July 11 and July 31, 1786, both in *NDBW*, p. 12.

[7] Jefferson to Adams, July 11, 1786, *NDBW*, p. 10.

[8] Adams to Jefferson, July 31, 1786, *NDBW*, p. 12.

[9] D. Humphreys to Edward Church, October 12, 1793, *NDBW*, p. 47.

[10] Washington's Address to Congress, December 3, 1793, in *A Compilation of the Messages and Papers of the Presidents*, James D. Richardson, ed (Washington: Government Printing Office, 1896-99), 1:140.

[11] *Annals of Congress*, 3rd Congress, 1st session, pp. 143, 154.

[12] *Annals of Congress*, 4th Congress, 2nd session, p. 2122.

[13] *Annals of Congress*, 3rd Congress, 1st session, p. 449; Madison to Jefferson, March 9, 1794, in James Morton Smith, ed., *The Republic of Letters: The Correspondence Between Thomas Jefferson and James Madison, 1776-1826* (New York: W.W. Norton, 1995), vol. 2, p. 835. For an extended discussion of the Congressional debates over the Act of 1794 see Marshall Smelser, *The Congress Founds the Navy, 1787-1798* (South Bend, IN: Notre Dame University Press, 1959), 12-24; and Craig L. Symonds, *Navalists and Antinavalists: The Naval Policy Debate in the United States, 1785-1827* (Newark, DE: Delaware University Press, 1980), 27-38.

[14] U.S. Congress, *The Public Statutes at Large of the United States of America* (Boston: Little and Brown, 1859), 1:350-51.

[15] The text of the treaty is printed in *NDBW*, pp. 107-116. The sum negotiated did not include "Peace Presents" totaling $36,028 nor the "Present to Hadgi Ali," that is, to Hassan, in the amount of $1,659.60. See Ray W. Irwin, *The Diplomatic Relations of the United States With the Barbary Powers* (Chapel Hill: University of North Carolina Press, 1931), 71-72.

[16] *Annals of Congress*, 4th Congress, 1st session, 873.

[17] Ibid., 878.

[18] *Annals of Congress*, 4th Congress, 2nd session, 2117.

[19] Ibid., 2119.

[20] Jefferson has long been credited with (or condemned for) the reduction of the Navy in 1801, but the Peace Establishment Act was one of the "midnight acts" passed by the lame duck Federalist Congress on March 3 before Jefferson took office, though it was intended to forestall an expected effort by Jefferson to make even deeper cuts once he took office.

[21] Karamanli demanded a lump-sum payment of $225,000 and an annual tribute of an additional $25,000. See Secretary of State to William Eaton, March 21, 1801, *NDBW*, p. 425.

[22] Symonds, Navalists and Antinavalists, 95.

[23] A.B.C. Whipple, *To the Shores of Tripoli: The Birth of the U.S. Navy and Marines* (New York: William Morrow, 1991), 248.

[24] Ibid.

[25] William Eaton to Isaac Hull, January 8, 1805, *The Hull-Eaton Correspondence* (Worcester, MA: American Antiquarian Society, 1911), p. 21; Whipple, *To The Shores of Tripoli*, 254-56.

In: Presidents and War
Editors: A. Eksterowicz and G. Hastedt, pp. 29-51
ISBN 978-1-61668-917-9


*Chapter 3*

# WARS OF CHOICE: JAMES MADISON, GEORGE W. BUSH AND THE PRESIDENTIAL LEGACY QUESTION

***Anthony J. Eksterowicz and Glenn P. Hastedt***

## INTRODUCTION

What can be noted about the legacy of a president who conducts a war of choice? To exemplify such a situation let us assume that a president has, at one time or another, stated various reasons for the conduct of such a war. So much so that average citizens find it difficult to ascertain the fundamental and real reasons for such an action. Furthermore, the president has cloaked the language justifying the war in the language of necessity (national defense) not choice. The president plays fast and loose with the facts to convince the public by using worst case analysis to bolster the need for war. The president has not prepared the nation for the waging of this war in that no direct individual taxes have been raised nor has the population been asked to sacrifice any material goods for the war effort. The president and his allies reassure the public that the war will be won with a minimal amount of violence and that the opposing forces will be defeated in short order. In addition, the economic costs of war will be low. The president appeals to the patriotism of the nation to unify citizens behind the cause. He simultaneously characterizes opposition figures and arguments as dangerous to the cause of victory at best and traitorous at worst. The president asserts executive powers that serve to provoke the opposition forces. He notes that all diplomatic efforts have been exhausted and the enemy still resists the nation's demands. There appears to be no alternative to war from the president's and his party's perspective. While the president portrays unity of purpose there seems to be concern in military circles about the effectiveness of our fighting forces. In addition, there is concern within the president's party and among the opposition for the nature of the president's leadership abilities. This is displayed by arguments among cabinet members about the necessity, justification, preparedness and leadership required of a successful war effort. The president is aware of such criticisms but asserts his justifications for war in no uncertain terms and acts as though making tough decisions reflects bold leadership.

Many of the above characteristics can be applied to President George W. Bush in his conduct of the Iraq war. However, we present them as not only applicable to President Bush but also applicable to James Madison in his conduct of the War of 1812. Wars of choice present presidents with similar circumstances and how they manage such circumstances contribute to their legacy.

In the last year of his presidency, President Bush was thinking of his legacy and particularly about the impact of the Iraq War upon such a legacy. In fact, a group of scholars and pundits have suggested that Bush will be treated better in history's long run than he is today. Some go as far as suggesting he might turn out to be another Truman. Harry Truman was a president who left office with extremely low popular approval ratings and yet somehow today is revered for his tough and decisive decisions. These decisions have withstood the test of time. All of this occurs before the Bush economic collapse but their analysis was limited to the foreign policy area.

Forgetting the fact that presidents do not get to choose which other presidents they will be compared to and that when these comparisons are made they usually encompass the entire policy realms of an administration, wars of choice have remarkably contributed to negative assessments for many presidents. We posit that understanding the problems associated with such efforts can go a long way in determining just how presidents are treated legacy wise. Thus, there is great utility in examining Madison's efforts in the War of 1812 and Bush's efforts in the Iraq War for similarities and contrasts.

In this article we discuss the problems associated with determining wars of choice and wars of necessity. Then we examine President Madison's War of 1812. We first discuss the international and domestic political environment within which the war takes place. We note the causes expressed for the war both real and contrived. We also attempt to ascertain the true causes as best we can. We cite the nature of expectations and leadership associated with the war. We cite logistical and military strategies and problems with the war. We also examine the nature of the opposition to the war. We then examine President Bush's Iraq war and scrutinize it among the lines above. Finally we draw some conclusions concerning wars of choice and their legacy upon presidents.

## Wars of Choice or Necessity

Early in the 2004 presidential election year President Bush was asked on *Meet the Press* if he considered the Iraq War a war of choice or necessity. Mr. Bush was not prepared for the question. He replied, "That's an interesting question," as if to give him time to think through the implications. He even asked the questioner to elaborate on that a bit. Finally he answered with certainty that it was a war of necessity [1]. One can forgive the president for hesitating because it is not an easy answer.

How can we distinguish wars of choice from wars of necessity? Any given war is to some extent in the eye of the beholder. So it is possible for two different people to see the same war but one may see it as a war of necessity and the other as a war of choice. Thus someone like a Charles Krauthammer sees the Vietnam War as a war of necessity [2] while another like Richard Hass views it as a war of choice [3]. The criteria for distinguishing the two are often cloaked by policymakers who wish to turn a perceived war of choice into a perceived war of necessity in order to rally the nation behind a noble cause which only they may see clearly. That is why the reasons for initiating such a war are often cloaked in the language of necessity. Furthermore, there may be many reasons for the initiation of the war articulated by various policymakers at various times. These reasons may swing from national defense to the promotion of democracy to the protection of resources vital to the functioning of a democracy. But which is the real and paramount reason? It is difficult to tell among the various reasons given by policymakers. It is also difficult to define what the national interest is at any given moment for great powers have many interests. Finally, can wars of choice turn into wars of necessity and vice versa? [4]. For example did the War of 1812, which we argue was a war of choice, turn into a war of necessity once the British invaded the United States and burnt the capital building and the White House?

On this last question we may have an answer. We would argue that it is the initial decision to go to war that is of paramount importance. One cannot blame a big bully for retaliating against a smaller foe if that foe deliberately poked him in the eye with a stick. It is the initial act of poking that is important. The other questions are much more difficult to handle. We would suggest that there are a number of criteria that distinguish a war of choice from a war of necessity. With regards to some wars it may be self evident that they are either one or the other. For example, World War II is generally believed to be a war of necessity despite Patrick J. Buchanan's arguments to the contrary [5]. There is a certain amount of "I know it when I see it" mentality here. Other wars are much more difficult to distinguish. For example, how would one characterize the Civil War? It would depend upon which perspective was stressed the North's or South's. In any event, there are a number of characteristics associated with a war of choice.

A war of choice is offensive in character. There is am emphasis upon the danger to national interests in waiting for an attack or invasion. There is much more of an emphasis upon prevention and even preemption. In addition all diplomatic means toward neutralizing the crisis may not have been exhausted even though top national policymakers may claim otherwise. In other words there are always a few more diplomatic steps left on the table. Wars of choice are often portrayed as low cost, low risk endeavors. A quick and easy end to them seems to be the watchword. Policymakers usually do not take draconian measures to prepare the nation for such wars. National taxes may not be raised. There may be little to no attempts at rationing goods necessary to the war effort. Standards of living will not take an immediate hit therefore the nation is not prepared for the longevity of the struggle by being asked to make sacrifices. It can be termed war on the cheap if not for the inevitable, long run, losses of life and investments. The protection of the state from physical attack or invasion is usually not of immediate concern although policymakers may threaten dire outcomes if nothing is done. Another characteristic of such wars is initial high public support because of the expectation of a quick victory and low costs. This, in turn, leads to an increase in opposition to such wars as they drag on and these initial expectations fail to be realized [6].

Another characteristic of these wars is their call for patriotism and characterization of the opposition as unpatriotic or even traitorous. This is especially the case if these wars are initiated during election years.

The great problem here is that wars of choice may not be perceived that way until they progress and begin to bog down. Their danger lay in their initial framing. We suggest that it may be useful to place wars along a continuum. At one end there are clearly the wars of choice like Vietnam, the War of 1812 and Iraq. At the other end, wars of necessity may be represented by World War II and the Revolutionary War. The more a war exhibits the characteristics of a war of choice it would fall closer to the choice side of the continuum. Thus any war may possess more or less of these characteristics but we may still be able to determine its nature.

Using this method both the War of 1812 and the Iraq War under the leadership of James Madison and George W. Bush appear to be wars of choice. We now turn to the analysis of these wars and what they portend for presidential legacies.

# Madison and the War of 1812

## The International and Domestic Environment

The international and domestic environment that led to the War of 1812 was one of war between France and England. For many years preceding Mr. Madison's war France and England were fighting for economic domination in trade and commerce in the European theater. Their colonies were producing goods and products that had to be protected from one another. The threat to Britain was Napoleon and his dreams of conquest. Empires literally collided from approximately the 1790s to Napoleon's defeat by the British at Leipzig in 1813 and again at Waterloo in 1815. The war was fought on land and sea. Two great naval armadas met for battle on the high seas. As such the burgeoning country of America, formally neutral, found itself caught between these two great powers. No matter what agreement was made with one country the other would take offense as did France after the United States signed the Jay Treaty with England in 1794. This treaty regulated commerce and defined neutral rights during the war between France and England. The French resented the treaty so much that there was a sort of mini naval war between America and France from 1798 to 1801 [7].

From the American perspective there was a changing of the guard politically with the election of Thomas Jefferson in 1800. Before this election the Federalist Party under Alexander Hamilton's influence wanted to prepare the nation financially for war and build up its defense establishment. There were various threats that existed on American boarders from the potential Spanish and French threats in the south and southwest to the British threat in Canada and their increasing alliance with Native American tribes in the north and northwest. However Jefferson's election changed the American response. Jeffersonian Republicans were against big government programs and worked to cut taxes and reduce national debt. This meant that defense spending declined under Jefferson. He preferred defensive measures such as gunboats to protect American ports. He believed them to be cheap and effective [8].

During this time American neutrality was severely tested by both the British and the French. They were competing economically by restricting each others' most important trading goods via quarantines and blockades. Napoleon's Continental System served to restrict British manufacturing and trade. The British Orders in Council sought to do the same to France [9]. These two decisions confounded Jefferson and America around 1806-07 but there was another important issue that would lead to Jefferson's embargo of British goods and that was the British practice of impressments.

Naval war consumed ships and as the War of 1812 approached the British fleet experienced shortages of lumber which England increasingly had to obtain from Canada due to French and Russian actions regarding the closing of Baltic ports exporting such goods [10]. During this time the British experienced shortages of material and other goods that hindered their ability to build and maintain a large fleet. As 1812 neared British shipbuilding declined [11]. As early as the issuance of Orders in Council the British experienced a shortage of sailors to man their ships. Many British sailors deserted the spartan quarters and harsh treatment aboard British vessels for the more accommodating American vessels. British ships began the practice of boarding American ships in search of such sailors but inevitably American sailors were *impressed* by the British to serve on their ships. This practice caused much distress between Britain and America and led to Jefferson's embargo of British goods in retaliation. Near the beginning of the War of 1812 nearly 6000 American sailors had been impressed by the British and nearly one quarter of the men aboard American ships were British [12].

Domestically, America was divided. The Federalist Party was strong in the northeast and in New England. They were opposed to the war and believed that President Madison was too close to France. They preferred the British Crown to the Emperor Napoleon. However, Madison's own party was split between his supporters and the supporters of the New York Republican Clintons; DeWitt and George. In fact George Clinton ran against Madison in 1808 as an Independent Republican and DeWitt Clinton ran against him in 1812 as a Federalist. The Clintons and their followers believed that the Republican Party should have adhered to greater Federalists principles. Thus they disliked Madison for not preparing properly for war. The so called "invisible Republicans" also wanted an increase in military preparedness and they despised Secretary of the Treasury Albert Gallatin. John Randolph of Roanoke Virginia, a Republican, disliked Mr. Madison for towing too much of a Federalist line [13]. The election of increasing numbers of Republican War Hawks to Congress after 1810 and Republican majority control of both houses of Congress in 1812 did much too politically spur on war [14].

Thus on the eve of the War of 1812, America had been dealing with her neutrality rights between two great powers fighting for economic superiority and world empire. Any move in this environment would be tricky at best and quite hazardous at worst. Tensions mounted between all three nations as the war approached. Domestically things were not much better. The nation was split three or four ways. There were splits in Mr. Madison's Republican party and he was not a well liked person within his party. In addition, the nation was not yet the *United* States of America. That would come only after a bitter Civil War. It was Mr. Madison's task to unify the nation and it would not be easy.

## The Causes for War

The War of 1812 has become known as Mr. Madison's war precisely because he made the choice. It was not strictly speaking a defensive war although President Madison attempted to cloak it in that language. The nation was not prepared for war. There existed no professional military in place [15]. The nation did not raise taxes to fund the effort preferring to borrow loans to finance the war [16]. In addition, there were expectations of a quick victory encouraged by government policymakers and Mr. Madison. Most of the criteria we developed for a war of choice apply to the War of 1812.

The causes for the war can largely be found in the objectives for war. We should note that scholars are still debating the primary cause for the war and at this time it may never be known with certainty. One reason for war was the British issuance of Orders in Council which affected American trade with other nations allied with either France or Britain. Closely related to this was the practice of British impressments of American sailors. As Hickey noted the war was fought for"free trade and sailors rights" [17].

There was an economic component to the need for war. America fought to free up trade with the European continent.

A second reason concerns the Northwest Territory. British officials in Canada were arming Indian tribes there. America feared the possibility of war from Canada and coercion of the increasing number of Americans settling in Canada [18]. While there were tensions along the boarder there also seems to be a bit of pre-emptive mentality in this reason.

A third reason flows from the second and can be attributed to the Federalists critics of the Madison administration. They believed that Mr. Madison wanted to annex Canada. This reason appears sound since the initial war plans called for an invasion of Canada. The protection of American settlers there was also one of the professed aims of the Republican War Hawks. Irving Brant claims that Madison disavowed this goal to the British shortly after the war began. According to Brant, the invasion was only strategic to defeat enemy troops within reach of America [19]. There is disagreement concerning this goal.

Stagg has argued that as the war approached the British believed that Canada could supply timber, fish and livestock that their West Indies colonies needed. Therefore the British could continue to obtain sugar and coffee from the West Indies. Canada's importance only increases after Russia denies the British access to her Baltic ports. At the same time American settlers rush to Canada where they find cheap land. With the American embargo failing Canada becomes even more crucial to American interests [20].

A fourth reason concerns the domestic political reality at the beginning of the war. President Madison was the leader of a deeply divided party doing battle with a Federalist Party. The war was one way of unifying all of these factions within the Republican Party and forging a governing base after the war. It would also have the effect of weakening the Federalist Party and silencing their opposition [21]. This view places much responsibility upon the "War Hawks" in Congress for the drumbeat to war.

Finally, there was the reason of national honor. We went to war to preserve our republican institutions. We went to war to demonstrate that we believed in our patriotic principles. We would not allow any empire to continue to disgrace us. Our prestige as a nation was at stake.

What can be noted of these reasons for war? Well they all appear to contain a grain of truth because all were expressed formally or informally encouraged by President Madison, his Republican Party leaders, members of his party in Congress, and the Federalist opposition among others. How do we determine the primary cause of the war after all of these years? It may be impossible for the scholarly community is still divided over this as a few of our cited sources demonstrate. One thing is clear, these objectives went largely unmet. The British government decided to stop the practice of impressments and revoked their Orders in Council before a shot was fired. Due to travel times in those days and a lag in communication Madison was unaware of this. War could have been avoided with further diplomatic overtures and more decision time for the Congress. It was an unnecessary war if we believe these reasons were the main ones. Ironically, Madison attempted to get the slow moving Congress to declare war a bit faster by revealing the letters of a man named John Henry who he portrayed as being in league with the British in Canada, Henry's purpose was to stir up trouble among the war resisters in New England. Madison actually paid for these dubious letters [22]. There was an impatience displayed by the Madison administration and a few diplomatic steps or maneuvers were left on the table.

Perhaps the closest we will get to the true cause of the war lies in the combination of political and economic reasons. Canada became crucial for American trade and the divisions within Madison's own party and the nature of the Federalist opposition all seemed to make war more likely. However, when assessing the success of the war, President Madison achieved very little beyond the unification of his own party and an increase in patriotism and national pride [23]. These are hardly reasons that justify the loss of life and national economic treasure that the war brought about. In fact, the cost of war was estimated at about 105 million dollars and it took, two decades to pay off this debt [24]. The war also failed to achieve its purpose of spreading republican institutions and democracy into Canada via conquest [25].

## National Expectations and Leadership

National military leaders, Republican Party leaders, the War Hawks in Congress and President Madison thought this would be a quick and decisive war. They believed that the British were too far away to protect Canada adequately and that the French and American settlements would help welcome Americans as they invaded Canada. In the eyes of some, Canada was there for the taking [26]. Others thought that the British were too occupied with Napoleon and would immediately give in when war was declared. Many American newspapers did not believe that Britain would invade America [27]. This would lead to a bloodless victory [28]. All of these beliefs were founded in wishful thinking and reflected the unwillingness to prepare seriously for war or at least a moderately long term struggle. This, in turn, reflected a lack of leadership in various circles.

The nature of the preparations for war or the lack thereof was stunning. We have already noted that the Republican Party was fiscally stringent eschewing keeping large numbers of men under arms during peacetime. There was also an unwillingness to increase taxes for the war preferring instead to borrow through loans for the effort. A naval build up was also needed but largely ignored for the preference of increasing the Army [29]. As a result, at the outset of the war the nation needed men, equipment, money, leadership, a realistic strategy for success and an appreciation that this endeavor might last a while. All of this reflected the type of leadership available to the nation.

Leadership suffered due to a number of problems. There were divisions within President Madison's own Republican Party which we have noted previously. It was a very difficult party to lead on the eve of war. It suffered from excessive argumentation and factions within its cabinet. These are problems that strong presidents must overcome but what type of a leader was James Madison?

Gary Wills notes that Madison was primarily a legislator whose best accomplishments came by working in secret. He was small in stature and prone to social isolation. While brilliant in drafting legislative and constitutional documents and in argumentation he was very provincial in his outlook. He was the only Secretary of State who never traveled abroad. This resulted in a naiveté about world politics and his fellow men. To Madison isolationism was a good thing [30].

These are not characteristics that foster leadership in presidential circles. Add to this that 1812 was an election year and Madison was pressing the Congress for action that would help to unify the Republican Party. But it is proper to ask if war for the sake of political unity is leadership? Therefore the unrealistic expectations surrounding the war effort, the necessity to act in an election year, the problems associated with leadership all lead to America's lack of preparation for war and inevitability for conducting it.

## Strategic and Military Problems

The first struggle the nation faced was the raising of an army for the war effort. There was a debate concerning troop levels. Madison wanted to rely upon short term volunteers and militia largely because he believed it would be a short war. However Congress raised the level of regular troops but they also engaged in a debate concerning the use of state militias. This threatened to decentralize the war to the leadership of governors in the states. There was also concern that militias could not legally engage in foreign wars on Canadian soil. In addition, Congress would not support a proposed expansion of the navy. Many believed that we simply could not compete with Great Britain on the high seas. The final compromise on troops was a combination of volunteers, regulars and militia in numbers hardly adequate for a long struggle [31]. The leadership of this army was also problematical.

In 1808 General Winfield Scott provided a scathing assessment of the military officer corps. He noted that the appointments to the officer corps were bad and influenced by party politics. Very few Federalists were appointed to the corps. The remainder of Republicans were not very educated leading to ignorant men as officers. This was the case particularly among New England Republicans. Other appointees were generally unfit for any duty [32]. Political patronage infected the appointment process so much that many believed the army was politicized. During the beginning of the war Madison's administration selected new generals from the pool of aging Revolutionary Republican veterans. Many of them were ex politicians [33]. There were no preparations for these officers to recruit for or organize their regiments. There were shortages of pay, supplies and equipment all of which directly led to early defeats in land battles in the north and northwest [34]. We should note that the army did get better as the war progressed. By the end of the war it was a professional, highly educated and socialized tool for defense [35]. This did not help the nation in the early going.

The military strategy was also a problem. Madison's administration thought a great deal about land war but the administration and the Congress neglected the Navy. Ironically some of the most accomplished military commanders like Perry and McDonough were in the Navy. Their exploits and defeats of the British along the Great Lakes were legendary. However, the British remained far superior along the east coast where they burned towns, plundered property and pillaged villages including Washington D.C. Mr. Madison was lucky to escape their wrath.

The land war strategy was lacking. The best plan was a frontal assault on Montreal with all available troops. However that would require the cooperation of the New England states through which invading forces would travel. This section of the country was heavily Federalist and opposed to the war effort. Therefore, a three pronged attack was launched through the New York/Niagra, Montreal, Dearborn/Detroit areas. All of which met with humiliating defeat and surrender of American troops. It did not help that the War Department was in disarray, payment of soldiers was lacking and there was a shortage of food and doctors [36]. A war of choice should offer opportunities for far superior organization and preparation but ironically history would seem to demonstrate the opposite.

## Federalist Opposition

As Hickey notes the War of 1812 provoked the most opposition of any American war effort. The grisly riot by Republicans against a Federalist newspaper and its staff and editor was but an example of this [37]. Federalist's arguments against the war were framed by the highly politicized environment of the times. Republicans, though divided, controlled the presidency and both houses of Congress. Mr. Madison did not obtain a single Federalist vote in the House of Representatives or the Senate for war. In fact only 61% of all votes in both houses were for war. The closest of any war vote in the nation's history [38]. Mr. Madison would lose support and Republican representatives in Congress all through the war until after the signing of the Treaty of Ghent.

Federalists had many reasons to oppose the war. They noted the obvious problems associated with preparation for the war. They did not buy the spreading of democracy to Canada argument. Federalists did not consider a conquered people fertile soil for republicanism. They argued that the federal government would become too big and unconcerned with civil liberties. In order to curtail smuggling of British goods through Canada and New England the Madison administration and Congress granted the Customs Department increased powers to search and seize illegal goods. Federalists, especially those on the boarder of Canada, deemed this an invasion of their rights. They considered it spying on Americans and became particularly agitated that it was done through an expansion of Madison's executive order power. Federalists also condemned the war as being political and exploitative of the divisions in the country. They warned of national control of state militias. Federalists complained bitterly that they were being portrayed as traitors who were unpatriotic to the American cause. They stressed their rights to free and open debate. Federalists also feared the effect of the war upon domestic politics [39].

The New York Federalists were particularly incensed. They railed against the projected costs of the war in money and lives. Because of the war Republicans lost control of the New York State legislature after 1812. The New Yorkers warned of confrontations between soldiers and civilians. In this way the war would be brought home against American citizens. They questioned their rights to free speech during this war. In 1814 the Republicans campaigned against New York Federalists and the Federalists lost control of the New York state assembly. Despite these circumstances the New York Federalists campaigned against the war electorally citing its unconstitutional nature. Peace societies sprung up throughout New York and New England after the war [40].

John Lowell produced a passionate but cogent critique of the war in his Dispassionate Inquiry entitled, Mr. Madison's War. He noted that this was a war against Great Britain due to Mr. Madison's preferences for France. He provided extensive reasons as to why the war was wrong least of which was its offensive nature. He noted that we could have settled with Great Britain over the issue of impressments and that the section of the nation hardest hit with impressments was the section most opposed to war. He questioned Mr. Madison's motives, strategies and moral judgment in conducting what he considered to be an immoral and unjust war [41]. The opposition to the war was concentrated in the New York/ New England area but as intense as any opposition ever seen since. With all of these problems how did Mr. Madison fare historically?

## Mr. Madison's Legacy

Immediately after the war the Republicans claimed that they had won the war. They fostered the political unity that the war brought about. The Republican Party was finally a unified force and the Federalist Party was in decline. There was a reveling in the new found patriotism which would be manifest in the Monroe Doctrine under yet another Virginia president. However the deep divisions between sections of the nation that the war revealed would come into play again in the decade before the Civil War. Did Madison win this war? He did not achieve most of his objectives and he was lucky to win the peace if not the war. The costs of the war were enormous; the divisions in the nation were not healed by the effort but rather muted for a time. Mr. Madison's judgment has been severely challenged by modern day historians. His saving grace was the Treaty of Ghent. Madison sent the best possible negotiating team to this conference. The British sent their second or third string team. They were concerned with the peace talks at the Congress in Vienna. To the British Ghent was a side show. The British were tired of the costs of the Napoleonic wars. While some of the British wanted to extract revenge others simply wanted it over. Besides the British had prevented the American conquest of Canada. When all was said and done both sides agreed to a peace treaty which reverted to the status quo before the war [42]. This made the concept of winning irrelevant. Mr. Madison may have won the peace but it was one he could have had at much less cost to the nation.

The scholarly assessment of Mr. Madison's effort has fluctuated a bit over the years. In the immediate aftermath of the war historians like Henry Adams castigated Madison for being a weak and unprepared leader. This affected his legacy in the negative direction. After World War II Irving Brant (cited here in this work) adopted a kinder explanation for Madison's usurpation of power and his abilities as commander in chief. However, more recently, scholars like Donald Hickey (also cited here) have taken the position that Madison lost the War of 1812 due to his inadequacies as commander in chief. What are we to make of this and Madison's legacy? As Wills notes, historians have not considered him a failure but have not seen fit to move him from the average category [43]. One must wonder if that rating has anything to do with Madison's accomplishments before and after his presidency. In any event the War of 1812, a war of choice probably has a lot to do with this average assessment. Is this a celing for war choice presidents? We now turn to another president at another time engaged in a war of choice.

# Bush and the Iraq War

## Domestic and International Environment

George W. Bush assumed the presidency under highly polarized circumstances, a condition that did not change for his entire tenure in office except for a period of national unity following the terrorist attacks of September 11, 2001. He was the first candidate since 1888 elected president with less than a majority of the popular vote and his election was affirmed by the Electoral College only after Florida began a controversial recount of the votes cast for president and the Supreme Court ordered the recount suspended.

George W. Bush was the first Republican president since Dwight Eisenhower to have a majority in both Houses of Congress on taking office, even though it was by the slimmest of margins, 10 seats in the House of Representatives and the tie breaking vote by Vice President Dick Cheney in the Senate. This working majority did not last long as in 2001 Senator Jeffords switched sides and joined the Democratic caucus. Bush regained a majority with the 2002 midterm elections which saw him campaign more vigorously for his party's candidates than was the norm for a sitting president. It was also a campaign marked by highly partisan language in which Democratic incumbents were widely and loosely condemned as soft on terrorism and had their patriotism questioned.

Bush was reelected in 2006 by the slimmest margin of any president since the Civil War and the Republican Party continued to hold a majority in Congress. As in 2000 his election owed far more to the outpouring of support from the Republican Party base than it did to support from swing voters [44]. In 2000, 52% of his vote came from party stalwarts while in 2004 it rose to 59%. Democrats regained control of Congress in the 2006 mid term election in what was generally held to be a nationwide vote repudiating his policy on Iraq.

Once again polarization was evident in the voting patterns of the American public. In May 2006 only 4% of Democratic voters approved of Bush's performance as president. No previous president had ever recorded an approval rating in the single digits from members of the opposition. In stark contrast, in January 2007 89.5% of Republicans approved of the job he had done as president. The average difference between Democratic and Republican respondents in the last quarter of 2004 was 79 points, 13 points higher than it had been during the Clinton administration [45].

The international environment that greeted the Bush administration when it took office looked anything but daunting. It was in most respects quite calm although the storm that would become 9/11 was already brewing beneath the surface. With the end of the Cold War now a decade removed the agenda of American foreign policy seemed increasingly preoccupied by "B" list threats rather than core national security problems. The most troubling military engagements of the Clinton era had either been brought to a conclusion such as Haiti and Somalia or were reaching that point as was the case in the former Yugoslavia. It was the calm and not the coming storm that the Bush administration's national security team (along with virtually all others) focused on as the 2000 presidential election neared.

National Security advisor Condoleezza Rice wrote in *Foreign Affairs* in January 2000 that the United States was "in a remarkable position [46]. Powerful secular trends are moving the world toward economic openness and –more unevenly—democracy and individual liberty…In such an environment, American policies must help further these favorable trends by maintaining a disciplined an consistent foreign policy that separates the important from the trivial." The failure to do so was the Republican Party's primary critique of Clinton's foreign policy. His administration Rice went on had replaced the national interest with humanitarian interests which she defined as there being "nothing wrong with" but as also being of a "second order effect." Perhaps most tellingly, in criticizing Clinton's "epidemic" penchant for seeking out "largely symbolic agreements and its pursuit of, at best, illusory 'norms' of international behavior" Rice pointed to the need to focus on the behavior of the few big powers that can radically affect international peace, stability and prosperity. Nowhere to be found in her discussion of the U.S. national interest was a reference to terrorist groups.

Rice promised that a new Republican administration would 1) ensure that America's military could deter war, project power and fight in defense of its interests if deterrence fails 2) promote economic grown and political openness by fostering free trade and a stable international monetary system 3) renew strong and intimate relations with allies who share American values 4) focus U.S. energies on comprehensive relations with big powers and 5) deal decisively with the threat of rogue regimes an hostile powers. She cautioned that the military is a special instrument and one not designed to be used as a civilian police force, political referee and "certainly not designed to build a civilian society."

This complacent view of the international system was shaken to its core by the terrorist attacks on the World Trade Center and Pentagon so much so that not long after 9/11 Deputy Secretary of State Richard Armitage asserted "history starts today"[47]. In focusing on the terrorist threat the Bush administration cast the attack on the U.S. in global terms embracing a world view in which there was no middle ground. They were not just directed at the U.S. but against freedom, democracy and human rights. "Either you are with us or you are with the terrorists" stated President Bush.

The new more muscular U.S. foreign policy initially encountered little opposition. Traditional allies came to the U.S.'s side as did current adversaries such as Russia. Even those the Bush administration had labeled as rogue states such as Iran and Syria provided the U.S. with quiet support as it prepared for the invasion of Afghanistan and overthrow of the Taliban regime. The first U.S. Special Forces entered Afghanistan on October 19. Conventional forces arrived on November 25, and the last Taliban stronghold fell on December 16. Osama bin Laden, whose group al Qaeda was held responsible for the 9/11 attacks, remained at large. By year's end a multiethnic interim government led by Hamid Karzai was in place.

The climate of widespread international support for the U.S. began to change as the administration turned its attention to Iraq and sought to build the case for war against it at the United Nations in 2002 and 2003. In making its case the U.S. relied upon both behind the scenes arm twisting and the public presentation of intelligence. Central to the administration's argument was Iraq's possession of weapons of mass destruction. When these diplomatic efforts failed the U.S. to sway key Security Council members China, Russia, Germany and France the U.S. along with Great Britain proclaimed they would create a "coalition of the willing" to remove Saddam Hussein from power.

On March 16, 2003 President Bush met with British Prime Minister Tony Blair and leaders from Spain and Portugal in the Azores to announce that the "moment of truth" had arrived for Saddam Hussein. The following day Bush issued an ultimatum requiring Saddam to leave Iraq in 48 hours, and on March 19 Brush ordered the invasion of Iraq. A "shock and awe" military campaign was begun that was designed to overwhelm and demoralize Iraqi forces, allowing the coalition forces to move swiftly to Baghdad. On April 9 Baghdad came under the control of U.S. forces, and on May 1 President Bush declared an end to major combat operations on the USS Abraham Lincoln against the backdrop of a huge banner declaring "mission accomplished."

Expecting to be greeted as liberators, U.S. forces soon came to be viewed as occupiers and became the target of terrorist attacks. Looting and vandalism were common. In September 2004 U.S. casualties had reached the 1,000 mark. As American casualties mounted, the nature of the conflict changed as well. Terrorist attacks directed at the United States and its Iraqi allies now took place alongside a heightened sectarian conflict between the Shia and Sunnis that increasingly took on the character of a civil war.

The conflict also brought forward vivid images of mistreatment of prisoners by American military personnel at Abu Ghraib prison, which served to enflame anti-American sentiment in Iraq and antiwar feelings in the United States. American casualties reached the 3,000 mark by the end of 2006; the United Nations estimated that 34,452 Iraqi civilians died in 2006 and that 30,842 people were detained in Iraq, including 14, 534 in U.S. military–run prisons.

Two years later the political-strategic landscape of Iraq looked very different. The Bush administration's decision after the November 2006 midterm elections to sending additional forces to Iraq, popularly known as the "surge," along with a change in strategy put into place by General David Petraeus that emphasized counterinsurgency tactics against U.S. enemies and working with Iraqis rather than trying to secure victory through battlefield successes against them led to a reduction in the violence and increased political stability. By the time President Barak Obama took office there was widespread agreement that U.S. troop withdrawals from Iraq could take place.

What did not look different in 2008 were continued problems with Iran and North Korea, the two other members of the axis of evil identified by President Bush. Neither had been dissuaded from their pursuit of nuclear power by attempts at diplomatic isolation, economic sanctions, or veiled threats of preemptive military action. Problems also began to resurface in Afghanistan where the Taliban had regrouped and were now once again viewed as a significant national security threat that demanded a U.S. military presence there. More generally a sense had developed that the administration's goal of spreading democracy through the region had been replaced by a support for stability.

Finally because the Bush Doctrine had been so heavily focused on terrorism it seemed to provide little guidance for other national security threats. A case in point was Russian intervention into Georgia during the 2008 Summer Olympics on the side of pro-Russian separatists. The U.S. response was little more than a series of declaratory policy statements of disapproval and support for Georgia. Nothing was done to change the situation on the ground.

## Causes of War

The shifting rationales provided by the Bush administration about its urgency is a major contributing factor to the assessment that the Iraq War was one of choice and not of necessity. The two overarching arguments provided by the administration centered on a link between Iraq and al Qaeda along with its possession of weapons of mass destruction. Although invoked repeatedly neither claim was substantiated, a failure that gave rise to the assertion that administration had either politicized intelligence or simply ignored.

A third frequently expressed rationale for war was the need to bring democracy to the region. Global democratization formed a key tenet in the neo-conservative foreign policy agenda. A world of democratic states was held to be critical to furthering U.S. security in the region. Just as critical to the neo-conservative perspective was the belief that the U.S. had the ability to do so. While the democratic peace argument had already become a central fixture of the debate on U.S. foreign policy before Bush took office it remains a contested position with some arguing there are important differences between liberal and illiberal democracies and between new and established democracies in their peacefulness. Terrorism experts are similarly divided over the relationship between democracy and the origins of terrorist movements.

The subjective nature of the Bush administration's most frequently argued reasons for why the Iraq war was necessary gave rise to speculation that other reasons were really at work. One such argument focused on access to (cheap) oil. A second argument was that George W. Bush was driven to complete the removal of Saddam Hussein from power that his father began but did not finish in the Persian Gulf War. A variant of this argument held that his obsession with Saddam Hussein from power stemmed from a failed assassination attempt on his father. Still another conspiracy theory harkened back to arguments about the influence of the military-industrial complex. In this view the war was designed to provide large profits to companies doing business with the military. Fueling this view were the huge profits earned by Halliburton. Vice President Dick Cheney had served as its Chief Executive Officer from 1995-2000.

## National Expectations and Leadership

The tragic events of 9/11 led to a dramatic reversal of the public's evaluation of George W. Bush. Where prior to that day his approval rating was at or near 50% after 9/11 it hovered near the 90% mark. Neither Bush personally nor his administration as a whole was able to translate this leap in public standing into a long term working foundation on which to govern. It did, however, provide support for a series of national security measures such as the USA Patriot Act in the short term. Long term, his administration's domestic agenda stalled and his personal approval rating decreased steadily as the Iraq War progressed spiking occasionally after such positive events as the capture of Saddam Hussein in 2003 and the Iraqi election in 2005.

Perhaps most significantly Bush was never able to overcome the polarized context within which his actions were evaluated. Far more than was the case with the Korean War, the Vietnam War, the Persian Gulf War, fighting in Kosovo or the invasion of Afghanistan a gap existed between Democratic and Republican support for this war. The average difference in support level from July 2004 through the end of 2005 was about 62 percentage points [48].

Echoes of the polarized pubic attitudes toward the Bush administration were found in the Bush administration's view of the public and its opponents. Governing from his Republican Party base Bush employed "binary rhetoric" in dealing with its opponents. Criticism and debate were characterized as undercutting the war effort, unpatriotic and bordering on treasonous [49]. Perhaps not surprisingly Republicans tended to stand by Bush and the Iraq War effort even as evidence mounted that the principal arguments for going to war, Saddam Hussein's possession of weapons of mass destruction and his links to al-Qaeda, were flawed while Democrats abandoned him. Just after the war began over 80% of Republicans agreed that Iraq was a national security threat to the U.S. and at least 60% would continue to hold this belief. In contrast, only 46% of Democrats saw Iraq as a threat at the start of the war and by October 2004 this number had fallen to 12% [50].

This leadership strategy for engaging his opponents was at variance with that promised by Bush in his campaign for the presidency in 2000 and after taking office in 2001. Then he spoke of being a unifier and not a divider. By 2004 his public rhetoric had taken on a very different quality. After winning re-election he announced in his first press conference "I earned capital in the campaign, political capital, and now I intend to spend it. It is my style." It was not one, however, that Bush invented. As Richard Skinner notes the presidency was becoming increasingly partisan since the Reagan administration [51].

The partisan and binary nature of Bush's approach to dealing with opposition was also evident in how he structured his White House decision making system [52]. White House appointees overwhelmingly tended to have personal ties with the Bush 2000 presidential campaign or his term as governor of Texas. Some 30% of Executive Office of the President staffers hailed from Texas and more than 80% had worked on the campaign. Collectively they ran interference for him in dealing with the bureaucracy or ran offices from the White House that made policy in their stead. For example, Chief of Staff Andrew Card was a key driving force in an early administration initiative on immigration reform that was widely seen as an effort to attract Hispanic voters to the Republican Party. As war with Iraq approached Card organized the White House Iraq Group to coordinate policy and ensure that the administration spoke with one public voice.

Partisan staffing was reinforced by a centralized decision making process that ensured as one staffer put it, the president would get the information he wanted but not necessarily the information he needed. A poignant example comes from a meeting between national security advisor Stephen Hadley and a strategy review group appointed to review Iraq policy at the same time that the Iraq Study Group was conducting its inquiry. As the meeting progressed Hadley spoke up: "you have got to give the president the option of a surge in forces…he will want to see it and he'll want to know what it means. You can take your positions for or against or in between, but you have to present him that as an option.

Moreover that information would not necessarily come through formally established channels but often through direct one-on-one conversations with key decision makers such as vice President Cheney and Secretary of Defense Donald Rumsfeld. Bob Woodward recounts one White House foreign policy meeting in the following terms:

> Rice began going through a long paper on issues that everyone was supposed to have read and understood. Rumsfeld leaned back and made it pretty clear he was not paying much attention. The president also seemed bored. "Don, what do you think about this?" Bush asked, interrupting Rice. . . . the discussion drifted off and the decision was left hanging. . . . It was as if Rice and the NSC had one serious, formal process going on while the president and Rumsfeld had another one—informal, chatty and dominant [53].

Firm in his convictions, Bush did not seek out debates or an exchange of views on policy matters. His preference was to make a quick decision based on his personal assessment of the problem and then move forward. Meetings were designed to inform not elicit information. Two incidents highlight the resulting dynamics of Bush's leadership style for his administration's decision making processes. First, before the Iraq War Richard Haass who headed the State Department's policy planning unit met with national security advisor Condoleezza Rice and raised the need to discuss the pros and cons of war. Rice responded to the effect that Haas shouldn't bother because the president has made a decision [54]. Second, is another description of a White House foreign policy meeting by Woodward:

> Rumsfeld made his presentation while looking at the president, while Powell looked straight ahead. Then Powell would make his presentation to the president with Rumsfeld looking straight ahead. They didn't even comment on each other's statements or views. So Bush never had the benefit of a serious, substantive discussion between his principal advisors. And . . . the president did not force a discussion [55].

## Strategic and Military Problems

Pre 9/11 the Bush administration's foreign policy could be defined one of two ways. From the perspective of foreign leaders it was the equivalent of the saying "no" strategy employed with great effect during the early Cold War years by Charles DeGaulle and more recently by Alexander Putin. Whatever was asked of the United States the answer was "no." Where DeGaulle and Putin sought to reestablish the image of France and Russia respectively as major world powers, Bush said "no" in order to drive home the hegemonic power of the U.S. From the perspective of American domestic politics the essence of his foreign policy was captured by the phrase "ABC," anything but Clinton. Consistent with Condoleezza Rice's view of the American national interest the U.S. would no longer engage in the type of multilateral undertakings of its predecessor.

After 9/11 the Bush Doctrine would become the signature statement of the administration's strategy to deal with terrorism and the challenges of world politics more generally. It does not emerge in full form from any one document but rather is found throughout a series of statements made by George W. Bush beginning with his 2001 State of the Union address which predated the 9/11 terrorist attacks in which he identifies terrorists and rogue states as "emerging threats" but does not put forward a strategy for responding to them nor did he identify a linkage between the two. In his nationwide address following the 9/11 attacks Bush proclaims that the U.S. is now involved in a war against terrorism and those who support it.

The first statement of a strategy for dealing with terrorists and other hostile threats to the U.S. came in his June 2002 speech to the graduating class at West Point where Bush stated, "Our security will require all Americans to be forward-looking and resolute, to be ready for preemptive action when necessary to defend our liberty and to defend our lives." He also asserted that "the gravest danger to freedom lies in the crossroads of radicalism and technology." To these observations the September 2002 *National Security Strategy* added, "We cannot let our enemies strike first," that the United States will use its power to encourage free and open societies, and that it will never allow its military supremacy to be challenged [56]. Bush's January 2002 State of the Union Address further developed the linkage between terrorist and their supporters when he identified Iran, North Korea and Iraq as members of an axis of evil.

Observers disagree as to characterize the actual content of the Bush Doctrine although its essential features are generally agreed upon. Steven Hook identifies two core pillars on which it is based [57]. The first is American primacy in world politics. The world is unipolar and the U.S. is the dominant power. The second is preemptive war, the right to attack first in self defense. Together, American primacy and preemptive war laid the foundation for what Hook describes as an American protectorate over the interstate system. Ilan Peleg constructs a more expansive definition of the Bush Doctrine and divides its key elements into three parts [58]. Substantively the Bush Doctrine calls for opposition to terrorism, preemptive military action to defend U.S. security and promoting the spread of democracy. In terms of methods it relies upon unilateral action and where necessary the construction of coalitions of the willing instead of acting through international institutions. Finally, in terms of tone, the Bush Doctrine adopts a moralistic stance in which the American definition of values and goals is taken as a given to be the correct definitions.

Several aspects of the Bush Doctrine brought forward questions about the strength of its intellectual foundations with some asserting that it was not a strategic road map that guided policy but an opportunistic response to the events of 9/11 that allowed the administration to address real and longstanding foreign policy problems in the Middle East.

At its most general level the debate over the Bush Doctrine has pitted conservative realists against neoconservatives. Five key themes form the foundation for neoconservative thinking about world politics [59]. First, the internal character of regimes matters. Second, American power should be used for moral purposes. Third, neoconservatives are skeptical about the legitimacy and effectiveness of international law and institutions to achieve security and justice. Fourth, the United States should act unilaterally whenever possible. And fifth, military power ought to be considered as a primary instrument of American foreign policy. Conservative realists are in partial agreement with neoconservatives on such matters as the importance of military power in world politics and a de-emphasis on the role of international organizations and international law in world politics. But they take exception elsewhere. For realists there is a fundamental difference between national interest and global interest. Any foreign policy that does not recognize the difference will result in overreaching and in the long run result in dilution of a country's power, which will, in turn, threaten its ability to protect its national security. Moreover, what matters in world affairs is the nature of a country's foreign policy and not its domestic policies in areas such as human rights and democracy. They argue that the link between democracy and peace is not as iron-clad as many world make. New democracies, for example, tend to be prone to war. Finally, realists assert that although international law and institutions cannot protect countries from national security threats, they do provide a means for legitimizing the use of power, thus reducing both resistance to it and the costs of using it.

Specific aspects of the Bush Doctrine have also brought forward challenges. The most prominent point of controversy is the concept of preemption. At issue here was the blurring of a long-standing distinction in international politics between preemption and prevention. Both are based on the principle of striking first in self-defense. In the case of preemption, the feared attack is imminent. In the case of prevention, it is more general and future-oriented. International law recognizes the legitimacy of preemptive strikes but not necessarily of preventive strikes on an enemy. Critics argued that in casting the Iraq War as a preemptive one, the Bush administration used the imagery of preemption in a situation that was more legitimately characterized as prevention, especially when it was later found that Iraq did not possess weapons of mass destruction [60].

Another line of criticism questioned the assertion that containment deterrence could not work against rogue regimes and supporters of international terrorism [61]. Defenders of these strategies argued that they continued to be useful, and they attributed Libya's decision to abandon its quest for weapons of mass destruction to them. Critics also questioned the assertion that deterrence could not work because of the irrational nature of these regimes; making the argument that rationality is a matter of degree and not an all-or-nothing quality. Rogue regimes concerned with their survival could be expected to act rationally enough in the face of U.S. deterrence threats.

## Democratic Opposition

Formulating a single policy stance on the Iraq War proved to be a challenge that the Democratic Party was never fully able to master during the Bush administration. In part, the problem involved tactics and timing. The terrorist attack of 9/11 along with the immediate success of the invasion of Afghanistan led to a rally-around-the-flag effect put opponents of the war on the defensive. By casting opposition in unpatriotic terms President Bush was able to secure passage of the USA Patriot Act and regain Republican control of the Senate in the 2002 midterm election. Bush did encounter opposition in his plans for creating an Office of Homeland Security in the White House but it was largely institutionally based and not partisan in nature. Placed in the White House this office would be beyond the reach of congressional overseers.

Later Democratic opposition to war related policies such as warrantless wiretaps and the selection of interrogation tactics was hindered by the rules put in place for briefing key congressional leaders. The "Gang of Eight" (the leaders of the two parties from the House and Senate and the ranking majority and minority members of the two intelligence committees) were sworn to secrecy and briefed in the absence of their aides.

Political memories also undercut Democratic attempts at crafting an opposition position on Iraq. Not only were the Democrats the party of Vietnam, they were also associated with the highly politicized anti-war movement of that era. Polls leading up to the 2004 presidential election showed that while Kerry was rated higher by the public on such domestic issues as health care, social security and the economy, Bush received higher ratings on his ability to handle Iraq and terrorism. At the same time as the Iraq War progressed pressure from grass roots Democrats for ending it mounted placing pressure on the Democratic Party leadership to address the issue if they wished to hold on to their electoral political base.

Senator Russ Feingold was first to openly challenge the Bush administration in August 2005 calling for the withdrawal of U.S. troops from Iraq by December 31, 2006. John Kerry would later join Feingold and other Democrats in the Senate in calling for a July 1, 2007 withdrawal date. Representative John Murtha along with Senate Minority leader Harry Reid proposed a redeployment of U.S. forces from Iraq to other cites in the region. In contrast Senator Joe Lieberman, while still a Democrat, called for supporting the president stating "it is time for Democrats who distrust President Bush to acknowledge that he will be the commander-in-chief for three more critical years and in matters of war we undermine presidential credibility at our nation's peril."

Absent the ability to formulate a unified position on Iraq the Democrats pursued a second-based opposition strategy of calling for Secretary of Defense Donald Rumsfeld's removal and the creation of a bipartisan committee to examine U.S. policy toward Iraq and the options open to it. Such a committee, the Iraq Study Group was created by Congress on March 15, 2006 and issued its report on December 6, 2006. Just over one week later Rumsfeld resigned. The Iraq Study Group's report painted a bleak picture of the situation in both Iraq and Afghanistan. It strongly urged a large pull back of U.S. forces from Iraq and a stepped-up transfer of power to Iraqi officials so that a more rapid withdrawal of U.S. forces might be arranged.

It should also be noted that opposition to going to war with Iraq also existed within the Republican Party. This opposition was expressed most openly by Brent Scowcroft who served as President George H.W. Bush's national security advisor. In a *Wall Street Journal* essay he cautioned that attacking Iraq at this time would threaten to undermine if not destroy the global anti-terrorist campaign the U.S. had begun [62]. More generally President George W. Bush's Iraq policy created a split within the Republican Party between traditional realists (who lost) and neo-conservatives (who won).

## Madison and Bush Compared

As we noted in the beginning of this article the similarities between the Madison and Bush are remarkable. With respect to the causes for war both presidents justified their action for numerous different reasons or causes. For Madison it was the British impressment of American sailors or an invasion of Canada or the protection of the Northwest territories. For Bush it was weapons of mass destruction, the inhumane Iraqi regime, peace in the Middle East. There were also the rumored reasons like the protection of the Iraqi oil fields and other economic considerations or perhaps a personal vendetta against the inhumane leader of Iraq who attempted to assassinate his father. With so many reasons it was difficult to isolate one that served as the true cause in either Madison or Bush's case. The reasons for war in both cases are muddled and are likely to remain so.

In terms of national expectations and leadership both Bush and Madison suffered from perceived leadership problems. Madison was a legislator with no battlefield experience. Bush was someone who supposedly flew fighter jets over American airfields and not Vietnam targets. Both naively believed that American forces would be welcomed with open Canadian and Iraqi arms. Both wrongly believed that their war efforts would be short. Both suffered from a lack of preparation for the war effort; Madison in the very beginning of his war and Bush after the initial "shock and awe" campaign. Both were surprised by these sets of circumstances. Neither president asked the nation to suffer either economically nor individually for the war effort. Both left national debts as a result of their war efforts.

As far as the international setting goes both Madison and Bush failed to understand that neither international system demanded the kind of U.S. involvement that it received. In Bush's case the link between international terrorism and Iraq was manufactured. In Madison's case the British would have and did resolve the impressment situation over time. Domestically both faced political opposition. Madison faced severe opposition from the Federalist Party and there were rifts within his own party which he successfully navigated.

Bush faced Democratic opposition especially as time passed after the initial campaign. Both presidents dealt with the opposition by characterizing opponents as being unpatriotic or treasonous.

In terms of strategy and military problems these abounded in both cases. Madison's original strategy was faulty. Bush's plans for a long occupation of Iraq were virtually non existent. In addition, the war effort of both presidents faced significant politicization rather than national unity.

## Conclusion

We have isolated a number of variables or factors that can be used to assess whether a president engages in a war of choice. We have also suggested that this takes place on a continuum. In other words, the more of these factors that are present the more likely the war in question is one of choice. We have also suggested that Madison and Bush both engaged in wars of choice. What does this imply for their historical legacies?

The more a president engages in this type of activity the higher the chance he or she will damage their historical legacy absent other redeeming actions. Madison fares much better than Bush here. He probably gets some credit for luck with respect to the War of 1812. After all the British were mainly concerned with Napoleon and European politics thus Madison escapes the potential harsh British retributions for the war. In addition, Madison probably gets a bit of a pass for being the "Father" of the Constitution and other significant legislative accomplishments. Despite all of this Madison has never risen above an average rating as president.

President Bush is in worse shape as far as his legacy goes. Not only do we have the criticisms surrounding the effort in Iraq ,which we have cited, there are other developments that subtract from his legacy. For example two of the greatest accomplishments touted by the Bush Administration are the No Child Left Behind Act and the Bush tax cuts. By 2009 both accomplishments are viewed as problematical. The act was not fully funded and the tax cuts were leading to heavy budget deficits. When one adds the near fiscal collapse, the nationalization of the American financing system and the disastrous emergency response to the Katrina hurricane there seems to be no where to go but down in legacy for the Bush administration. Unlike Madison there appears to be a paucity of redeeming circumstances that could aid the Bush legacy.

We close by noting that presidents cannot pick the previous presidents they wish to be compared to. That is up to historians. Thus George W. Bush has less in common with President Truman (the president he wishes to be compared to) and more in common with James Madison. Unfortunately, this comparison holds the promise of diminutive historical returns.

## Acknowledgment

Dr. Eksterowicz would like to thank his Graduate Assistant, Andrew Sullivan for his research efforts on Madison and the War of 1812.

## References

[1] Joe Klein, "Why the 'War President' Is Under Fire," *Time* (February 15, 2004).

[2] Charles Krauthammer, "Wars of Choice, Wars of Necessity'" *Time* (November 5, 2001).

[3] Richard N. Hass, *Wars of Choice; Wars of Necessity*, New York: Simon and Schuster, 2009.

[4] See the discussion of this point in John Schuessler, "When Wars of Necessity Become Contested as Wars of Choice," Paper delivered at the 2004 Annual Meeting of the American Political Science association, September 2-5.

[5] Patrick J. Buchanan, *Churchill, Hitler and "The Unnecessary War": How Britain Lost Its Empire and the West Lost the World*, New York: Crown Publishers, 2008.

[6] For a discussion of these and other reasons see, Schuessler, "When Wars of Necessity..." 1-19.

[7] Donald R. Hickey, *The War of 1812: The Forgotten Conflict*, Chicago: Illinois University Press, 1990, pp. 1-9.

[8] Gary Wills, *James Madison*, New York: Times Books, 2002, pp. 109-110.

[9] John K. Mahon, *The War of 1812*, Gainesville: University of Florida Press, 1972, p.7.

[10] J.C.A. Stagg, "James Madison and the Coercion of Great Britain: Canada, the West Indies and the War of 1812," *The William and Mary Quarterly,* Third Series, Vol. 38, No. 1, p.26, 32-34.

[11] Richard Glover, "The French Fleet, 1807-1814; Britain's Problem; and Madison's Opportunity," *The Journal of Modern History,* Vol. 39, No. 3, pp.235-236.

[12] Hickey, The War of 1812: A Forgotten Conflict, p. 11.

[13] Ibid. pp.29-33.

[14] J.C.A. Stagg, "James Madison and the 'Malcontents': The Political Origins of the War of 1812," *William and Mary Quarterly,* Third Series. Vol. 33, No.4, pp.557-585.

[15] For a discussion of the plight of the officer corps before and after the war see, William B. Skelton, "High Army Leadership in the Era of the War of 1812: The Making and Remaking of the Officer Corps," *The William and Mary Quarterly,* Third Series, Vol.51, No.2, pp.253-274.

[16] Irving Brant, *James Madison: The President 1809-1812*, (New York, The Bobbs Merrill Company, Inc., 1956), p.402.

[17] Hickey, *The War of 1812...,* p.1.

[18] Irving Brant, "Madison and the War of 1812," *The Virginia Magazine of History and Biography,* Vol. 74, No. 1, Part One, p.56.

[19] Ibid. p.56.

[20] Stagg, "James Madison and the Coercion of Great Britain..." pp. 5-6, 7, 26-27, 32-34.

[21] Hickey, *The War of 1812...,* p.1.

[22] Reginald Horsman, *The War of 1812,* (New York: Alfred A. Knopf, 1969), p.21.

[23] For a discussion of national pride and patriotism as a reason for the war see, Norman K. Risjord, "1812: Conservatives, War Hawks and the Nation's Honor," *The William and Mary Quarterly*, Third Series, Vol. 18, No.2, pp. 196-210.

[24] Mahon, *War of 1812,* p. 385.

[25] Hickey, *The War of 1812,* p. 27.

[26] Robert Allen Rutland, *The Presidency of James Madison,* (Lawrence: The University Press of Kansas, 1990), p. 88.
[27] Lawrence S. Kaplan, "France and Madison's Decision for War 1812," *The Mississippi Valley Historical Review,* Vol. 50, No. 4, p. 662.
[28] Hickey, *The War of 1812, p.47.*
[29] Rutland, *The Presidency of James Madison,* p. 89.
[30] Wills, *James Madison,* pp.3-7.
[31] Hickey, *War of 1812,* pp. 30-35.
[32] Skelton, "High Army Leadership...," p. 253.
[33] Ibid. 255.
[34] Ibid. pp. 264-65.
[35] Ibid. p. 273.
[36] Hickey, *The War of 1812,* pp. 75-90.
[37] Ibid., pp.52-71
[38] Ibid. p. 46.
[39] For a discussion of these and other Federalist criticisms see, Lawrence Delbert Cress, "Cool and Serious Reflection': Federalist Attitudes toward War in 1812," *Journal of the Early Republic,* Vol. 7, No.2, pp. 123-145.
[40] Harvey Strum, "New York Federalists and the Opposition to the War of 1812,"
[41] John Lowell, *Mr. Madison's War. A Dispassionate Inquiry,* (Boston: Russell and Cutler, 1812), passim.
[42] For a discussion of the Treaty of Ghent see, Francis F. Beirne, *The War of 1812*(Hamden, Connecticut: Archon Books, 1965), pp. 374-387.
[43] Wills, *James Madison,* p.153.
[44] James E. Campbell, "Presidential Politics in a Polarized Nation: The Reelection of George W. Bush in Colin Campbell, Bert Rockman and Andrew Rudalevige (eds.), *The George W. Bush Legacy* (Wasnington, D.C. Congressional Quarterly Press, 2008), 21-44.
[45] Gary C, Jacobson, "George W. Bush, Polarization and the War in Iraq," in Campbell, et. al., *The George W. Bush Legacy*, pp. 62-91.
[46] Condoleezza Rice, "Promoting the National Interest," *Foreign Affairs* 79 (2000), 45-62.
[47] Quoted in Andrew Bacevich, "The Real World War IV," *Wilson Quarterly* (Winter 2005), 60.
[48] Jacobson, "George W. Bush, Polarization and the War in Iraq."
[49] Colin Campbell, Bert Rockman and Andrew Rudalevige, "Introduction," in Campbell, et. al., *The George W. Bush Legacy,* p.11.
[50] Jacobson, "George W. Bush, Polarization and the War in Iraq."
[51] Richard Skinner, "George W. Bush and the Partisan Presidency," *Political Science Quarterly* 123 (2008-9), 605-622.
[52] Andrew Rutalevige, "The Decider: Issue Management and the Bush White House," in Campbell, et. al., *The George W. Bush Legacy,* 135-163.
[53] Bob Woodward, *State of Denial, Bush at War, Part III* (New York: Simon and Schuster, 2006), p. 276.
[54] Glenn Kessler, "U.S> Decision on Iraq has Puzzling Past," *Washington Post,* January 12, 2003.
[55] Woodward, *State of Denial,* p. 241.

[56] White House, *"The National Security Strategy of the United States of America,"* September 2002, www.whitehouse.gov/nsc/nss.
[57] Steven Hook and John Spanier, *American Foreign Policy Since World War II,* seventeenth edition (Washington, D.C.: Congressional quarterly Press, 2009), pp. 324-28.
[58] Ilan Peleg, *The Legacy of George W. Bush' Foreign Policy: Moving beyond Neoconservatism* (Boulder: Westview Press, 2009).
[59] G. John Ikenberry, "The End of the Neo-Conservative Moment," *Survival,* 46 (2004), 7–22; Francis Fukuyama, *America at the Crossroads* (New Haven: Yale University Press, 2006).
[60] On the distinction between preemption and prevention, see Lawrence Freedman, "Prevention, Not Preemption," *Washington Quarterly,* 26 (2003), 105–114.
[61] Robert F. Trager and Dessislava P. Zagorcheva, "Deterring Terrorism: It Can Be Done," *International Security,* 30 (2005/6), 87–123; and Jeffrey Record, "The Bush Doctrine and War with Iraq," *Parameters* (Spring 2003), 4–21.
[62] Brent Scowcroft, "Don't Attack Saddam," *Wall Street Journal.* August 15, 2002, p. 22.

In: Presidents and War
Editors: A. Eksterowicz and G. Hastedt, pp. 53-64
ISBN 978-1-61668-917-9


*Chapter 4*

# ABRAHAM LINCOLN: THE PRESIDENT WHO CHANGED THE ROLE OF COMMANDER-IN-CHIEF

***Frank J. Williams****

## INTRODUCTION

When he became Commander-in-Chief in 1861, Abraham Lincoln lacked serious military experience, especially in contrast to Jefferson Davis, a West Point graduate and Mexican War hero. Indeed, Lincoln often joked about his brief Army career: four months' service with several rag-tag militia companies in the Black Hawk War. After he was elected a captain by his New Salem friends, Lincoln inspired more humor than gallantry as a leader. Once, when marching his company toward a narrow gate, he forgot the proper command to form his troops to in a single column so they could advance. "Halt!" Lincoln finally shouted. "This company will break ranks for two minutes and form again on the other side of the gate." Lincoln was a civilian by habit, experience, and vision. Yet, his background served him well when he led the citizen soldiers who fought in the Civil War.

In truth, Lincoln's service in the Black Hawk War should not be underestimated. His election as captain led him to reflect almost 30 years later that no subsequent success of his life gave him as much satisfaction. It was a defining moment in his life, much like Captain Harry Truman's experience during World War I. Both drew many lessons from their experiences, the most important for young Lincoln was that exuberant young men could not make the transition from civilians to soldiers overnight, and would never fully transform themselves into full-time military men. He also learned that raw recruits came from a democratic culture with a high disregard for authority. Many of these civilian soldiers in the end simply could not, and would not, recognize the right of the military to keep them in service longer than they wished to stay. Such attitude owed little or nothing to cowardice, laziness, or lack of patriotism, but had a great deal to do with a cultural instinct for independence.

* The author is indebted to William D. Pederson, Director of the International Lincoln Center at Louisiana State University in Shreveport for his editorial assistance.

Lincoln shared their privations, especially hunger: the military supply system worked imperfectly at best, and the soldiers often went without rations. When his men went hungry, so did he, on one occasion passing two days without food. Instinctively he understood that good humor, patience, a willingness to share equally in the hardships of the privates, and an absence of self-importance were the primary basis to provide leadership and to bind the men to him. Fortunately, these characteristics were already a part of his mid-western nature.

Photo by The Frank & Virginia Williams Collection of Lincolniana.

"I Want You" by James Montgomery Flagg. The artist and illustrator created the Uncle Sam recruiting poster for both World Wars. The painting (oil, 47¾" X 25¼") has been described as showing President Lincoln waiting for news from the second Battle of Bull Run. It certainly demonstrates Lincoln's intensity of emotion as Commander-In-Chief as he waits nervously for reports from the front.

## Captain to Commander-in-Chief

But, in the War Between the States, circumstances existed which required a full exercise of the President's power as Commander-In-Chief. For a considerable time, its outcome remained highly uncertain. Initially, many of the Union commanders were incapable or unlucky leaders. Their military plans frequently miscarried so that changes in strategy had to be swiftly devised and implemented. Abraham Lincoln, a strong and active president, had little choice but to take part in the conduct of the war. And he did so from the outset. His first major problem arose in regard to Union forts in the South. Should they be surrendered or held? If held, should men and supplies be sent to relieve and replenish the troops? Lincoln sent a relief expedition to Fort Sumter in Charleston Harbor. Jefferson Davis ordered General Beauregard to open fire and the war began.

From the beginning, Lincoln set a pattern. His war power would not be limited to strictly military measures. On April 20, 1861, he ordered United States marshals to seize, from the principal telegraph offices in the northern states, the originals of all telegrams sent and copies of all received during the preceding year. The following day, without congressional authorization, he directed Secretary of the Treasury Salmon P. Chase to advance $2 million dollars for the arming of ships. Shortly thereafter, again without action by Congress, he suspended the writ of habeas corpus and simply ignored the individual ruling of the long-time Chief Justice of the United States, Roger B. Taney, that his action was unconstitutional. The ex-captain soon felt it was necessary to disregard his professional military advisors, too. Both General Winfield Scott, who headed the Army, and General Irwin McDowell, the field commander, advised against fighting the first battle of Manassas on the ground that more time was required for disciplining and drilling the troops. The public, however, clamored for action, and Lincoln always in tune with political necessity, overruled the generals. The battle was fought -- with disastrous results. Not daunted, the following night, Lincoln went ahead and prepared a detailed plan of strategy.

He did not always attempt to force his tentative strategy on others. Often he submitted to the advice of his generals. Occasionally they disregarded his wishes if not his direct orders. Early in the war Lincoln was eager for General Don Carlos Buell to capture Cumberland Gap, from which his grandfather and grandmother had once made their way westward. Buell, more than once, promised to take this course, but in the end turned his back on the Gap and moved toward Nashville.

As the war developed, Lincoln became even more concerned with questions of strategy. He was greatly troubled by his inability to stir into action General George B. McClellan, the commander of the Army of the Potomac. The ever serious Commander-in-Chief went so far as to educate himself on military strategy. The autodidact read military treatises, which he procured from the Library of Congress, and held long conversations with officers on the art of war. In December 1861, he presented an elaborate memorandum to McClellan which asked technical questions and made suggestions about an advance. The over-confident McClellan returned it with penciled replies and a note rejecting all the suggestions.

On January 27, 1862, Lincoln issued his General War Order No. 1, in which he fixed February 22 as "the day for a general movement of the land and naval forces of the United States against the insurgent forces." The Army of the Potomac and others, as well as certain naval forces, were named as ordered to "be ready to move on that day." Four days later he supplemented this with "President's Special War Order No. 1," commanding the Army of the Potomac, after providing for the defense of Washington, to move on February 22 to seize Manassas Junction. This was followed on February 3 by a note to McClellan insisting upon Lincoln's own plan for an attack on the Confederate army near Washington rather than an expedition by water against Richmond. However, plans, suggestions, and orders were alike ineffective to move McClellan or his Army.

Shortly after this, Lincoln told John Hay of his impulse to take charge of the Army of the Potomac and see what he could do as a field commander. He did not yield to this impulse at this time or later, though on May 23, 1863, the *Chicago Tribune* urged him to take the field as actual commander. During the week of May 5, 1862, however, he did assume personal command of the operations that resulted in the capture of Norfolk. The President not only ordered the advance on Norfolk but personally selected the place where the attack was to begin and gave the order to fire. Moreover, he countermanded the orders of Major General John E. Wool as to the disposal of some of his troops.

Perhaps encouraged by this success, when Stonewall Jackson made one of his forays into the Shenandoah Valley, Lincoln gave specific orders to Generals Irwin McDowell, Don Carlos Buell, and John Fremont to surround and capture Jackson and his army. Fremont disobeyed two of Lincoln's orders, resting his men one day when they were ordered to march and again taking a different route from the one selected by Lincoln. Even if the orders had been obeyed, the capture of Stonewall Jackson's army would not have been a simple task. After this experience, Lincoln did not again attempt to direct the field movements of several armies a long distance from the White House.

Several Presidents have faced major crises either in bringing their field generals to engage in battle or in keeping them within bounds, not simply on the battlefield but within the framework of Constitutional government. General McClellan, the most lagging of field generals, was a great trial to Abraham Lincoln in both spheres. Bold in his strategic conceptions, McClellan nevertheless dreaded the actual execution of his plans. A repetitive pattern for him was to demand more reinforcements after overestimating the enemy's strength and depreciating his own. He was a wonderfully imaginative procrastinator. If he had Robert E. Lee at a disadvantage, he almost invariably failed to exploit it. He must wait, McClellan would report to his impatient superiors at Washington, until the Potomac rose to be sure that Lee would not recross it; he must finish drilling new recruits, reorganize his forces, and procure more shoes, uniforms, blankets, and camp equipment.

McClellan compensated for battlefield inaction by spending his battle-idle time pouring his irrepressible arrogance into his letters, including one to Lincoln on July 7, 1862, pointing out that it was high time the government established a civil and military policy to cover the full canvass of the nation's troubles and "generously" informed the President what precisely that policy should be. McClellan's behavior became critical after his failure to follow up his victory at Antietam by pursuing Lee's fleeing Army. Lincoln worked mightily, as his secretary John Nicolay put it, at "poking sharp sticks into little Mac's ribs." When the General included among his ingenious excuses that an epidemic had afflicted the horses with sore mouths and weary backs, Lincoln was goaded into a sharp reply. "I have just read your dispatch about sore tongued and fatigued horses," he telegraphed. "Will you pardon me for asking what the horses of your Army have done since the Battle of Antietam that fatigues anything?"

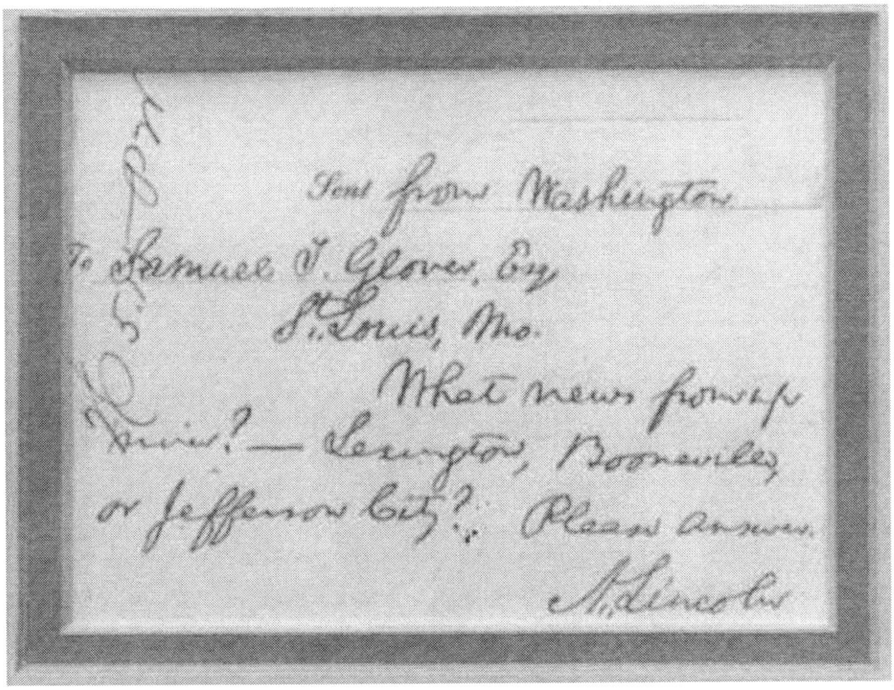
Sent from Washington
To Samuel T. Glover, Esq
St. Louis, Mo.
What news from up river?— Lexington, Booneville, or Jefferson City? Please answer.
A. Lincoln

Photo by The Frank & Virginia Williams Collection of Lincolniana.

"What news?" Abraham Lincoln autograph telegram (Washington, September 28, 1861). The Commander-In-Chief's concern about the crisis in border state Missouri is obvious in this telegram to a friend in St. Louis. The President would often telegraph officers and civilians asking, "What news?" His ability to convey his question succinctly was another attribute acquired from the practice of law.

Lincoln and his administration were now at a critical juncture. Winter was approaching and would assure that, with the exception of Antietam, the long record of Eastern defeat and stalemate would remain intact. Congress, restive with this state of affairs, was soon to convene. Governors were nervous, the cabinet was divided, and both the extreme war and peace men were thundering against the President. Nor was Lincoln unmindful of McClellan's personal softness toward the South, and the presence on his staff of some who advocated a waiting game to prolong the war until both sides were exhausted and the Union might be preserved with slavery intact. Should he replace McClellan? Alternative generals were a sorrowfully undistinguished lot, many already scarred with failure, and others abysmally inexperienced.

After serious deliberation, Lincoln relieved McClellan on November 5, 1862 and appointed General Ambrose E. Burnside in his place. Upon reading the President's order, McClellan explained, "Alas for my poor country!" Some among his officers even urged him to disobey the presidential order. McClellan later wrote that he could easily have marched his troops into Washington and taken possession of the government. If so, it would have been the first successful forward movement of the war! Instead, McClellan turned over the command of his 120,000 men in an elaborate ceremony. But this was by no means the last encounter between McClellan and Lincoln. In 1864, two years after his removal, McClellan met Lincoln on new terrain – as the Democratic nominee for the presidency. He lost that battle too.

## An Active Commander-in-Chief

Functioning as he does in a democratic state, the President requires legal authority to pursue military purposes. In wartime, of course, the need and the quest become most compelling. Presidents in the nation's major wars have invoked two contrasting patterns of legal justification for their acts. One, the Lincolnian, asserts an expansive view of the president's independent authority based on the Commander-in-Chief Clause [Article II, Sections 2 & 3] of the Constitution and on the duty "to take care that the laws be faithfully executed". In the ten weeks between the outbreak at Fort Sumter and the convening of Congress in special session on July 4, 1861, Lincoln employed these clauses to sanction measures whose extraordinary magnitude suggests dictatorship.

In the ten-week interval, Lincoln added 23,000 men to the regular Army and 18,000 to the Navy, called 40,000 volunteers for three years' service, summoned the state militias into a ninety-day volunteer force, paid $2 million dollars from the Treasury's unappropriated funds for purposes unauthorized by Congress, closed the Post Office to "treasonable correspondence," imposed a blockade on Southern ports, suspended the writ of habeas corpus in certain parts of the country, and caused the arrest and military detention of persons "who were represented to him" as engaging in or contemplating "treasonable practices." He later instituted a militia draft when voluntary recruiting broke down and extended the suspension of the habeas corpus privilege nationwide for persons "guilty of any disloyal practice." Lincoln did not intend to fight a rebellion with a powder puff.

His first Emancipation Proclamation was also couched as a military order from the Commander-in-Chief. It freed the slaves in states in rebellion against the United States and pledged "the Executive Government of the United States, including the military and naval authority thereof," to protect the freedom conferred. Lincoln invited Congress to "ratify" his enlargement of the armed forces, which it did, and it bolstered his handling of the writ of habeas corpus. Lincoln's actions, as Edward S. Corwin wrote, "assert for the President for the first time in our history, an initiative of indefinite scope and legislative in affect in meeting the domestic aspects of a war emergency." Yet, how else does one confront the most serious challenge to the Union?

All wartime Presidents had to reckon, too, with a favorite preoccupation of Congress in the military realm: investigation. Harry Truman's Senate Committee to investigate the defense program was a model of searching, but constructive criticism, that produced positive change in the administration of World War II. Success as a wartime investigator established Truman's chief claim upon his subsequent vice presidential nomination in 1944. A contrasting view of the investigatory power was the great cross Lincoln had to bear in the Civil War: the Joint Committee on the Conduct of the War. Spotty and arbitrary, the committee concentrated upon the Army of the Potomac and investigated selected specific generals – George B. McClellan, Charles P. Stone, Fitz-John Porter, and William B. Franklin – as their investigative targets. In contrast, John C. Fremont and Benjamin Franklin Butler were favorites who could do no wrong. The committee investigated its selected victims with preconceived notions of guilt, employed rumor and irresponsible publicity, and became a factional instrument of the Radical Republicans.

## Civil Liberties and Rights in a Civil War

As Commanders-in-Chief, presidents face additional tensions with the remaining governmental branch's concern with military affairs, the federal courts, with their high duty in a democratic state to protect the Constitution and the laws against encroachment. The most perplexing and consequential issues between the executive and the courts may arise during actual war, when the president is driven to curtail, or even suppress, key liberties sanctioned in the Bill of Rights. To further the progress of war, to safeguard the nation's imperiled safety, the president may have to set aside political and economic liberties which in peacetime are inviolable.

The Civil War, fought within the nation's borders and jeopardizing its capital, was actually resisted in many sectors of the North, to the point that President Lincoln promulgated several orders and proclamations restrictive of individual liberty. The most important of these was his suspension of the Constitutional privilege of the writ of habeas corpus, protecting the civilian against arbitrary arrests. Lincoln's first habeas corpus proclamation, issued in the war's early weeks, was triggered by events in Maryland. In early 1861, underground resistance and open defiance were rampant in that state. Federal troops were attacked by mobs in Baltimore, communications to the capital were severed, and the mayor and police chief were unabashedly pro-Confederate and anti-Lincoln. Bridges were destroyed to hamper the passage of Union troops, and newspapers hostile to the administration fanned disunion sentiment. The state legislature was soon to convene, with some of its members seeking to have the state secede from the Union.

To their credit, Union generals moved to nip the growing conspiracy by arresting the mayor, the chief of police, and several police commissioners. Even more sensational was the arrest of members of the Maryland legislature. To forestall the passage of an act of secession, Union General Nathaniel P. Banks barred the legislature from meeting and arrested nine of its members and the chief clerk of the Senate. Still other Marylanders were arrested, including one John Merryman "charged with various acts of treason." Merryman, was languishing in Fort McHenry when the Chief Justice, Roger B. Taney, on circuit duty, ordered the "body of John Merryman [produced] and . . . the day and cause of his [capture and detention]" made known. A head-on clash between the President and the Court between the war and the Constitution was in the making. Taney, to the administration's great relief, confined himself to declaring that the power to suspend the writ, which should be exercised with "extreme caution," belonged to Congress, and not to the President. Taney's opinion, nevertheless, put the administration under the cloud of the likelihood of a hostile Supreme Court decision, an event Attorney General Edward Bates said would "do more to paralyze the executive . . . than the worse defeat our Armies have yet sustained."

The administration's position was strengthened when Congress, after much struggle, passed the Habeas Corpus Act of 1863, affirming the president's power to suspend the writ. Despite several procedural devices incorporated to placate the courts, the act left to the executive the setting of policy concerning arrests and imprisonments. As before, prisoners were tried by military tribunal and punished or released under authority of the War Department. Arrests continued apace. Clement L. Vallandingham, the well known Copperhead, after his arrest, trial, and sentencing by a military commission, appealed to the United States Supreme Court to transfer his case to civil court, but the Supreme Court ruled that it had no jurisdiction, since a military commission was not a "court" over which the federal judiciary had no jurisdiction [1].

Although Vallandingham never lived to see it, his legal position was ultimately vindicated in the celebrated case of Ex parte Milligan, Milligan too was a Copperhead, tried by a military commission for "treasonable" speeches. Condemned to hang, he invoked the habeas corpus writ. But by then the war was over, and the Court was prepared to act boldly. It ruled that Indiana, where Milligan resided and spoke, was not part of the "theater of war" and that the civil courts there were "open" and therefore available to conduct his trial. Under such a combination of circumstances, the writ could not be Constitutionally suspended. The Milligan case, needless to say, has become the source of permanent consternation to the friends of Presidential power. It establishes the principle that the courts shall determine, even to the point of overriding the executive, what is the area of war and public danger, a principle that could well cause havoc with Presidential effectiveness in an actual emergency.

## Lincoln's Adaptive Methods

But a wartime President's principal role, as Lincoln came to see it, was to press his generals into action. McClellan was not the only commander who tested the President's patience. On October 16, 1863 he sent to George Gordon Meade, through his Chief of Staff General Henry Halleck, a curious letter which was in effect an order to attack Lee, and which concluded: "The honor will be yours if it succeeds and the blame with be mine if it fails." The letter was widely publicized and administration newspapers hailed the President as a great strategist.

Lincoln himself laid no claim to military genius and frankly admitted that his interference with his commanders was partly the result of their dilatoriness and ineptitude, and partly the result of political pressure. As capable commanders emerged Lincoln interfered less and less. He became less inclined personally to direct the strategy of the various campaigns but he became more insistent upon generals who could work out a plan of campaign and fight.

In the beginning, hundreds of commissions were issued, many to high ranking officers, for purely political reasons – because they had powerful friends, could raise troops, or because it was desired to obtain their full support of the war. The criticism was made – not without justification – that favoritism had officered the Army with incompetence. Even when such men as Benjamin Butler and George McClellan had repeatedly demonstrated their incapacity, there was long hesitation in removing them for fear of unfavorable political reaction. Butler had Radical Republican friends. McClellan had Democratic admirers. Both elements were crucial to maintain the coalition support for the war at home. After Donelson, Shiloh, and Vicksburg, Ulysses S. Grant had Lincoln's complete confidence and his reply to voluble criticism of him was: "I can't spare this man – he fights." After Grant moved to Virginia, there was little interference and, indeed, on no other basis could the President and his chief commander have worked together. Grant was determined to go his own way and, though he attempted to conceal his feelings, was not particularly pleased when Lincoln visited his headquarters.

In the latter months of the war, finding in Grant, William T. Sherman, and Phillip Sheridan a triumvirate upon whom he could depend, Lincoln, while he keenly followed the movements of the Armies, permitted his commanders free conduct of their own campaigns. On one occasion he said to Secretary of War Edwin M. Stanton, who was insisting that Grant was exceeding his authority: "Now, Mr. Secretary, you know we have been trying to manage the Army for three years and you know we haven't done much with it. We sent over the mountains and brought Mr. Grant, as Mrs. Grant calls him, to manage it for us and now I guess we'd better let Mr. Grant have his own way."

Lincoln withheld from Grant only the decision or questions that were within the political zone as when he instructed him to have no conference with Robert E. Lee except for the surrender of Lee's Army or upon some minor or purely military matter. All proposals for peace were to be passed on by Lincoln.

Lincoln had reason to believe that sentiment in the Army favored his reelection in 1864, so he was not reluctant to take advantage of this factor. No restriction was placed upon electioneering for the soldier vote – the first in history. Leaves of absence were fully granted to officers that they might participate in the campaign. Many of them spoke at public meetings on behalf of the Lincoln-Johnson ticket. Furloughs were given privates that their influence might be felt in their home districts. Men on detached service and convalescents in hospitals were sent home to help. The situation in Indiana was a special problem since it was the only large state whose soldier-citizens could not vote in the field. It was felt that the loss of the state election in October would be a severe blow to the Republicans. Because General Sherman's Army contained twenty-nine regiments and two batteries of Hoosiers, Indiana Governor Oliver Morton pressured Lincoln to write Sherman to permit the Indiana soldiers to return home to cast their ballots. Sherman, feeling that their absence would endanger his Army, declined to order the soldiers home, and Lincoln refused to overrule him. Nonetheless, a few Indiana regiments from posts in Tennessee and Kentucky did return home for the state election. In addition, Lincoln ordered all Indiana soldiers either hospitalized or unfit for service sent to their home state. Moreover, he sent from Sherman's Army six prominent Hoosier officers along with Major Generals John Logan and Frank Blair to stump Indiana and nearby states. Logan later wrote Sherman that "When I left on leave after the Atlanta Campaign to canvass for Mr. Lincoln, I did it at the special and private request of the President."

Lincoln justified this conduct, just as he justified his yielding to political pressure and granting pardons and cotton trading permits, on the ground that in seeking his own re-election and strengthening the political influence of his administration, he was working not for personal ends but for the salvation of the Union.

The greatest exercise of Lincoln's power as Commander-In-Chief was in regard to subjects which he could not delegate to any general. There was no other basis for the governments which during the war were set up in the occupied Southern states. Congressman Olin of New York had declared in the House of Representatives that in occupied territory in wartime the President had the power to do what must be done. "Of that necessity," he added, "the President is alone the judge: as Commander-in-Chief of the Army." It was on this theory that Lincoln proceeded.

The Emancipation Proclamation was, of course, the culmination of Lincoln's exercise of his power as Commander-in-Chief. Only on this ground could it be valid and on this ground alone Lincoln defended it: "You dislike the Emancipation Proclamation. You say it is unconstitutional. I think differently. I think the Constitution entrusts the Commander-in-Chief with the law of war in time of war."

Some of Lincoln's acts as Commander-in-Chief may have been questionable, some unwise, and others of doubtful constitutionality, but in retrospect it seems clear that he was in each instance motivated not by any thought of personal aggrandizement but by his desire to save the Union and that taken together they contributed greatly to that end.

Expediency shaped Lincoln's military thought. He recognized that he had to break with the old tenets of war. Among the President's more radical moves was his decision to free and arm the slaves. With this bold strike at the South's "peculiar institution" Lincoln accomplished three goals: he provided needed manpower for the Union armies (170,000 African-Americans); he weakened the South's labor force; and he inspired African-Americans, North and South, to suppress the rebellion.

Other innovations reveal Lincoln's understanding of the concept of total war. He authorized the devastating marches led by Sherman in Georgia and North Carolina and Philip H. Sheridan in Virginia. Late in the war he refused to exchange prisoners with the Confederacy. Each rebel soldier returned to his unit, reasoned Lincoln, would help prolong the war. Lincoln also was the first Commander-in-Chief to declare medicines contraband of war.

Photo by The Frank & Virginia Williams Collection of Lincolniana.

"The Door is Open to All" The Last Offer of Reconciliation – In Remembrance of Pres. A. Lincoln (Published by Henry & Wm. Vought, New York, 1865, Lithograph 24½" X 167/8"). Forgiveness and restoration of the Union are the messages in this print, which present sympathetic portraits of Gen. Robert E. Lee and Jefferson Davis that sharply contrast with the angry public mood immediately after Lincoln's assassination.

## INNOVATIVE COMMAND LEGACY

Although Lincoln made mistakes as a war leader, he learned from them. Lincoln grew as a strategist; he asked questions; he read; he probed – anything within his power to win and shorten the war. Ironically it was Lincoln, a most unlikely military man, who became America's apostle of modern war.

When George B. McClellan took the field in the spring of 1862, Lincoln relieved him as General-in-Chief on the grounds that one man could not direct an Army engaged in active operations and at the same time plan moves for other Armies. The President did not appoint another officer to the position until July 1862. In the interim, Lincoln acted as his own General-in-Chief. There can be little doubt that by this time he had come to have serious misgivings about the judgments of professional soldiers. Inclined at first to defer to their opinions, he now felt a growing confidence in his own powers to decide military questions, and he was perhaps a little too ready to impose his opinions on his Generals.

Nevertheless, even in this period, Lincoln did not presume to dispense completely with expert advice. Secretary of War Edwin M. Stanton had convened an agency known as the Army Board, consisting of the heads of the bureaus in the War Department. This was only the general staff brought together under a Chairman, but the transformation of the bureau chiefs into a collective body was a forward step in command. Lincoln frequently consulted the Board before arriving at an important decision.

Lincoln seemed to sense that there was something wrong in the existing arrangement. He, a civilian, was doing things that should be done by a military man. Again he decided to fill the post of General-in-Chief. In July 1862, he named to the position Henry W. Halleck, who had been a departmental commander in the Western Theater.

General Halleck seemed to be the ideal man for the job. Before the war he had been known as one of the foremost American students of the art of war and a capable departmental administrator. Lincoln intended that Halleck should be a real General-in-Chief, that he should, under the authority of the President, actually plan and direct operations.

At first Halleck acted up to his role – but not for long. His great defect was that he disliked responsibility. He delighted to provide technical knowledge and to advise, but he shrank from making decisions. Gradually he divested himself of his original function and deliberately assumed the part of an advisor and an informed critic.

Halleck's refusal to perform the requirements of his position forced Lincoln to act again as General-in-Chief, but he kept Halleck as titular head of the office. The President had discovered that Halleck could do one valuable service for him – in the area of military communications. Often Lincoln and his generals had experienced serious misunderstandings because, almost literally, they spoke different languages: Lincoln the words of the lawyer-politician, and the generals the jargon of the military. Halleck had lived in both the legal and military worlds, and he could speak the language of both. Increasingly, Lincoln came to entrust the framing of his directives to Halleck.

In those years of lonely responsibility when Lincoln directed the war effort he grew steadily in stature as a strategist. Usually he displayed greater strategic insight than most of his commanders. But he was willing, as he had been earlier, to yield the power to frame and control strategy to any general who demonstrated that he could do the job -- if he could find the general. By 1864 both he and the nation were certain they had found the man – Ulysses S.

Grant. And in that year the United States finally achieved a modern command system to fight a modern war.

But Lincoln's most important legacy as a strategist was his establishment of the modern command system: a Commander-in-Chief (Lincoln) to establish overall strategy; a General-in-Chief (Grant) to implement plans; and a Chief of Staff (Halleck) to relay information. Thus Lincoln, without recognizing his long-range contribution to our modern command system, laid its foundation in 1864.

Under this new system, a joint product of Lincoln and Congress, Ulysses S. Grant was named General-in-Chief, charged with the function of planning and directing the movements of all Union Armies. Because he disliked the political atmosphere in Washington, Grant established his headquarters with the field Army and the Eastern Theater, but did not technically command that Army. In the new arrangement Hallack received a new office, "Chief of Staff." He was not, however, a Chief of Staff in today's sense of the term. Primarily, he was a channel of communication between Lincoln and Grant and between Grant and the 17 departmental commanders under Grant. The perfect office soldier, he had found at last his proper niche.

As General-in-Chief, Grant justified every belief Lincoln had in his capacities. He possessed in superb degree the ability to think of the war in overall terms. But his grand plan of operations that ended the war was at least partly Lincolnian in concept. Grant conformed his strategy to Lincoln's known ideas: hit the Confederacy from all sides with pulverizing blows and make enemy armies, not cities, his main objective. The General submitted the broad outlines of his plan to Lincoln and the President trusting in Grant approved the design without seeking to know the details.

The 1864 command system embodied the brilliance of simplicity: a Commander-in-Chief to lay down policy and grand strategy, a General-in-Chief to frame specific battle strategy, and a Chief of Staff to coordinate information. It contained elements that later would be studied by military leaders and students in many nations. Abraham Lincoln, without fully realizing his part, had made a large and permanent contribution to the story of command organization.

## REFERENCES

[1] Ex parte Vallandingham, 68 U.S. 243, 1864.

In: Presidents and War
Editors: A. Eksterowicz and G. Hastedt, pp. 65-78
ISBN 978-1-61668-917-9


*Chapter 5*

# Ex Parte Milligan: Lincoln's Use of Military Commissions

***Joseph R. Thysell, Jr.***

## Introduction

President George W. Bush's response to the terrorist attacks of September 11, 2001 has been called unprecedented in American history. Bush using the full weight of his office has initiated extraordinary wartime measures to protect what he deemed the national interest. One hundred forty years earlier in April 1861, President Abraham Lincoln initiated similar extraordinary wartime measures for the same reason. Both Bush and Lincoln, using their powers as Commander-in-chief and as Chief Executive, sought to ensure the survival of the nation while at the same time protect the Constitution and its democratic institutions. Both Presidents resorted to restrictions and even suppression of important civil liberties as guaranteed in the U.S. Constitution, and in particular Bill of Rights [1].

One of the most controversial measures of the Bush Administration has been the authorization of military commissions. On November 13, 2001, Bush signed a presidential order entitled *Detention, Treatment and Trial of Certain Non-Citizen In The War Against Terrorism* authorizing their use to try suspected international terrorists [2]. Under Bush's order, defendants were denied certain constitutional rights normally given in civil courts and were granted a limited right to appeal the military commission's final decision. In past cases, similar defendants charged with terrorist-related offenses were tried in federal district court. The Bush Administration concluded that trying Al Qaeda members in civil courts could place judges and jurors at risk. Security would have to be extended not only to the courtroom but to the entire building and adjacent streets. Much of the evidence introduced would be classified, having been gathered through covert sources [3].

In addition to military commissions Bush issued several different executive orders that he judged vital for safeguarding national security and aiding law enforcement. These executive orders, including military commissions, were made without prior consultation with Congress or the courts. They included: allowing the interrogation of Middle East men who had recently come to the U.S., circumventing the issuance of visas to Muslim men and eavesdropping of confidential conversations between defendants in federal custody and their lawyers. In justifying the government's actions, U.S. Attorney General John Ashcroft has argued:

> Foreign terrorists who commit war crimes against the United States, in my judgment, are not entitled to and do not deserve the protections of the American Constitution, particularly when there could be very serious and important reasons related to not bringing them back to the United States for justice. I think it's important to understand that we are at war now [4].

The Bush Administration's adoption of military commissions came despite intense criticism from Congress, especially Democrats, who charged that his actions were contrary to a long history of bipartisanship. Vermont Senator Patrick J. Leahy, Chairman of the Judiciary Committee, charged that using military commissions to try "foreign nationals" on charges of suspected terrorism would send the wrong message both at home and around the world. Military commissions if conducted in secret and where execution is summary and judicial review is nonexistent, would be strongly condemned.

In the months after the September 11, 2001 bombing, the Bush Administration believed that the public would overwhelmingly support their adoption, and that Congress would only hamper their anti-terrorist activities through extended debate [5]. When compared to other Presidents; the Bush detainees are fewer in number, and are limited to aliens, and confined for more specific reasons. The Bush Administration was concerned that the detainees, if released, would leave the country, preventing the U.S. government from treating them as defendants or witnesses [6].

## Lincoln's Actions

One hundred forty years earlier Lincoln also authorized the use of military commissions. Lincoln had just assumed office in March 4, 1861, and Congress was not in session. One by one eleven Southern states would secede from the Union and eventually form the Confederate States of America. Lincoln would be forced to act on the home front hoping to avert a permanent break between the North and the South, and at the same time win Congress' approval for his actions after the fact [7].

During a ten week period beginning with the surrender of Fort Sumter, South Carolina on April 14, 1861, through the convening of a special session of Congress on July 4 1861; Lincoln adopted a series of unprecedented wartime measures. Lincoln's measures included: combining state militias into ninety day volunteers; transferring 40,000 volunteers into three year enlistments; enlarging the regular army by 23,000, and the navy by 18,000; spending two million dollars which Congress had not yet appropriated to pay for the war; preventing the Post Office from delivering "treasonable correspondence"; enacting new restrictions upon foreign travelers, such as passports; ordering the blockage of all Southern ports; suspending the right of habeas corpus; and arresting and detaining in military custody political opponents on charges of "treasonable practices." These and other wartime measures were done without prior congressional authorize action, which was eventually granted [8].

Lincoln's predecessor James Buchanan had adopted a view of the Presidency diametrically opposed to that of his own. Buchanan's view, better known as the *strict constructionist* approach, held that the President had *no* more power than what was specifically set down in the U.S. Constitution or in federal law [9]. In 1861, Buchanan believed that as President he could not constitutionally or statutorily intervene to resolve the Southern act of secession. He was "bound by solemn oath, before God and the country, 'to take care that the laws be faithfully executed', and from this obligation he cannot be absolved by any human power" [10]. The President, Buchanan argued, had no legal authority or grant of discretion to intervene into the relationship between the national government and the states. To entrust the President with such powers would go beyond his constitutional mandate. Buchanan wrote:

> This would be to invest a mere executive officer with power of recognizing the dissolution of the confederacy among our thirty-three sovereign States. It bears no resemblance to the recognition of a foreign de facto government, involving no such responsibility. Any attempt to do this would, on his part, be a naked act of usurpation. It is therefore my duty to submit to Congress the whole question with all its bearings [11].

Lincoln's view, better known as the *prerogative* approach, held that a President may use his constitutional powers liberally when responding to a national crisis or emergency. Recent presidents, especially Franklin D. Roosevelt, have adopted Lincoln's approach. Inherent within this approach is that the President may act decisively and use the full weight of his office in the performance of his duties [12].

In his first major address to the nation as president on March 4, 1861, Lincoln warned the Southern states that the United States of America was a permanent entity. This permanence, or rather "perpetuity," must be seen as "implied, if not expressed, in the fundamental law of all national governments." No government has written into its laws the means to its own destruction. No state can voluntarily secede from the Union. Legislative acts allowing for secession "are "legally void, and that acts of violence within any State or States against the authority of the United States are insurrectionary or revolutionary, according to circumstances" [13]. Lincoln called the whole idea of secession "anarchy." The rule of the majority adheres to "constitutional checks and limitations" and is shaped through "deliberate changes of popular opinion and sentiments" guaranteeing their liberties, had instead become hostage to the rule of the minority [14].

Lincoln justified his wartime measures in a July 4, 1861 message to Congress. In that message, Lincoln adopted a more warlike and less conciliatory tone toward the seceding Southern states. Lincoln again brought up the issue as to whether the majority had become hostage to the minority and whether the majority can use its power to ensure its preservation against that minority. Lincoln asked the question as to whether a constitutional republic or democracy can ensure its territorial existence against enemies at home. In the impending crisis a nation faces a faction of discontented persons who lack the required votes to form an administration and are intent upon bringing down that government. Lincoln spoke:

> It must force us to ask, Is there, in all republics this inherent and fatal weakness? Must a government, of necessity, be too *strong* for the liberties of its own people, or too *weak* to maintain its own existence? So viewing the issue, no choice was left but to call out the war power of the Government and so to resist force employed for its destruction by force for its preservation [15].

Lincoln explained that his wartime "measures whether strictly legal or not," resulted from what appeared to be "a popular demand and a public necessity," and the belief that Congress would approve them. All his measures were constitutionally within the scope of Congress. His administration decided that with the calling up of the state militias the military authorities should have the "discretion" to suspend the writ of habeas corpus, and "to arrest and detain without resort to the ordinary processes and forms of laws such individuals as he might deem dangerous to the public safety."

This power to suspend and to arrest and detain was exercised, though only "sparingly." The "legality and propriety" of his administration's actions had been openly challenged. One third of the states had defied or failed to carry out the nation's laws. He asked the question as to whether a nation based upon a rule of law should be compelled to enforce a particular law protecting an individual's liberties, even when the overall effect of enforcing that law favors the guilty over the innocent. Lincoln spoke:

> To state the questions more directly, Are all the laws *but one* to go unexecuted, and the Government itself go to pieces lest that one be violated? Even in such a case, would not the official oath be broken if the Government should be overthrown when it was believed that disregarding the single law would tend to preserve it? [16]

The major constitutional issue at stake is that which provides that "the privilege of the writ of habeas corpus shall not be suspended unless when, in cases of rebellion or invasion, the public safety may require it." A "rebellion" has taken place and the "public safety" mandates a "qualified suspension" of this right, which he authorized. The argument is made that the Congress, and not the President, has the power to suspend. On this issue, the Constitution was "silent." Suspension was intended to take place during a "dangerous emergency." In the event that Congress was not in session, the framers of the Constitution could not possibly have wanted a "rebellion" to go unabated, without taking action [17]. In the latter part of his July 4, 1861 message, Lincoln spoke:

> Our popular Government has often been called an experiment. Two points in it our people have already settled—the successful establishing and the successful administering of it. One still remains—its successful maintenance against a formidable internal attempt to overthrow it. It is now for them to demonstrate to the world that those who can fairly carry an election can also suppress a rebellion; that ballots are the rightful and peaceful successors of bullets, and that when ballots have fairly and constitutionally decided there can be no successful appeal back to bullets; that there can be no successful appeal except to ballots themselves at succeeding elections [18].

In a letter to A. G. Hodges, Editor of the Frankfurt Kentucky *Commonwealth* dated April 4, 1864 Lincoln gave a more descriptive interpretation as to how he viewed his constitutional powers upon assuming the office of president with the onset of the Civil War. Lincoln abhorred the whole institution of slavery: "If slavery is *not* wrong, nothing is wrong." He wrote that whatever his personal views on slavery were he was bound by constitutional oath to protect its legal existence. The "ordinary civil administration" prohibited him from indulging into "abstract" moral judgments on slavery. On the broader issue as to the nation's survival in the impending crisis, Lincoln wrote that his constitutional oath to preserve the

Constitution imposed on him "the duty of preserving, by every indispensable means, that government-that nation, of which that Constitution was the organic law." Lincoln spoke:

> Was it possible to lose the nation and yet preserve the Constitution? By general law, life and limb must be protected, yet often a limb must be amputated to save a life; but a life is never wisely given to save a limb. I felt that measures otherwise unconstitutional might become unlawful by becoming indispensable to the preservation of the Constitution through the preservation of the nation. Right or wrong, I assume this ground, and now avow it. [19].

Throughout the Civil War, especially the early years, the Lincoln Administration's major concern on the home front was the presence of pro-South Northerners. Though most professed loyalty, the military authorities were concerned that they could pose a threat to the Union war effort. Their wartime activities could involve spying, sabotage, supplying troops to the embattled South, passing treasonable materials, encouraging acts of secession in the North, and giving aid and comfort to the enemy.

Even if they remained peaceful, they could still do political damage to the Lincoln Administration. Their activities could include hindering enlistments, encouraging desertions, handing out disloyal material, and criticizing the President and the Republican Party. Existing statutes and court rulings on treason, and conspiracy to commit treason were seen as inadequate for the impending crisis. Convictions would be very difficult in civil courts, especially before pro-Southern or indifferent juries. Also, many anti-war activities did not qualify as violations of federal law. Grand jury indictments would be very difficult in many Northern jurisdictions. Convictions would be few in number [20].

The military authorities in lieu of charging for treason would arrest potential violators and suspend their writ of habeas corpus. Early in the war, arrests were based on presidential proclamations covering certain areas. The U.S. State Department whose function was to arrest relied upon various sources such as secret service, federal marshals and the military authorities. Violators were often not informed as to the reasons for the government's actions. Arrests were made without adequate investigation or evidence. Violators without habeas corpus suspended had no legal recourse to challenge their terms of their confinement. Release came only after the emergency had ended. On occasion judges would order prisoners to be released, but the provost marshals or the military authorities would ignore their rulings. When military and civilian jurisdictions clashed, the military inevitably held the upper hand [21].

The Lincoln Administration used military commissions to try civilians in both free and border states. Military security became the ultimate justification given for the government's actions. During General Robert E. Lee's July 1863 invasion of Pennsylvania resulting in the Battle of Gettysburg, Lincoln responded to citizens' fears and imposed martial law.

A year later in July 1864, he imposed martial law on all of Kentucky. Military commissions were set up in full recognition of the civil authorities and civil courts. Interference was kept to a minimum. Among the major wartime offenses tried were spying and sniping. In the border states; the punishment varied in severity. One of the most controversial aspects was the trying of civilians who were arrested for offenses committed considerable distances from actual Union military operations. In all Northern jurisdictions, the civil courts were open and in session.

During the years 1863 and 1864, opposition was especially strong among many Northern Democrats from the states of Ohio, Indiana and Illinois, who openly opposed Lincoln's war policy. These dissident Democrats, better known as Copperheads, supported an early end to the war with the South. They became the target of the military authorities in their campaign to root out disloyalty and treason [22].

On February 14, 1862, Secretary of War Edwin Stanton was given the task of enforcing the Lincoln Administration's policy of detainment, arrest and trial of civilians, which included dissident Democrats. As the civilian head of the U.S. War Department, Stanton was seen as the most logical choice. He was seen as being the least judicious of all the Cabinet Secretaries, as well as the most aggressive and partisan on wartime policy. Two other Cabinet Secretaries were considered but dismissed as unsuitable to the task. U.S. Attorney General Edward Bates was seen as "too old, slow and erratic" as well as being a staunch opponent of military arrests. Secretary of State William Seward, though competent, was too involved in foreign policy and frequently acted in a "distressing casual, circuitous, and flippant manner" [23].

Lincoln authorized Stanton in *Executive Order No. 1 Relating To Political Prisoners* to use his discretion (as Secretary of War) to detain "as spies any persons in the service of the insurgents, or others whose release at the present moment may be deemed incompatible with the public safety." Stanton's order called the Southern "insurrection" a clash of "political ideas" unknown in U.S. history. His order proclaimed: "Every department of the Government was paralyzed by treason." Defection" was the order of the day. That included: Congress, federal judges, diplomats, the armed forces, territories and many state officials. Dissension existed even in most loyal Union states in the form in political organizations and "secret societies." Northern groups were supplying men, money and war material to the Southern insurgents. Congress did not anticipate the Southern "insurrection" and did not plan for this emergency. Courts which were intended to support the administration were hesitant when called to act [24].

Stanton's order conceded that the recent reversals on the field of battle had disheartened loyal Union supporters and gave new optimism to its opponents. The most obvious indicator was the decrease in enlistments and the increase of desertions. The President concluded that it was "his duty to employ with energy the extraordinary powers which the Constitution confides to him in cases of insurrection."

The armed forces were used as he felt necessary, even though "existing law' provided for no such use. Suspension of habeas corpus was also exercised. Stanton order declared that the President "caused persons who were represented to him as being or about to engage in disloyal and treasonable practices to be arrested by special civil as well as military agencies and detained in military custody when necessary to prevent them and deter others from such practices." The detainee was examined and released when conditions held that the "public safety" was no longer at risk. Lincoln's wartime measures were intended to clearly define the difference between loyal and disloyal conduct [25].

Ten days later on September 24, 1862; Lincoln issued a proclamation aimed at those persons who interfere with the calling up of Union volunteers and draftees and those which the civil law cannot adequately persecute for military offenses. Such offenses impede the war effort and "give aid and comfort in various ways to the insurrection." Lincoln's wartime measures were to include "all rebels and insurgents, their aiders and abettors, within the United States, and persons discouraging volunteer enlistments, resisting militia drafts, or guilty of any disloyal practice, affording aid and comfort to Rebels against the authority of the United States...." Offenders were subject to martial law and were to be tried and punished before courts-martial or military commissions. In addition, the writ of habeas corpus was to be suspended during the "rebellion" and the imprisonment was to include "any fort, camp, arsenal, military prison, or other place of confinement by any military authority or by the sentence of any Court-Martial or Military Commission" [26].

Lincoln's September 1862 proclamation created a firestorm of criticism. Lincoln was charged as having acted as a despot totally ignoring the will of Congress. Critics charged that his actions showed no respect for the rule of law, but was rather based on military expediency. Former U.S. Supreme Court Justice Benjamin Curtis believed that Lincoln had entrusted himself with powers which only Congress and the Judiciary enjoyed. Lincoln's actions created offenses unknown in U.S. jurisprudence, such as discouraging volunteers and encouraging disloyal acts. Prisoners were unlawfully removed from the jurisdiction of the civil courts. Also, grand jury indictments were substituted for provost marshal reports and military commissions for trial by jury. As for the latter, military commissions used uncontrolled discretion, determining the punishment imposed rather than relying upon the will of Congress [27].

Curtis believed that the President's powers, even in wartime, were constitutionally limited to the conduct of his office.

> In time of war, a military commander, whether he be the commander-in-chief, or one of his subordinates, must possess and exercise powers both over the persons and property of citizens which do not exist in time of peace. But he possesses and exercises such powers, not in spite of the constitution and laws of the United States, or in derogation from their authority, but in virtue thereof and in strict subordination thereof [28.]

To ensure that Lincoln's September 24, 1862 proclamation enjoyed the full color of law, Congress passed the Habeas Corpus Act on March 3, 1863. Through its actions, Congress sanctioned the president's actions after the fact. The 1863 Act required that the military authorities provide a list of prisoners to the civil authorities within twenty days of their capture otherwise the prisoners must be released from custody. Upon release, the prisoners must swear allegiance to the U.S. government and give evidence of future good behavior. In the event that the list is not given to the civil authorities, the prisoners may petition the civil courts through writ of habeas corpus. The effect of the 1863 Act was to speed up the release of prisoners charged where no violations of federal law occurred. After twenty days and no grand jury indictment, the prisoners must be granted immediate release [29].

One year later on September 15, 1863, Lincoln issued a second; and more detailed proclamation, suspending the writ of habeas corpus. His September 1863 proclamation reaffirmed the validity of the 1863 Act passed a year earlier. Like 1862, Lincoln authorized the suspension when in his judgment the "public safety" was at risk. The 1863 proclamation was expanded to include all persons under the command or in the custody of the military, naval or civil authorities. A wide number of potential offenders were again covered: prisoners of war, spies, aiders and abettors of the enemy; all U.S. military personnel including deserters, draft dodgers and any person who commits military-related offense. Lincoln declared that suspension was to remain for the duration of the rebellion or until this proclamation was revoked or modified. All magistrates, attorneys and civil officers, as well as all military and naval authorities, were "to take distinct notice of this suspension, and give it full effect…." [30].

The year 1863 saw the Lincoln Administration become even more stringent in its position against anti-war Northern opponents. The two main reasons were increased Union defeats and Confederate military operations in the vicinity of Washington., D.C. A year earlier in 1862 the nation's first conscription law was passed resulting in widespread evasion and blatant opposition. The U.S. War Department arrested would-be violators whether leaving town or aiding a draftee. Northern public opinion, on the whole, supported conscription, labeling violators as 'skeedaddlers' [31].

The Civil War saw Lincoln and Chief Justice Roger Taney supporting opposite positions on the issues of law and war. Lincoln symbolized war and military expediency whereas Taney symbolized the letter of the law. This clash of positions came to a head in the case of *Ex Parte Merryman*. In that case, the military authorities acting upon Lincoln's authority ignored Taney's court order of release of the prisoner Merryman. Eighteen sixty four saw a new Chief Justice (Salmon P. Chase), and four new Associate Justices (Noah H. Swayne, Samuel F. Miller, David Davis and Stephen Fields) all appointed by Lincoln. The remaining four Justices were holdovers from previous Presidents. They included: James M. Wayne (Andrew Jackson - 1835), Samuel Nelson (John Tyler - 1845), Robert C. Grier (James Polk - 1846) and Nathan Clifford (James Buchanan - 1858). On the issue of military commissions, both the Lincoln appointees and the holdovers were split.

## THE MILLIGAN CASE

The most famous case of the Lincoln's use of military commissions was the trial of Lambdin Milligan, a Northern Democrat, who opposed the war. On October 4, 1864; the military authorities acting under the 1862 proclamation arrested Milligan; and several others at their homes in Indiana, and imprisoned them in a military stockade. Less than a month later, Milligan was tried, convicted, and sentenced to death before a military commission held in Indianapolis, Indiana which Lincoln upheld [32].

During the military trial, evidence was brought out that Milligan belonged to a secret organization known as the Sons of Liberty. Milligan and others had conspired to commit various illegal acts such as: capturing federal and state arsenals in the Northern states of Ohio, Indiana, and Illinois; releasing prisoners of war at Camp Douglas (Chicago), Camp Morton (Indianapolis), Camp Chase (Columbus, Ohio) and Johnson's Island on Lake Erie; arming freed Southern prisoners; starting a reign of terror including arson and pillage; and resisting Union forces stationed in Missouri and Kentucky [33]. Though Milligan could have been tried for violations of federal law, Secretary of War Stanton and Indiana Governor Oliver P. Morton desired more drastic measures than what the civil law provided [34]. His date of execution was set for May 19, 1865 [35].

On January 2, 1865; after the military commission had completed its findings the U.S. Circuit Court in Indianapolis authorized a grand jury to hear his case to see if any federal laws were violated. After almost a month, the grand jury failed to issue a bill of indictment or a presentment. Milligan appealed his case to the U.S. Circuit Court claiming that the military commission lacked jurisdiction to hear the charges against him or any charges in the future.

Milligan also claimed that the military commission violated his right of trial by jury. The lower federal court ruled that military authorities arrested, tried and sentenced him all in violation of the 1863 Act. On May 10, 1865, nine days before his execution his petition was granted. The two judge federal panel split on the final result, forcing a question of law before the U.S. Supreme Court [36].

A similar case on military commissions occurred in *Ex Parte Vallandigham*, where the Supreme Court ruled in favor of the military authorities. Though the facts in *Vallandigham* appeared similar to *Milligan*, the Justices saw a major factual difference. In *Vallandigham*, the petitioner appealed directly from a military commission to the U.S. Supreme Court which federal law did not provide for, whereas in *Milligan* the petitioner appealed from a federal circuit court in violation of a federal law, the Habeas Corpus Act of 1863. Milligan argued successfully that the military authorities should have transferred him forthwith to the civilian authorities [37].

On April 3, 1866; one year after Lincoln's death, the U.S. Supreme Court announced its unanimous decision. The U.S. Supreme Court ruled that the President had exceeded his constitutional powers when he established a military commission to try Milligan, a civilian, for the offenses charged. The civil courts of Indiana were open and in session. Lincoln's actions were taken without proper authorization from Congress [38]. Where the Justices in *Milligan* differed was the *extent* of the President's power to establish military courts (commissions) in wartime. The language of the majority was sweeping in the negative on the President's power, whereas the language of the concurring was more circumspect. Better known as *Ex Parte Milligan*, this case stood as a historical reminder that limits do exist on the war-making power of the President as spelled out in Article II of the Constitution. Prior to the World War II case of the eight Nazi saboteurs, *Milligan* had little or no significance [39] .

Justice Davis, a close personal friend of Lincoln and one of his four appointees to the U.S. Supreme Court wrote for the majority. He was joined by Justices Nelson, Grier, Clifford, and Fields. Davis ruled that the military commission did *not* have proper jurisdiction to try and to punish Milligan. Milligan was not a resident of any of the rebelling states, nor was he a prisoner of war, nor did he serve in the U.S. armed forces. Rather, he was a citizen of the state of Indiana for over twenty years at the time of his arrest. The military commission, in Milligan's case, tried, convicted and sentenced him to die for criminal offenses. The actions of the military authorities stripped from him the protection of the law which placed him "at the mercy of wicked rulers or clamor of an excited people" [40].

The framers of the U.S. Constitution understood the historical struggle against tyranny, and that the Bill of Rights was the best guarantee against the abuses of government. The framers knew that during troubled times leaders, and people seek to sever government restraints and, instead, try to accomplish their goals through "sharp and divisive measures." Important constitutional liberties were at risk unless the rule of law prevailed. Davis wrote: "The history of the world had taught them [framers of the U.S. Constitution] that what was done in the past might be attempted in the future. The Constitution of the United States is a law for rulers and people, equally in war and in peace, and covers with the shield of its protection all classes of men, at all times, and under all circumstances" [41].

Davis ruled that Milligan was denied his right to trial before a civil court. The military commission trying Milligan lacked proper jurisdiction, having been established without valid congressional or presidential authority. The President, in war as in peace, is empowered to execute, rather than legislate, the law. In addition, the "laws and usages of war" cannot be substituted for proper jurisdiction. U.S. citizens cannot be tried before military commissions when the civil courts are open and in session. The civil courts of Indiana were handling routine judicial business deciding criminal cases and redressing grievances. The trial judges hearing Milligan's case must be appointed for terms of "good behavior" [42].

Davis was emphatic in his ruling that Milligan should have been transferred to the civil authorities. Congress had already set down into law the offenses, the punishment, and the court to hear the case. The civil courts were "peaceful," not needing "bayonets" or "military aid to execute its judgments."

The trial would be held in a loyal Union state before judges who were "eminently distinguished for patriotism," and juries who were "upright, intelligent," and lawfully selected. Davis ruled: "The government had no right to conclude that Milligan, if guilty, would not receive in that court merited punishment; for its records disclose that it was constantly engaged in the trial of similar offenses, and was never interrupted in its administration of criminal justice" [43].

Davis ruled that Milligan's right of trial by jury was also denied. Milligan was a civilian and entitled to be treated as such. Trial by jury does not apply to a person who is "attached to the army, or navy, or militia in actual service." The discipline essential for running efficient armed forces demands a "swifter" trial than what the civil courts provide. Congress has the constitutional power to decide the type of trial which the armed forces will use when trying military-related offenses. Both soldiers and sailors subject themselves to the jurisdiction of Congress which makes the rules [44].

Martial law can never be used when the civil authorities and civil courts remain in power undisturbed. States, such as Indiana, having once invaded were designated as a "theatre of operations." On this point, Davis responded that the threat of invasion was past. Any reason for martial law had ceased. Mere threat is not enough. Davis reasoned: "The necessity must be actual and present; the invasion real, such as effectually closes the courts and deposes the civil administration." Martial law can be used only in a "real war" situation. The president can use such wartime measures in states like Virginia where lawful authority, especially the courts, was overthrown. The same cannot be said for Indiana [45].

Chief Justice Chase wrote the concurring opinion. He was joined by Justices Wayne, Swayne and Miller. Chase agreed with the majority's conclusion that the military authorities lacked jurisdiction to detain, and to try Milligan for the offense charged. The grand jury failed to indict after the close of its session, making his continued imprisonment unlawful. The government clearly violated the Habeas Corpus Act of 1863 Act. Chase expressed major reservations as to the majority opinion.

First, the president, like the Congress, has the power to detain and to arrest in the event that habeas corpus is suspended. Second, Congress may establish military courts to exist alongside civil courts with full powers even though habeas corpus is suspended [46].

Chase believed that Congress, though not exercising such, did have the power to establish military commissions in the state of Indiana. The Constitution gives the Congress the power to raise and support the armed forces and the power to make the rules and regulations for their use. This same power extends to the state militias when called into active service. Inherent within these powers is to establish military courts to try and to punish without trial by jury. The guarantees of the Bill of Rights, especially the Fifth Amendment right of presentment or grand jury indictment, were not extended to armed forces [47].

Chase believed that limits do exist on the war-making power of Congress. When a nation is at peace "the laws of peace must prevail." But when a nation is at war and all or part is invaded the power rests with Congress to respond. Congress must decide those jurisdictions where "great and imminent public danger" reign which justify military courts to try offenses against the national interest. Contrary to what the majority says, the official record shows that when Milligan was arrested, Indiana was in a military district within a "theatre of operations." Indiana was previously invaded and was subject to further invasion. Chase wrote:

> It appears, also that a powerful secret association, composed of citizens and others, existed within the state, under military organization, conspiring against the draft, and plotting insurrection, the liberation of prisoners at various depots, the seizure of the state and national arsenals, armed cooperation with the enemy and war against the national government [48].

Chase believed that Congress did have the constitutional power to establish military courts to try civilians charged with conspiracy offenses. He disagreed with the majority's conclusion that since the civil courts were open, Congress was somehow prohibited from exercising this power. The civil courts can be hearing cases and rendering decisions and, at the same time, be ill-prepared to try and to punish a conspirator, such as Milligan. Chase called the judges and the judicial officers of Indiana "loyal" to the present administration. Under different circumstances, the opposite can be true. Judges can conceivably sympathize with the conspirators and even rule in their favor [49].

## THE *MILLIGAN* LEGACY

The full *Milligan* opinion was not made public until December 1866. When the case was handed down, Lincoln's wartime actions were called into question. Though the opinion was split, all the Justices agreed that Lincoln had exceeded his constitutional powers. The entire Court in *Milligan* sided with Taney over Lincoln in *Ex Parte Merryman* earlier in the war that the President cannot substitute military courts for civil courts when trying civilians for military related-offenses [50]. *Milligan* influenced the on going post-Civil War conflict between President Andrew Johnson, and the Radical Republicans in Congress on the issue of Southern Reconstruction.

Johnson supported a policy of terminating military governments throughout the South. *Milligan*, so Johnson believed, strengthened his case for ending all trials of civilians before military commissions within the occupied South. U.S. Supreme Court Justices had stopped hearing appeals before the federal circuit courts due to the Union occupation [51].

In contrast, the Radical Republicans supported a policy of continued military governments. Johnson and various federal judges had implied through their actions that the Lincoln assassination conspiracy trial was unlawful. Republican Senator Thadeus Stevens of Pennsylvania argued that *Milligan* "places the knife of the rebel at the throat of every…loyal Union man in the South." Federal judges would abuse their powers over writ of habeas corpus through their release of Lincoln's "assassins" [52].

Reacting to *Milligan,* the Radical Republicans proposed new laws, all aimed at circumventing the U.S. Supreme Court's powers to hear cases on appeal. They included:

limiting its appellate jurisdiction, requiring unanimity whenever constitutional issues were involved, and even voiding the *Milligan* case itself. One proposal *did* pass Congress. The Radical Republicans passed a law revoking the U.S. Supreme Court's appellate jurisdiction to hear cases challenging Congress' Reconstruction legislation.

When brought before the Court, the Justices ruled in a unanimous decision that Congress' policies and motives concerning the defeated South could not be challenged. (*Ex Parte McCardle*) [53]. Occurring at the same time as *Milligan* was the death of the two remaining Justices from the South, William Catron and James M. Wayne, both appointed by President Andrew Jackson. In part because of *Milligan,* but also because of Johnson's tenure, Congress rescinded the ninth seat and decreased the number of Justices to eight [54].

*Milligan* was *not* the only famous case of military commissions during the Civil War. Eight civilians, including one woman, were tried and convicted before a nine member military commission in the Lincoln assassination conspiracy trial. As a result of the Lincoln assassination, Secretary of War Stanton began a "reign of terror" in his attempt to apprehend the conspirators. On May 1, 1865, President Johnson issued a proclamation declaring that "all persons implicated in the murder" of the president, and "the attempted assassination" of Secretary of State Seward and other government officials, as well as "their aiders and abettors (were to be) subject to the jurisdiction of and legally triable before a Military Commission." The trial of the eight conspirators lasted from May through July 1865. Four conspirators, including the lone woman Mrs. Mary Surratt, were hanged whereas four others received long prison terms [55].

Historically, cases dealing with military commissions and martial law are limited to national emergencies. Events such as Fort Sumter, Pearl Harbor and the World Trade Center bombing of September 11,2001; inevitably force government to initiate wartime measures which would be seen as both unlawful and unpopular in peacetime. In all three instances, the government resorted to using national security as justification however unpopular. Lincoln set the example that later Presidents, such as Franklin D. Roosevelt and George W. Bush, would follow.

Lincoln showed that nothing would prevent him from ensuring the survival of the Union and that the government would use, if necessary, extraordinary wartime measures to protect itself, including military commissions. Lincoln's wartime measures in many cases, if not violating the letter of the law, at least stretched the law to its outer limits.

## REFERENCES


[1] Walter Koenig, *The Chief Executive* (New York: Harcourt, Brace and World, 1964), pp. 248-249

[2] "Military Order of November 13, 2001–Detention, Treatment, and Trial of Certain Non-Citizens in the War Against Terrorism," *Federal Register*, November 16, 2001, Vol. 16. n. 222.

[3] "Justice in the Shadows," *Newsweek*, November 26, 2001, p. 39

[4] "White House Push on Security Steps Bypasses Congress," *The New York Times*, November 15, 2001, p. 1

[5] *Ibid.*, p. 1

[6] War Powers: Is Bush Making History?" *Time*, December 3, 2001, p. 1.
[7] *Ibid.*, p. 1
[8] Edwin S. Corwin, *The President–Office and Powers* (New York: New York University Press, 1957), p. 229
[9] James Pfiffner and Roger H. Davison, *Understanding the Presidency*, 3rd. ed. (New York: Longman, 2003), pp. 23-24
[10] *Messages and Papers of the Presidents* (New York: Bureau of National Liberature, Inc., 1897), p. 3165
[11] *Ibid.*, p. 3166
[12] Pfiffner and Davison, *Understanding the Presidency*, pp. 25-27
[13] Messages and Papers of the Presidents, p. 3208
[14] *Ibid.*, p. 3210
[15] *Ibid.*, p. 3224
[16] *Ibid.*, pp. 3225-3226
[17] *Ibid.*, p. 3226
[18] *Ibid.*, p. 3231
[19] Pfiffner and Davison, *Understanding the Presidency*, p. 35
[20] Alfred H. Kelly and Winifred A. Harbison, *The American Constitution–Its Origin and Developments*, Vol. 1 (New York: W.W. Norton and Co., 1948), pp. 437-438
[21] *Ibid.*, pp. 438-439
[22] *Ibid.*, pp. 443-444
[23] Allan Nevins, "The Case of the Copperhead Conspirator," *Quarrels that have Shaped the Constitution*, ed. John A. Garraty (New York: Harper and Row Publishers, 1962), pp. 106-107.
[24] Messages and Papers of the Presidents, pp. 3303-3304
[25] *Ibid.*, pp. 3304-3305
[26] *Ibid.*, pp. 3299-3300
[27] Homer Carey Hockett, *The Constitutional History of the United States 1826-1876* (New York: The Macmillan Co., 1939), pp. 284-285
[28] *Ibid.*, p. 285
[29] *Ibid.*, pp. 286-287
[30] Messages and Papers of the Presidents, pp. 3299-3300
[31] Nevins, "The Case of the Copperhead Conspirator," *Quarrels that have Shaped the Constitution*, pp. 110-111
[32] "The Military Commission in 1942," *Virginia Law Review*, 29 (1942), p. 326.
[33] Nevins, "The Case of the Copperhead Conspirator," *Quarrels that have Shaped the Constitution*, pp. 110-111
[34] William H. Rehnquist, *The Supreme Court–How it was, How it is* (New York: William Morrow and Co., Inc. 1987), pp. 158-159
[35] *Ex Parte Milligan* 71 U.S. (4 Wall) 2, p. 107
[36] *Ibid.*, p. 107; Nevins, "The Case of the Copperhead Conspirator," *Quarrels that have Shaped the Constitution*, p. 112
[37] Carl Brent Swisher, *American Constitutional Development* (Boston: Houghton Mifflin Co., 1943), pp. 287-288
[38] 71 U.S. (4 Wall), 2, pp. 121-122
[39] *Ex Parte Quirin*, 317 U.S., 18 (1942).

[40] 71 U.S. (4 Wall), pp. 118-119
[41] *Ibid.*, pp. 120-121
[42] *Ibid.*, pp. 120-121
[43] *Ibid.*, p. 122
[44] *Ibid.*, pp. 122-123
[45] *Ibid.*, pp. 125-126
[46] *Ibid.*, p. 137
[47] *Ibid.*, p. 137-138
[48] *Ibid.*, p. 140
[49] *Ibid.*, pp. 140-141
[50] Elder Witt, *Guide to the U.S. Supreme Court*, 2nd ed. (Washington, DC: Congressional Quarterly, Inc., 1990), p. 21
[51] *Ibid.*, p. 21
[52] Hockett, The Constitutional History of the United States 1826-1876, p. 298
[53] *Ibid.*, p. 298
[54] Witt, Guide to the U.S. Supreme Court, p. 21
[55] "The Military Commission in 1942," *Virginia Law Review* 29 (1942), pp. 323-325

In: Presidents and War
Editors: A. Eksterowicz and G. Hastedt, pp. 79-101
ISBN 978-1-61668-917-9


*Chapter 6*

# FOR LOVE OR FOR MONEY?: WILLIAM MCKINLEY AND THE SPANISH-AMERICAN WAR

***Jeffrey Bloodworth***

## INTRODUCTION

In the spring of 1892, news of a calamitous famine in Russia reached American shores. While Congress groused about the Tsar's lackluster famine relief and even threatened to sever diplomatic relations over his government's poor efforts, the lives of an estimated 20 million peasants hung in the balance. With Congress dithering, Iowans sprang to action. Spurred by the *Davenport* (Iowa) *Democrat's* editor, Benjamin Franklin Tillinghast, and Governor Horace Boies's "Iowa Russian Famine Relief Commission," the Hawkeye State's farmers donated 3,000 tons of grain. Though Congress eventually refused to ship the foodstuffs the grain reached the starving before summer's end [1].

The bounty's arrival elicited much hue and cry. To one hungry Russian the unsolicited aid from faraway strangers meant "Christ is risen," while Leo Tolstoy claimed Iowa's beneficence signaled the "dawn of universal brotherhood" [2]. Hyperbole aside, the connection between Tillinghast, Iowa's farmers, Tolstoy, and Russia's peasants complicates a typical dichotomy in the history of American foreign policy: 19$^{th}$ century isolationism followed by 20$^{th}$ century internationalism [3]. Indeed, the episode reveals that even during the supposed "isolationist" nineteenth century, humanitarian concerns fueled a nascent internationalism and American interventionism.

"Isolationism" originally entered the political lexicon as a partisan cudgel wielded against opponents of the Spanish-American War. Thus, the term was and remains problematic [4]. Though any number of foreign policy specialists regularly debunk "isolationism" as a myth which has never accurately described US foreign relations, many historians regularly employ the term, nevertheless. From Arthur Schlesinger, Jr. who describes US foreign policy during the 1920s, as a return to the "womb[of] familiar and soothing isolationism," to Frank Ninkovich who terms late nineteenth century America "hopelessly isolationist," if nothing else, the concept's sheer ubiquity forces historians to grapple with it [5].

Since many specialists still take the term's existence for granted and relatively few actually study it, "isolationism" generally remains what *Washington Post* editor Felix Morley once called, "something highly reprehensible that nobody attempts to define" [6]. Moreover, when historians have sought to identify its sources, they have drawn a specious and poorly buttressed connection between it and the agrarian Midwest. The paucity of work on the Midwest and isolationism should hardly surprise. Decades ago, Richard Leopold presciently warned his fellow diplomatic historians, "[by] ignor[ing] the international aspects" of the Midwest, "glib generalizations" would eventually replace well-resourced understandings of the region [7]. Thus, textbooks and monographs not only routinely depict the nineteenth century as an isolationist era; they identify the Midwest as its haven.

With the still-entrenched assumption that isolationism reigned throughout the "long nineteenth century," the 1898 Spanish-American War has become a natural point of departure separating America's non-interventionist tradition from the twentieth century's swash-buckling internationalism. Mirroring this belief, Walter McDougall cleaves US foreign policy into an Old and New Testament, in which the long nineteenth century was marked by neutrality and non-intervention while the twentieth century featured a "Crusader State" mentality and action [8]. To McDougall, the Spanish-American War was the watershed moment where "a newly prideful United States began to measure its holiness by what it did, not just by what it was" [9]. Likewise, Alan Dawley pinpoints the Spanish-American War as the spot in time where the "new internationalism" replaced the "isolationist moorings" of George Washington's Farewell Address and the Monroe Doctrine. [10].

As both a watershed moment separating isolationism from internationalism and the proverbial ugly imperialist stepchild of American diplomatic history, the Spanish-American War occupies complicated historiographical territory. Because foreign policy specialists realize the war's imperialist results and assume an isolationist influence upon the Midwestern-born William McKinley, their histories bear this imprint [11]. Despite the allure of categorizing eras into "isolationism" versus "internationalism," an examination of the 1890s milieu and McKinley's foreign policy reveals the bankruptcy of simple foreign policy dichotomies, regional stereotypes, and tidy morality plays.

It is clear that nineteenth century American foreign policymakers avoided Jefferson's "entangling alliances," however, it does not necessarily follow that nineteenth century Americans were then isolationist [12]. Rather than interpreting the federal government's reluctance to enter into alliances as proof of "isolationism," a number of scholars: George Herring, James Field, and David Hendrickson, have looked beyond state officials in their assessment of US foreign policy. According to them, during the long nineteenth century, individual Americans were thoroughly involved with and committed to transforming the wider world: the very definition of internationalism [13].

In light of this more nuanced interpretation of US foreign policy, Tillinghast's humanitarian efforts and Congress's refusal to ship the foodstuffs are explicable, as both hew to the dominant themes of early diplomatic history: individual internationalism and governmental detachment. Tillinghast's labors reveal more than this. His activism reflects the emergence of an "international humanitarian" zeitgeist which appeared in—of all places—the American Midwest. This nascent humanitarian sensibility became so powerful, on both sides of the Atlantic, that humanitarian considerations influenced the foreign policies of democratic nations. Thus, even though Congress refused to ship famine relief to Russia, Iowa's governor responded to popular pressure by creating the "Iowa Russia Famine Relief Commission." In a similar fashion, McKinley heeded public outrage at Spain's gross human rights violations by launching a humanitarian intervention.

"Humanitarianism" does not usually play a significant role in most historical treatments of nineteenth century international history. Indeed, the nineteenth century has a well-deserved reputation as the heyday of European imperialism and *realpolitik*. In spite of this reality, humanitarian sensibilities did influence Western foreign policies. Whether it was British agitation against Ottoman atrocities and the Indian suttee (the self-immolation of widows), the multilateral 1885 Berlin Treaty eradicating the slave trade, or American aid to Russian peasants, a distinctly modern version of "humanitarianism" informed many Western citizens' views of the world in the mid-to-late nineteenth century. Consequently, and in democratic societies, humanitarians influenced policy [14].While William McKinley's decision for war was not solely prompted by humanitarian concerns, the president's policymaking occurred in a complicated international milieu in which humanitarianism increasingly influenced public opinion and American foreign policy.

Spanish atrocities in Cuba and humanitarian concerns significantly shaped McKinley's path to war. From grassroots church leaders who wrote thousands of letters urging intervention to political elites close to the president, calls for a "humanitarian intervention" were major factors in McKinley's decision-making. Thus, even though the conflict had an imperial consequence, the president's rationale should be considered separate from the war's results. Rather than judge the forces for war distinct from the conflict's consequences, the dominant historiographical interpretations fail to make this division. Instead, historians assume the conflict's architects always sought an imperial outcome. Instead, they pinpoint global capitalism's inherent imperial structure and/or McKinley's expansionist designs as the war's prime causes [15].These views are not only reductionist; they betray an *inverted* Whig interpretation of history. In contrast to the classic Whig interpretation of inevitable societal progress, the inverted Whigs emphasize the opposite. In their histories, the children of darkness continually, almost inevitably, triumph over the progeny of goodness and light; a pattern of which McKinley's war was yet another example.

In addition to a general inverted Whigishness coloring the dominant interpretations, most historians of the 1898 Spanish-American War stress four basic causal categories: international, national, regional, and individual. Scholars bandying the international analytical perspective look at the "macro-analytic" global viewpoint to reveal how shifts in geopolitical structures shaped events. From the macro-analytic position, the late nineteenth century was an era of living and dying powers during which ascendant nations; the United States, challenged descending empires: Spain. For macro-analytics, the Spanish-American War was predictable [16].

Emphasizing the intersection of the national *and* international context, William Appleman Williams and Walter LaFeber of the Wisconsin School, argue that war with Spain was part and parcel of a conscious program of imperial expansion designed to expand markets and reduce domestic tensions [17]. In league with the Wisconsin School's national and international context are regionalists, like Louis Perez, who emphasize the capitalist and imperialist structure of the world system which shaped McKinley's drive for regional hegemony. For Perez, McKinley's decision for war was a "[s]hrewd, purposeful, and calculated" move to secure a "dependent socio-economic system" before Cuban freedom fighters could gain independence from Spain [18].

The macro-analytic, Wisconsin School, and regional perspectives all share a presentist bias. Since the scholars realize the imperial war's imperial outcome, they naturally assume McKinley harbored expansionist tendencies from the start. The Spanish-American War had imperial consequences and led to a gruesome American counter-insurgency in the Philippines. This historical reality does not necessarily mean the conflict's architect, McKinley, was guided by nefarious motives. Instead, the war is a prime example of the role "irony" plays in the course of human events.

McKinley took America to war under the banner of righteous humanitarianism, only to succumb to the lures of empire once the conflict ended. In this way, the Spanish-American War neatly jives with Reinhold Niebuhr's definition of irony and history: "[t]he powerful person…is involved in an ironic contrast only if his weakness is due to some pretension of strength…it is clear that the great evils of history are caused by human pretensions" [19].

In this way, McKinley's humanitarian motives and hubris led him to war while also blinding him to the dangers of its aftermath. McKinley's declaration that his war would be fought "[i]n the cause of humanity and put an end to barbarities, bloodshed, starvation, and horrible miseries now existing there," should not be cynically viewed as a smokescreen for ulterior motives [20]. Rather the Spanish American War is part and parcel of a rich and ironic tradition in American foreign policy that George Kennan identifies. Echoing Niebuhr, Kennan claims that American moralism "rooted as it unquestionably is in a desire to do away with war and violence, makes violence more enduring, more terrible, and more destructive…than did the older motives of national interest" [21].

Unlike a Niebuhrian reading of McKinley's motives, which understands how quickly high moralism quickly devolves into selfishness and self-interest, the inverted Whigs ignore irony and moral complexity. To them, McKinley was always guided by "populism, jingoism, and imperialism," and little else [22]. Thus, the accrued weight of Social Darwinism, cultural chauvinism, missionary zeal, and American big business rendered McKinley's decision predestined and inevitable [23]. Taken together, the accumulated mass of the isolationist-internationalist dichotomy, unsupported regional stereotypes, and the inverted Whigs have so skewed the historical treatments of McKinley's Spanish-American War that James Field has rightly termed the writings on conflict and the 1890s, "The Worst Chapter in Almost Any Book" [24].

## Individual Perspective

In terms of the Spanish-American War and William McKinley, the individual perspective has undergone the most profound interpretive transformation. For decades, historians regarded William McKinley as little more than a tool of northeastern business interests and his political handler, Mark Hanna. Since the 1980s, revisionists, led by Lewis Gould, have successfully resuscitated McKinley's reputation. In their view, he was the first "modern" president who used the bully pulpit to shape public opinion and bend Congress to his will. For them, it was McKinley—rather than GOP philosophy, an imperialist world system, or business interests who spelled the difference between war and peace. The president historical context also substantially shaped his policy. As the leader of an emergent power which sought to expunge European imperialism from the Western Hemisphere, McKinley operated within the framework of the Monroe Doctrine and the nation's long-held, yet ambiguous, desire to "control" Cuba.

## INTERNATIONAL LEVEL

Though regional and national factors were substantial, this article argues that the international context and individual level were the most significant factors shaping McKinley's decision for war. In the mid-nineteenth century, international organizations and agreements dedicated to humanitarian ideals were founded and signed across the North Atlantic world. Starting with the "World Anti-Slavery Convention" in 1840, and extending to the "International Red Cross" and the "Geneva Conventions" in 1864, Western European and American activists lobbied and convinced their governments to sign onto a series of humanitarian-inspired treaties and agreements.

Initially catalyzed by the "teeming mass of ideas" linked to the American and French Revolutions, the humanitarian "association mania," as the *London Times* dubbed it, reflected the materialization of humanitarian ideals and movement [25]. Humanitarianism was a decidedly liberal project premised on the Enlightenment's fundamental hypothesis that all human life is equal [26]. The American and French Revolutions' emphases on "natural rights" along with the emergence of the mass press, public opinion, and democratic (responsive) governments helped transform humanitarianism into a mass movement. More importantly, these ideological and institutional developments made humanitarian interventionism, governments acting to protect human life beyond its borders, both politically possible and popular [27].

Contemporary observers have dubbed public outcry at images of human suffering and attendant calls for governmental action the "CNN effect." However, media's ability to depict individual anguish, shape public opinion, and create calls for intervention existed prior to cable news. Indeed, rising literacy rates across Western Europe and America caused the proliferation of mass media in the form of newspapers and magazines which enabled nineteenth century print media to perform the same function as television does today. In this way, Benedict Anderson's pioneering work, *Imagined Communities*, which details the ways in which media built "imagined" national communities, helps account for the creation of transnational identities and the emergence of humanitarianism [28].

It was in this technological, cultural and intellectual milieu that a Swiss businessman, Henri Dunant, successfully founded the International Red Cross. In the summer of 1859, Dunant stumbled into the gory aftermath of a battle between French and Austrian forces. Without proper medical care available, Dunant witnessed the slow and torturous death of wounded soldiers who after days of suffering finally expired where they fell. Deeply affected by what he saw, Dunant penned a memoir of the battle's aftermath, *Memory of Solferino,* which became an unexpected bestselling sensation across Europe. Dunant sensed he had touched a nerve. Thus, in 1863, Dunant, Gustav Moynier, and other European humanitarians convened the Geneva Convention. There, they founded the International Red Cross and unveiled the Geneva Treaty [29]. As the first codified humanitarian principles of international law governing war, the sixteen signatory nations to the "Geneva Treaty and Convention" gave the International Red Cross unfettered access to treat and aid the wounded on the battlefield [30].

At the very time Dunant was organizing the Geneva Convention, Clara Barton was also leaping into the humanitarian fray across the Atlantic. Similar to Dunant's reaction to Solferino, Barton was horrified at the primitive level of care available for Union soldiers. She took it upon herself to provide medical aid for the wounded and care for prisoners-of-war, thus, becoming a folk hero in the North [31]. After the war, Barton spent the better part of the 1870s unsuccessfully lobbying presidents to sign the Geneva Convention [32]. In the 1880 election, Barton used her considerable cache with Union veterans to campaign for James Garfield, whom she believed might support the treaty and an American branch of the Red Cross [33].

Reflecting America's status as an emergent power and increasing dependence on foreign trade, Garfield and his Secretary of State, James Blaine, devised a foreign policy that looked beyond the Western Hemisphere. Though Garfield signaled his intent to ratify the Geneva Convention, he was felled by an assassin's bullet [34]. Garfield's successor, Chester Arthur, however, was even more committed to cultivating ties with Europe [35]. From standardizing postal regulations and time zones to finally ratifying the Geneva Convention, Arthur made US foreign policy more closely mirror Americans' individual internationalism.

The administration backed the Geneva Convention as little more than an afterthought. Nevertheless, Barton used Arthur's treaty endorsement to found and champion an American chapter of the Red Cross [36]. By 1892, the Red Cross had become America's *defacto* provider of domestic humanitarian relief, an activity the federal government had foresworn. Indeed, in 1890, Congress had rebuffed calls for federal relief to drought-stricken Great Plains farmers. A mere two years after Congress claimed it had "no [constitutional] authority" to aid its own citizens, the Senate voted to transport relief to Europe. The House defeated the Senate measure, leaving the Red Cross to transport Iowa's foodstuffs. Nonetheless, the vote revealed how popular humanitarian sentiment was slowly changing Congressional conceptions of federal power, relief, and foreign policy [37].

Though Congress refused to ship famine relief, it did eventually commission the "Russian Famine Relief Committee of the United States." Headed by a former President, Rutherford B. Hayes, and Vice President, Levi Morton, as well as senators, congressmen, and Supreme Court Justices, The commission's very existence exemplified the famine relief movement's effectiveness in pushing the federal government into the international humanitarian fray [38]. Moreover, the entire Russian famine relief effort raised Barton's and the American Red Cross's visibility further convincing humanitarian activists of their ability to mobilize voters and move government to ameliorate the world's ills.

Though Tillinghast, who was involved with the Red Cross and close to its leaders, and Barton slowly brought government toward international relief work, events slowly made "humanitarian intervention" palatable to the public and policymakers. Because Russia was a signatory to the Geneva Conventions and Leo Tolstoy was literally begging for international aid, the Tsar had little choice but to accept Barton's help. Two years later, when Americans called for the Red Cross to relieve Armenians in the Ottoman Empire, Barton dealt with a government that was not only the perpetrator, Turkish officials believed American missionaries were to blame for the "troubles" in Armenia [39].

In large part, humanitarians pushed for global action, due to the influx of news enabled them to read about and view images of human suffering as never before. During the 1890s, the international telegraph, along with the maturation of *Reuters* and *Associated Press* news services, enabled newspapers and magazines to more easily report international news [40]. For example, the *Christian Herald* and *Harper's* regularly publicized Turkish atrocities committed against Armenians. In tandem with new communication systems were advances in photographic technologies, which rendered human suffering all the more real to readers. For example, *Harper's* 1895-96 series "The Troubles in Armenia," editors used photographic reproductions and image-making to bring Armenian anguish to life.

With eleven-by-sixteen photolithographs and drawings graphically depicting the Armenians' "utter extinction," American opinion leaders, like Julia Ward Howe and Charlotte Gilman Perkins, called for American intervention [41]. Gilman believed American intervention in Armenia would "usher in the new age of global social consciousness... [by] using her great strength to protect it [liberty] everywhere" [42]. In conjunction with newspapers and magazines were books, like Frederick Greene's bestseller, *The Armenian Crisis in Turkey,* which further highlighted the slaughter. Similar to Gilman and Howe, Greene called also for American involvement: "I care not what parties are in power, or how the games stands on the diplomatic chessboard, the Eastern Questions will be settled...and one more blot will be wiped out from the annals of the world" [43].

Despite the activism, Grover Cleveland refused to act. Mirroring Congress's refusal to aid Great Plains farmers in 1892, the president claimed he lacked the constitutional power to act [44]. After years of Cleveland ignoring pleas for American involvement, the 1896 Republican Platform explicitly called for action to "bring these atrocities to an end" [45]. With scores of local Armenian relief organizations raising money and calling for intervention, including Tillinghast's Davenport Iowa Relief Committee, a reluctant Clara Barton finally negotiated access to the Armenians and directed the Red Cross's first "intervention" [46].

Barton's move into Ottoman territory was a significant first step toward establishing the precedent of humanitarian interventions with the American public. For example, the *New York Tribune's* editors believed the "Armenian venture" had "established the precedent that it is not necessary that two countries should be at war in order to admit of the intervention of the Red Cross on behalf of the suffering" [47]. Moreover, the "right of humanitarian interventionism" was not invented in American. In the 1880s, Britain's Prime Minister William Gladstone received Parliamentary approval for armed intervention to stop Turkish atrocities against Bulgarian Christians [48]. In this way, the concept of "humanitarian interventionism" was well entrenched during the 1890s [49].

Despite the Red Cross's intervention, an estimated 186,655 Armenians died in the autumn of 1896 alone [50]. Thus, the memory of "Armenia" loomed large in Americans' collective consciousness when their attention turned to Cuba. Indeed, in the days leading to McKinley's declaration of war, the *New York Times* equated Armenia with Cuba: "The barbarities of the Spaniard, like the barbarities of the Turk, are...essential to his rule...[a]s Europe recognizes that to put a stop to Turkish misrule it is necessary to put a stop Turkish rule...so we must recognize that to pacify Cuba Spain must go" [51]. In this way, Cuban rebel leaders used the specter of "Armenia" as a propaganda tool to maintain the American public's interest in the conflict. Maximo Gomez, the leader of the Cuban insurgency, told the *New York Journal's* readers "[t]he horrors of Armenia are not as deserving of the attention of the American Congress as the barbarous and atrocious conduct of the butcher, Captain-General Weyler" [52].

In McKinley's "declaration of war" message to Congress, he referred to the "many historical precedents where neighboring States have interfered…to check the hopeless sacrifices of life by internecine conflicts beyond their borders." [53]. He directly addressed the issue of violating sovereign borders in the name of humanitarian ideals, "[i]t is no answer to say this is all in another country, belonging to another nation, and is therefore none of our business. It is specially our duty, for it is right at our door" [54]. In this way, the Red Cross's intercession into the Armenian crisis was yet another model and precedent for intervention into another state's internal affairs. Concurrently, it revealed the impotency of doing so solely through a humanitarian agency.

## The Individual Level: McKinley's Path to War

Taken together, the emergence of the Red Cross, international news services, and a coherent humanitarian movement set the stage for McKinley's humanitarian intervention into Cuba. Americans' long held designs on the island coupled with domestic politics undoubtedly played a role in the president's decision-making. Still, the precedent and public support for humanitarian action existed and proved decisive in McKinley's decision for war. McKinley, though, entered office both publicly and privately forswearing any intent to intervene in Cuba or wage war against Spain: A seeming carbon copy of his predecessor's policy. While Cleveland is given credit for revitalizing the Monroe Doctrine, restraint largely defined his foreign policy and sense of executive authority. Whether he was resisting pressure to annex Hawaii, refusing to ship famine relief to Russia, or refusing to intervene in Cuba, Cleveland retained a limited vision of presidential powers. Nonetheless, during discussions with Spanish authorities and in public statements it was he who originally made humanitarianism America's primary pretext for war [55].

The evening prior to his inauguration, McKinley dined with Cleveland and praised the outgoing president for his restraint, telling his soon-to-be predecessor, "if I can only go out of office…with the knowledge that I have done what lay in my power to avert [war]…I shall be the happiest man in the world." [56]. Though inverted Whigs dismiss this oft-cited statement as little more than cornpone, at best, and a smokescreen, at worst, historians should look no further than to McKinley's military service for proof of his sincerity.

McKinley's intimate familiarity with war made him quite hesitant to launch one of his own. Though he looked back on his service in the Union army with pride, his experience at Antietam and other minor, yet bloody, skirmishes led the president to recount "as I have grown older, I have come to understand…[that] it [war] means empty houses, empty hearts, and empty futures" [57]. Despite his efforts to avert conflict, 13 months into his presidency, he signed a congressional resolution that amounted to a declaration of war. Though revisionists have restored the 25$^{th}$ president's reputation through a handful of balanced and sober works, insofar as the Spanish-American War is concerned, the inverted Whigs remain dominant. In their accounts, McKinley remains either a secret imperialist, feckless, or a combination of the two.

McKinley revisionists and the inverted Whigs share one thing in common, however: Little direct documentation of the president's private deliberations [58].

In life, McKinley was famous for "the masks he wore," shielding even his closest associates from his intimate thoughts [59]. The tribune of Middle America, the *Emporia Gazette's* William Allen White, once complained even he could not penetrate "that plaster cast which was his public mask" and find the "real" McKinley [60]. The president's biographers believe a series of personal tragedies rendered the president more reserved and aloof than what was "normal" for his era. Thus, aside from his early stance against intervention, McKinley left little in the way of a personal written record through which to understand his evolving policy on Cuba [61]. Consequently, historians are left to piece together the evolution of his policy via an array of eye-witness accounts, speeches, memoranda, and educated conjecture.

With a foot in both the nineteenth and twentieth centuries, the source of William McKinley's popular appeal and basic personality has eluded many of his biographers. The modern half of McKinley might have successfully restructured the presidency; but the nineteenth century portion remained decidedly Victorian. Thus, when the president used media to build support for his agenda, he appears familiar. However, the personal side of the final Civil-War-vet-cum-president appears antiquated, especially when measured against his high-flying successor: Theodore Roosevelt.

McKinley assumed office at a key juncture in the history of American foreign policy. The nation's messianic vision to transform the world had always animated Americans' individual view of their role in the world. But by the late nineteenth century, the emergence of the United States as a significant global power alongside the materialization of mass media and non-governmental organizations made increased diplomatic activism inevitable. In this way, intervention into the Spanish-Cuba conflict was likely, if not inevitable.

While McKinley forged a modern foreign policy, his entrée into international policy, tariffs and reciprocity were the political fault lines of a different era. Similar to the way in which McKinley occupies the intersection of two political eras, in hailing from Canton, Ohio, the president's hometown straddled the junction of a modern industrial era and an agrarian America. As a Congressman, McKinley's voters were mostly farmers. However, his constituents and district also included B.F. Goodrich and Harvey Firestone, who transformed Akron into the world's rubber capitol, Joshua Gibbs, who made Canton America's foremost producer of farm machinery, and William Hoover, who based his vacuum cleaner company out of McKinley's adopted hometown [62].

As a Congressman and Governor, McKinley focused almost exclusively upon domestic issues, such as tariffs. As a staunch protectionist advocating stiff duties on imports, McKinley was hardly distinct from his Republican brethren, who elevated such a stance to party orthodoxy [63]. As chair of the powerful Ways and Means Committee, he mastered the issue by authoring the landmark 1890 tariff bill, was commonly called the "McKinley Tariff" [64]. Some critics might dismiss the Congressman's policy bailiwick as little more than carrying water for Ohio's business interests. Still, McKinley believed high tariffs protected American farmers and workers against low foreign wages [65].

McKinley's single-minded focus upon high tariffs was only altered by James Blaine's concept of "reciprocity." Reciprocity was the brainchild of the contentious two-time Secretary of State who popularized the idea as a legislative crow-bar to pry foreign markets open to American goods. Contemporary reciprocal trade agreements are commonly associated with liberalized trade policies. For McKinley, though, reciprocity was a means to stop "free trade" which he believed resulted in "sending too much money out the country, or getting too little in, or both" [66].

While McKinley's embrace of reciprocity merely reemphasizes his long-held protectionism, it would be a mistake to narrowly associate the president's trade policy with isolationism. As America's world trade boomed, McKinley and other Republican protectionists realized they would have to allow more foreign goods into America as a carrot for reciprocity agreements and access to international markets. In a strange twist of fate, McKinley's protectionism actually led him and his administration toward greater internationalism and bi-lateral cooperation [67].

As president, McKinley remained an internationalist and emphasized reciprocity agreements as a key to economic growth, claiming the nation could "no long[er] indulge in the sentiment that we can sell everything and buy nothing" [68]. While McKinley came into office focused on relieving "the glut" through foreign trade, the issue of Cuba demanded his immediate attention. Though his formative governing experience was overwhelmingly comprised of domestic affairs, he was no small town rube controlled by business interests. As McKinley's experience with reciprocity reveals, he was a quick study who could learn and embrace new theories with relative aplomb. Moreover, McKinley ran and "dominated" his government's foreign policy, yet another attribute of the first "modern" president [69].

The president's Cabinet revealed both his Midwestern roots and his desire to pursue Cleveland's Cuba policy: home rule (autonomy) and an end to the civil war. Indeed, with tariff policy and an international conference on bimetallism as his most pressing and immediate foreign policy issues, McKinley's choices for Secretary of War, Russell Alger, and State, John Sherman, reflects a president preparing for the hum-drum work of bi-lateral trade agreements rather than imperial expansion. [70]. As a general in the Civil War and former governor of Michigan, Alger might have appeared fit for his position on paper. However, he lacked the bureaucratic and organizational capacity for the job. John Sherman's choice for State was similarly uninspired. Sherman revealed his shortcomings when he suggested threatening American intervention into Cuba for the president's inaugural address, leaving McKinley to rely upon his personal friend William Day, who served as the assistant secretary of state, to handle Cuba [71].

McKinley sincerely wished to avoid war with Spain. The president, unlike his predecessor, had realistic hopes of maintaining party unity in the highly partisan and closely fought electoral thicket of the day even as he advanced America's strategic and moral interests. Nevertheless, his sense of presidential powers combined with the political calculus of the situation and the ongoing conflict made war likely, if not inevitable.

Historians posit that Spain's newly installed liberal government could only remain politically viable if it maintained its most prized colonial possession, a position increasing the likelihood of American intervention. Since the Cuban rebels lacked the firepower to expel the estimated 60,000 Spanish troops, who occupied well-entrenched positions in the island's urban centers, and Spain lacked the power to defeat the rebels or the political will to admit defeat and end 400 years of colonial control, McKinley's program of "escalating pressure" could only lead in one direction [72]. Further complicating the situation was the Cuban Junta, which operated in New York City. As the leaders of the Cuban rebels-in-exile, the Junta raised money and sent arms to its forces on the island, a situation that the Spanish government called for McKinley to stop [73].

If the president had merely cared only about acquiring Cuba, he had ever geo-strategic and political reason to immediately launch a war. In addition to Cleveland's prescient warning to McKinley that "[n]othing [could] stop" war from coming, it was in the president's political interest to launch the conflict [74]. Armed with the economic and military firepower to enforce the Monroe Doctrine, if the policy were to retain any meaning, McKinley had to end the bloody anti-colonial conflict located at America's doorstep.

With Americans consistently supporting anti-colonial independence movements throughout the nineteenth century from the Greeks to the Armenians, war was a political winner. In the bubble-and-boil of Gilded Age partisan politics, control of Congress was at stake in every election. In the twenty years following Reconstruction's end and McKinley's election, Republican presidential candidates had never earned a majority of the vote and only held the Congress and the White House simultaneously for one congressional session, 1889-1891 [75]. Thus, from McKinley's perspective, if the recent past was indicative of the future, the 1898 midterms could spell the end of a united GOP government. It was not only Democrats McKinley had to worry about, but the six so-called "silver" Republicans who were McKinley's implacable foes over bimetal currency *and* Cuba, and up to thirteen Senate otherwise loyal Republicans who were ready to buck their president in support of the Cuban rebels[76].

Though historians' claims that Republican congressional leaders pushed for war to control Washington, rather than Cuba, has merit, domestic political considerations played a minor role in shaping McKinley's policy [77]. A Democratic Congress was not the equivalent of a political earthquake. The president surely wanted a Republican Congress, but he had come of age in a time where divided government was the norm rather than the exception. More importantly, McKinley had already fought in a bloody civil war and had no taste for sending American troops into war unnecessarily [78]. Indeed, McKinley told General Leonard Wood "I shall never get into a war until I am sure that God and man approve. I have been through one war; I have seen the dead piled up; and I do not want to see another"[79].

While political and geo-strategic considerations pushed McKinley toward war, moral concerns over the human costs of continued Spanish rule, more than any other single factor, account for the timing of McKinley's decision for war. By 1897, the full humanitarian consequences of Weyler's latest offensive were coming to light and the August assassination of Spanish Prime Minister Antonio Canovas left an already anarchic political scene in even greater chaos [80].

Similar to any other incoming president, McKinley used his initial months in office to reassess his predecessor's policy and configure his own positions. He stalled while Congress pressed the president to recognize the "belligerent rights" of the rebels. Under the paper-thin guise of investigating the death of Dr. Ricardo Ruiz, a Cuban-born naturalized American citizen who died while in custody of Spanish authorities, McKinley sent a personal envoy, William Calhoun, to investigate and report. But if McKinley were so primed for conflict, as many inverted Whigs claim, why send Calhoun? After all, America's consul-general in Havana, Fitzhugh Lee, who favored intervention, would have supplied the White House with pro-invasion arguments. [81].

Though McKinley claimed Calhoun's report would have to "differ very materially from the overwhelmingly facts already in my possession," to alter his Cuba policy, his decision to send a personal envoy is revealing. Far from an executive pushed by yellow journalism, jingoism, and big business, McKinley cautiously collected facts and calibrated policy.[82].

Rather than hit the administration like a bombshell, Calhoun's May, 1897 report merely re-emphasized what McKinley already understood: with Cuba "wrapped in the stillness of death and the silence of desolation," Spain had lost sovereignty and the ongoing humanitarian nightmare had no end in sight [83]. Significantly, Calhoun believed the rebels would reject the compromise of "autonomy" meaning the bloodletting and violence would continue until Spain capitulated.

Calhoun's report, however, helped prepare the way for McKinley's turn toward war. Though the president refused to recognize the Cuban insurgency, he maintained the option to intervene on behalf of suffering Cubans. Regardless, McKinley used the report as a pretext to call for Spain's actions in Cuba to "at least be conducted according to the military codes of civilization" [84]. In authorizing funds to feed and clothe destitute Americans in Cuba, McKinley might have meddled in Spain's internal colonial affairs but he stopped well short of what his pro-war foes wanted [85].

McKinley showed similar flexibility when his Ambassador to Spain, Stewart Woodford, first reported the new president's policy to the Spanish government. The president's blunt call for a resolution "in conformity...with the feelings of our people, the inherent rights of civilized man, and...of advantage both to Cuba and Spain" seemingly set the two nations on a collision course toward war; at the time, an eventuality Woodford believed would occur before December, 1897 [86]. Ironically, Spanish leaders were relieved to hear McKinley's "demands." The newly installed liberal government, headed by Prime Minister Práxedes Sagasta, believed its autonomy program could meet McKinley's hopes for "Cuban peace...and protection of American interests" [87]. Moreover, once Sagasta recalled Weyler from Cuba, McKinley believed Spain was committed to Cuban autonomy [88]. After hearing these encouraging signs, the president did call "intervention upon humanitarian grounds" the rationale receiving his "most anxious and earnest consideration," but he refused to recognize the Cuban insurgents as "belligerents" or endorse Cuba's outright independence [89].

While McKinley was committed to avoiding war via Sagasta's autonomy program, he was constrained by domestic politics from fully aiding the program's success. In December, 1897 Spain's Queen Regent, Maria Cristina, begged Ambassador Woodford to stop the New York-based Junta from sending arms to Cuba, a reasonable request in light of her government's rapid shift toward autonomy [90]. Though Madrid could not stop the rebellion and implement autonomy without Washington's help, McKinley, could not impede the Junta without creating a political firestorm at home. Rather than a cynical ploy to prompt war while appearing innocent, McKinley's refusal to buttress Spain's autonomy program reveals the extent to which any president is constrained by domestic politics. Unfortunately for both sides, without an American crackdown on the Junta, autonomy was destined to fail; a reality the Spanish government understood.

In the interim between Sagasta's October, 1897 negotiations with Woodford and the April, 1898 outbreak of war, McKinley's major policy moves regarding Cuba were exclusively devoted to humanitarian measures. From sending aid to American citizens living in Cuba to a wholesale aid program overseen by Clara Barton, the president might have been privately mute about his motives, but his actions reflect a leader who was unsure about the resolution of the crisis but resolutely sought to ameliorate Cubans' suffering.

## McKinley's Religiosity

Inverted Whigs may see the president's humanitarianism as little more than a smokescreen for his "real" aims, but McKinley's religiosity matters. Separated from their subject by time and cultural distance, many historians have failed to fully value McKinley's decidedly middle class sensibilities. Central to understanding McKinley moral worldview is Methodism: The most popular nineteenth century American denomination. In McKinley's youth, nearly 12,000 Methodist preachers evangelized the American Midwest and frontier bringing over a million Americans to the Christian faith and the Methodist Church. Among these converts was a young Will McKinley.

In comparison to his ebullient successor, Theodore Roosevelt, McKinley is a boring fuddy-duddy. The president's Methodism, while a significant source of his deep religious faith, merely reemphasizes McKinley's Middle American roots, a cultural context which, as Christopher Lasch has noted, most scholars either implicitly distrust or refuse to understand [91]. Methodism was the religious equivalent of kudzu, growing from four ministers and 300 lay people in 1771 to 8,000 preachers and 1.5 million members 1850, making it most numerous of all American denominations [92].

Spread by the energy and zeal of itinerant frontier preachers, Methodism found most of its converts among the newly settled frontier's petty bourgeoisie. The defining feature of American Methodism, lay preachers, leveled the differences between "gentlemen and commoner" by offering leadership positions and other trappings of social mobility to otherwise humbly-born congregants [93]. Like thousands of other upwardly mobile Americans, the McKinleys switched from Presbyterianism to become founding members of their Niles, Ohio congregation and were so active it was said "they ran the church" [94]. No longer the "boiling hot religion" of the eighteenth century, McKinley's Methodism was a mass social movement fit for those "hungry for advancement" and spiritual nourishment [95].

While the McKinley's denominational switch had a worldly dimension, the family and young Will were deeply devout. Teetotalers, fervently anti-slavery, yet religiously tolerant, the McKinley clan were the quintessential mid-century Yankee Protestants. Indeed, the minister who oversaw young McKinley's conversion and baptism, Reverend Aaron Morton, was quietly active in the Underground Railroad. Moreover, McKinley's hometown, Poland, Ohio, was not only a veritable hotbed of abolitionist sentiment his brother-in-law was a former bodyguard for John Brown [96].

Though McKinley's Methodism might seem milquetoast to contemporary observers, his religious faith was both deep and sincere. Though he did not become a minister, as his mother had hoped, he remained a committed Christian throughout his life. As a self-described "soldier of Jesus" who served in "the psalms-singers of the Western Reserve" Civil War regiment, McKinley claimed "I felt more of the love my God in my heart at these [church] meetings than I have felt for some time" [97]. In his postwar career, McKinley remained active as president of his local YMCA [98]. Indeed, the YMCA embodied McKinley's straight-arrow Protestant reformism. Ostensibly a vehicle for evangelizing unattached young men, in the decades following the Civil War the YMCA lost its proselytizing zeal in favor of a more generic "social betterment" [99].

It was McKinley's spiritual life and Christian moorings, which proved decisive in his decision to launch a humanitarian intervention into Cuba. Both McKinley's brother and his political adviser, Mark Hanna, noted that the outpouring of petitions, letters, and pressure for intervention put forth by "religious people" played a significant role in pushing the president to war [100]. Thus, it was not merely McKinley's personal spirituality that drove his Cuba policy, but that of his constituents as well. McKinley was operating in an environment in which middle class sentiment had made charity and humanitarianism the "highest achievements of civilization" [101]. In this way, McKinley's hopes of stopping Spain's brutality in Cuba made intervention both viable and politically popular.

The president was a committed churchgoer whose religiosity was influenced by what Henry May called "Progressive Social Christianity." A middle class movement dedicated to enacting the New Testament's social principles via reform, the Social Gospel (as it is commonly called) had become a powerful force in late nineteenth century American Protestantism [102]. Thus, whether McKinley literally embraced the Social Gospel is irrelevant because the movement shaped the entire climate of intellectual and religious opinion. Insofar as the Spanish-American War is concerned, Protestant church leaders, influenced by this perspective, offered stirring moral endorsements for war.

One leading Social Gospel adherent, Josiah Strong, reveals the way in which church leaders brought their religious worldview to the foreign policy. Seeking to contrast America's role in the world with that of Europe, Strong called for an "imperialism of righteousness" rather than an imperialism of conquest [103]. Strong's "imperialism of righteousness" and his influential book, *Our Country* reeks of chauvinism and racist language to contemporary eyes. While Strong was undoubtedly naïve and filled with hubris, *Our Country* was a clarion call for an American foreign policy to serve as a source of good in the world. With the Social Gospel and Strong's "imperialism of righteousness" gaining sway with America's middle class and educated Protestants, a climate of opinion supportive of humanitarian activism paved McKinley's path to war.

## McKinley's War

In conjunction with Calhoun's visit and the increasing public scrutiny of the situation in Cuba, in May, 1897, McKinley asked Congress to appropriate funds to aid 800 "destitute" Americans living in Spain's notorious *reconcentrados* compounds [104]. The policy, wholly consistent with international law, was also a first step toward intervention [105]. Soon after and with Armenia still fresh in the memories of humanitarian activists and American politicians, McKinley urged Clara Barton to visit Cuba to assess the situation and report to him. Upon her return, Barton called the island's situation tantamount to a war zone and asked for the president's endorsement to organize relief. McKinley gave his explicit and implicit approval to Barton's request. Pushing Spanish sovereignty aside, McKinley claimed "he would ignore any objection that might come from…the sending of food…and let Spain take the initiative by any overt act she might choose" [106] .In late December, 1897, the president formed the Central Cuban Relief Committee (CCRC), and anonymously donated $5,000 to it. Under the direction of Barton, the CCRC was a coalition of philanthropic organizations designed to solicit and funnel charitable aid to Cuba [107].

When historians consider non-governmental organizations (NGOs) in diplomatic history, they usually study contemporary bodies. The Red Cross and the CCRC were, however, early prototypes of what has now become ubiquitous. Lacking any legal clout, the CCRC and Barton possessed the very same "moral authority" to act and intervene that contemporary NGOs have. Thus, once both organizations entered Cuba in early 1898, the processes that Samuel Huntington terms the "transnational organizational revolution," were set into motion. Transnational organizations are founded upon values emphasizing the international bonds binding all humans together, and therefore represent ideas and values antithetical to national sovereignty. Thus, NGOs, by their very existence and nature, "act as a solvent against the strictures of sovereignty" [108]. Consequently, with McKinley demanding that Spain conduct its warfare under "military codes of civilization," and then forming and sending the CCRC to ameliorate and monitor the existing crisis, the US had already compromised Spanish sovereignty over Cuba months before the war began [109].

The CCRC's fundraising efforts lagged until Barton made vivid accounts of *reconcentrados'* suffering central to her appeals. Barton wrote of the *reconcentrados* children "[a]lmost every living child among them represents the sacrifice of a heroic mother. When there was little food the mother went without and died. The children ate and lived" [110]. Though money soon poured in, officials estimated the CCRC required $20,000 per day to feed Cuba's 200,000 *reconcentrados*, a sum most considered beyond the reach of a private charity [111.] Thus, as Americans grew more involved in Cuba, the government realized private charity alone could not ameliorate the situation.

The De Lome letter and the *Maine*'s explosion are rightly credited with rousing mass sentiment for war. However, elite opinion regarding the humanitarian situation in Cuba was much more significant in shaping McKinley's policy than headlines in the penny press. Since the president had always sought the peaceful separation of Cuba from Spain and pursued policies designed to realize these ends, he had shown a disregard for popular pro-war sentiment from the time he had taken office. Deliberate and focused on ending Spain's domination over Cuba, the president slowly pursued what he believed to be an achievable goal. Hardly rushing headlong into war, it was the first-hand reports from Clara Barton and Senator Redfield Proctor which decisively proved that Spain's autonomy program had failed [112].

The war's proponents could have scarcely chosen a better spokesman for intervention than Proctor. The reserved and conservative Vermont senator was highly-regarded among his Senate colleagues, the White House, and the northeast business community. Consequently, those most opposed to intervention, conservatives and businessmen, were those most likely to be swayed by Proctor. The founder of what became the world's largest marble producing operation, Vermont Marble Company, and a political giant in his state, Proctor was a quintessential conservative [113]. While his conservatism was unquestioned, Proctor was privately and adamantly supporting the Cuban rebels [114]. Thus, when he announced his impending fact-finding trip to Cuba, many assumed the quiet and unassuming senator was disposed to counter American intervention.

Proctor's significant role was an accident of coincidences, false assumptions, media hype, and the senator's own sensibilities. Far from journeying to Cuba at the president's behest, Proctor extended his Florida vacation to include a tour of the island at the very last possible moment. By chance, Proctor's vacation coincided with the February 15, 1898 explosion of the *Maine*, which only increased media scrutiny of the senator's trip. Despite intense public interest in the *Maine*, the senator was in no hurry to capitalize on the combustible situation. After a week of fishing, Proctor finally set sail for Cuba from Key West [115].

The much ballyhooed "Yellow Press" did hype Proctor's Cuba visit. Hearst's newspapers made all sorts of extravagant and unfounded claims, speculating that the former Secretary of War went to the island to plan invasion routes [116]. Rather than diagramming invasion scenarios, Proctor's two weeks were spent meeting with officials, attending a bullfight, visiting the wreck of the *Maine* and most significantly, observing *reconcentrados* conditions. In Matanzas, a city 50 miles north of Havana, Proctor saw what Barton called "all the diseases, incident to exposure, physical want and mental woe, from gaunt, lingering hunger down to actual starvation and death typical of the *reconcentrados*" [117]. While visiting *reconcentrados* hospitals, the senator came upon several dead who still lay in their beds. Proctor described what he saw: "all my conception of wrong that could be inflicted on people falls short of this reality" [118].

After visiting four of Cuba's six provinces, meeting with Barton, and touring some of the worst of the *reconcentrados* camps, Proctor returned to the Capitol more convinced than ever of the necessity for intervention. Significantly, he kept his own counsel and remained mute on the subject—a stance that only added to media speculation. The senator's visit and belief in intervention hardly made him distinct. Nonetheless, his conservative bona fides, perceived relationship with the president, and the sense of drama rendered his pronouncement favoring intervention into a political bombshell. After refusing interview requests, Proctor penned a simple "statement" which he planned to release to the press. By happenstance on a Friday morning, March 18, Proctor bumped into Senator William Frye. According to Proctor, Frye literally "pushed me into the Senator chamber" to deliver his report [119].

After a roll call which ensured Proctor of a full senate and plenty of gallery watchers, the understated New Englander let loose. Describing the "desolation and distress, misery and starvation" that was Cuba, Proctor painted the picture of a full-fledged humanitarian nightmare. He was known for his quiet, conservative, and understated manner. Thus, the senator's claim, "[t]orn from their homes, with foul earth, foul air, foul water and foul food or none, what wonder that one half have died and that one quarter of the living are so diseased that they can not be saved," rebutted those who believed the conditions were the creation of the yellow press. It was not only the religious and the moralists who were swayed; but also the business community, which finally backed intervention.

Proctor's speech rallied the business community and wary business journalists to the cause. Convinced that "an American Armenia" was festering 100 miles away, the *Wall Street Journal* and the *New York Commercial Advertiser* threw its weight behind intervention. As one New York banker, R.J. Kimball, said of Proctor's speech, "I do not remember of a speech, or document receiving in my observation and association among business men, such universal commendation" [120]. Proctor's speech further solidified the moral and religious justifications for war and firmly brought the business community into the interventionist camp. With conservatives and the business community firmly backing what one Protestant journal called "the will of Almighty God that by war the last trace of this inhumanity of man to man shall be swept from this Western Hemisphere," McKinley had the moral backing of the religious and business elites [121].

## Conclusion

After 13 months in office, McKinley finally opted for war. Though it is impossible to completely separate humanitarian considerations from domestic political and foreign policy concerns, the former were fundamental to the president's policy. If McKinley was solely concerned with domestic politics or simply in acquiring territory, he had ample opportunity to launch a war upon his inauguration. Why wait and further alienate silver Republicans and give Democrat's an issue? What if Spain's autonomy program would have worked and the US would have lost its chance to grab Cuba? The president chose war to end a bloody and seemingly irresolvable conflict that lay 90 miles from American shores. Indeed, with the humanitarian impetus at high tide and the Cuban revolution threatening to continue into the foreseeable future, how could McKinley have acted otherwise?

McKinley, like any human being, was pushed and pulled by self-interest, moral concerns, and above all an overweening faith in his own goodness and benevolent intentions. In the weeks between the end of the fighting and the 1898 Treaty of Paris, which officially ended the war, Americans organized "Peace Jubilees" to celebrate the conflict' close. First organized in 1869 by composer Patrick Gilmore to commemorate the American Civil War, "Peace Jubilees" were celebrations of what Gilmore called the coming "permanent tranquility." Though Boston and Atlanta hosted their own celebrations, President McKinley chose Philadelphia's "Peace Jubilee" for a major address [122].

In his keynote, the president claimed America waged Spanish-American War so "that oppression at our door should be stopped" while warning his countrymen to "face the obligations that came with victory" [123]. Echoing McKinley's self-righteous apology were the editors' of the Christian magazine *The Advance* who wrote "most Christian men believe that there are worse things than war, and that it [war] may be resort[ed] to as a last resort...for the overthrow of great wrongs, and for the defense of justice and humanity" [124].

The editors, like McKinley, remained convinced of their moral clarity and humanity's ability to pursue just ideals without contamination by base motives.

Within weeks of the "Peace Jubilee," however, McKinley struck a treaty which definitively set the nation on an imperialist path. In addition to adding Cuba, Puerto Rico, and Guam, by1899, the US, like the Spanish before them, was fighting its own an anti-colonial rebellion in the Philippines.

## References

[1] Merle Curti, *American Philanthropy Abroad: A History*, New Brunswick: Rutgers University Press, 1963 p. 114; "Another Cargo for Russia," *New York Times* April 21, 1892 , p. 8; Clara Barton, *The Red Cross, A History of this Remarkable International Movement in the Interest of Humanity; a Vivid and Authoritative Account of Relief from Suffering by War, Pestilence, Famine, Flood, Fires and other National Calamities*, Washington, D.C.: American National Red Cross, 1898, p. 178; Francis Reeves, *Russia Then and Now, 1892-1917; My Mission to Russia During the Famine of 1891-1892, With Data Bearing Upon Russia of Today*, New York: Putnam's Sons, 1917; *Final*

*Report of the Russian Famine Relief Commission to the Governor of the State of Iowa*, June 1, 1892, Davenport: The Democrat Company, Printers, 1892.

[2] Curti, *American Philanthropy Abroad*, p. 113.

[3] Curti, *American Philanthropy Abroad,* p. 117; Barton, *The Red Cross*, p. 178.

[4] Walter McDougall, *Promised Land, Crusader State: The American Encounter with the World Since 1776*, Boston: Houghton Mifflin, 1997 p. 40-41.

[5] George Herring, *From Colony to Superpower: U.S. foreign Relations Since 1776*, New York: Oxford University Press, 2008, p. 1, 482; Frank Ninkovich, *The Wilsonian Century: U.S. Foreign Policy Since 1900,* Chicago: University of Chicago Press, 1999, p. 20; See Wayne Cole's *Senator Gerald P. Nye and American Foreign Relations*. Cole makes Europe the linchpin of American isolationism by defining "isolationists" as, people "opposed to [American] intervention in European wars." Broadening the term's applicability beyond US-European relations, Justus Doenecke claims "isolationists" are perfectly willing to act abroad but prefer do so without the constraints of multilateral agreements.

[6] David Hendrickson, *Union, Nation, or Empire*, Lawrence: Kansas University Press, 2009, p. 360-361; Ronald Powaski, *Toward An Entangling Alliance*, Santa Barbara: Greenwood Press, 1991 p. xi-xii; Justus Doenecke, "The Strange Career of American Isolationism," *Peace and Change* 3 (Summer-Fall 1975): 79. With mid-century historians such as Charles Chatfield declaring "no prominent [nineteenth century] American c[ould] be meaningfully described as [an] internationalist" and Hans Morgenthau calling the whole era an "intellectual, barren…political desert," nineteenth century isolationism has become a truism. Taken from, "Internationalism as a Current in the Peace Movement: A Symposium," in *Peace Movements in America*, ed. Charles Chatfield, New York, Schocken Books, 1973, p. 174-175; Hans Morgenthau, *In Defense of the National Interest*, New York: Knopf, 1951, p.4.

[7] Richard Leopold, "The Mississippi Valley and American Foreign Policy," *The Mississippi Valley Historical Review*, Vol. 37, No. 4 (Mar., 1951), p.626; Wayne Cole, *Senator Gerald P. Nye and American Foreign Relations*, Minneapolis, University of Minnesota Press, 1962, p. 7; Glen Smith, *Langer of North Dakota: A Study in Isolationism, 1940-1959,* New York: Garland Pub., 1979, p. 212-213.

[8] McDougall, *Crusader State*, p. 120-121.

[9] McDougall, *Crusader State*, p. 120-121.

[10] Alan Dawley, *Changing the World: American Progressives in War and Revolution*, Princeton: Princeton University Press, 2003 p. 14-16 and 107-108.

[11] James Field, "American Imperialism: The Worst Chapter in Almost Any Book" *American Historical Review* 83 (June 1978): 644-83.

[12] Bradford Perkins, "Interests, Values, and the Prism: The Sources of American Foreign Policy," *Journal of the Early Republic,* Vol. 14, No. 4 (Winter 1994), p. 466; George Herring, *From Colony to Superpower: U.S. foreign relations since 1776*, New York: Oxford University Press, 2008, p. 2-3.

[13] Hendrickson, *Union, Nation, or Empire,* p. xiv-xv; James Field, *America and the Mediterranean World, 1776-1882*, Princeton: Princeton University Press, 1969, p. 25-26; Herring, *From Colony to Superpower*, p. 4-5.

[14] Nancy Cassels, "Bentinck: Humanitarian and Imperialist—The Abolition of the Suttee," *The Journal of British Studies*, Vol. 5, No. 1, November 1965, p. 77-87; Peter

Marsh, "Lord Salisbury and the Ottoman Massacres," *The Journal of British Studies*, Vol. 11, No. 2, May, 1972, p. 63-83; Gary Bass, *Freedom's Battle: The Origins of Humanitarian Intervention*, New York: Alfred A. Knopf, 2008, p. 7; Geoffrey Robertson, *Crimes Against Humanity: The Struggle for Global Justice*, New York: New Press, 2000, p.12-13.

[15] Field, "The Worst Chapter in any Book," p. 645.

[16] Michael Mandelbaum, *The Fate of Nations: the Search for National Security in the Nineteenth and Twentieth Centuries*, Cambridge; Cambridge University Press, 1988.

[17] Joseph Fry, "From Open Door to World Systems, Economic Interpretations of Late-Nineteenth-Century American Foreign Relations," *Pacific Historical Review* 65 (May 1996): 277-303 p. 279.

[18] Louis Perez, *Cuba between Empires, 1878-1902,* Pittsburgh: University of Pittsburgh Press, 1983, p. 378-379; Louis Perez, *Cuba and the United States: Ties of Singular Intimacy,* Athens: University of Georgia Press, 1990.

[19] Reinhold Niebuhr, *The Irony of American History*, New York: Scribner, 1952, p. 154-155, 158-159.

[20] Message of POTUS Communicated to Congress 'Relations of the United States to Spain by Reason of Warfare in the Island of Cuba, April 11, 1898, p. 11.

[21] Alan Geyer, *Piety and Politics: American Protestantism in the World Arena*, Richmond, Virginia: John Knox Press, p. 60.

[22] James Field, "American Imperialism: The Worst Chapter in Almost Any Book," *American Historical Review,* Volume 83, No. 3, June 1978, p. 644.

[23] Louis Perez, *Cuba Between Empires*, p .178.

[24] James Field, "American Imperialism: The Worst Chapter in Almost Any Book," *American Historical Review,* Volume 83, No. 3, June 1978, p. 644.

[25] Douglas Maynard, "Reform and the Origin of the International Organization Movement," *Proceedings of the American Philosophical Society*, Vol. 107, No. 3, June, 1963, p. 220.

[26] Karen Halttunen, "Humanitarianism and the Pornography of Pain," *American Historical Review,* Vol. 100 No. 2, April, 1995, p. 303; Kevin Rozario, "'Delicious Horrors': Mass Culture, the Red Cross and the Appeal of Modern American Humanitarianism," American Quarterly, Vol. 55 No. 3, September, 2003.

[27] Gary Bass, *Freedom's Battle*, p.8 and 22-23.

[28] Benedict Anderson, *Imagined Communities: Reflections on the Origin and Spread of Nationalism,* London: Verso Editions, 1983.

[29] Caroline Moorehead, *Dunant's Dream: War, Switzerland and the History of the Red Cross*, New York: Carroll and Graf, 1999, p. 8.

[30] Moorhead, *Dunant's Dream* p. 23.

[31] Moorhead, *Dunant's Dream* p. 88-89.

[32] Moorhead, *Dunant's Dream* p. 92; Elizabeth Pryor, *Clara Barton: Professional Angel*, Philadelphia: University of Pennsylvania, 1988, p. 190; Moorhead, *Dunant's Dream* p. 93.

[33] Pryor, p. 202.

[34] Ira Rutkow, *James A. Garfield*, New York: Times Books, 2006 p. 73-74.

[35] Hendrickson, *Union, Nation, or Empire*, p. 261; John Rollins, *Frederick Theodore Frelinghuysen, 1817-1885: The Politics and Diplomacy of Stewardship*, Ph.D.

dissertation, University of Wisconsin, Madison, 1974, p. 358-361; Pryor, *Clara Barton: Professional Angel*, p. 207-209; Clara Barton: What is the Red Cross?, Reel 68, File: International Red Cross Conferences, Sixth International Red Cross Conference, Vienna, Austria, Sept., 1897-97, Clara Barton Papers, Library of Congress.

[36] Pryor, *Professional Angel*, p. 263-65, 266; Bass, *Freedom's Battle*, p 28; George McMichael, *Journey to obscurity; the life of Octave Thanet*, Lincoln: University of Nebraska Press, 1965, p. 127; Moorhead, *Dunant's Dream*, p. 96-98; B.F. Tillinghast, "A Far-Reaching Charity," *The Midland Monthly*, p. 325-339; William Barton, *The Life of Clara Barton: Founder of the American Red Cross*, New York: Houghton Mifflin, 1922, p. 271.

[37] Extract from House Proceedings, William Jennings Bryan, Speech, January 6, 1892, Reel 81, Series IV, William McKinley Papers, Library of Congress.

[38] *Report of the Russian Famine Relief Committee of the United States*, Washington, D. C., John Hoyt, Washington, D.C., 1893, p. 1; Pryor, *Professional Angel*, p. 270.

[39] James Eldin Reed, "American Foreign Policy: The Politics of Missions and Josiah Strong, 1890-1900," *Church History*, Vol. 41, No. 2, June 1972, p. 234.

[40] Gary Bass, *Freedom's Battle*, p. 316; Pryor, *Professional Angel,* p.315-1317.

[41] Peter Balakian, *The Burning Tigris: The Armenian Genocide and America's Response*, New York: Harper Collins, 2003, p. 126; Bass, Freedom's Battle, p. 316.

[42] Balakian, *Burning Tigris*, p. 132.

[43] James Eldin Reed, "American Foreign Policy: The Politics of Missions and Josiah Strong, 1890-1900," *Church History*, Vol. 41, No. 2, June 1972, p. 235.

[44] *The Armenian Massacres, 1894-1896: U.S. Media Testimony*, ed. Arman Kirakossian, Detroit: Wayne State University Press, 2004, p. 41.

[45] Balakian, *Burning Tigris*, p. 64.

[46] Moorhead, *Dunant's Dream*, p. 99-101; Pryor, *Professional Angel*, p. 298-300; Balakian, *Burning Tigris*, p.70.

[47] Moorhead, *Dunant's Dream,* p. 103.

[48] Robertson, *Crimes Against Humanity*, p. 14-15.

[49] Ibid.

[50] *The Armenian Massacres, 1894-1896: U.S. Media Testimony*, ed. Arman Kirakossian, Detroit: Wayne State University Press, 2004, p, p. 51.

[51] "Armenia and Cuba," *New York Times*, April 15, 1898, p.6.

[52] New York Journal: The Purpose to Exterminate Rural Population, p.1" Reel 97, Series 12, Volume 20-26 William McKinley Paper, LOC.

[53] Message of POTUS Communicated to Congress 'Relations of the United States to Spain by Reason of Warfare in the Island of Cuba, April 11, 1898, p 11.

[54] Message of POTUS Communicated to Congress 'Relations of the United States to Spain by Reason of Warfare in the Island of Cuba, April 11, 1898, p. 11.

[55] Henry Graff, *Grover Cleveland*, New York: Times Books, 2002, p. 124-126.

[56] Lewis Gould, *The Spanish-American War and President McKinley*, Lawrence: University Press of Kansas, 1982, p.1.

[57] William Armstrong, *Major McKinley: William McKinley and the Civil War*, Kent, Ohio: Kent State Press, p. 127.

[58] See John Offner *An Unwanted War, The Diplomacy of the United States and Spain Over Cuba, 1895-1898*, Chapel Hill: University of North Carolina Press, 1992.

[59] Lewis Gould, *The Presidency of William McKinley*, Lawrence: University Press of Kansas, 1982, p.6.
[60] William Armstrong, *Major McKinley: William McKinley and the Civil War*, Kent, Ohio: Kent State University Press, 2000, p. 2.
[61] Thomas Paterson, "United States Intervention in Cuba, Interpretations of the Spanish-American-Cuban-Filipino War," *History Teacher* 29, May, 1996, p. 348.
[62] Kevin Phillips, *William McKinley* (The American Presidents), New York: Times Books, October, 2003 p. 14.
[63] Gould, *The Presidency of William McKinley*, p.6.
[64] Ibid.
[65] *Ideas and Foreign Policy: Beliefs, Institutions, and Political Change*, edited by Judith Goldstein and Robert O. Keohane, Ithaca: Cornell University Press, 1993, p. 91-93; McKinley Speech, The North West and Middle West in Foreign Trade, Series 4, Reel 81, William McKinley Papers, Library of Congress.
[66] "Letter Accepting Republican Nomination for President, 1896, p 12, Series 4, Speeches Reel 85, William McKinley Papers, Library of Congress; William McKinley, *The Tariff in the Days of Henry Clay and Since: An Exhaustive Review of Our Tariff Legislation, From 1812-1860*, New York: Kraus Reprint Co., 1970.
[67] Phillips, *William McKinley*, p. 113-115.
[68] Speech, The Mississippi Valley and Latin American Trade, p. 17, Series 4, Speeches, Reel 81, William McKinley Papers, Library of Congress.
[69] Offner, p. 38. Richard Hamilton, *President McKinley, War and Empire, Volume I*, New Brunswick: Transaction Publishers, 2006, p. 95-98.
[70] Gould, *The Presidency of William McKinley*, p. 16-19.
[71] Gould, *The Presidency of William McKinley*, p. 18-19; Offner, p. 227-228.
[72] Gould, *The Presidency of William McKinley*, p. 66.
[73] Offner, p.226.
[74] Offner, p. 41.
[75] Paul Kleppner, *The Cross of Culture: A Social Analysis of Midwestern Politics, 1850-1900*, New York: Free Press, 1970, p. 5-6.
[76] Offner, p. 43.
[77] Offner, p. 233-234.
[78] Armstrong, p. 18-20.
[79] Armstrong, p. 127-128.
[80] Offner, p. 51-53.
[81] Gould, *The Presidency of William McKinley*, p. 66; Newspaper Article, Starvation in Cuba, in *The Baltimore American*, Reel 97, Series 12, Volume 20-26, William McKinley Papers, Library of Congress.
[82] Newspaper Article, Preemptory Demand Will be Made that Independence of the Island Be Acknowledged, by Herbert Jervin Browne, *New York Journal*, Reel; 97, Series 12 Volume 20-26, William McKinley Papers, Library of Congress
[83] Newspaper Article, The Light Breaking in Cuba, *New York Journal And Advertiser*, June 1 ,1897, Reel 97, Series 12, Volume 20-26, William McKinley Papers, Library of Congress.
[84] Gould, *The Presidency of William McKinley*, p. 67.

[85] Relief of Destitute American Citizens in Cuba, 55TH Congress 1st Session, Senate, Document No. 86 Message from the President of the United States "Appropriations for the Relief of Desstitute American Citizens in the Island of Cuba, May 17, 1897.
[86] Offner, p. 57-58.
[87] Offner, p. 62-63.
[88] Offner, p. 77.
[89] Message of the POTUS Communicated to Houses of Congress at the Beginning of the 2nd Session of the 55th Congress, 55th Congress, 2nd Session, Document No. 1, Washington Government Printing Office , 1897. Series 14, Box 6, F Message of POTUS to Congress, December 6, 1897. Message of the POTUS Communicated to Houses of Congress at the Beginning of the 2nd Session of the 55th Congress, 55th Congress, 2nd Session, Document No. 1, Washington Government Printing Office , 1897, p. 12.
[90] Offiner, p. 92.
[91] Christopher Lasch, *The True and Only Heaven: Progress and Its Critics*, 1991.
[92] Nathan Hatch, "The Puzzle of American Methodism," Church History,Vol. 63, No. 2 (June, 1994): p 178.
[93] Hatch, p. 180.
[94] William Armstrong, *Major McKinley: William McKinley and the Civil War*, Kent, Ohio: Kent State University Press, 2000, p. 7; Quentin Skrabjec, *William McKinley, Apostle of Protectionism*, p. 44.
[95] Hatch, p. 181; Skrabjec, p. 44.
[96] Armstrong, p. 7.
[97] Armstrong, p. 11.
[98] Phillips, *William McKinley*, p. 15-17.
[99] Zald, *The Political Economy of the YMCA*, p. 54-57.
[100] Hamilton, *President McKinley, War, and Empire*, p. 113.
[101] Kevin Rozario, "'Delicious Horrors': Mass Culture, The Red Cross, and the Appeal of Modern American Humanitarianism," *American Quarterly*, Vol. 55, No. 3, (September 2003): p. 418.
[102] *The Social Gospel in America, 1870-1920*, edited by Robert T. Handy, New York: Oxford University Press, 1966, p. 10-11.
[103] *The Social Gospel: Religion and Reform in a Changing America*, by Ronald C. White, Jr. and C. Howard Hopkins, Temple University Press, p. 115-116.
[104] "A Policy from the Senate," May 15, 1897, *New York Times*, p. 6A; Teemu Ruskola, "Canton Is Not Boston: The Invention of American Imperial Sovereignty," *American Quarterly*, Volume 57, Number 3, September 2005, p. 859-884.
[105] Gould, *The Spanish-American War and President McKinley*, p. 30-31.
[106] "President Plans to Stop Suffering" Reel 112, File 1898- Spanish American War a charitable act that remained secret until his death.
[107] "Minister De Lome on Charity," *New York Times*, December 29, 1897, p. 2.
[108] Steve Charnovitz, "Nongovernmental Organizations and International Law," *The American Journal of International Law*, Vol. 100, No. 2, April, 2006, p. 348; Samuel Huntington, "Transnational Organizations in World Politics," *World Politics*, Vol. 25, No. 3, (April, 1973) p. 365-368.
[109] Clara Barton, *The Red Cross*, p. 365.

[110] Clara Barton, "Relieving the Cuban Reconcentrados," The Indpendent, Clara Barton Ppaer, Seriew IV Civil War and Relief, LOC.
[111] "Cubans Dying of Hunger," *New York Times*, January 12, 1898, p.4; Offner, p. 92.
[112] Moorhead, *Dunant's Dream*, p. 104.
[113] Chester Winn Bowie, *Redfield Proctor: A Biography*, Ph.D. dissertation, University of Wisconsin, Madison, 1980. p. 1.
[114] Ibid, p. 356.
[115] Ibid, p. 356-360.
[116] Ibid, 360-362.
[117] "Cuba as Proctor Saw It," *New York Times*, March 18, 1898,p .1. Ibid, 363-364.
[118] Ibid, 363-364.
[119] Ibid, p.368.
[120] Ibid. 373-375.
[121] McDougall, *Crusader State*, p. 112.
[122] "The Jubilee at Boston," *New York Times*, Jun 16, 1869; pg. 1.
[123] Ibid, p. 5.
[124] The Advance, p. 1, Box 1, Series 13, F "Peace Jubilee" Clara Barton Papers.

In: Presidents and War
Editors: A. Eksterowicz and G. Hastedt, pp. 103-119
ISBN 978-1-61668-917-9


*Chapter 7*

# War Counsel: Military Advice in the White House

***Brent A. Strathman***

## Introduction

The night of February 15, 1898 was quiet and calm, as sailors of the USS Maine returned from a bullfight in Havana. At 9:40 in the evening, an explosion in the aft of the ship lifted the hull out of the water and tossed scores of sailors into the air. Out of 354 officers and men assigned to the ship, over 2/3 (266 in total) died in the explosion. Within six months, the United States joined the pantheon of world sea powers by defeating Spain in Cuba and the Philippines. As the American ambassador to London would go on to say at the time, "It has been a splendid little war, begun with the highest motives, carried on with magnificent intelligence and spirit, favored by that fortune which loves the brave" [1].

President William McKinley viewed the war in a different light. When looking back at the events of April 1898, McKinley saw himself as the victim of war fever. The president did not want a war, even after an independent inquiry into the explosion of the Maine implicated Spain. Though the public wanted to fight (urged on by a sensationalist press and eager Congress), the president stalled for time, hoping diplomacy would force Spain to relent. As the crisis in Cuba deepened, the president became more uncertain in the solution to the crisis. Imperialists in Congress and the administration used this strategic uncertainty to place the United States on a war footing. In the end, McKinley approved a decision that he believed was wrong. The president confided in a former secretary that the "declaration of war against Spain was an act which has been and will always be the greatest grief of my life. I never wanted to go to war with Spain. Had I been let [alone] I could have prevented [it]" [2]. For McKinley, this was a "dirty little war" [3] that he wanted to avoid.

The decision to go to war in Cuba highlights an important question of foreign policy making in the White House: who advises the president? Presidents perceive advisors differently, and these personal beliefs limit or constrain the inner circle. President George W. Bush, for example, relied heavily on those around him to make foreign policy decisions; in effect, he 'out-sourced' decision making to his inner circle. Like-minded advisors – the self-named 'Vulcans' – in the Bush Administration used their placement in the foreign policy hierarchy to support a war in Iraq [4]. But other presidents are not as dependent on their inner circle. President Kennedy famously questioned the utility of military advisors after the Bay of Pigs fiasco, warning future presidents to "watch the generals and to avoid feeling that just because they were military men their opinions on military matters were worth a damn" [5]. The perception of bias limited the role of the inner circle in decisions for war [6].

What is the role of advisors in the decision for war? How does competition between members of the inner circle impact presidential decisions? And most importantly, how does trust in advisors change executive level deliberations? This article continues in several parts. First, the paper examines the politics of advice in the White House. Political advising is an interaction between what a president wants to hear, and what an advisor can provide. But leaders are naturally wary of their advisors, concerned with personal and professional bias. As a result, presidents learn to structure the foreign policy hierarchy to limit bias by either quieting or encouraging competition between advisors. Decisions of war and peace are connected to how presidents manage trust in the inner circle.

The logic of the argument is explored in a case study of the Spanish-American War. McKinley was unsure of the proper solution to the Cuban problem. Unfortunately for the president, his inner circle was unable to ease the endemic uncertainty surrounding the crisis on the island. Though Congress, members of the media, and the American public wanted war, McKinley was unconvinced that force could solve the 'Cuba problem.' The attack on the USS Maine changed the decision. Political elites used the sinking of the Maine to push a new doctrine of American power, putting "their shoulders to the wheel of the wagon of jingoistic ballyhoo" [7]. The inability of McKinley to manage the process allowed imperialists to execute their vision of American grand strategy. This drive for empire, hidden behind a moralist veneer, led McKinley to approve a war that he dreaded.

An examination of the Spanish-American War is important for two reasons. First, conventional explanations of the "splendid little war" argue that public opinion – aroused by Congress and the media – was responsible for the decision. But a focus on advisors provides a different interpretation. Internal debate between competing conceptions of American interest split the McKinley Administration. Importantly, McKinley's mismanagement of the advisory system magnified the disagreement. The president was unable to find a solution to the 'Cuba problem', mostly due to the selection of the inner circle and his management style. The Spanish-American War is a prime example of how unchecked competition within the White House can lead to a military adventure.

And second, an exploration of the McKinley White House provides leverage on the question of who is responsible for quagmires: leaders or advisors? While the Spanish-American War was successful, the aftermath was not, as the United States becomes trapped in a lengthy engagement in the Philippines. In American foreign policy, it is common to blame advisors for quagmires. For example, McMaster argues that advisors did not do their duty, unable or unwilling to persuade President Johnson to change his Vietnam strategy [8]. Failed advising was responsible for the adventure in Southeast Asia. Likewise, conventional explanations of the Iraq War focus on the competition and machinations of neo-conservative advisors. According to these accounts, advisors played a large role in both planning the war, and persuading the president to approve their plan. A case study of decision making in the Spanish-American War examines the validity of the claim, while answering why these engagements persist.

## THE CREDIBILITY PROBLEM IN THE WHITE HOUSE

French President Georges Pompidou once remarked there were three ways for a politician to ruin his career: chasing women, gambling, and trusting experts. He continued, saying "The first . . . was the most pleasant and the second the quickest, but trusting experts was the surest" [9]. Pompidou realized experts and advisors have their own biases, and leaders who fail to question their inner circle risk mistakes. The question of who to trust – what I call the credibility problem of advising – is a constant feature of presidential decision making.

The dilemma facing presidents is not different from other, more mundane choices that feature information asymmetries and biased advisors. One example is investment planning. For most individuals, investment planning is complex and uncertain. Individuals not only lack basic knowledge of the available options, but the variety of choice is prohibitively large. More importantly, most of us do not have the time or resources to fill this information gap. The decision is too difficult without outside counsel. The solution is to hire an expert, such as an investment manager, to recommend a set of options that maximize returns. In other words, most individuals out-source their decisions to an expert. The decision making process closely resembles 'Judge-Advisor' models from organizational psychology [10]. Instead of comparing and contrasting specific options, the decision maker evaluates the validity of the expert. Experts, in effect, act as cognitive shortcuts, collecting relevant information and generating a recommendation. In terms of investment planning, the decision to invest in a stock is tied to perceptions of the investment manager.

Decision making in the White House follows a similar process. Whenever a decision arises, bureaucracies mobilize to collect information and forward policy recommendations. These alternative policies are then relayed to the president through key members of the foreign policy team. In making the decision, presidents solicit two types of information: incoming intelligence on the strategic problem, and advice on which policy option would be most successful. But the credibility problem changes the decision, and leaders attribute sinister motives to members of the inner circle [11]. As a result, decision makers discount or under-weigh contributions from counselors because they are unable to trace the reasoning behind the recommendation; a psychological effect known as egocentric discounting [12]. More importantly, dysphoric cognition increases mistrust and paranoia [13]. Instead of collecting all relevant information and constructing a decision that best serves the nation, presidents are forced to evaluate their inner circle. In effect, decision making is a task of selecting which advisor (or advisors) to follow, and leaders who do not have faith in their advisors suffer from decision making errors [14]. Foreign policy is a product of nested and competitive social relationships between advisors and leaders where trust is the coin of the realm [15].

One of the main tasks of presidential decision making is to inculcate trust by eliminating the bias created by the advisory process. Presidents traditionally reduce bias by either minimizing or encouraging conflict. In the first approach, leaders limit the competition between advisors by emphasizing consensus. Debate and disagreement are kept at a minimum, and leaders pressure advisors to create consensus. Advisors do not persuade or compete with other members of the White House; instead, counselors bolster a decision or policy that a president has previously made. By keeping debate at a minimum and dominating their subordinates, presidents minimize bias.

In this view, advisors censor discordant views, hoping to make the decision making process easier and more efficient. In effect, presidents that dominate their advisors limit their role in decisions for war. For example, President Lyndon Johnson silenced dissenters in his administration through his dominating personality and 'Tuesday lunches' [16]. By quieting dissent, the president could concentrate on his plans for the 'Great Society' and maintain a positive view of Vietnam. Daalder and Lindsay argue that the Bush Administration followed a similar pattern [17]. The Bush inner circle was responsible for verifying central pillars of neo-conservatism. Advisors simply mimicked the beliefs already held by the president.

But consensus is difficult to enforce or guarantee. Some presidents instead prefer multiple advocacy, encouraging an array of viewpoints supported by motivated proponents [18]. Instead of eliminating disagreement, presidents structure the process to guarantee active competition among bureaucracies. In these structures, advisors fill 'institutional roles,' representing their bureaucracies as faithful agents [19]. The pulling and hauling among advisors creates a marketplace for opinion that dilutes or balances individual bias. Successful and effective presidents learn to use the competition within the inner circle as a sounding board, matching the structure of the advisory process to their personality [20].

The key to effective decision making in this perspective is the experience of the president in managing competition. For example, President Kennedy changed his advisory process after the Bay of Pigs fiasco to compensate for group decision making errors [21]. Kennedy recognized the danger of consensus, implementing new rules for ExComm to produce better decisions. The president took an active role in guaranteeing the free flow of ideas, and minimizing the conditions that quieted debate. But the mere presence of competition does not guarantee effective advocacy. Instead, leaders must judiciously and carefully arrange advocates to limit any bias introduced by an unequal distribution of advisor capacity and viewpoints [22]. By opening up the decision making process to many actors, leaders cancel out advisory bias.

Presidents ease the credibility problem – the question of who to trust – either by limiting advisory opinion, or diluting it. But solutions for the credibility problem present their own difficulties. For example, presidents with too much control of the process will unduly quiet or limit valid viewpoints; they receive bad advice from counselors who refrain from speaking truth to power. Policy stagnates, unable to evolve and change. Moreover, a competitive inner circle is difficult to control. Effective advising requires a hierarchy that complements the strengths of the president [23]. Though competition among advisors minimizes the effect of bias, it places a strain on presidents who must balance the egos of the inner circle. A competitive advisory structure can backfire on presidents without prior experience, leading to problems such as groupthink or deadlock [24]. Presidents can create a marketplace of ideas that rewards well-considered foreign policy, but only when they force advisors into specific roles. Otherwise, competition increases backbiting and discontent in the inner circle.

The Spanish-American War illustrates the problems associated with an inexperienced president that incorrectly manages the advisory system. McKinley was unsure of what to do regarding the Cuba problem. The president realized the United States was at a military disadvantage, as Spanish forces outgunned the American military. But McKinley's advisors did not ease his uncertainty. The president was confident in his leadership, appointing advisors that were unprepared for the rigors of foreign policy. In effect, the president eliminated bias by appointing weak advisors that he did not intend to follow. As a result, the president ignored the advice of his inner circle, and as the crisis on the island deepened, McKinley stalled the decision to go to war.

More importantly, the decision to rely on his own judgment provided a space for rivals who supported an expansionist foreign policy doctrine. As diplomacy continued, media reports of Spanish atrocities inflamed American public opinion. Imperialist allies in Congress and the Department of Navy used this opportunity to push a new offensive grand strategy.

## Military Advice and the Spanish-American War

What convinced the president to go against his better judgment and commit the United States to war? A decision that not only went against his own pacifism, but also created an empire that many in the United States did not want? The case study is divided into two parts. The first section reviews the events leading up to the explosion of the USS Maine. The debate over the 'Cuba problem' reflected a growing division within the government over the future of foreign policy. McKinley and his allies believed the United States did not have enough military power for an offensive grand strategy; he was wary of Spanish power in the Caribbean, and believed diplomacy provided the best solution to the conflict. But his imperialist opponents (best personified by Theodore Roosevelt, Henry Cabot Lodge, and Alfred T. Mahan) disagreed.

The United States needed a new, offensive grand strategy to not only protect the Caribbean from European influence, but also gain access to Asian markets. War provided the best means to accomplish both. The second part of the case study argues McKinley wilted in the face of his opponents, largely due to his own failures in selecting and using his advisors. In general, McKinley never solved the credibility problem, and the muddled decision to commit to war was soon followed by a quagmire in the Philippines.

## A Disagreement of Doctrine

American interest in Cuba began well before 1898. In 1820, Thomas Jefferson echoed popular sentiment when he told Calhoun that "[we] ought, at the first possible opportunity, to take Cuba"[25]. In the years leading up to the Civil War, many political elites considered an expansion into Cuba – with its large slavery population and natural resources – as economically and militarily wise. The United States gained territory and supported the Monroe Doctrine by forcing the Spanish out of the Caribbean. Several presidents even approached Spain to purchase Cuba, with the most serious proposal coming from Polk who offered $100,000,000 for the island [26].

American foreign and domestic policy struggled with the 'Cuba problem' in the years directly prior to the Maine explosion. As the insurgency in Cuba gained strength, conflict between Americans and the Spanish fleet increased. American gun-runners were frequently fired on by the Spanish navy as they fled their docking ports. On several occasions, these confrontations nearly ended in war. For example, Spanish authorities captured the Virginius off the coast of Jamaica in 1873. Spain charged the crew with piracy, eventually executing over 50 crewmembers. The capture and trial of the ship enraged the American public, but

President Ulysses Grant resisted using force. The crisis ended after officials discovered the ship's registry was fraudulent [27].

A bigger problem for American diplomacy was the humanitarian crisis on the island. Continued domestic instability encouraged Spanish leaders to strong-arm insurgent groups. In February 1896, 'Butcher' Weyler was given control of the island. To end guerrilla activities, Weyler began a program that herded rural Cubans into camps, where starvation and torture were common. Soon, a majority of Americans received daily reports of Spanish atrocities from the cadre of bored reporters sent by Hearst's Journal and Pulitzer's World. Weyler instituted harsh censorship policies as a response – which only forced reporters to fabricate stories for an eager public [28]. Personalized accounts of Spanish policies convinced the masses that a response was morally necessary. Leagues and groups arose across the American West pleading for action and collecting money to help the cause. Relief agencies even persuaded McKinley to donate money [29].

The president was not immune to the current of opinion. On the contrary, McKinley carefully studied mass opinion for direction, reading newspaper editorials and making public appearances [30]. Some historians argue this fascination with the electorate and the public mood was the secret to his success as a politician. By understanding what the public wanted, McKinley could deftly change his policies to match trends in public attitudes [31]. Yet the president did not relent to the war fever gripping the country. Personal experiences during the Civil War traumatized McKinley, convincing him that war was not to be celebrated. When speaking with confidantes, this pacifist streak stood out. As the president remarked to a friend, "I shall never get into a war until I am sure God and Man approve. I have been through one war; I have seen the dead piled up; and I do not want to see another"[32].

But there were other reasons for his lack of enthusiasm. First, the American military was weak and poorly funded. In 1898, the army stood at 28,000 troops with roughly 100,000 members in the National Guard. In comparison, Spain had 80,000 to 150,000 troops in Cuba [33]. Some newspapers even compared American uniforms to "cavemen" skins and their weapons to clubs [34]. Though the American Navy fared better (enjoying newer technology, a better trained corps, and more 'modern' battleships), Spain had more ships (in tonnage and number), and they were more maneuverable in battle. On the eve of the war, one American admiral wrote his wife "It is impossible for me to give you an idea of the surprise and consternation experienced by all on the receipt of the order to sail ... for nothing can be expected of this expedition except the total destruction of the fleet or its hasty and demoralized return ... With a clear conscience I go to the sacrifice" [35]. Moreover the American economy continued to struggle in the aftermath of the 1893 economic depression. War would be bad for business, and powerful business groups urged the president to withstand the public clamor. Henry Cabot Lodge noted this reluctance in his account of the war, arguing the only brake on the march to war were business interests who "exerted their great force to stop every forward step along the inevitable path"[36].

Yet there was a deeper issue within the Administration. Officials struggled with defining the role of the United States in world affairs, and the instability in Cuba brought this disagreement into relief. For McKinley, the United States was unprepared for the demands of an empire. Militarily and economically, the United States could not compete with other great powers. Supporting an insurgency in Cuba did not advance American interests, nor did it improve commercial and military power. The best balance between the demands of the public and the wishes of business groups was diplomacy. As a result, McKinley hoped to pressure Spain to change their Cuba policy without resorting to the use of force.

Influential imperialists in Congress and government disagreed. War would be good for the country and satisfy the demands of Manifest Destiny. McKinley was too timid, and many agreed with Theodore Roosevelt's characterization that the president had "no more backbone than a chocolate éclair" [37]. More importantly, war justified greater military spending and a stronger role in international affairs. Cuba was an opportunity to extend American power and implement a new, global policy that balanced European gains [38]. The greatest threat to American power was not Spain, but rather a rising German presence in the Caribbean. Roosevelt told Captain Alfred Mahan "Until we definitely turn Spain out of those islands (and if I had my way that would be done tomorrow), we will always be menaced by trouble there . . . by turning Spain out [we] should serve notice that no strong European power, and especially not Germany, should be allowed to gain a foothold by supplanting some weak European power" [39]. The United States would best be served through military action and an offensive military doctrine; the greatest threat to American power was the failure to not do enough.

Cuba presented a dilemma for the president. The growing discontent in the public and government could best be satisfied through war. An offensive strategy in the Caribbean not only ended the humanitarian crisis on the island, but also served notice to European powers. But war with Spain was risky. A failed effort to release Cuba from the Spanish -- a likely outcome considering the weak American military -- would encourage other European states to extend their influence into the region, sap American military and economic strength, and weaken McKinley's chances for re-election.

The dilemma was particularly acute for the president. McKinley was inexperienced in foreign relations, and his political rivals used this inexperience to their advantage. His real forte was domestic politics and outflanking his opponents through public opinion. More importantly, McKinley preferred to micromanage decision making, trusting his own ability to read the political environment [40]. In choosing his cabinet, McKinley opted for well-known public figures, hoping to weaken domestic political opponents and minimize disagreement within the White House. For his Secretary of State, McKinley appointed John Sherman, a noted Senator and member of the Senate Foreign Relations Committee who was widely seen as the most able statesmen for the post. Though critics noted his advanced age (74), many believed Sherman increased the international and domestic stature of the president [41]. Secretary of War Russell A. Alger (a war hero, successful businessman, and a candidate for the Presidency) and Secretary of the Navy John Long (a popular governor of Massachusetts and Congressman with no previous experience with matters of the Navy) were chosen for similar reasons. By placing Sherman, Alger and Long in the cabinet, McKinley maintained control of the decision making process and ended the critiques of his inexperience.

McKinley's cabinet was a carefully constructed political ploy to quiet his critics. Yet his own foreign policy inexperience, combined with the inexperience of his main advisors, only complicated the Cuba decision. These factors would come to a head after McKinley ordered the USS Maine to Havana in late January 1898 as a response to rumors of a German-Spanish treaty [42]. Within 45 days of the explosion, Congress increased defense spending; within 70 days, Congress declared war.

## From Peace to War

On December 6, 1897, McKinley delivered his annual address to Congress. A significant portion of the speech reviewed Administration policy concerning Cuba. Though popular opinion and certain elements of Congress pushed war, the incremental approach favored by McKinley was effective. Diplomatic pressure and military threat forced Spain to recall Weyler, end the policy of concentration camps in the cities, and granted the release of American prisoners [43]. More importantly, a change in policy risked war. The most dangerous option – and the one favored by many in Congress – was recognition of the insurgents as legitimate representatives of Cuba. In the speech, McKinley connects recognition to war; a step that he was unwilling to take [44]. War was too risky, the benefits were too few, and in his speech, the president reminded Congress that few options just short of armed conflict remained on the table.

But the argument of the president changes. By March 26, 1898, McKinley offered ultimatums, urging the Spanish to give up its fight against guerrillas and institute reforms. “The concentration of men, women, and children in the fortified towns and permitting them to starve is unbearable to a Christian nation,” he wrote. “All this has shocked and inflamed the American mind, as it has the civilized world” [45]. On April 11, 1898, McKinley asked Congress for the authority to commit war. The speech outlined Spain's broken diplomatic promises. For McKinley, it was now necessary to end the humanitarian crisis on the island, extend rights of self-determination to the Cuban people, protect American commercial activities, and end the threat to the homeland caused by the conflict on the island. The explosion of the Maine was “impressive proof of a state of things in Cuba that is intolerable … thus shown to be such that the Spanish government cannot assure safety and security” of their own seaports [46]. Diplomacy failed to solve the Cuban problem, and war was justified by the continued failures of Spanish authorities.

What caused the dramatic change in American policy? How did McKinley – the noted pacifist – become a proponent of an offensive strategy? Previous explanations of the war generally focus on the political pressure brought to bear by domestic actors. Congress realized the explosion of the Maine presented an opportunity, and imperialists in both legislative bodies pressured the president. Congress simply needed to reflect the mood of the day to push the president into war, since the public “had made up their minds that the only real and possible solution was the end of Spanish rule in Cuba” [47]. Soon, Congressmen began to frame the intervention as a moral crusade. The most notable political ploy was a speech delivered by Redfield Proctor on March 17. Proctor, who visited the Cuban reconcentrado camps in December 1897, spoke of his travels, combining appeals to national security with moral truth – war would open “opportunities among a capable people whose racial and temperamental characteristics were compatible with those of Americans” [48]. The speech continued by denouncing McKinley and his connection to American big business. McKinley clearly felt the impact of the speech, lamenting to a friend “Congress is trying to drive us into war with Spain ... and we haven’t enough ammunition on the Atlantic seacoast to fire a salute” [49].

More importantly, members of the media used the Maine tragedy to stoke anti-Spanish public opinion. The 'Cuba problem', hyped by newspaper headlines, was a microcosm of the frustration at social and economic conditions at home. Sensational reports provided by the media only confirmed popular perceptions of Spain. As a result, many histories of the Spanish-American war argue that McKinley was forced to declare war. President McKinley had no other choice but relent to popular demand arising everywhere in the United States [50].

But for others, this was McKinley's war. The image of McKinley as an inexperienced president pushed around by an agitated public does not fit with historical accounts. McKinley did have control of the process, and he continued to resist the call to arms by pushing back at political rivals. For example, on April 13, the Senate Foreign Relations Committee (moved by powerful imperialists such as Lodge) recommended the president intervene in Cuba and support the independence movement, introducing legislation that would essentially force the president to take action. Though Congressional imperialists advised the president that war was the surest and best way to solve the Cuban crisis, McKinley recognized the weakness of the American military. The president believed the United States would get involved "when it could fight in a manner that would allow it to shape foreign affairs in crucial and long lasting ways" [51]. Diplomacy was a stalling tactic that protected business interests, while providing time for a military buildup. A much weaker Joint Resolution eventually passed both legislative bodies on April 19$^{th}$, but only after Congress relented by dropping the call for recognition [52].

War became "unavoidable" only after McKinley made the decision that Spain needed to relinquish Cuba [53]. The question, then, turns to what changed in McKinley's mind; what made war unavoidable. Indeed, very little had changed on the ground. The arguments used by McKinley to resist war did not waver in the months following the explosion in Havana harbor: the military balance continued to favor Spain, business interests were still threatened by an independent Cuba, and war with Spain favored the expansionists. A better explanation for McKinley's change is found in the relationship between the president and his inner circle.

McKinley's choice of advisors haunted him on the eve of war. To limit biased opinion, the president appointed weak and inexperienced advisors; advisors that he could easily dominate. But as diplomacy stalled and conditions on the island worsened, McKinley became confused over the direction of foreign policy. Unfortunately, the inexperience of the inner circle could not help the president in his decision making, and McKinley began making strategic missteps. For example, Alfred Mahan argued the fascination with Havana was a mistake. An attack on Puerto Rico should have been the first move, due to its geo-strategic position as a base for supplies and reinforcements. The US would have been better off by dropping the cause of Cuban independence and competing with the declining Spanish empire. If the US used a strategic rationale for war, "our leading object in such case would not have been to help Cuba, but to constrain Spain" [54]. By not appointing experienced advisors, McKinley was unable to formulate an efficient policy.

More importantly, problems in war planning were exacerbated by the mismanagement of the military. The navy, while professional and top-heavy with an experienced officer corps, suffered from a lack of ships and ammunition. The destruction of the Maine reduced the American fleet to seven armored battleships, giving the Spanish navy a large advantage in the Caribbean. The United States not only had fewer ships, but also no reserve forces on the east coast. According to Mahan, the Spanish did not realize "the fact that we had not a battleship in the home ports that could in six months be made ready to replace one lost or seriously disabled" [55]. He continued, "If we lost ten thousand men, the country could replace them; if we lost a battleship, it could not be replaced" [56]. The War Department and Department of the Navy rushed to purchase more ships, only to find a bidding war with Spain [57]. A bigger problem for the navy was a lack of ordnance. Even with an imminent war, the navy could not adequately arm their ships. Indeed, Dewey began the Battle of Manila with his ammunition holds half full [58].

The army was likewise poorly funded, ill-prepared, and disorganized. Army supplies could not meet demands, and soldiers confronted too little food, too few cots, and too few supplies for war. As Gould remarks, "Had all the soldiers who had been mobilized seen combat, there would not have been enough bullets for them" [59]. And more importantly, officers were unable to deal with the mass of men that they now commanded. Officers could not even efficiently load troops onto boats, stalling the invasion several times. As conditions worsened at army camps in Tampa (the staging area for the invasion), McKinley grew frustrated, finally ordering the flotilla to leave with whatever force they could in early June. Though McKinley was the first modern war president (directing the war from the White House), he was continually thwarted by a pre-modern requisition system that weakened troop strength and mobility.

The choice of military advisors not only created uncertainty and military mis-management, but also exacerbated competition within the administration. The critics were correct in their judgment of both Sherman and Alger. Secretary Sherman began to experience memory less and decaying mental acuity, largely due to the added stress of the foreign policy crisis [60]. More and more duties fell to the Assistant Secretary of State, William R. Day. While Day was a longtime friend and confidante of McKinley, [61] he was inexperienced in foreign policy; his only previous experience in government was his post as a federal district judge. Secretary of War Russell A. Alger suffered a similar fate, wilting under the demands of his position. A declaration of war required a reorganization of the Department of War to equip a military that would become ten times the size of current force structures [62]. Alger was not up for the job, and instead, Elihu Root took on many of the duties of the Secretary.

John Long likewise struggled with the pressures of his office, often looking to medical doctors to ease his pains. As a result, Long was often absent from the decision making. The real power belonged to his Assistant Secretary, Theodore Roosevelt. While McKinley disagreed with Roosevelt's approach to politics, he was experienced in naval affairs and many supported the young Roosevelt's position. Roosevelt's first public address as the Assistant Secretary brought this difference into relief. Where McKinley dreaded war, Roosevelt celebrated it as an activity to strengthen the nation. "War is the most effective means to promote peace," according to Roosevelt, and "It is through strife … that a nation must win greatness" [63]. Importantly, Roosevelt had allies in government and Congress. His friendship with Mahan gave him an ally on the Board of Directors of the Navy, while Henry Cabot Lodge supported his imperial vision of American power in Congress. And when war seemed likely, Roosevelt took advantage of his position.

In January, the Assistant Secretary wrote a letter to Long outlining a deployment plan for the navy to destroy the Spanish fleet and invade Cuba, hoping to push an activist role for the navy in any upcoming conflict. And when Long failed to show up to his office (due to a doctor's visit) on Feb. 25th, 1898, Roosevelt used his position to implement a policy of expansion [64]. Without Long's knowledge, Roosevelt contacted Dewey, ordering him to assemble his fleet and prepare for offensive operations. Long was shocked by the actions of his undersecretary when he returned to his office the following morning, remarking that Roosevelt "has come very near causing more of an explosion than happened to the Maine …

the very devil seemed to possess him" [65]. Only the charisma and ambition of the Assistant Secretary was necessary to place the Navy on a course for war [66].

Roosevelt continued his push for an offensive doctrine, regardless of the president's intentions. For example, Roosevelt publicly attacked Senator Mark Hanna at a public appearance in March, imploring the White House and opponents in Congress to step away from business interests [67]. The advisory system, built from McKinley's belief in his own ability to read and respond to public pressure, provided a space for Roosevelt to compete successfully against the more staid, conservative diplomatic solution to the Cuban problem. McKinley eventually relented to the beat of war drums.

The decision to go to war with Spain did not emerge solely from national tragedy, nor from a sense of moral outrage. And it did not arise from a favorable balance of power; the United States did not have a material advantage in the sea or on the ground. Instead the decision for war resulted from an internal battle between competing conceptions of American empire. The president assumed he could dominate his cabinet and rely on his own policy judgments. Yet his choice of advisors, combined with his own inexperience in foreign policy, provided a space for imperialists to satisfy their own vision for American foreign policy. A war that began with freeing Cuba from Spain ended in a global war of expansion, fueled by imperialists in Congress and the foreign policy bureaucracy [68].

## CONCLUSION

This paper began by asking the question of how the competition between advisors impacts presidential decisions for war. Put simply, who do presidents trust in their decision making? In general, three broad conclusions can be drawn from the example of McKinley and his management of the advisory system.

### 1. Solutions to the Credibility Problem Present Their Own Difficulties

Conventional accounts argue that domestic actors were responsible for the Spanish-American War. Congress and the media used the humanitarian tragedy on the island and the explosion of the Maine to their advantage. Redfield Proctor's speech in March, combined with media accounts of Cuban atrocities, influenced public attitudes concerning war [69]. McKinley recognized his chances for re-election would increase with a declaration of war. It made political sense to pursue a military solution.

But the historiography provides a more complicated account of the decision. For example, public opinion was generally calm in the weeks following the destruction of the Maine. Instead, the precipitating event was the release of the report on the explosion in March 1898. Only after the board of inquiry released their findings did the public blame the Spanish [70]. In other words, Congress and the media did not create the public support of war; they followed a trend that was already present. More importantly, McKinley resisted public opinion. The president recognized the United States military was unprepared for war. A devastating military loss to the Spanish (a likely consequence) would hurt his chances for re-election. An offensive grand strategy only satisfied a vocal minority, while limiting his political future. Though public opinion was a contributing factor to McKinley's decision, it was far from decisive.

A focus on advisors provides a different interpretation of war-making in the White House. In general, the inner circle is a cognitive shortcut, collecting information and forwarding policy recommendations. Unfortunately, the information gap creates doubt and suspicion; what I termed the credibility problem. And in the McKinley White House, solutions to this credibility problem only created confusion. McKinley was a micro-manager, relying on his own political skill to read the political environment. But his top-down control of the foreign policy process manifested uncertainty. First, his major foreign policy advisors were inadequate, chosen for their political symbolism rather than their insight. His Secretary of War and Secretary of State were incapable of aiding the president. As a result, McKinley struggled with the decision, stalling the decision to commit war, even going so far as to ignore his advisors for days before committing to minor strategic decisions, such as the decision to send Dewey to the Philippines in April 1898 [71].

This lack of direction encouraged competition between members of the foreign policy bureaucracy. It was not uncommon to find lower levels of the administration flouting bureaucratic rules and going beyond their job descriptions [72]. And more importantly, an imperialist coalition rose to take advantage of the vacuum and push McKinley towards war. The offensive grand strategy that produced both the drive to Havana and occupation of the Philippines was a product of individuals with strategic positions in the government. First, Henry Cabot Lodge used his position on the Senate Foreign Relations Committee to rally Congressional support for war. Mahan, a well-known figure who published articles in popular magazines, was the intellectual energy behind the strategy. The ex-Navy flag officer supplied the strategic rationale behind an offensive grand strategy, and publicly supported Senator Lodge. But more importantly, Mahan gave political cover for Theodore Roosevelt. Roosevelt used his position to move the navy into a war-footing, while arguing within the Administration for an offensive grand strategy. In effect, this 'trinity' – Lodge provided the moral reasoning for war, Mahan the military doctrine and strategic rationale, and Roosevelt the 'push' within the administration – built a coalition that McKinley could not out-compete. By failing to properly manage his advisors, the president provided the incentive and the political space for his opponents to win. And the combined energy of the three men successfully bargained for a stronger navy and supported a colony in the Philippines.

## 2. Advice Is 'Sticky'

Before the explosion of the Maine, the president resisted an offensive grand strategy. But this changes after the war. McKinley instead defers to his advisors, supporting plans for overseas territories. And after the decision was made, McKinley never revisited the logic of empire pushed by the imperialists.

For some, this change is to be expected. For example, work in organizational psychology finds that advice is 'sticky.' Placing faith in the inner circle promotes certainty and increases confidence, and decision makers are hesitant to change course after a decision is made [73]. By connection, a president that follows their inner circle is hesitant to question their decision to accept advice, and as a result will ignore discordant evidence in order to maintain that trust. In the case of the Spanish American War, McKinley simply followed this heuristic. But while the war was short and successful, the aftermath was not, as the initial success in the Philippines is replaced by a quagmire.

First, an influential anti-war campaign (funded by Carnegie) challenged the plans for expansion. To Carnegie, European imperialism should not be replaced by American imperialism. The United States did not have a history of overseas expansion, and they were ill prepared to run a colony. Mistakes would naturally follow empire. More importantly, anti-war activists argued jingoists were leading the United States down a path that promoted greater conflict with the Europeans. Empire naturally entailed a greater chance for war.

Carnegie's warning would prove prophetic. After the successes of Dewey in Manila Harbor (May 1), the Battles of El Caney and San Juan Hill (both on July 1), and the destruction of a Spanish flotilla in Santiago, Chile (on July 3), the imperialists were proven correct. The success in the Caribbean allowed the coalition of imperialists to turn their attention to South Asia. But the planning for the Philippines was slapdash and confused [74]. The president never intended to occupy the island, only changing his plans after the rousing success of Dewey. Many in the Administration were unfamiliar with the politics of the island, the strength of the insurgency, and even the geography. McKinley hurriedly created a Pacific command, ordering 5000 troops to deploy to the Philippines (which would quickly grow) to help defeat the Spanish in a meeting on May 6th. The first 2500 arrived on June 4, followed by another 3500 on July 17th.

The initial optimism of a colony in Southeast Asia soon faded. Dewey believed the insurgents could help the United States take the Philippines at a lower cost; and as a result, Dewey supported Aguinaldo and his leadership of the insurgency. But the guerrilla leader turned against the Americans. Filipinos wanted self-rule, and as the Spanish left the island (from the summer through the fall), Aguinaldo's rebels became better armed and gained support from the population. The American agreement to take control of the island infuriated the insurgents, and they began targeting American soldiers. On Feb. 4, 1899, an American sentry fired upon insurgents, starting a revolt that would last for several years. When the war ended on July 4, 1902, the US had suffered 4200 casualties, while killing roughly 20000 insurgents [75]. And more importantly, the United States lost the moral upper hand. In fact, planners borrowed a tactic used by Weyler on Cuba: separating civilians from guerrillas by forcing populations into camps. Though the US gained a vital seaport, the cost was high.

In general, the case demonstrates the problem of too much trust. By following advice, leaders can become trapped, unwilling to question their advisors in future deliberations. On its face, this makes sense. Advisors are vital cognitive shortcuts that ease decision making. A good advisor can simplify foreign policy. But there is a cost to following the inner circle. Too much trust in an advisor creates the conditions for policy stagnation and foreign policy quagmires.

## 3. Advisors Matter to the Extent Leaders Let Them Matter

Presidents form an advisory system to control the flow of information in the White House, and advisors are constrained by the structure they populate. But there are tradeoffs. For example, presidents can limit competition by stressing consensus and appointing advisors that can be easily controlled. Advisors realize they serve at the president's leisure. Because advisors want to participate in decision making, they hold their tongues, unwilling to speak truth to power. But limiting advisory opinion leads to stagnant foreign policy. While consensus limits backbiting and competition in the inner circle, it promotes tunnel vision. As a result, presidents who limit debate are often given bad advice.

A president that encourages competition faces a similar tradeoff. Competition and multiple advocacy guarantee motivated proponents with differing policy positions. Advisors are not shy from giving their advice, and leaders are given more and better information. But this complexity taxes the president. While competition dilutes individual bias through a marketplace of ideas, it also encourages advisors to subvert the policy making process. Advisors begin to compete with each other for influence, rather than provide unbiased advice. And more importantly, a competitive system is difficult to control. Inexperienced presidents are unable to manage the bruised egos of the inner circle, and the quality of advice quickly declines. The competition eventually overwhelms the decision making system and creates a space for advisors to hijack the decision.

The problems of both approaches arise during the Spanish-American War. McKinley wanted an advisory council that he could dominate. He believed in his own capabilities, convinced that he would be able to make foreign policy decisions without the help of his advisors. Unfortunately, when he needed help – in choosing a policy path and in planning the war – these same advisors were unable to aid his decision making. More problematic for McKinley was the emergence of policy entrepreneurs. The failure of McKinley to control the process granted a space for imperialists to enact their own plans for war. By not taking control of the process, the president created a power vacuum that was filled by motivated political opponents.

Advisors matter to the extent that leaders allow; the important question for presidents is the manner and type of that participation. In general, the structures presidents use to constrain or control the advisory process present opportunities for participation. Advisory influence in decisions of war is connected to how presidents ease the credibility problem. Trust, in effect, is a two-way street. Leaders want to have faith in the inner circle to ease the demands of decision making and receive unbiased advice. But this can only occur if presidents give their advisors freedom to speak truth to power. Likewise, advisors want to have faith in the president to take control of the decision, and do what they think is best for the country. Unfortunately for presidents, the best policy is to limit competition and stress consensus. The solutions to credibility problems in the inner circle manifest their own problems. Each president chooses which costs to pay.

## References


[1] George J. A. O'Toole, *The Spanish War: An American Epic*, 1898 (New York: WW Norton and Co., 1984), 18.

[2] Quoted in Gerald F. Linderman, *The Mirror of War: American Society and the Spanish-American War* (Ann Arbor: The University of Michigan Press,1974), 35.

[3] Harvey Rosenfeld, Diary of a Dirty Little War: The Spanish-American War of 1898 (Westport, CT: Praeger, 2000), 2.

[4] James Mann, *Rise of the Vulcans* (New York: Viking, 2004).

[5] Benjamin Bradlee, *Conversations with Kennedy* (New York: Norton, 1975).

[6] Richard K. Betts, *Soldiers, Statesmen, and Cold War Crises* (Cambridge, MA: Harvard University Press, 1977).

[7] Gregory Mason, *Remember the Maine* (New York: Henry Holt and Co., 1939), 32.

[8] H. R. McMaster, Dereliction of Dury: Lyndon Johnson, Robert McNamara, the Joint Chiefs of Staff, and the Lies that Led to Vietnam (New York: HarperCollins Publishers, 1997).

[9] Guy Benveniste, *The Politics of Expertise*, 2nd edition (San Francisco: Boyd and Fraser Publishing Company, 1977), 4.

[10] Janet A. Sniezek and Timothy Buckley, "*Cueing and Cognitive Conflict in Judge-Advisor Decision Making*," Organizational Behavior and Human Decision Processes 62 (2): 159-174 (1995).

[11] Roderick M. Kramer, "Paranoid Cognition in social systems: Thinking and Acting in the Shadow of Doubt," *Personality and Social Psychology Review* 2:251-275 (1998), 262-263.

[12] See Michael Ross and Fiore Sicoly, "*Egocentric bias in availability and attribution*," JPSP 37:322-326 (1979); and Susan T. Fiske and Shelley E. Taylor, Social Cognition (Reading, MA: Addison-Wesley, 1984).

[13] See Roderick M. Kramer, "Paranoid Cognition in social systems: Thinking and Acting in the Shadow of Doubt," Personality and Social Psychology Review 2:251-275 (1998); and Roderick M. Kramer, "In dubious battle: Heightened accountability, dysphoric cognition, and self-defeating bargaining behavior." In Roderick M. Kramer and David M. Messick, eds., *Negotiation in its Social Context* (Thousand Oaks, CA: Sage, 1995).

[14] See Brian Uzzi, "Social structure and compeition in interfirm networks: the paradox of embeddedness," Administrative Science Quarterly 42:35-67 (1997); and Roderick M. Kramer, "Trust and Distrust in Organizations: Emerging Perspectives, Enduring Questions," *Annual Review of Psychology* 50:569-598 (1999).

[15] Ivo H. Daalder and I.M. Destler, *In the Shadow of the Oval Office* (New York: Simon and Schuster, 2009).

[16] See Robert Dallek, Flawed Giant: Lyndon Johnson and his Times, 1961-1973 (New York: Oxford University Press, 1998); and Henry F. Graff, The Tuesday Cabinet: Deliberation and Decision on Peace and War under Lyndon B. Johnson (Englewood Cliffs, NJ: Prentice-Hall, 1970).

[17] Ivo H. Daalder and James M. Lindsay, America Unbound: The Bush Revolution in Foreign Policy (Hoboken, NJ: Wiley and Sons, Inc., 2005).

[18] Alexander L. George, "The Case for Multiple Advocacy in Making Foreign Policy", American Political Science Review 66(3): 751-785 (1972).

[19] See I.M. Destler, Presidents, Bureaucrats, and Foreign Policy (Princeton, NJ: Princeton University Press, 1972) ; Colin Campbell, Managing the Presidency: Carter, Reagan and the Search for Executive Harmony (Pittsburgh, PA: University of Pittsburgh Press, 1986); and Charles E. Walcott and Karen Hult, "Organizing the White House: Structure, Environment and Organizational Governance," *American Journal of Political Science* 31(1): 109-125 (1987).

[20] See Margaret G. Hermann and Thomas Preston, "Presidents, Advisors and Foreign Policy: The Effect of Leadership Style on Executive Arrangements," Political Psychology 15(1): 75-96 (1994); and Thomas Preston, The President and His Inner Circle (New York: Columbia University Press, 2001).

[21] Irving L. Janis, *Victims of Groupthink* (Houghton-Mifflin, Boston, 1972).
[22] Alexander L. George, Presidential Decision-Making in Foreign Policy: The Effective Use of Information and Advice (Boulder, CO: Westview Press, 1980), 191-208.
[23] Ibid.
[24] Paul A. Kowert, Groupthink or Deadlock: When Do Leaders Learn from Their Advisors? (Albany, NY: State University of New York Press, 2002).
[25] Quoted in Richard Barnet, The Rocket's Red Glare: When America Goes to War (New York: Simonand Schuster, 1990), 107.
[26] Charles S. Olcott, William McKinley, Part of the American Statesmen, Second Series (Houghton Mifflin Company, New York, 1916), 383-384.
[27] Ibid., 386.
[28] Marcus M. Wilkerson, Public Opinion and the Spanish-American War: A Study in War Propaganda (Baton Rouge, LA: Louisiana State Press, 1932) 13.
[29] Olcott, William McKinley (1916), 396-397.
[30] Kevin Phillips, William McKinley, part of the series, The American Presidents, Arthur M. Schlesinger, Jr., editor. (New York: Times Books, Henry Holt and Company, 2003), 34-35.
[31] Paul T. McCartney, Power and Progress: American National Identity, the War of 1898, and the Rise of American Imperialism (Baton Rouge, LA: Louisiana State University Press, 2006), 117.
[32] Quoted in Phillips, William McKinley (2006), 92.
[33] See Mason, Remember the Maine (1939); and Jack Cameron Dierks, A Leap to Arms: The Cuban Campaign of 1898 (New York: J. B. Lippincott Company, 1970).
[34] Linderman, *The Mirror of War* (1974).
[35] Dierks, *A Leap to Arms* (1970), 46.
[36] Henry Cabot Lodge, *The War with Spain* (New York: Harper and Brothers, Publishers, 1899), 32.
[37] Mason, Remember the Maine (1939), 46.
[38] Lewis L. Gould, The Presidency of William McKinley (Lawrence, KS: The Regents Press of Kansas, 1980), 63.
[39] O'Toole, *The Spanish War* (1984), 99.
[40] Phillips, William McKinley (2003), 87.
[41] Olcott, William McKinley (1916), 329, 333-334.
[42] O'Toole, The Spanish War (1984).
[43] Phillips, William McKinley (2003), 91.
[44] Harry J. Sievers, ed., William McKinley, 1843-1901, Series Editor Howard F. Bremer (Dobbs Ferry, NY: Oceana Publications, Inc., 1970), 38.
[45] Ibid., 42.
[46] Ibid., 52.
[47] Lodge, The War with Spain (1899), 33.
[48] Linderman, The Mirror of War (1974), 42.
[49] David Traxel, 1898 (New York: Alfred A. Knopf, 1998), 120-121.
[50] David F. Trask, The War with Spain in 1898 (New York: Macmillan Publishing Co., Inc., 1981), 58.
[51] McCartney, Power and Progress (2006), 113.

[52] John A. Corry, 1898: Prelude to a Century (New York: Fordham University Press, 1998), 115-116.
[53] Gould, *The Presidency of William McKinley* (1980), 62.
[54] Alfred T. Mahan, Lessons of the War with Spain (and Other Articles) (Boston, MA: Little, Brown, and Company, 1899), 27.
[55] Ibid., 185.
[56] Ibid., 186.
[57] Traxel, 1898 (1998), 109-110.
[58] Ronald Spector, Admiral of the New Empire (Columbia, SC: University of South Carolina Press, 1988), 42.
[59] Gould, The Presidency of William McKinley (1980), 105.
[60] Olcott, William McKinley (1916), 335.
[61] Corry, 1898: Prelude to a Century (1998), 19.
[62] Olcott, William McKinley (1916), 337.
[63] Corry, 1898: Prelude to a Century (1998), 20.
[64] Gould, The Presidency of William McKinley (1980), 94-95.
[65] Traxel, 1898 (1998), 111.
[66] Corry, 1898: Prelude to a Century (1998), 188.
[67] Ibid., 97-98.
[68] Ibid., 121.
[69] See Wilkerson, Public Opinion and the Spanish-American War: A Study in War Propaganda (1932) 13; and John William Tebbel America's Great Patriotic War with Spain: Mixed Motives, Lies, and Racism in Cuba and the Philippines, 1898-1915 (Manchester Center, VT: Marshall Jones Co., 1996).
[70] Louis A. Pérez Jr., The War of 1898 (Chapel Hill, NC: The University of North Carolina Press, 1998), 66-68.
[71] Traxel, 1898 (1998), 123.
[72] Corry, 1898: *Prelude to a Century (*1998), 188.
[73] Janet A. Sniezek and Lyn M. Van Swol, "Trust, Confidence, and Expertise in a Judge-Advisor System," *Organizational Behavior and Human Decision Processes* 84(2): 288-307 (2001).
[74] Gould, *The Presidency of William McKinley* (1980), 97-103.
[75] Corry, 1898: *Prelude to a Century* (1998), 331-332.

In: Presidents and War
Editors: A. Eksterowicz and G. Hastedt, pp. 121-140
ISBN 978-1-61668-917-9


*Chapter 8*

# Regime Formation and Maturation in the White House: The Rise of Internationalism during the Administration of Theodore Roosevelt

***Tom Lansford***

## Introduction

The end of the nineteenth century marked the beginning of a transitional period in American foreign policy. With the interior of the continental United States essentially settled, the energies and power of the emerging nation would be unleashed on the global stage. The historian Ernest May once quipped that the United States had "greatness thrust upon it," reflecting the view that the nation's rise to superpower status was the result of its unique combination of geography and natural resources and not because of specific long-range policies. However, particular decisions made during the Roosevelt administrations ultimately laid the foundation for the country's emergence as a world power. Hence the roots of the "American Century" were in the few years preceding the turn of that century.

As the United States became a more influential actor in international relations, there was a change in the diplomatic regime that included the State Department and the nation's political elites. This essay traces the development of the new political regime in foreign policy that accompanied the increased American presence on the world stage which began with the McKinley administration and became solidified during Roosevelt's tenure. The work begins with an examination of the role and influence of domestic political regimes. The essay then specifically focuses on the role of the president in regime building and the adoption of new norms and values during the period in the context of foreign policy.

## REGIMES

Regimes may be defined as the "sets of implicit or explicit principles, norms, rules, and decision-making procedures around which actors' expectations converge in a given area . . ." [1]. Regimes encompass the common ideologies and beliefs which link together the people, institutions and policies of government. Significantly, regimes can serve as a means to maintain common policies during a change in administration or they can expedite the implementation of new or reformist ideas and policies. For instance, during the Cold War, there developed a foreign policy regime which was embraced by both the Democratic and Republican Parties and which helped maintain a remarkable degree of continuity in American diplomacy. This regime embraced the doctrine of containment of the Soviet Union, promotion of free trade, and American involvement in world affairs [2]. In order to accomplish the goals of the regime, new institutions, including the National Security Council and the Central Intelligence Agency, were developed.

Conversely, regimes can speed the adoption of new policies by providing a common framework for incoming administrations. As such, political regimes are often influence working arrangements among institutions fashioned by new governing cadres to elaborate their particular political commitments. As regimes transform new ideas about the purposes of government into governing routines, they carry on the reformer's central contention as the political common sense of a new era, a set of base assumptions shared (or at least accepted) by all major actors in the period. In this way, political regimes come to exercise an overarching influence over the affairs of state [3]. Once accepted, regimes speed the establishment of new norms, rules, and institutions because of the cohesiveness they furnish.

### Norms, Rules, and Institutions

While regimes represent ideals, norms are about behavior [4]. Norms are the "standards of behavior defined in terms of rights and obligations." Common norms include sovereignty or free trade [5]. Norms impact behavior since they are "collective beliefs that regulate the behavior and identity of actors" [6]. The relationship between regimes and norms is critically important since these constructs form the basis for political identity. Thomas Risse-Kappen defines identity as predicated on:

> norms firmly embedded in the political culture of . . . states and norms shape the identity of political actors through the processes of socialization, communication, and enactment. . . . Collectively held identities not only define who "we" are, but they also delineate the boundaries against "them," the "other." Identities then prescribe norms of appropriate behavior [7].

In regards to national security and foreign policy, norms serve several important functions. For example they have led to the acceptance of national boundaries and both established buffer zones and spheres of influence [8]. Historical examples of such norms include the 1885 Congress of Vienna, which established spheres of influence in Africa for the European states or the Root-Takahira Agreement of 1908, in which the United States and Japan recognized each other's possessions in the Pacific [9]. In addition, norms can also dissuade nations from "cheating" on global agreements by specifically detailing the conditions under which other actors are prepared to act [10]. Contemporary examples of this would include the various global treaties on nuclear, biological, and chemical weapons (NBC) [11]. Norms may also codify the procedures for international transactions. This has been especially apparent in the realm of global economics. Arrangements such as the General Agreement on Tariffs and Trade (GATT) and its successor the World Trade Organization (WTO) have significantly reduced the cost of business transactions for individual nations [12]. Finally, norms promote collective action. They provide justification for states to act as a group for implementation purposes [13].

Rules are the application of individual norms to specific circumstances. As such, they are "specific prescriptions or proscriptions for action" [14]. An example of such rules would be the practices established under the WTO to outlaw certain economic practices that run counter to free trade. These rules include provisions against subsidies, product dumping, and other discriminatory economic policies. In order for rules to be effective, they must have mechanisms to enforce them and they must be accepted (either passively or under duress). As Hedley Bull wrote, "a rule, in order to be effective in society, must be obeyed to some degree, and must be reckoned as a factor in the calculations of those to whom it applies, even those who elect to violate it" [15]. Bull went on to assert that the effectiveness of a rule was dependent on several factors including the manner in which the rule is communicated to the people and the enforcement potential of the rule as well as its "adaptability" [16].

Institutions are formalized versions of regimes [17]. The main difference between a regime and an institution is that regimes do not have the ability to act since they are made up of norms and principles [18]. Only institutions have enforcement capabilities. As a result, regimes rely on institutions to carry-out enforcement measures [19]. The distinction between regimes and institutions can be illustrated with the complex issue of free trade. Western Europe has developed a trade regime that encompasses tacit and explicit rules. This regime is characterized by institutions that formalize rules and employ multilateral decision making processes [20]. Hence, institutions may be defined more narrowly as "persistent and connected sets of rules and principles that prescribe behavioral roles, constrain activity, and shape expectations" [21] because of their enforcement abilities.

## Political Elites

The connection between regimes and institutions is represented by the common norms and rules shared by the two. The bridge which joins these two and ensures uniformity of principles is political elites. These elites form a disproportionate share of governmental employees and policymakers and also have a disproportionate influence in the formation and development of political opinion. In regards to foreign policy, Mark Lagon found that the American people often abrogate their control over the formation of policy and instead allow elites to develop initiatives while the populace concentrates on domestic policy. Lagon contends that "elites play a surprisingly significant role in democracies, especially in the foreign policy realm, where the mass public consciously or unconsciously cedes influence to experts and self-appointed experts" [22].

In a study on the responsiveness of the mass public to political communication from elites, Richard Herrera found that elites are generally "more sophisticated politically than the average voter"and have the capability to significantly influence opinion.[23]. This builds on the classic work of V.O. Key in which the noted scholar asserts that "mass opinion is not self-generating [but] a response to the cues, proposals, and the visions propagated by the political activists" [24]. During regime formation, elites may even bypass the public completely until the rules and norms of a new regime are established. The elites then work to garner public support and acceptance for the regime [25]. In some case, the elites may even abrogate their responsibility to disseminate information to bureaucrats or technocrats within the government [26]. Consequently, domestic political regimes are not "synonymous" with governmental institutions, instead they may be located:

> in the linkages that elites forge between governing institutions and political commitments. These linkages are composed of political norms, public discourses, decision-making procedures, and modes of intervention into socioeconomic relations. The formative element in any given regime is . . . not its trademark institutions but the governing cadre that manages them and acts within an intellectual milieu, infusing institutions with meaning, purpose, and direction [27].

The importance of political elites cannot be underestimated especially in regards to the acceptance and internalization of the new regime.

Jeffrey W. Legro asserts that when states change their fundamental ideas about international relations (a regime change) that change occurs in a two-step process: "First, social actors [elites] must somehow concur, explicitly or tacitly, that the old ideational structure is inadequate, thus causing its collapse. Second, actors must consolidate some new replacement set of ideas, lest they return to the old orthodoxy simply as a default mechanism" [28]. Hence, political elites are responsible for not only initiating regime change, but also for securing the broad acceptance of the regime by domestic interests. Such acceptance is most likely to occur under three conditions including: "1) when events generate consequences that deviate from social expectations; 2) when the consequences are undesirable; and 3) when a socially viable replacement idea exists" [29]. For instance, during the post World War II era, the end of the conflict did not produce the period of global peace that most in the United States expected. Instead the tensions generated by the initiation of the Cold War ushered in a period of global strife. However, the renewed challenge presented to U.S. interests was met with a renewed domestic commitment to global involvement centered around the drive to contain the Soviet Union.

The role of elites in American politics is heightened because of the role of the Congress, and particularly the Senate, in developing and implementing foreign policy. In many ways, the Congress serves as the mechanism to reconcile domestic and foreign policy and it is the arena in which the two are often intertwined. On an economic level, Peter Katzenstein asserts that "the main purpose of all strategies of foreign economic policy is to make domestic policy compatible with the international political economy" [30]. David A. Baldwin goes further and contends that "economic statecraft" or "foreign economic policy" has begun to supplant the traditional emphasis on security-based diplomacy, as contemporary states promote their domestic economic interests [31]. Robert Putnam best summarized the connections between foreign and domestic policy as a "two-level" game:

> The politics of many international negotiations can usefully be conceived as a two level game. At the national level, domestic groups pursue their interests by pressuring the

> government to adopt favorable policies, and politicians seek power by constructing coalitions among those groups. At the international level, national governments seek to maximize their own ability to satisfy domestic pressures, while minimizing the adverse consequences of foreign developments. Neither of the two games can be ignored by central decision makers, so long as their countries remain interdependent, yet sovereign [32].

In this fashion, government and elites serve as the intermediaries between domestic and international actors.

In the United States, statesmen do not formulate foreign policy in a vacuum. They are constrained in their policy options by domestic groups that can bring significant political pressures and resources to the promotion of their interests. Policymakers have also had to balance the potential costs of security policies and programs in regards to national economies and social policies [33]. This leads to actions which may appear irrational because endeavors which are rational at the international level may be "impolitic" at the domestic level, and thus may not be taken [34]. The leadership and persuasion capabilities of elites are the keys to reconciling domestic and foreign interests.

At the end of the nineteenth century, there was a small, but very powerful foreign policy elite in the United States. Members of this elite dominated the nation's diplomatic service and often moved easily between business and government service. Theodore C. Sorenson contends that the foreign policy elite at the turn of the century was "the closest thing to a governing aristocracy" in the United States [35]. This elite was "led by Protestant white male graduates of Ivy League universities with close family and business toes to each other" and existed mainly in the corridor that was made-up of Boston, New York, and Washington [36].

Theodore Roosevelt was an ardent supporter of an internationalist foreign policy for the United States. He sought to establish a new regime in foreign policy which was based on an expanded role for the emerging superpower. The challenge for Roosevelt was not just to develop new policies, but to ensure the continuation of internationalism through regime change. In order to accomplish this, Roosevelt had to gain acceptance of his new international vision of the United States by both existing political elites, including the leadership in Congress, then by the public at large. Concurrently, Roosevelt had to actually implement the polices that corresponded with his central goal of a greater global presence for the United States.

## THE OLD REGIME

Throughout the eighteenth and nineteenth centuries, American foreign policy was directed primarily toward the Western Hemisphere. The resources of the nation were concentrated in the drive to develop the interior sections of the continental United States while trade considerations dominated American global diplomacy. The westward drive to develop the interior of the nation was rooted in the belief in the superiority of the "American way." John O'Sullivan coined the phrase "Manifest Destiny" to reflect the nation's claim to the continental areas of the West. Hence new territories belonged to the United States "by right of our manifest destiny to overspread and possess the whole of the continent which Providence has given us for the great experiment of liberative and federative self-government entrusted to us" [37]. The principle of Manifest Destiny became a powerful piece of political rhetoric that was used by elites to not only justify expansion, but to garner enormous public support for the acquisition of new areas – especially as these territories were meant to be fully integrated with the rest of the nation through the application of established political and cultural norms [38]. Throughout the nineteenth century, manifest destiny formed one of the core myths of American society [39]. Political elites use the commonalities of a culture to establish national myths which incorporate the norms, rules, and principles of existent regimes.

George Washington's oft-quoted admonishment to "avoid permanent alliances" and the principles of the Monroe Doctrine acted as dual constraints on any efforts to project American influence outside of the hemisphere [40] .Michael Dunne suggests that the term most used to describe U.S. foreign policy during this period – "isolationism" – should be replaced with the more accurate phrase "hemispheric unilateralism" [41]. This concept holds that Americans may have actively sought to avoid political or security entanglement with Europe, but successive administrations were able to garner public support for expansion and interaction in Central and South America [42]. The ability of elites to rally public opinion lay in the nature of American attitudes toward foreign policy. For instance, Gabriel Almond asserts that for the most part Americans are, and have traditionally been, "indifferent" to foreign affairs, but that indifference could quickly turn to "anger" with the right motivations (leading to "dangerous overreactions" on the part of the populace) [43].

This facet of the nation's foreign policy was rooted in the longstanding belief in American exceptionalism – the idea that the United States was unique among the nations of the world. This uniqueness was the combination of a variety of factors including geography, politics, and culture. The idea of American exceptionalism was expressed domestically in the doctrine of manifest destiny [44]. Joseph Lepgold and Timothy McKeown contend that the belief in this exceptionalism lay in the longstanding manner in which "Americans depreciate power politics and old-fashioned diplomacy, mistrust powerful standing armies and entangling peacetime commitments, make moralistic judgements about other people's domestic systems, and believe that liberal values transfer readily to foreign affairs" [45] .

As a result of this exceptionalism, Richard Kerry asserts that successive "American presidents have been addicted to citing the absence of territorial claims as evidence of the high purpose and moral purity with which the U.S. projects power to far places. This virtue is believed by Americans to distinguish the U.S. from any other power in the world, including other democracies" [46]. For those such as Theodore Roosevelt, and later Woodrow Wilson, who believed in American internationalism, exceptionalism also carried with it an implicit duty to apply uniquely American qualities such as democracy and individual rights to other nations. This belief in "democratic universalism" reflected that the political ethnocentrism at the core of most Americans' view of the world – "everyone ought to be like us" [47]. Such beliefs would be used to justify intervention in Central and South America and the acquisition of territories such as the Philippines since it was incumbent upon the United States to foster democracy in these developing nations [48]. Emily Rosenberg employs the term "liberal developmentalism" to describe American efforts at economic and democratic universalism [49]. Years after Roosevelt left office, the self-declared anti-imperialist president Woodrow Wilson would justify American intervention throughout the hemisphere by claiming that the United States was deploying troops in nations such as Nicaragua in an effort to "teach them to elect good men."

This universalism became prominent within the nation's foreign policy elite toward the end of the nineteenth century. Nonetheless, hemispheric unilateralism enjoyed one final period of prominence during the second administration of Grover Cleveland (1893-1897). Cleveland and his secretaries of state Walter Q. Gresham (1893-1895) and Richard Olney (1895-1897) reversed the internationalist efforts of Benjamin Harrison's secretary of state, James G. Blaine. For instance, Cleveland withdrew the 1893 annexation treaty with Hawaii from Congress and sought to avoid entanglement in Cuba (despite increasing public domestic pressure to respond to economic losses by U.S. citizens). The administration's policies were rooted in the principle that the Western Hemisphere represented the "new" world and were open to American influence and power, while Europe, Africa and Asia were the "old" world and the U.S. should avoid commitments or involvement in these regions. Olney used the Monroe Doctrine as justification for diplomatic brinkmanship which almost led to war between the United States and Great Britain during the Venezuelan Boundary Controversy [50].

Even as the nation acquired territory during the expansionist periods of the nineteenth century, there was not a formal regime which supported the annexation of new territory [51]. Instead, while there were often economic imperatives for the acquisition of specific areas, other underlying factors including strategic interests or domestic political reasons, were just as likely to prompt territorial expansion. The second Cleveland administration followed time-adhered policies which sought to promote American economic interests, but not necessarily advance a heightened global role for the emerging nation.

## The McKinley Administration

The election of 1896 led to dramatic changes in U.S. foreign policy. The new President, William McKinley, espoused a much more assertive foreign policy than had his predecessor (including favoring the annexation of Hawaii). Concurrent with the beginning of McKinley's tenure was a series of events which would draw the United States into a more visible global role. The real turning point was the Spanish-American War of 1898. While the United States clearly had the capability to be a world power relatively early in its history, the Spanish-American War demonstrated the nation's military power and led to a recognition by the established great powers of the young democracy's nascent potential. The conflict also marked the redirection of American imperialism outside of the Western hemisphere. For instance, Michael Dunne contends that the war marked:

> an American form of imperialism, for American power (in its broadest sense) was projected abroad and imposed over unwilling subjects; and in taking American power overseas so forcefully and dramatically, the war represented both the continuity of American territorial expansion and its discontinuous passage into the Caribbean and western Pacific [52].

For the most part, the onset of American imperialism outside of the continental United States was merely the continuation of Westward expansion. The aggressive acquisition of territory had marked the nation from its very beginning and the closing of the frontier merely prompted a redirection of American power projection outside of the continental United States.

Richard W. Van Alstyne even contended that the United States was an imperium or expanding imperial power from its very foundation [53.]

Within the United States the acquisition of new territories overseas elicited considerable domestic debate. The rise of groups such as the American Anti-Imperialist League was demonstrative of the strong sentiment which opposed American colonialism. This opposition was based on traditional isolationist sentiments as well as moral grounds. The 1899 League Platform summarized the moral objections:

> We hold that the policy known as imperialism is hostile to liberty and tends toward militarism, an evil from which it has been our glory to be free. We regret that it has become necessary in the land of Washington and Lincoln to reaffirm that all men, of whatever race or color, are entitled to life, liberty and the pursuit of happiness. We maintain that governments derive their powers from the consent of the governed. We insist that the subjugation of any people is "criminal aggression" and open disloyalty to the distinctive principles of our Government [54].

Anti-imperialist sentiment was embraced by a number of prominent Americans including such diverse figures as Andrew Carnegie, William Graham Sumner, William Jennings Bryan, and Samuel Gompers. However, while elite opposition to imperialism remained strong throughout the Spanish-American War and afterward, elite support for the expansionist policies of the McKinley administration would initiate a regime change in the nation's foreign policy. The most prominent and public advocate for an enhanced global role for the United States was Theodore Roosevelt.

## The New Regime

Long before he entered the political spotlight, Roosevelt became convinced of the need for a more assertive foreign policy. By the late 1880s, Roosevelt had gained some fame as a historian and writer (including a work on the War of 1812). After he read Alfred Thayer Mahan's *The Influence of Sea Power Upon History, 1660-1783*, Roosevelt became firmly convinced of the need for the United States to become a global naval power. In a review of Mahan's work, Roosevelt wrote that the nation needed a navy that excelled above all others:

> Our ships should be the best of their kind–this is the first desideratum. But in addition, there should be plenty of them. We need a large navy, composed not merely of cruisers, but containing also a full proportion of powerful battleships, able to meet those of any other nation [55].

Such a navy would serve not only to protect the national interests of the United States, but it would also allow Washington to project its power anywhere around the globe.

Roosevelt, Mahan, and Massachusetts Senator Henry Cabot Lodge became the core of the elite group that advocated expansionist policies. The group was headquartered at New York's prominent Metropolitan Club. In his biography of the young Roosevelt, Edmund Morris points-out that eventually the circle of expansionists would include "Senators and Representatives, Navy and Army officers, writers, socialites, lawyers, and scientists–men linked as much by Roosevelt's motley personality as by their common political belief, namely, that Manifest Destiny called for the United States to free Cuba, annex Hawaii, and raise the American flag supreme over the Western Hemisphere" [56] .

Partially through the efforts of Senator Lodge, Roosevelt was appointed Assistant Secretary of the Navy in 1897. Almost at once, Roosevelt began to agitate for war against Spain over Cuba. In his autobiography, Roosevelt wrote that "soon after I began work as Assistant Secretary of the Navy I became convinced that war would come" [57]. When war broke-out in April of 1898, Roosevelt resigned his post and rode to fame at the head of the Rough Riders [58]. He parlayed his popularity into a successful campaign to be governor of the state of New York. This in turn served as a stepping stone to the vice-presidency in 1900.

Meanwhile, the Spanish-American War had resulted in an American empire. As a result of the conflict, the United States gained the territories of Puerto Rico, Guam, and the Philippines. Cuba was granted nominal independence, but remained an American protectorate through the adoption of the Platt Amendment which gave the United States the rights to two naval bases in the island and the legal right to intervene in its southern neighbor's domestic politics. The war also led to a Congressional resolution to annex Hawaii. The rapid expansion of the United States into the Pacific affirmed that the nation would be both an Atlantic and Pacific power. The new territories also permanently drew the nation into the affairs of Asia.

The United States fought a bloody and repressive war to prevent Filipino independence, and participated in the military operations against the Boxers in China during the summer of 1900. Concurrently, McKinley's second Secretary of State, John Hay, promulgated the Open Door Notes by which the United States refused to recognize the European and Japanese spheres of influence in China. The Notes marked a major turning point in the nation's diplomatic history and began the process by which the Washingtonian policy of hemispheric isolationism began to erode. Dunne provides this summation:

> These paper commitments aligned the US and British governments; but they went against German as well as Japanese and Russian interests. Hindsight shows us that, not for the last time, the US government had adopted a policy towards China which set it against two regional powers (Japan and Russia). More to the point, contemporaries appreciated that the American drive for markets, naval bases and coaling stations, and for greater political influence in the Pacific and along the shores of Asia, entailed an examination of traditional policies. As was astutely noted at the time, the very ease of American success obscured the need to reflect on the reasons and conditions for this pre-eminence and encouraged Americans to avoid a re-evaluation of their unilateralist practices [59].

The role of the foreign policy elite in the transformation of American diplomacy was significant. Roosevelt and his circle, including judge and future president William H. Taft, were the ideological leaders of the movement which championed both the acquisition of new territories and an increased global presence. They also acted to coordinate policies and craft legislation to support a more robust foreign policy.

In his autobiography, Roosevelt asserted that one of the reasons that he accepted the vice-presidency was "the need, after 1898, of meeting in manful and straightforward fashion the extraterritorial problems arising from the Spanish War" [60]. In other words, Roosevelt wanted to make sure that there was no retreat from the nation's new global prominence which was occasioned by the war with Spain.

## Roosevelt's Foreign Policy

When Roosevelt became president in 1901 following the assassination of McKinley, the transformation of American foreign policy had begun and the nation had emerged onto the world stage as a major international power following its defeat of Spain and its military involvement in the Boxer Rebellion of 1900 [61]. Nonetheless, in spite of the nation's increased overseas commitments, domestic opposition to internationalism remained significant in the United States. While Roosevelt's brand of internationalism (based on democratic universalism) was embraced by many within the foreign policy elite, it would only be through his efforts as President that the norms, values and ideas of internationalism became formalized. His efforts to strengthen the U.S. Navy and changes in the State Department led to the development of the institutions necessary to support a new foreign policy regime.

Once in office, Roosevelt pledged to maintain the policies of his predecessor and even asked all of the assassinated president's cabinet members to remain. During his first annual address to Congress, Roosevelt reiterated his belief in the virtue of annexing the Philippines, Hawaii, Puerto Rico, and Guam. In regards to the ongoing revolt in the Philippines, the new President also emphasized his belief in the universal mission of the nation to "help these people upward along the stony and difficult path that leads to self-government" [62]. He also expressed his wish to see the current American battleship fleet increased from nine to seventeen. The President stressed the importance of the fleet as a means to enforce the Monroe Doctrine and forestall European intervention in the Western Hemisphere. Most important, Roosevelt emphasized the need for the construction of a canal across the Panamanian Isthmus. Concerning the canal, the new President claimed that "no single great material work which remains to be undertaken on this continent is of such consequence to the American people" [63].

Throughout his tenure, Roosevelt's foreign policy would be centered around these themes. He would justify the military repression used in the Philippines as necessary to instill democracy–an argument that would also be used to rationalize American military interventions in the Caribbean. For instance, Roosevelt actions in fostering a revolution in Panama were explained away through his assertions that Colombia was ruled by a dictator and that the people of the Isthmus of Panama were governed by a government "without their consent" [64]. The main reason for U.S. support of the revolution was the Colombian Senate's rejection of the original canal treaty between that nation and the United States. With Panama an independent nation, Hay was free to negotiate the Hay-Bunau-Varilla Treaty which gave the United States the right to construct a canal and maintain sovereignty over a ten-mile-wide zone in exchange for $10 million and an annual payment of $250,000.

He used a similar rationale for intervention in Santo Domingo in 1904. However, the intervention in Santo Domingo was mainly the result of Roosevelt's desire to protect American bankers and business interests from German and French creditors and the possibility of domestic revolution. Roosevelt justified his actions in the Caribbean with the promulgation of the Roosevelt Corollary to the Monroe Doctrine. In the Corollary, Roosevelt declared that:

> all that this country desires to see the neighboring countries stable, orderly, and prosperous. . . . Chronic wrongdoing, or an impotence which results in the general

> loosening of the ties of civilized society, may . . . require intervention by some civilized nation, and in the Western Hemisphere the adherence of the United States to the Monroe Doctrine may force the United States, however reluctantly, in flagrant cases of such wrongdoing or impotence to the exercise of an international police power. . . . We would interfere with [Latin Americans] only in the last resort [65].

The Corollary gave the United States the right, indeed the duty, to intervene in the domestic affairs of Latin American nations when revolution or European intervention appeared imminent. The Corollary also highlighted the high degree of autonomy that American Presidents have in the realm of foreign policy. In his efforts to change the diplomatic orientation of the United States, Roosevelt extensively utilized the broad powers of the presidency, both to direct foreign policy and to oversee the military. In the Senate, Roosevelt could count on the support of his friend and mentor, Henry Cabot Lodge. Meanwhile, in the House, the President found a willing ally in Illinois Congressman Robert Hitt who was chairman of the House Foreign Affairs Committee [66].

## The Navy

In order to meet the increased commitments occasioned by his policies, Roosevelt needed to improve the capability and increase the size of the American military – mainly the Navy. Historian James R. Reckner points out that "perhaps no other President has exerted such intimate influence on the U.S. Navy as Theodore Roosevelt" [67]. The importance of the Navy was underscored early in Roosevelt's Administration when in 1902 German and British warships blockaded Venezuela over that country's nonpayment of debts. Roosevelt had a fleet assemble off Puerto Rico, ostensibly for maneuvers. Roosevelt informed the German Ambassador that he intended to dispatch the fleet to Venezuela if Germany did not agree to arbitration. The threat had the desired impact and the matter was turned over to arbitration. Nonetheless, the incident underscored for the new President the potential for European intervention in the Hemisphere.

Throughout the remainder of his tenure, Roosevelt believed that Germany represented the greatest foreign threat to American interests. In April of 1901, Roosevelt wrote that "it seems to me that Germany's attitude toward us makes her the only power with which there is any reasonable likelihood or possibility of our clashing" [68]. Besides potential problems in Latin America, Roosevelt also judged that Germany could cause problems for the United States elsewhere around the globe. From 1904 to 1906, tensions between France and Germany over spheres of influence in Morocco brought the two nations repeatedly to the verge of war. Roosevelt offered to mediate the crisis. The result was the 1906 Algeciras Conference which found in favor of French claims. Roosevelt's influence at the Algeciras Conference came in the wake of a 1904 incident in which a bandit leader, the Raisuli, took two Americans hostage. Roosevelt deployed the fleet off the coast and eventually pressured the Sultan of Morocco into securing the release of the hostages. In the midst of the crisis, came the 1904 Republican National Convention. Roosevelt brought the Convention to its feet when he had the chairman read a demand for either the return of the Americans or the death of the Raisuli.

In fact, Roosevelt used his foreign policy successes, including the Corollary and the Panama Canal Treaty to great success during his reelection campaign. Roosevelt appealed to the nation by stressing his activism in both domestic and foreign policies. His actions in regards to Panama and Santo Domingo were very popular with the American people as Roosevelt emphasized the nation's role in promoting democracy and protecting the Hemisphere from European intervention in his campaign speeches. When the election was over, Roosevelt won by the largest margin in the popular vote that had yet been recorded in a presidential election [69]. His victory further emboldened Roosevelt and his second term was marked by an increased assertiveness in foreign affairs.

## The Far East

In 1905, Roosevelt achieved a dramatic diplomatic success when he mediated an end to the Russo-Japanese War. Roosevelt's impatience and his impetuousness worked in his favor after he became personally involved in the negotiations between the warring powers. At the peace conference in Portsmouth, New Hampshire, Roosevelt sought to maintain a balance of power between the nations. Therefore, although Japan was clearly winning the war militarily, Roosevelt wanted to ensure that Russia would not be so weakened that it could not counterbalance Japan in the future. This would continue the policy begun under McKinley of maintaining a regional balance of power in Asia.

The Portsmouth Conference and its resultant peace treaty were critically important in validating Roosevelt's heightened global role. For his role in the negotiations, Roosevelt became the first American President to win the Nobel Peace Prize. The international recognition that Roosevelt gained, and the fact that he was highly effective, legitimized the President's internationalism in the eyes of the American public and especially in regards to the nation's political elites.

When Roosevelt's first secretary of State, John Hay, died in 1905, the President asked former Secretary of War, Elihu Root to replace him. While Hay had served as a bridge between nineteenth and twentieth century diplomacy, Root emerged as a prototype of the professional secretary of state that became common in the twentieth century. Root deftly negotiated an accord with Japan, the "gentlemen's agreement," in 1906 after San Francisco passed legislation which segregated Japanese students. In the accord, Japan agreed to stop emigration to California in exchange for a repeal of discriminatory laws in California. Roosevelt had to use political pressure to enforce the agreement in California [70]. Fortunately, the governor of California, James Gillett, was a Republican and Roosevelt was able to persuade him to pressure the state senate to block additional anti-immigrant legislation. The Democrats used the anti-immigrant sentiment in the 1906 congressional elections to some success [71].

The Gentleman's Agreement provides an example of a two-level game whereby Roosevelt and Root had to balance domestic and international issues. Roosevelt understood the domestic dangers of the agreement, but he was more concerned with the possibility of conflict with Japan. Therefore, he was willing to accept the domestic backlash and its consequences in return for the maintenance of relations with Japan [72]. Nonetheless, relations with Japan would continue to occupy a central role in Roosevelt's foreign policy throughout the remainder of his term. In May of 1907, there were anti-Japanese riots in San Francisco and tensions between the two nations surfaced again.

## Manifestations of the New Regime

In the meanwhile, Roosevelt quickly overcame the minor electoral losses in the 1906 midterm elections with another major foreign policy success. On November 9, 1906, Roosevelt set sail for Panama with his wife Edith to view the progress made thus far on construction of the canal. He became the first American president to travel outside of the continental United States while in office. The trip was an overwhelming triumph. The idea of Roosevelt traveling to inspect the nation's greatest engineering feat to date had widespread public appeal [73]. By breaking the unofficial taboo on presidential voyages, Roosevelt opened the door for future presidents to travel (including his successor, William Howard Taft who also visited Panama while in office). Upon his return to the United States, Roosevelt delivered a special message to Congress on the progress of the Canal, complete with pictures and movie footage. As such, Roosevelt changed one of the central norms surrounding presidents and their ability to conduct foreign policy.

Roosevelt's concern with Japan would be chiefly responsible for his decision to dispatch an American fleet on an around-the-world voyage. He saw this as an opportunity to demonstrate to the world the capability of the United States to deploy its fleet anywhere in the world. In his autobiography Roosevelt claimed that:

> In my judgement the most important service that I rendered to peace was the voyage of the battle fleet round the world. I had become convinced that for many reasons is was essential that we should have it clearly understood, by our own people especially, but also by other peoples, that the Pacific was as much our home waters as the Atlantic, and our fleet could and would at will pass from one to the other of the great oceans [74].

Specifically, Roosevelt saw the circumnavigation as means to demonstrate to the Japanese that the United States could deploy its forces to the Pacific quickly. The force, known as the "Great White Fleet," consisted of 16 battleships and dozens of escort vessels with a total of 18,000 sailors and marines. The fleet departed from Norfolk Naval Station in Hampton Roads, Virginia in 1907 and completed its excursion in 1909.

The Fleet's voyage was a resounding success, both strategically and in the realm of public opinion. The greatest obstacles the operation faced were domestic. Roosevelt found that Eugene Hale, the Chairman of the Senate Naval Affairs Committee, opposed the mission on grounds that it might antagonize or provoke the Japanese. Roosevelt declared that "I have almost as much trouble with our own people, like Senator Hale, who are always giving the impression to Japan that we are afraid of them, as with the other people, who insult the Japanese" [75]. However, the overwhelmingly domestic public approval of the voyage easily compensated for the limited disapproval of some in Congress or members of such groups as the Anti-Imperialist League [76].

# CONCLUSION

When the Great White Fleet returned to port, Roosevelt had already left office. He was followed by his hand-picked successor, William Howard Taft. While in office, Roosevelt greatly dramatically changed the nation's foreign policy regime. He emerged as the leader of a foreign policy elite that embraced new norms and values and attempted to alter the very basis of U.S. diplomacy and engagement in the world. Roosevelt also deftly utilized this new regime to manage a series of two-level games. From his actions in initiating construction of the Panama Canal to his balancing of foreign and domestic interests in regards to Japanese immigration, the President was able to maximize the political payoffs of these situations.

By the end of his tenure in office, the public and foreign policy elites had embraced the assertive foreign policy of Roosevelt. Under his leadership, a regime developed with its requisite institutions, including an expanded Navy and other military components necessary to oversee the nation's new territories and expanded role in Asia and Latin America. In addition, as a result of his use of the "bully-pulpit," the majority of the U.S. citizenry accepted the aggressive norms and ideals of Roosevelt. Under Roosevelt, the public accepted an enhanced role for the United States as the perceived "guardian" of the Western Hemisphere. As a consequence, public support for military interventions in the Caribbean remained strong into the Wilson presidency. In addition, Roosevelt's actions at the Portsmouth Conference and the Algeciras Conference served to legitimize the status of the United States as a world power and that of the American president as the equal of the heads of state of Europe. By traveling outside of the U.S., Roosevelt also helped to elevate foreign policy to a more equal plane with domestic policy. Underlining all of these policies was Roosevelt's sense of mission – his belief in what he termed the "strenuous life." This was an extension of the general belief in democratic universalism and would form the core of Wilson's progressive idealism.

Roosevelt's accomplishments and innovations in foreign policy had a long-lasting impact on the office of the presidency. First, Roosevelt successfully established the United States as major actor on the global stage. Building upon the military success of the United States in the Spanish American War, the new President projected American power in a highly visible fashion through actions such as the construction of the Panama Canal and the circumnavigation of the Great White Fleet. Second, Roosevelt used the "bully-pulpit" to garner public support for his assertive diplomacy and lead the effort to introduce the norms, rules and principles of a new foreign policy regime. In doing so, he adroitly managed the transition to a new regime and ensured its acceptance by the nation's contemporary political elites. Roosevelt became the first president to successfully combine the trends of exceptionalism and universalism as the long-term basis for his foreign policy. Roosevelt's new regime provided the foundation for the internationalist foreign policies of Roosevelt's successors, Taft and Wilson. Third, and finally, Roosevelt's personal involvement in foreign affairs foreshadowed the later summit diplomacy whereby presidents ranging from Franklin D. Roosevelt to Ronald Reagan personally negotiated international agreements or met with their counterparts to address global issues. Roosevelt's tenure marked the decline of the strong secretary of state and the corresponding dominance of the president in foreign policy (a change that was finalized under his nephew, Franklin and his successor, Harry S. Truman, and the post-World War II division of foreign and security policy as manifested by the creation of the office of National Security Advisor).

Nonetheless, while Roosevelt's policies centered around an expanded and aggressive role for the U.S. in world affairs, Taft's foreign policy would concentrate on economic issues. Taft would term his new diplomatic outlook "dollar diplomacy" and base foreign policy on the nation's economic interests in both Asia and Latin America [77] .Still, the new president would continue to use military force to protect business and commercial interests.

Conversely, it would be Wilson who took the greatest advantage of the foreign policy regime that had been established by Roosevelt. Yet, under Wilson, the nation also rejected the broad aims of democratic universalism which formed the basis of the regime and the expanded global role of the United States. The leader of the opposition to Wilson's view of a new global order based on the League of Nations was Henry Cabot Lodge who ironically helped form Roosevelt's new regime.

## REFERENCES

[1] Stephen Krasner, "Structural Causes and Regime Consequences: Regimes as Intervening Variables," in *International Regimes*, ed. Stephen Krasner (Ithaca: Cornell University,1983), 2.

[2] John Gerard Ruggie asserted that the new foreign policy regime which developed in the post-World War II era was the nation's "third try" at implementing a broad multilateral security order (the first was Woodrow Wilson's post-World War I effort and the second was Franklin Roosevelt's endeavor to bring together the "four horsemen," the U.S., Great Britain, Russia and China, to establish a collective security regime through the United Nations); see John Gerard Ruggie, "Third Try at World Order," *Political Science Quarterly*, 109, no. 4 (Fall 1994): 553-70.

[3] Karen Orren and Stephen Skowronek, "Regimes and Regime Building in American Government," *Political Science Quarterly*, 113, no. 4 (Winter 1999), 694.

[4] Andrew Farkas, "The Evolution of International Norms," *International Studies Quarterly* 40, no. 3 (September, 1996): 362.

[5] Andrew P. Cortell and James W. Davis, Jr., "How Do International Institutions Matter? The Domestic Impact of International Rules and Norms," *International Studies Quarterly* 40, no. 4 (December 1996): 452.

[6] Robert Herman, "Identity, Norms, and National Security," in Peter J. Katzenstein, ed. *The Culture of National Security: Norms and Identity in World Politics* (New York: Columbia University, 1996), 274.

[7] Thomas Risse-Kappen, "Collective Identity in a Democratic Community," in Katzenstein, 366-67.

[8] Gregory A. Raymond, "Problems and Prospects in the Study of International Norms," *Mershon International Studies Review* 41, no. 2 (November 1997): 214.

[9] On the Root-Takahira Agreement, see Robert Bacon and James Brown Scott, *The Military and Colonial Policy of the United States, Addresses and Reports by Elihu Root* (Cambridge: Harvard, 1916).

[10] As an example, norms can determine prearranged courses of action for transgressions of international agreements: if state A violates agreement B, then the other signatories to B pledge that C course of action will result.

[11] These treaties provide mechanisms that prompt multilateral action against violators of the norms, as well as encourage compliance through incentive programs. U.S., Department of Defense, *Weapons of Mass Destruction: Reducing the Threat From the Former Soviet Union*, NSIAD-95-7 (Washington, D.C.: GAO, 1995); U.S., House of Representatives, C. Bruce Tarter, testimony, "Stemming the Proliferation of Nuclear

Weapons and Other Weapons of Mass Destruction," *The Department of Energy's Budget Request for FY 1996: Hearing of the Subcommittee on Military Procurement* (Washington, D.C.: GPO, 1995), 1.

[12] As an example, the Tokyo round of the GATT negotiations in the mid-1980s, linked trade and monetary policy in such a way as encourage exports to the United States following a decision by the Reagan administration to weaken the dollar; Charles Pearson and Nils Johnson, *The New GATT Trade Round,* FPI Case Studies, no. 2 (Washington, D.C.: Johns Hopkins, 1986), 22-23.

[13] For examples of this type of behavior see Axelrod and Keohane.

[14] Krasner, 2.

[15] Hedley Bull, The Anarchical Society: A Study of Order in World Politics (New York: Columbia University, 1977), 56.

[16] Ibid; 56-7.

[17] Charles A. Kupchan, "The Case for Collective Security," in *Collective Security Beyond the Cold War*, ed. George W. Downs (Ann Arbor: University of Michigan, 1994), 48.

[18] Andreas Hansenclever, Peter Mayer, and Volker Rittberger, "Interests, Power, Knowledge: The Study of International Regimes," *Mershon International Studies Review* 40, no. 2 (October 1996): 179.

[19] Robert O. Keohane combines principles, norms and rules into a single category with his definition of international regimes: "institutions with explicit rules, agreed upon by governments, that pertain to particular sets of issues in international relations;" Robert O. Keohane, "Neoliberal Institutionalism: A Perspective on World Politics," in *International Institutions and State Power: Essays in International Relations Theory*, ed. Robert O. Keohane (Boulder: Westview, 1989), 4. However, Keohane's narrow definition has been subject to much criticism, especially over its inability to account for the relationships between the factors within a regime.

[20] In addition, this regime has allowed for non-security expansion, or economic augmentation, for nation-states, which has ameliorated the security dilemma, and hence prevented security rivalries by channeling economic competition through regime norms; Randall L. Schweller, "Neorealism's Status-Quo Bias: What Security Dilemma?" *Security Studies*, Special Issue, Realism: Restatements and Renewal, 5, no. 3 (Spring 1996): 92.

[21] Robert O. Keohane, Peter Haas, and Marc Levy, eds., Institutions for the Earth: Sources of Effective International Environmental Protection (Cambridge: MIT, 1993), 4-5.

[22] Mark P. Logan, "Elite Analysis of Democracies' International Policy," *Perspectives on Political Science*, 29, no. 1 (Winter 2000), 5.

[23] Richard Herrara, "Understanding the Language of Politics: A Study of Elites and Masses," *Political Science Quarterly* 111, no. 4 (Winter 1997), 620.

[24] V.O. Key, *Public Opinion and American Democracy* (New York: Alfred Knopf, 1961); quoted in Herrara, 620.

[25] An example of such "bypassing" occurred during the negotiations which ended Apartheid in South Africa; Jeffrey Herbst, "Prospects for Elite-Driven Democracy in South Africa," *Political Science Quarterly* 112, no. 4 (Winter 1998), 614.

[26] Juan D. Lindau contends that the ruling political elite in Mexico provides an example of this trend where the distinction between the political elite and technocrats has been

blurred to the point of indistinguishability; Juan D. Lindau, "Technocrats and Mexico's Political Elite," *Political Science Quarterly* 111, no. 2 (Summer 1996): 295-322.

[27] Orren and Skowronek, 694.

[28] Jeffrey W. Legro, "Whence American Internationalism," *International Organizations* 54, no. 2 (Spring 2000), 254.

[29] Ibid.

[30] See Peter J. Katzenstein, ed., Between Power and Plenty: Foreign Economic Policy and Advanced Industrial States (Madison: University of Wisconsin, 1978), 4.

[31] David Baldwin, *Economic Statecraft* (Princeton: Princeton University, 1985), 29-50

[32] Putnam, "Two-Level Games," 434.

[33] Paul A. Papayoanou, "Economic Interdependence and the Balance of Power," *International Studies Quarterly* 41, no. 1 (March 1997): 117.

[34] Putnam, "Two-Level Games," 436.

[35] Theodore C. Sorenson, " Foreign Policy in a Presidential Democracy," *Political Science Quarterly* 109, no. 3 (Special Issue, 1994), 521.

[36] Ibid.

[37] Quoted in Frederick Merk, Manifest Destiny and Mission in American History: A Reinterpretation (New York: Vintage, 1963), 31-2.

[38] This theme forms the core of Frederick Merk's seminal work, see ibid. Also see Norman Graebner, ed., *Manifest Destiny* (Indianapolis: Bobbs Merrill, 1963) or William Earl Weeks, *Building the Continental Empire: American Expansion from the Revolution to the Civil War* (Chicago: Ivan R. Dee, 1996).

[39] James Oliver Robertson underscores the importance of national myths when he states: "no human society is a rational construct. All societies depend for their continuation, for their very existence, on common assumptions, common forms of communication , common referents for thoughts and ideas, common patterns of behavior and ritual , and a common inheritance;" James Oliver Robertson, *American Myth, American Reality* (New York: Hill and Wang, 1980), 17.

[40] The quote from Washington's Farewell Address served as a constant reminder to successive administrations to shun political or military ties to foreign nations. However, bilateral and multilateral economic treaties were common during the nineteenth century. The Monroe Doctrine pledged American non-interference in European affairs in exchange for European non-interference in the Western Hemisphere (including no new colonization).

[41] Michael Dunne, "US Foreign Relations in the Twentieth Century: From World Power to Global Hegemony," *International Affairs* 76, no. 1 (January 2000), 27.

[42] Examples of public endorsement for such assertive policies in the Western Hemisphere included expansion into the Mexican territories and support for the purchase of Cuba.

[43] This indifference was the result of the tendency for Americans to became self-absorbed in their own lives and localities, leaving little time to pay attention to world events; Gabriel Almond, *The American People and Foreign Policy* (New York: Praeger, 1960), 53, 76. Conversely, reflecting traditional Marxist analyses, Richard Barnet contends that the 'manipulation" of American public opinion on foreign policy matters is the result of broad efforts by political and economic elites to ensure access to, and often control of, overseas markets; Richard Barnet, *The Roots of War* (New York: Atheneum, 1972).

[44] Robertson asserts that the basis for the notion of American exceptionalism was rooted in the broader myths that undergirded the society; see Robertson, 12-18.

[45] While the idea of American exceptionalism is a long-standing component of U.S. foreign policy, the authors conclude that there is a disconnect between the political rhetoric of elites and the actual implementation of foreign policy. In other words, elites use the idea of exceptionalism as a means to justify actions or to garner public support; Joseph Lepgold and Timothy McKeown, "Is American Foreign Policy Exceptional? An Empirical Analysis," *Political Science Quarterly*, vol. 110, 3 (Fall 1995), 369.

[46] Richard J. Kerry, *The Star-Spangled Mirror: America's Image of Itself and the World* (Savage, Maryland: Rowman & Littlefield, 1990), 3.

[47] Ibid.

[48] Following this line of reasoning, manifest destiny was rooted in the drive to spread American political and economic values throughout the continent, not in the simple drive for territory. Once the "Americanization" of the continent was fairly secure, ideological forces drove the nation to endeavor to spread these same values throughout Asia and the Caribbean; see Michael H. Hunt, *Ideology and U.S. Foreign Policy* (New Haven: Yale, 1987).

[49] Rosenberg contends that political elites in the United States used the rhetoric of peace, prosperity, and democracy as a means to satisfy domestic audiences while the nation pursued an expansionist foreign policy designed to Americanize the world. Liberal developmentalism was based on five principles: 1) the belief that other nations could copy the development patterns of the U.S.; 2) the promotion of free enterprise; 3) championing global free trade and open markets; 4) staunch support for the free flow of information (including an open and free media); and 5) an "acceptance" of government actions to protect and promote American business interests; Emily S. Rosenberg, *Spreading the American Dream: American Economic and Cultural Expansion, 1890-1945* (New York: Hill and Wang, 1982).

[50] The boundary controversy centered on a dispute between Venezuela and the British Colony of Guiana over a border area where gold had been discovered. Olney threatened to use military force against the British if they intervened in the region. British diplomatic isolation during the Great Anglo-Boer War led London to seek accommodation with the U.S. and the dispute was ultimately settled through arbitration (Great Britain was granted most of the region). The dispute also led to a general arbitration treaty between the two nations over future territorial disagreements, the Olney-Pauncefote Convention which was signed in January of 1897.

[51] David M. Pletcher, The Diplomacy of Trade and Investment: American Economic Expansion in the Hemisphere, 1865-1900 (Columbia: University of Missouri, 1998), 2-3.

[52] Dunne, 26.

[53] On this theme, see Richard W. Van Alstyne, *The Rising American Empire* (New York: Blackwell and Mott, 1960).

[54] Anti-Imperialist League, *League Platform 1899*; reprinted in Constance Jones, Derris L. Raper, and John J. Sbrega, eds., *The American Experience: Documents and Notes*, 2nd ed., (Dubuque, Iowa : Kendall/Hunt Pub. Co., 1987), 160.

[55] Theodore Roosevelt, "Review," *Atlantic Monthly* (October 1890); quoted in H. W. Brands, *TR: The Last Romantic* (New York: Basic Books, 1997), 238.

[56] Edmund Morris, *The Rise of Theodore Roosevelt* (New York: Coward, McCann & Geoghegan, 1979), 568.

[57] Theodore Roosevelt, *Theodore Roosevelt: An Autobiography* (New York: Scribner's, 1913); reprinted by New York: De Capo Press, 1985, 213.

[58] Roosevelt's heroics during the Spanish-American War led to his promotion to colonel and the recommendation that he be awarded the Medal of Honor for his actions in the capture of San Juan Hill. He returned to the United States as one fo the most popular heroes of the conflict.

[59] Dunne, 20; as an example of contemporary observations, Dunne cites John B. Henderson, Jr., *American Diplomatic Questions* (New York: Macmillan, 1901).

[60] Roosevelt, 366.

[61] During the summer of 1900, an anti-foreign society, the Boxers, rose-up in open revolt against the foreign powers. In response, the major international powers sent troops into China. McKinley dispatched 5,000 American soldiers. Secretary of State Hay used the presence of these forces as a bargaining tool to ensure acceptance of the second set of Open Door Notes. The deployment demonstrated the military capability of the United States and its ability to dispatch troops quickly to areas of the Pacific.

[62] Theodore Roosevelt, *Annual Message to Congress*, December 3, 190; in Theodore Roosevelt, *The Works of Theodore Roosevelt*, vol. 17, Hermann Hagedorn, ed., (New York: Scribner's, 1926) 93-160.

[63] Ibid.

[64] Roosevelt, *Autobiography*, 533.

[65] "Roosevelt Corollary" in Ruhl J. Bartlett, ed., *The Record of American Diplomacy*, 4th ed. (New York), 539.

[66] Roosevelt was so pleased with Hitt's support for his policies, that he endeavored to have the Illinois Congressman placed on the ballot as vice-president in 1904. However, the nomination went to Republican insider Senator Charles Fairbanks of Indiana.

[67] James R. Reckner, " TR and his Navy," *Naval History* 15, no. 1 (February 2001), 41.

[68] Theodore Roosevelt to G. Meyer, April 12, 1901, quoted in Brands, 465.

[69] In the election, Roosevelt received 7,628,461 popular votes and 336 electoral votes. His opponent, Democrat Alton B. Parker, received 5,084,223 popular votes and 140 electoral votes.

[70] For instance, Roosevelt brought the mayor and school board of San Francisco to Washington to personally lobby them to accept the agreement.

[71] In the 1906 Congressional elections, the Democrats increased their number of seats in the House from 136 to 164 while the Republican numbers decreased from 250 to 222. However, Roosevelt's Party gained 3 seats in the Senate (moving from 58 to 61 while the Democrats declined from 32 to 29 seats).

[72] For a good overview of the balancing act between domestic and international concerns, see Brands, 578-83.

[73] In the seminal work on the construction of the Canal, David McCullough's *The Path Between the Seas*, the author points out that even conservative newspapers such as the Washington *Star* endorsed the trip; David McCullough, *The Path Between the Seas: The Creation of the Panama Canal, 1870-1914* (New York: Simon & Schuster, 1977), 492.

[74] Roosevelt, *Autobiography*, 563.

[75] Theodore Roosevelt to Andrew Carnegie, July 15, 1907; quoted in Brands, 609.

[76] Opposition also came from groups who were afraid that the nation would not be able to respond to a crisis if the fleet was on the other side of the world.

[77] For an overview of the divergent development of Taft's foreign policy beliefs, see Ralph Eldin Minger, *William Howard Taft and United States Foreign Policy: The Apprenticeship Years, 1900-1908* (Chicago: University of Illinois Press, 1975).

In: Presidents and War
Editors: A. Eksterowicz and G. Hastedt, pp. 141-152
ISBN 978-1-61668-917-9


*Chapter 9*

# THE WILSON PRESIDENCY, THE U.S. NAVY, AND HOMELAND DEFENSE

***George H. Quester***

## INTRODUCTION

In the aftermath of the terrorist attacks on the World Trade Center and the Pentagon on September 11, 2001, some analysts have proclaimed the United States as now entering upon an entirely new situation in foreign and defense problems, with the American homeland seen as being under direct physical attack for the first time. By such an interpretation, the implications for the presidency, and for the United States Navy, would be basically unprecedented, with the future of American policy thus becoming enormously difficult to predict, as "homeland defense" suddenly has become a centerpiece of American military policy. This article will argue that there are indeed some close analogs and precedents in the past evolution of American foreign policy, and in the debates on whether the United States should invest in a powerful navy, illustrated quite well in the American 1917 entry into World War I, preceded by a 1916 decision to build "a navy second to none" [1]. "Homeland defense," – a defense against the threats that came in from the seas – thus was related quite closely to decisions about a navy, and therefore may have been a driving force in American policy decisions for a longer time than is generally appreciated.

The largest explosion to rock Manhattan before the 2001 attack on the World Trade Center occurred just across the Hudson River in New Jersey on July 30, 1916, at a dock stockpiled with munitions to be shipped to Britain and France. The dock, which was not very far from the Statue of Liberty, bore the name of "Black Tom" [2.] The explosion was the result of sabotage instigated by agents of the German Imperial Embassy, at a time when the United States was still neutral in World War I but was engaged in exporting substantial shipments of munitions to the Entente (Americans being unable, because of the British maritime blockade, to make any parallel sales to Germany and its allies).

These German sabotage attacks, parallel to the German submarine attacks on ships going to Britain and France, might have been portrayed as a simple attempt to deny munitions to an enemy, a legitimate target in war. Alternatively, such attacks could have been characterized as attempts to impose enough hardship on the British to erode their resolve for the war, or similarly, to impose hardship on the American homeland and on things Americans hold dear, so as to reduce American willingness to sell Britain what it needed.

The sabotaging of munitions plants and shipment points within the United States was, by any definition, an attack on the American homeland. But the sinking of merchant and passenger ships on the high seas also had been such an attack, by the way that Americans all along have seen the high seas. The United States since its inception has been a maritime nation and a trading nation, regarding "freedom of the seas" as almost as important as the physical security of its ground at home, with the War of 1812 having been a classical illustration of this principle [3].

Just as with the 9/11 attacks on New York and Washington, the German campaigns of 1914 to 1917 thus could have been calculated as perhaps seeking to intimidate Americans to induce them to cease supporting any causes in the outside world. The shock of Americans at such threats to what they hold dear, on shore and on the seas, undoubtedly was quite significant. Yet the Germans surely faced the risk (just as did Osama bin Laden) that such an attack, rather than intimidating and deterring Americans, would enrage them and cause them to launch a military counter-attack [4].

Submarine warfare, and terrorism on-shore, thus definitely amounted to the crucial factors in leading the United States to declare war on Germany in 1917, settling the outcome of the war in 1918 when Germany had to sue for peace. Yet the American decision in the same years to build "a navy second to none," a navy of big battleships rather than smaller anti-submarine warfare vessels, was related to an even broader American tradition of concern for homeland security, a tradition of concern that merely matured during World War I, with overtones that might often have been as much anti-British as anti-German. This article will review the interaction of presidential leadership, naval power, and homeland security as it evolved before and during World War I, tying this evolution to earlier American fears and traumas, and then relating it to today's concerns about "homeland defense."

## Before Sarajevo

The major thrust of the argument here is that Americans have felt concerns about the physical security of their homeland all through their history. It is simply not true to say that America has never had to fear what the Europeans so often experienced – the threat of foreign invasion. In 1814, the British occupied the American national capital, Washington, D.C., burning the White House and the Capitol building, and then laid siege to Baltimore [5]. The successful defense of Baltimore against the British amphibious force is hardly erased from the American collective memory (although American students are notorious for how little history or geography they are taught), for this defense is commemorated in our national anthem, the Star-Spangled Banner.

The United States, throughout the Nineteenth Century, did not try to match the power of the British fleet, but this was hardly because Americans regarded the British as their natural friends and cousins, with the seas being no source of threat so long as the Royal Navy dominated them. Rather, the explanation for the lack of American investment in a navy was that the task of matching and beating the British always looked too daunting. After Trafalgar in 1805, the British Navy was larger than all the other navies of the world combined, and the British, right up to World War I, proclaimed a national policy of having a navy larger than the next two fleets combined.

To try to match the British, when they were so far ahead, would have been a most difficult task; to try to challenge Pax Britannia would have been to provoke a serious political and military conflict with the British, with the risk of a British preemptive attack. The British Navy, in its analyses of the possibility of the growth of any hostile foreign navy, used to refer to "Copenhagening" such an upstart, referring back to Nelson's preemptive destruction of the Danish Navy when the risk had emerged of this force being put at the disposal of Napoleon [6]. Indeed, the same British rocket-launching sailing ships that had set fire to Copenhagen had been brought across the Atlantic and up the Chesapeake for the attack on Baltimore.

The vulnerability of American port cities to a British or other naval attack was thus a continuing part of the scene until the end of the Nineteenth Century. If one is asked to explain what worked to deter an American invasion of Canada through these decades, when the Canadians were still often portrayed in American 4$^{th}$ of July speeches as being held against their will under British colonial rule, it was hardly the presence of any substantial ground forces north of the 49$^{th}$ parallel. In the calculations of the British government, the reliable deterrent was instead what the Royal Navy could do to American high seas commerce and to American port cities [7]. During the 1898 Spanish-American War, great concern similarly was voiced along the Atlantic seaboard about what the Spanish fleet might do to these cities [8]. If the Royal Navy's capability for attacking American commerce and coastal cities might thus have been seen as the deterrent to an American invasion of Canada, the American ability to invade Canada might similarly have served as the reassuring deterrent against any particularly arrogant use of British naval power. Until the last decade of the Nineteenth Century, the United States thus largely had no choice but to live with this continuing threat to the safety of the homeland, the threat embodied in the "rocket's red glare."

But there were three important changes in this picture after 1890. First, in what is often seen as the basic sign of an American shift from isolation to playing a major global role (a shift then to be reversed again in the 1919 rejection of the League of Nations), the United States began building a major navy. Second, in the same decades, the president's leadership role and visibility increased dramatically. Woodrow Wilson had made his original reputation by publishing *Congressional Government*, [9] a book decrying the weakness of the presidency compared to the chairmen of the key committees of the Congress, but we all remember assertive presidents like Theodore Roosevelt and Wilson himself much more vividly than the presidents who had followed Abraham Lincoln in the latter half of the Nineteenth Century. A third factor of change, more than a little paradoxically, was that relations between Britain and the United States basically improved, in part because Americans came to realize that Canada was not being held under British rule against its will (it helped when Canada finally established its own Embassy in the United States, rather than having its affairs handled by a section of the British Embassy). The British, seeing their naval hegemony challenged by Germany, Japan, the United States and other powers, were forced to try to make friends with some of these potential adversaries, and in effect chose to appease Tokyo and Washington rather than Berlin.

The United States' decision to begin building a powerful navy after 1890 is often credited to the influence of the great book *The Influence of Sea Power on History*, published that year by Captain Alfred Thayer Mahan [10]. This American shift toward a naval role has been alternatively depicted by radical or "revisionist" historians such as Walter Lafeber [11] as reflecting the closing of the American western frontier, which might have served as a safety-valve earlier for periodic bouts of unemployment. By an analysis that has been very appealing to Marxists and other radical critics of American foreign policy in general, the defects of capitalism thus required a shift to imperialism, and the growth of the U.S. Navy therefore could be explained by domestic factors rather than by international threats.

The argument in this article instead focuses on the perceived international threats to the security of the American homeland, as stressed by Mahan, rather than on any defects of capitalism. The United States for all its history had sensed such threats coming from the sea. And the timing here might relate not simply to the influence of a particular book or to the closing of the western frontier, but to a major change in the technology of naval warfare, a change that would begin an entirely new round of the naval competition. After 1890, after the shift to steam-propulsion and steel warships rather than wooden fighting ships of sail, the United States, like such other powers as Japan, France and Germany, was finally in a position where it could challenge the British monopoly at sea rather than simply having to accept it.

Frank Klingberg published an analysis in 1952 [12] of the ins and outs of American involvement in foreign policy that argued that the United States had continually oscillated back and forth over its history, in a pattern in which the outward swings averaged 27 years in length, while the inward swings averaged 21:

| "Introvert" | "Extrovert" |
|---|---|
| 1776-1798 | 1798-1824 |
| 1824-1844 | 1844-1871 |
| 1871-1891 | 1891-1918 |
| 1918-1940 | 1940- |

Klingberg's analysis was based on many factors, including the number of references to foreign threats and foreign affairs in congressional debates and presidential speeches, and the appropriations voted for support of the U.S. Navy. (One enormously engaging feature of Klingberg's analysis is that it seemingly, some 15 years in advance, predicted the date of America's retreat from Vietnam, exemplified in Lyndon Johnson's decision to not to seek reelection in 1968.)

By Klingberg's analysis, the years from 1891 to 1918 were thus a period of extroversion for American foreign policy, as the United States began building a serious navy, fought a war with Spain, became engaged in a round of imperialism with the acquisition of the Philippines, Guam, and Hawaii, and possessions in the Caribbean, and then got drawn into World War I, with this phase being terminated by the American rejection after 1919 of President Wilson's League of Nations.

But the years from 1891 to 1918 were not quite such a steady period of American investment in a very active defense of the homeland. While President Theodore Roosevelt favored a larger navy, [13] his successor William Howard Taft was not nearly as supportive of such expenditures, and Woodrow Wilson came into office similarly leaning against naval growth, and even hoping that foreign policy would not occupy a major portion of his presidency. The threat of foreign attack on the American homeland could always be envisaged, but it was no surprise that there were interior portions of the United States that felt much more secure against such threats, and hence disinclined to spend tax moneys on warding them off. And, even along the exposed coasts, the argument could be made that one did not have to immediately respond to a foreign *capability* for attack if one did not see any immediate *inclination* to attack.

It is thus paradoxical indeed that the American post-1890 decision to begin challenging the British monopoly of high seas power came at a time when relations between the two English-speaking powers were generally improving rather than worsening. American congressmen after 1900 no longer gave speeches looking forward to the amalgamation of Canada into the United States. Yet the improvement in relations was hardly yet so pronounced that Americans would forget the War of 1812 and the issue of freedom of the seas. When the United States, together with the other smaller maritime states, had pressed Britain to renounce the interruption of high seas commerce in future wars, the British government had done so only very reluctantly, and London reneged on such commitments when World War I broke out [14].

In the years leading up to World War I, Americans thus were not freed of their inherent fears of what could be inflicted on their homeland from the seas. Almost as importantly, Americans' fears of what could be inflicted on their commerce out on those seas also endured. As American presidents were to become more prominent in the making of domestic policy, they were called upon to assert a greater leadership role in addressing these threats.

## Varying Perspectives

As always with any issue of foreign policy, Americans would differ in how they saw the threat to the homeland. One can sketch out at least four dimensions of such differences of evaluation.

One classic interpretation pits the coastal regions of the United States against the inherently more "isolationist" interior [15]. The residents of the Midwest would not feel the pain of naval bombardment nearly as directly as the people in New York or Baltimore, and hence would be much more likely to scoff at the need for American investment in a navy. Here we might find a significant difference from today's reactions to the new terrorist attacks, since tall buildings in Chicago are just as vulnerable to a 9/11 type of attack as those in New York. Even earlier, during the Cold War, the United States Air Force expended a major effort on getting Americans to refer to polar-projection maps of the world, rather than Mercator projection maps, with the message being that, in an age of intercontinental-range bombers and missiles, the interior of the United States shared the perils of the coasts. Concerns about what a terrorist group might do with an atomic bomb or with biological weapons thus are not to be limited to the coasts. Yet the maritime focus of American concerns looms up again when one realizes that perhaps the easiest approach for a terrorist attack will come now by means of the freight containers carried aboard a modern container-ship, or by a cruise-missile fired from some tramp steamer, with the U.S. Coast Guard and U.S. Navy having to be quite concerned about how such an attacker could be spotted in advance and intercepted.

A second kind of issue related to partisan politics, for the notion of bipartisan foreign policy had not yet won general acceptance in the United States, and indeed was not to settle in until the eve of World War II. If a Republican president favored naval appropriations,

Republicans in Congress might be generally inclined to support their president, in hopes of strengthening their appeal for the next election. Democrats, however, might be just as tempted to snipe at such proposals, with a view to similarly laying the groundwork for the next election. And the same might hold true in reverse when a Democrat was president. One can find examples of Democrats disagreeing with Democratic presidents in one direction or another on naval spending, and Republicans disagreeing with Republican presidents, because of the regional differences cited above, or analytical differences. But there was always also an argument for parties hanging together on this issue, as on any other issue in politics when the substantive disagreements on the issue were not too great, because of the inherent importance of winning over the voters.

Third, the issues of protecting against foreign attacks on the homeland relate more broadly to the strength of the national government vs. the states, and the strength of the presidency vs. the Congress. There were thus always members of Congress who saw any move towards greater military preparedness as a threat to their own share of decision-making power, or to American liberty in general, as "militarism" and "navalism" were the diseases of the Prussians and the British and to be avoided for the United States if at all possible [16]. If a stronger navy and a stronger military were to tend to coincide with a stronger presidency, under either Theodore Roosevelt's or Woodrow Wilson's versions of "progressivism," there would be opposition to such preparations on very basic domestic and constitutional grounds.

A fourth and final major argument about the perennial naval threat related to the analysis of the motivation of foreign powers, and of the basic nature of the international system. If one assumed that relations with Britain were improving, or that a balance-of-power on the high seas would keep foreign navies tied up in confronting each other, so that they would have no time to attack the American coasts, did one really have to build up a large U.S. Navy? [17]

Alfred Thayer Mahan's case for American naval growth went well beyond traditional American concerns for the safety of the homeland and the sanctity of commerce. His argument was that historical experience showed that the United States needed to expand if it were not to decline – that imperialism and a very extended naval presence, out and away from the American mainland, were now the natural course of things. In the age of sail, which Mahan so vividly recounted, Britain's naval superiority around Europe had led to its being paramount everywhere around the globe, for the wind-driven warships of the Royal Navy were virtually unlimited in range.

Yet the introduction of steam-propelled steel warships had not merely opened up a new round of naval competition, in which every power in effect had to begin again from scratch. Such ships would be tied much more closely to their coaling stations, with the result that each navy might now have a local preponderance in its own waters close to home base, with no navy any more able to achieve a global preponderance. An analytical disagreement thus was opened here about whether it was necessary for the United States to be so very much concerned about the German or French Navy ever coming across the Atlantic in force. How much American naval investment was now really needed, even if one could not count on the good intentions of other powers?

In Mahan's analysis, however, each separate naval power would not be so secure in its home waters because of the need for coaling stations, for he still saw the possibilities of a grand naval hegemony, just as in the days of sail, by which one battle fleet or another would come to dominate the seas. By Mahan's analysis, an analysis very appealing to Theodore Roosevelt, [18] America might have to establish such coaling stations and advance naval bases around the globe, as America might face an inherent choice of dominating or being dominated.

Here differences of analysis about *American* values and motivation would play a most central role. Woodrow Wilson, however much he favored a strong presidency and a strong and active federal government, did not come into office intent on playing and winning some game of global naval power politics [19]. Wilson's instincts were more in line with the American traditions of defending America itself; beyond this, they would turn to reforming the international system so that wars would be eliminated.

## THE ONSET OF WORLD WAR I

The year 1914 would have been an appropriate year for Americans to celebrate an entire century passing since the last foreign invasion of their homeland, 100 years since the British occupation and burning of Washington. Yet, this was more importantly the year of the outbreak of World War I, inducing at least two new rounds of feeling of homeland vulnerability. Americans had always felt a certain kind of such vulnerability, as already noted, simply because of their commitment to trade on the high seas. The exposure of coastal cities to attack from these seas was a more directly "homeland" threat. But international trade increasingly had occasioned foreign nationals to reside within the United States, selling their own goods and buying those made by Americans – and perhaps carrying a military threat into the homeland.

As the war began, British warships intercepted American ships trying to go to Germany, followed by a German use of submarines to sink ships going to Britain. The first kind of action, very reminiscent of 1812, damaged the material interests of the United States, while the second took a toll as well of human life, but both caused indignation among Americans, and great frustration about how best to respond. Particularly shocking was the sinking of huge passenger liner *Lusitania* early in 1915, with almost 1,200 passengers losing their lives, including some 128 Americans [20]. The Germans could claim, with some justice, that the *Lusitania* was carrying British munitions, but Americans would see such a submarine attack as much worse than a simple counter-military act of war.

As the ground war in Europe settled into an ongoing stalemate, American manufacturers of munitions sold larger and larger quantities of weapons to the British and French, while being kept by the intervening British naval blockade from doing the same for the Germans. Americans then experienced the closer-in threat to the homeland in a round of sabotage fomented by the German and Austrian embassies, with the most dramatic example of this being the Black Tom explosion just across the river from Manhattan. Exemplifying what Americans have had to fear since the Anthrax attack late in 2001, German agents also utilized a form of biological warfare in this sabotage campaign, seeking to infect American horses destined for the British or French cavalry with a disease called "glanders" [21] .The German Embassy always disclaimed responsibility for any of this sabotage, and some of the actual agents involved could have been Irish opponents of British imperialism, or anarchist or Bolshevik opponents of the capitalist system, simply encouraged by the German or Austro-Hungarian Embassies, with the ultimate guilt being difficult to prove. The question of assigning responsibility for terrorist attacks, so much a part of the scene in 2001, was thus similarly a part of the American problem here.

The earliest pro-Allied propaganda in 1914 had conjured up visions of a German victory in Europe bringing the German Navy to attack American shores. While this version of the future could easily be dismissed, as it was likely that the German fleet would be very much weakened even if it ever could win a naval battle with the British, the generic prospect of battleships attacking American ports had never been as easy to dismiss, and this was to account for some of the American policy that ensued.

British surface warships interfered with American commerce more than did any German surface warships, but the German U-boat response conjured up a new threat, amid rumors, both before and after the United States entered the war, that German agents were flashing signals from locations on the American shores out to waiting U-boats. Even if no such light signals were ever flashed, German U-boats did several times sink British merchant ships just outside the American three-mile limit, and German agents surely did engage in sabotage. An attack on the American homeland (broadly or narrowly defined) seemed underway, amid American suspicions of hostile agents that had slipped into the country.

If the German plan in launching the sabotage and submarine attacks had been to frighten the United States out of selling war material to the British and French, Berlin was to be very much disappointed. The end result was to bring the United States to declare war on Germany in April of 1917, and then to send a substantial force of ground soldiers to France – soldiers who staved off a German breakthrough in the summer of 1918 and then sealed the German defeat by fall of that year [22].

Terrorist attacks on a homeland are typically part of an endurance contest, as the attacker is betting that the victim will not be able to bear the suffering imposed, and will choose to back away from the conflict. One can recount a long series of instances in which a foreign adversary has underestimated the willingness of the American government or people to endure such a confrontation of wills, with the German miscalculations in World War I being matched later by the Japanese expectations of what they might achieve at Pearl Harbor, and Josef Stalin's expectations about Korea, Mikhail Gorbachev's assumptions about Afghanistan, Saddam Hussein's suppositions about Kuwait, and Osama bin Laden's 2001 assumptions about post-Cold War America. Democracies may be bad at advertising clearly enough in advance their willingness to persist in endurance contests and games of "chicken," and the United States may be particularly bad at this. But the historical experience is that Americans in general (the Vietnam War perhaps being a major exception) have indeed been willing to hang on through the pain of an endurance contest, and the foreign adversaries contemplating new rounds of terrorist attacks would do well to take note of this.

For the entire period of American neutrality in World War I, President Wilson was regularly accused of being too timid and weak by his Republican opponents, in particular by former President Theodore Roosevelt. Wilson's detractors accused him of advertising an aversion to war, which thereby invited the assaults of the bullies of the world, including the German attacks on things Americans held dear. When the United States at length opted to enter the war, the manner in which it did so was nonetheless somewhat paradoxical, illustrating some of the particular feelings and values of President Wilson (as contrasted sharply with those of Theodore Roosevelt) and demonstrating a basically defensive concern about the safety of the American homeland and extended rights at sea.

Woodrow Wilson had come into office opposed to large investments in the U.S. military, unconvinced of the imperialist argument that a country like the United States had no choice except to grow if it were not to decline. Wilson's view, very much reinforced by the specter of World War I as it became prolonged, was that war was a disaster for mankind, something to be avoided. Over time this conviction became Wilson's commitment to a League of Nations, to a collective security system that would make war much less likely by directing punishment at any power that initiated war. The United States, under Woodrow Wilson, thus was to enter World War I not as one of the Allies, a member of the Entente, but as an "associated power" pursuing its own agenda [23].

Theodore Roosevelt would have had the United States behaving like any other power, pursuing its own national interest. Woodrow Wilson saw the United States as behaving as a more noble and beneficent power, serving global interests. Protecting America itself against attack had always had priority, of course, but beyond that, the goals of America's participation in World War I were to be nobler than mere American imperialism.

Consistent with this world view, and with all the older concerns about American homeland security and the security of American shipping on the high seas, Wilson, a year before asking for a declaration of war against Germany, had asked the Congress to lay down a naval building program for "a navy second to none." With an emphasis on capital ships, on dreadnought battleships, this could be seen as directed against some possible German threats (if Germany ever decisively won something like the Battle of Jutland), but it just as easily could be perceived to be directed against the British, and against the generic threat of damage to America that always had come from the sea. The new U.S. battleships being built were hardly required for immediate reinforcement of any British fighting force facing off against the Germans. Neglected in this building program were the anti-submarine vessels that were to be much more specifically appropriate to countering the kind of naval warfare Germany was waging [24].

In 1916, therefore, the United States was definitely more sympathetic to Britain and the rest of the Entente than to Germany and the Central Powers. But, as late as 1916, the United States was advertising its resentment of what *all* the warring powers had been doing to damage important American interests – a resentment of the British blockade alongside its resentment of the German U-boat campaign and sabotage, and a resentment of the folly of war itself, in which the stubbornness in Berlin and Vienna seemed matched by that in London and Paris.

The American decisions of 1916 and 1917 thus reflected much more than a commitment to the side of Britain and France in the war. The kinds of warships procured for the U.S. Navy (in a program that President Wilson in fact decided to continue after the German surrender, and which was not to be cut back until the Washington Naval Disarmament Conference convened by President Harding in 1921) were in fact functionally more of a challenge to Britain and British "navalism" than to Germany [25]. The new fleet was an investment in more generic "homeland defense." The German U-boat attacks and the German-instigated sabotage attacks had indeed prodded America to come into the war, but the British interference with American commerce on the high seas also had been a provocation, activating Americans' historical memories of their vulnerability to attacks from the seas.

The worldview of the President was most important here, for Wilson did not share the perceptions of Mahan or Theodore Roosevelt that America should become engaged in the games of international power politics. Rather, Wilson's view was that America at the minimum needed to be defended against attack, and at the maximum should work to eliminate the power politics game entirely. When opponents of naval appropriations in the Congress after 1918 questioned the need for a navy now that the Germans had been defeated, Wilson repeatedly proposed to them a choice: Join the League by ratifying the Versailles Treaty, or instead build a large navy.

## Some Lessons for the Present

In the years since the Cold War ended, many observers have expressed doubts and confusions about where American foreign policy is headed. Would the United States seek to dominate the world as a "hegemon," as the only superpower? Or would it seek to withdraw from such burdens, tending more basically to its own affairs, giving up on any instincts of reforming the world?

President George H.W. Bush's campaign to force Iraq out of Kuwait in 1991 struck many as the realization finally of Woodrow Wilson's intentions for the League of Nations and a system of collective security. But Bill Clinton defeated the elder Bush in 1992 on the accusation that he had devoted too much energy and attention to international affairs. When George W. Bush defeated Al Gore in 2000, he did so on the parallel campaign argument that America should look after its own narrow interests more, and be less concerned with the welfare of the world.

If Americans were thus displaying a tendency to turn inward after 1989, with a series of presidential elections demonstrating that they were less concerned with the outside world, then the attacks of September 11, 2001, amounted to a very rude awakening – a signal that their homeland would be physically vulnerable even if Americans wanted to isolate themselves from an unpleasant world. Yet the analogy to World War I is strong, because the American homeland has been physically vulnerable for a longer time. The American people, and American presidents, have wrestled for a longer time with choices about what role to play in the world, and about how American naval power would fit into this. When the outside world impacts so directly on the United States itself, some of these choices then become simplified.

If nothing else produces clarity for American foreign policy choices, a threat to the homeland indeed serves this purpose. Beyond this elementary prod to action, it has never been clear that the United States would aspire to power or world domination, to being a "hegemon." Even if Mahan or Theodore Roosevelt aspired to this, they may not have had any majority of Americans behind them.

This very reticence, by which Wilson's view of the world was perhaps much more in synch with ordinary Americans, may explain why the world would be ready to tolerate the presence of the U.S. Navy off its shores, ready to tolerate an exertion of American power. United Nations General Assembly speeches aside, the world fears American military power or naval power much less than it fears the power of any other state. For as long as the basic character of American motivation does not change from what Wilson took it be in World War I, the world will be ready to tolerate whatever the United States has to do to defend and respond to attacks on its homeland.

The United States today, as during World War I, faces a threefold choice in responding to attacks on its homeland: 1) it can withdraw from world affairs as a way of avoiding such attacks, and this remains the unlikely choice; 2) it can respond militarily on its own, acting like any other militarily strong power, this being more or less what Theodore Roosevelt advocated; or 3) it can attempt to coordinate with other democracies and peace-loving states to establish a global system discouraging wars and aggressions, shielding all the homelands and all the international waters against attack, this being what Woodrow Wilson envisaged (and what many gave President George H.W. Bush credit for accomplishing in 1991).

## REFERENCES


[1] On the evolution of American commitment to a major navy, see Harold and Margaret Sprout, The Rise of American Naval Power: 1776-1918 (Princeton, NJ: Princeton University Press, 1939).

[2] This particular event, and German-sponsored sabotage in general, are detailed in Jules Witcover, Sabotage at Black Tom (Chapel Hill, NC: Algonquin Press, 1989).

[3] On the history of American feelings about the high seas, see Forrest Davis, The Atlantic System: The Story of Anglo-American Control of the Seas (New York, NY: Reynal and Hitchcock, 1941).

[4] The American feelings leading to entry into World War I are analyzed in Patrick Devlin, Too Proud to Fight (New York, NY: Oxford University Press, 1971).

[5] A very readable account of these events can be found in Walter Lord, The Dawn's Early Light (New York, NY: Norton, 1972).

[6] On the memory of "Copenhagening", see Jonathan Steinberg, Yesterday's Deterrent: Tirpitz and the Birth of the German Battle Fleet (London: McDonald, 1965).

[7] The interlocking of these political and strategic considerations is outlined in Kenneth Bourne, Britain and the Balance of Power in North America (Berkeley, CA: University of California Press, 1967).

[8] On these fears of the Spanish fleet, see Sprout, The Rise of American Naval Power: 1776-1918, p. 234.

[9] Woodrow Wilson, Congressional Government (Boston, MA: Houghton-Mifflin, 1896).

[10] Alfred Thayer Mahan, The Influence of Sea Power Upon History (Boston: Little Brown, 1890).

[11] Walter Lafeber, The New Empire (Ithaca, New York: Cornell University Press, 1963).

[12] Frank Klingberg, "The Historical Alternation of Moods in American Foreign Policy," World Politics, Vol. IV, No. 2 (January, 1952), pp. 239-273.

[13] On the attitudes of Theodore Roosevelt on naval expenditures, see Gordon Carpenter O'Gara, Theodore Roosevelt and the Rise of the Modern Navy (New York, NY: Greenwood, 1943).

[14] Britain's 1914 lack of commitment to international restraints on the Royal Navy's blockade options is outlined in Bernard Semmel, Liberalism and Naval Strategy (Boston, MA: Allen and Unwin, 1986).

[15] On the significance of perceived geography here, see Ray Allen Billington, "The Origins of Middle Western Isolationism," Political Science Quarterly, Vol. 60, No. 1

(March, 1945), pp. 44-64, and Henry Nash Smith, Virgin Land (Cambridge, MA: Harvard University Press, 1950).

[16] On the perceived links between fears of a strong presidency and fears of militarism, see John Milton Cooper, The Vanity of Power: American Isolationism and the First World War: 1914-1917 (Westport, CT: Greenwood, 1969).

[17] On the improvement in relations between Britain and the United States, see Stephen R. Rock, Why Peace Breaks Out (Chapel Hill, NC: University of North Carolina Press, 1989) Chapter 2.

[18] On the largely parallel thinking of Mahan and Roosevelt here, see Richard Turk, The Ambiguous Relationship: Theodore Roosevelt and Alfred Thayer Mahan (New York, NY: Greenwood Press, 1987).

[19] Wilson's initial fears of seeing America drawn into world power politics are outlined in John Dos Passos, Mr. Wilson's War (Garden City, NY: Doubleday, 1962).

[20] On the Lusitania sinking, and conflicting accounts of whether it was loaded with munitions, see Patrick O'Sullivan, The Lusitania: Unraveling the Mysteries (Dobbs Ferry, NY: Sheridan House, 2000).

[21] This early CBW attack on American soil is noted in Witcover, Sabotage at Black Tom, pp. 126-127, and 136-137.

[22] The German calculations about American resolve are given a detailed analysis in Karl Birnbaum, Peace Moves and U-Boat Warfare (Hamden, CT: Archon Books, 1970).

[23] The very distinctive nature of American war aims as presented by Woodrow Wilson is discussed in Edward Buehrig, Woodrow Wilson and the Balance of Power (Gloucester, MA: Peter Smoth, 1968).

[24] On the very late adjustment of American naval preparations for the particular nature of the German threat, see Sprout, The Rise of American Naval Power: 1776-1918, pp. 359-369.

[25] The motivation of America's continued naval buildup after the German surrender is analyzed in Harold and Margaret Sprout, Toward a New Order of Sea Power (Princeton, NJ: Princeton University Press, 1943).

In: Presidents and War
Editors: A. Eksterowicz and G. Hastedt, pp. 153-180
ISBN 978-1-61668-917-9


*Chapter 10*

# Franklin D. Roosevelt's First Trip to the West Coast: A President Prefigured

***David T. Leary***

## Introduction

Arguably the twentieth century's best U.S. president, Franklin D. Roosevelt (1882-1945) made many visits to the Pacific Coast over his memorable life [1]. Some were doubtless of greater consequence than others. But the first, during April 1914, while he was the assistant secretary of the navy in Woodrow Wilson's administration, is a window through which to view not only the FDR who was, but also, and more importantly, the FDR who was to be. Love of the sea, a measure of deceptiveness, the will to act boldly, a talent with people, concern for social equity, and a belief in national cohesion were qualities either just dimly visible or already quite apparent [2].

As its assistant secretary, Roosevelt was the navy's main business officer. Supply and construction fell within his purview, as did labor relations at over two dozen major shore facilities. Understandably, then, he was concerned with a good part of the navy's $140 million annual budget [3]. All this at age thirty-two, without previous management experience! But if he was eager, he was also diligent. That the Democrats chose him to run for vice president in the 1920 election—chose him in San Francisco, by the way—on balance attests the record [4].

Effective management entailed inspection. And according to the 1914 trip's announcement, FDR would look over navy properties from San Diego to Puget Sound. Implied was at least one opportunity for politics, though there would be more. Left unannounced was a diversion into southwestern New Mexico [5].

Eleanor Roosevelt (1886-1962) accompanied her husband on the trip. Up to this point, she had been a model political wife. The couple were already parents of two children, and another was on the way. She and Franklin had become bright stars in Washington's social firmament, with well-placed friends in both Democratic and Republican Party ranks. Alas, what seemed idyllic turned sour just three or four years later, when Franklin and Lucy

Mercer, Eleanor's social secretary, began an affair which did not end the Roosevelts' marriage but altered it essentially [6].

Remaining in Washington, but by extension a participant in the trip, was Roosevelt's assistant, Louis M. Howe (1871-1936). A former journalist, Howe was convinced FDR had the makings of a president and undertook to guide him. Together with Eleanor Roosevelt, Howe was as much responsible as anyone except the candidate himself for FDR's political ascendancy and 1932 presidential election victory [7].

Also in Washington was the only real boss FDR ever had, Navy Secretary Josephus Daniels (1862-1948). A North Carolina newspaper editor and member of William Jennings Bryan's wing of the Democratic Party, Daniels was inclined to restraint in naval and diplomatic matters. Roosevelt, by contrast, was out for a "big navy" and ready to use one. Daniels was in charge, however, so the juxtaposition required patience on his part and discretion on Roosevelt's. But the two got along, and FDR came to admire Daniels, not least because of the way he related to fellow Southerners in Congress. Indeed, Daniels became Roosevelt's ambassador to Mexico in 1933 [8].

In Washington, too, was President Woodrow Wilson (1856-1924). FDR had backed Wilson at the 1912 Democratic Party nominating convention and supported him in his three-way race with William Howard Taft and FDR's own cousin, Theodore Roosevelt. Thus Wilson had a political obligation to satisfy, and FDR's nomination as the assistant secretary of the navy did so [9].

Although Theodore Roosevelt had been president when the Panama Canal was started, Wilson would be in the White House when it was completed. And the West Coast was alive to the occasion: San Diego was at work on the Panama-California Exposition, as was San Francisco on its Panama-Pacific Exposition. Both events would have not only economic importance, but also social and cultural impact, despite the outbreak of World War I in 1914 [10].

More immediately significant, though, was Wilson's policy toward Mexico's Great Revolution of 1910-11 and the tumult following it. Early in 1913 Victoriano Huerta had used intrigue and violence to make himself Mexican president; by late 1913, outraged morally, Wilson was bent on Huerta's ouster. An excuse came during April 1914, at Tampico and Veracruz [11]. This was while FDR was traveling and out of close touch with Washington—the latter fact one which would prove especially pertinent.

## Toward the Coast

The Roosevelts departed Washington by train on the morning of Friday, April 3. But instead of proceeding directly, at Albuquerque on April 5 they turned south-southwest. The object was a three-night stay with family friends Robert ("Bob") Munro Ferguson (1867-1922) and his wife, Isabella Selmes (1886-1953). This at Tyrone, N.M., where the Fergusons were "homesteading" [12].

The friendship was close, rooted in ties to Theodore Roosevelt: each of the four, in fact, probably knew TR before knowing any of the others. It actually commenced in 1903, however, when Eleanor was back from school in Britain. Bob, the older brother she never had, introduced her to Isabella, and the young women really bonded. After Bob was diagnosed with tuberculosis and the Fergusons sought health in New Mexico, the Roosevelts traveled to them on three occasions: the present trip constituted the second [13].

The stay at Tyrone was unquestionably both personal and brief. Even so, it warrants mention here because of what was happening nearby, right then, and what would come not too much later.

At hand was the tumult of Mexico's Great Revolution, spilling across the border and impacting the lower Rio Grande Valley [14]. The Fergusons, early on, must have known of this: the New Mexico newspapers were certainly covering it. And anyway the border lay less than a hundred miles south [15]. It can thus be assumed the Roosevelts heard about events in Mexico when they visited the Ferguson homestead. Not that FDR was previously ignorant [16]. Yet they would hear much more: Mexico was going to loom large during the rest of their tour.

A few years later came Bob's death, after which Isabella was married twice again—first to John C. Greenway, and on his passing to Harry O. King. She bought a cattle ranch, headed an airline, and started Tucson's acclaimed Arizona Inn. Meanwhile, she successfully entered politics and in 1933 became the first woman to represent Arizona in Congress [17]. One can easily understand how she and Eleanor, both *femmes engagées,* might bond. But the friendship hit a bad patch in 1940, and, as will be seen, the details illustrate something noteworthy about FDR's way with people.

## LOS ANGELES

The Roosevelts left Tyrone on Thursday, April 9. Traveling west, most of the time just north of the border, they reached Los Angeles the next night and checked into the Hotel Alexandria. At that point the Alexandria was a hotel of choice. For example Woodrow Wilson stopped there in 1919, on his campaign to promote the League of Nations [18].

Los Angeles was dedicating its new municipal harbor, and FDR was to be part of the event. "Part" is an important word, because sharing the focus was U.S. Representative Joseph R. Knowland, Republican of Alameda. Knowland was not only the lone Californian on the House Interstate and Foreign Commerce Committee, but also had a U.S. Senate seat in mind [19]. The city was either acknowledging help in the past or trying to ensure help in the future—or both.

Even though the Port of Los Angeles is now one of the world's busiest, it is largely man-made. During much of the nineteenth century, San Pedro or Redondo or Santa Monica, all of which served the Southland, were little more than roadsteads [20]. But boosters realized that meaningful development would require a deep-water port. Thus, never mind abstract concepts of frontier individualism, they began seeking federal aid to improve San Pedro and nearby Wilmington. Washington responded: as early as 1871, Congress voted $200,000 for dredging at San Pedro, and over the ensuing decades, it approved additional measures [21].

Still there was more. In 1909 Los Angeles annexed San Pedro and Wilmington, and the following year the city's voters passed a $3 million bond issue for harbor improvement. By 1914—just in time to reap commercial reward from the new Panama Canal—the first projects, notably a municipal wharf, were at least partially complete [22]. It was enough to justify the "dedication," at which Knowland and Roosevelt were present.

Saturday, April 11, began with an automobile tour of Los Angeles and Pasadena, followed by a lunch at the Alexandria [23]. Roosevelt spoke both there and at San Pedro later in the day. On each occasion he said many of the same things, addressing what was closest in time, what was a few years away, and what was really, hopefully, for the future. One can identify a similar pattern in his remarks as he traveled along the coast.

About the near term, with the opening of the Panama Canal in mind, he said, "If the unpleasantness in Mexico is settled by next year . . . I hope you will have a fleet of seventeen first-class battleships, twenty destroyers and eight [or] ten auxiliary vessels here for six months during the Exposition" [24]. Although turmoil in Mexico had been a concern for several years, news of the arrest of U.S. personnel at Tampico on April 9 had just appeared in the Los Angeles papers [25]. As things turned out, dealing with the matter would prove more immediate than the fleet's coming in 1915.

About the longer term he stated, "I am here to make a thorough investigation of the naval needs of the Pacific Coast . . . . We have two well-equipped naval stations on the Coast, the yards and supply stations on Puget Sound and San Francisco Bay, and another is to be established at this end of the Western Coast line. When this will be I cannot say" [26]. At least as regards time, he was openly hedging.

About the ideal future, Roosevelt said, "It is the ambition of the Navy Department to make the navy a great national institution." More broadly he continued, "The fairs to be held on the Coast will bring hundreds of thousands of people, who have never been to the Coast before. It will teach the people of all the nation that this is a unified, a coherent nation and it will obliterate any lingering sectional feeling" [27]. The Civil War had ended just a half-century earlier; perhaps this was in FDR's mind, perhaps there was more.

## San Diego

The Roosevelts departed Los Angeles on the evening of April 11, taking an overnight train to San Diego. Thus far they had been traveling alone. Now, they were joined by W. Jefferson Davis, attorney and commissioner-at-large of the Panama-California Exposition, who had journeyed up the coast just to meet them [28]. And when the train reached its destination, among those on hand were Comdr. Cleland Davis (1869-1948) and Lt. Comdr. George C. Sweet (1877-1953) [29].

An Annapolis graduate, Davis specialized in radio. For the moment, though, he commanded the recruiting station in San Diego, and the Roosevelts were to stay with him and his wife, Mabel [30]. While the travelers might have enjoyed more sumptuous quarters at the Hotel del Coronado, Davis, beforehand, had prevailed on them to accept home hospitality [31]. Actually, it turned out that Davis had served with distinction aboard the battleship *Missouri* when Eleanor's uncle-in-law, Capt. William S. Cowles, commanded the vessel [32].

Sweet would be more pertinent than Davis. Also an Annapolis graduate and a specialist in radio, he was inspector of radio stations on the Pacific Coast [33]. Earlier, he had been the first navy officer to fly and had pressed the cause of naval aviation with William Cowles, when the latter, by then an admiral, headed the navy's Bureau of Equipment [34]. How Sweet first met FDR is uncertain (it was at least as early as 1913), but he served as his aide for the remainder of the West Coast trip. In fact the two kept up a lifelong friendship, on a first-name basis even when FDR was president [35].

After breakfast at the Davis home, everyone drove to the site of the Panama-California Exposition. "I consider the Panama-California Exposition buildings, grounds and the scope of its exhibits perfectly remarkable," Roosevelt declared. "I have been to many expositions a few months prior to their opening, but never saw the work so nearly completed as this one" [36]. Because it was Easter Sunday, Eleanor and Mabel next attended church; FDR, on the other hand, began inspecting [37].

First he visited the coaling station at La Playa. The navy was converting from coal- to oil-burning vessels, and FDR was impressed that La Playa's facilities could accommodate the transition. Then he moved on to a radio station at Pt. Loma. Here Sweet was the one to supply technical information. But at both La Playa and Pt. Loma Roosevelt apparently did a good deal of hinting that San Diego was destined for a greater future as a navy base [38].

The Chamber of Commerce sponsored a lunch for everyone at the Hotel del Coronado, after which the principals clambered into four automobiles for a hundred-mile trip through the countryside. As far as Roosevelt was concerned, visiting Chollas Heights had to be significant. The navy was planning to build one of the world's most powerful radio stations there. Opened in 1917, it would connect the U.S. with Hawaii and the Philippines [39].

The next day, April 13, was more leisurely, devoted to a harbor cruise and golf [40]. But in the evening, Franklin, anyhow, returned to public affairs. Local Democrats were holding a Jefferson Day celebration at the U.S. Grant Hotel, and he was the featured speaker. He stated that the fleet was coming in 1915 and that he was its "advance agent" [41]. This last, though probably true enough in principle, seems to have been something of a self-awarded designation.

Then he projected. "There is a naval station at Bremerton on Puget Sound, a navy yard at San Francisco and there is one other logical point for a big naval base on the Pacific coast. This point is San Diego" [42]. He had been intimating as much for two days; now he came out with it.

Projecting again he argued the big navy concept. "I do not believe in war, but the surest way to avoid war is to be prepared for it," he reasoned. "The reports tell you that we have thirty-nine battleships, but we have not. We have from sixteen to twenty real battleships." In any case, he said, "The Pacific coast will in the future have a fair share of battleships." Here he gave heart to those who worried about the positioning of U.S. warships once the Panama Canal was opened [43].

Roosevelt developed a fondness for San Diego. In 1938 he said that he felt like its "godfather," and as to the statement's sincerity a case can be made. Certainly he returned there several times, the last being in 1944, less than a year before he died [44].

## San Francisco

The travelers left San Diego just after the Jefferson Day event, taking a train to Los Angeles, changing there for one to San Francisco, arriving late in the evening of Tuesday, April 14. Reporters were waiting at the depot. "I am simply making a tour of the naval stations on the Pacific coast," FDR told them. "I am really an advance agent for the fleet which will assemble here in honor of the World's Fair." Having thus dealt with the press, the couple proceeded to the Palace Hotel [45].

By the next morning, events in Mexico were on everyone's mind. A U.S. Navy paymaster and nine marines had been arrested on April 9 at Tampico. The Mexicans quite soon released the Americans and apologized, but Adm. Henry T. Mayo, on the scene, demanded a salute to the U.S. flag, and Wilson backed him. When Mexican President Huerta balked at Mayo's mandate, Wilson ordered Adm. Charles J. Badger and much of the Atlantic Fleet to Mexico's eastern coast [46].

FDR's schedule that morning called for an inspection of Yerba Buena Island. Meeting reporters beforehand he was in an embarrassing position. The best he could do was decline comment on the Mexican situation because he had not received details from Washington. "At present I know only what I have read in the papers," he said lamely [47].

Excluded, caught out, Roosevelt fired off a telegram to Adm. Bradley A. Fiske, the department's aid [*sic*] for operations. "Surprised have not received information since departure. Telegraph such information as you have care commandant Mare Island" [48]. Fiske was one of FDR's big navy allies. He had been at Hampton Roads, Va., conferring with Badger [49] and might well have passed word along.

The visit to Yerba Buena Island went forward, nevertheless. FDR was reportedly pleased with what he saw, saying that the island's wireless station was to be made the government's main one on the coast [50]. Yet San Diego already had not only a station operating at Pt. Loma, but also, more importantly, a very powerful one destined for Chollas Heights. To believe he just forgot these facts is a stretch.

At noon Roosevelt addressed a lunch at the Palace Hotel, sponsored by the Panama-Pacific Exposition's directors. "The fleet will be here about a year from now," he said, dealing with the near term. "Its size may depend a good deal upon the events of the next few weeks," he continued, with Mexico clearly in mind. But preparing for the arrival was, as he had been repeating, a focal point of his trip [51].

Looking farther ahead he stated, "All the naval boards have agreed that two naval stations on the Pacific Coast are necessary. One is to be built on the Puget Sound and the other [on] San Francisco Bay. Beyond that we need in time, not a yard of the first magnitude, but an outpost in the southern part of the State." This last would not have excited boosters of the Southland nor squared with what he had said in San Diego. FDR had a local audience at hand, however, so he added, "We are going to have a great naval base on San Francisco Bay" [52].

Really looking ahead he declared, "On the Pacific Coast the Navy has had strong support since the time when it may be said to have brought California into the union. We have always counted on the people here as understanding why we had to have a Navy." Yet, he said, "I believe the exposition will go further than that. I think it will make this understanding national." Moreover, he asserted, "Your exposition is good for the citizenship and ideals of this country, and will do more for a better national understanding than anything in our history" [53]. Here again was the theme of the nation.

The next day, Thursday, April 16, aboard the destroyer *Lawrence*, the Roosevelts were off to the Mare Island Navy Yard where Capt. and Mrs. Frank M. Bennett, the yard commandant and his wife, would host them [54]. The government had $455,000 in work there, either just finished or still in progress, over half of which was dredging the Mare Island Strait [55]. Inspecting was the nub of FDR's real business, and inspect he did—ships and barracks and shops. Meanwhile, after lunch, Mrs. Roosevelt boarded *Lawrence* and returned to the city [56].

On the evening of April 16, Roosevelt attended a lengthy dinner and conference at the Vallejo home of attorney F.R. Devlin. (Vallejo was Mare Island's parent city.) The upshot was local belief that the government would be spending some $20 million at the yard, the bulk of the money going for the construction of a dreadnought and dreadnought drydock. During the evening FDR issued some qualifiers, though, as well he might, inasmuch as *California*, the vessel in question, was scheduled for the New York Navy Yard. Nevertheless, before departing Mare Island the next day, he declared, "There is no question but that Mare Island will be given a dreadnought to build" [57]. And so it happened: *California* was built at Mare Island over the years 1916-19 [58].

A concluding note about FDR at Mare Island. This was still a time when the cities about San Francisco Harbor were interconnected by ferryboats. One of the lines served Vallejo. The navy yard workers had been fighting for control of the service, and they won out during Roosevelt's visit. He lauded the workers and promised that the government would continue to subsidize the service [59].

On the morning of April 17, again aboard *Lawrence*, FDR had a cruise about upper San Francisco Bay, concluding at Richmond where he visited the Standard Oil Co. refinery. That done, he motored to Berkeley and met Mrs. Roosevelt for lunch with University of California President Benjamin Ide Wheeler. Following lunch, once more in *Lawrence*, the Roosevelts made for San Francisco, where federal money was to help finance a new drydock at the Union Iron Works on Hunters Pt. [60].

Meanwhile, the telegram to Fiske had gotten results—from three people. On April 15 Howe wired to say all dispatches received in Washington had been given to the press, ask if duplicates were wanted, and note a coded message had just been sent to FDR [61]. This last was apparently a quote from Daniels' signal to Adm. Thomas B. Howard, commanding the Pacific Fleet, alerting Howard to the fact that Admiral Badger and six battleships had been ordered to the eastern coast of Mexico [62].

The next day, April 16, Fiske wired that he thought FDR was informed of everything, inasmuch as all important matters had been given to the press. Yet perhaps defensively he added a good many details, both about ship movements and about a deployment of marines to San Diego [63]. Regarding the latter, at least, FDR would have known roughly as much from the morning papers.

Most significant were two telegrams from Daniels. In the first, which was uncoded, the secretary said, "All important facts concerning Mexican matters have been published in newspapers. Confer with Doyle and make such suggestion [*sic*] to department as you think wise"[64]. As will be seen, Adm. Robert M. Doyle was the commander of the Pacific Reserve Fleet at Bremerton, Wash. In the second, which was coded, Daniels said that he thought Huerta was going to render the salute, that Roosevelt would be advised of developments, and that Roosevelt was to "keep in conference" with West Coast officers [65]. Optimists in Washington, for the moment, believed Huerta would comply with the demand for a salute [66]. And FDR did get more latitude—though not much.

FDR responded to Daniels' first telegram, telling the secretary that he would confer with Doyle. Presumably he wired Doyle at the same time, though the admiral did not confirm the meeting until April 19 [67]. Also, he told Cleland Davis, "Make arrangements for quartering marines on North Island in case they are sent there soon." This got rapid, affirmative action [68]. And FDR let Daniels know [69].

Much more importantly, however, FDR used what Daniels had told him—just in the first, uncoded, message—to magnify himself. Heretofore, he had been the advance agent of the fleet; now, he indicated he was responsible for its West Coast operations. Several papers carried the item, one quoting him directly: "It is true that Secretary Daniels has wired me to assume charge on the Pacific coast, but that does not mean there will be any definite change."[70]. It was wise to add the caveat, because sailing orders were clearly emanating from Washington.

The Roosevelts departed San Francisco for Puget Sound on the morning of Saturday, April 18. From Red Bluff, two hundred miles and six hours north, he sent a coded message to Daniels recommending that in possible operations against western Mexico, naval and marine forces on the Pacific Coast seize Magdalena Bay and La Paz. The former, he argued, would be a valuable strategic asset; the latter would control Lower California [71]. The importance of Magdalena Bay had been asserted for years, and La Paz was the capital of all of Lower California through 1951 [72]. .

Why FDR waited so long is puzzling. Howe had sent him a message indicating Wilson was going to Congress on April 20 if Huerta had not yielded by 6:00 p.m., April 19 [73]. FDR should have received this before leaving San Francisco.

What might have energized his recommendation was a second message from Howe. It repeated some of what Howe sent earlier in the day and contained much that Roosevelt would have found in the newspapers. Yet one element leaps out: "W[ilson] finishing H[uerta]." The problem is that, while Howe's wire was directed to Mare Island, it was forwarded to FDR at Dunsmuir, a hundred miles and, because of the mountains, nearly four hours north of Red Bluff [74]. Thus FDR's recommendation stands as his own doing; why it was sent so late in the day is unclear, though the gravity of committing more U.S. forces to Mexican soil surely warranted reflection. It seems to have fallen on deaf ears, anyhow.

## SEATTLE

The Roosevelts reached Seattle about 9:00 p.m. on Sunday, April 19. Greeting them, along with newspaper reporters, were members of both the Seattle Commercial Club and the King County Democratic League [75]. Also on hand was Lt. Milo F. Draemel: besides George Sweet, he would assist FDR during the stay. Thus Draemel, whose naval service extended through World War II, probably accompanied the visitors to the New Washington Hotel [76].

Immediately the next day came the meeting with Admiral Doyle, called for by Daniels [77]. Doyle had enjoyed a lengthy career. One of his seagoing assignments had been command of the battleship *Missouri* during the global voyage of the Great White Fleet in 1908. But by 1913 he had run afoul of Daniels, who put a letter of admonition in his file [78]. Perhaps that explains why he was managing the Pacific Reserve Fleet: it was hardly a prestigious post, and Admiral Howard was really in charge of fighting vessels on the Pacific Coast.

What resulted from the conference, if anything, is uncertain. Although Doyle did weigh anchor and make for Mexican waters several days later, his sailing orders appear to have come from Washington [79]. This despite reports in the newspapers that FDR was supervising affairs on the Pacific Coast [80].

In fact FDR was simply out of touch! Probably on April 19, using code he wired Howe, "Advise by telegraph at earliest possibility probable scheme of operations on Pacific side. Is blockade only suggested, or will ports be taken?" [81]. Howe responded in plain text that FDR's question could not be answered until Congress acted finally on Wilson's April 20 message, and that Daniels would wire on April 21. Then, in code, he went on to convey Daniels' assurance that the government would do what was necessary to prevent the landing of a cargo of ammunition aboard a ship about to begin discharging. Despite some confusion on Howe's part, the ship was likely the inbound *Ypiranga* [82].

Wilson did go to Congress on April 20, for authority to intervene. But early the next morning, prior to full congressional authorization but fearful that Huerta would receive *Ypiranga's* cargo, he ordered the navy to seize Mexico's chief port, Veracruz. Doing so, he got far more than he expected: nineteen Americans and some two hundred Mexicans were killed. The arms, moreover, were landed elsewhere [83]. This time Roosevelt had been alerted, however.

Meanwhile, on April 20 FDR continued his rounds. At noon he addressed the Seattle Commercial Club [84]. Formed in 1905 by civic enthusiasts who were on the young side, the group coexisted with the Seattle Chamber of Commerce for about a decade [85]. Roosevelt said that the battleship fleet would be visiting Puget Sound in 1915, barring difficulties in Mexico; also, that the Pacific and Atlantic Coasts would be equal in naval affairs. In broader context he noted that the Commercial Club did not just represent Seattle's big business interests. "The big and the little sit side by side in its meetings," he said [86].

After lunch he moved along to Lake Washington [87]. Since the 1860's the government had had an interest there. The Washington Ship Canal, designed to link Puget Sound with the lake, was begun in 1911 and opened in 1917 [88]. While it was certainly an item of concern, whether anything eventuated from Roosevelt's visit is unclear: the newspapers offered no detail, FDR apparently made no written recommendation, and the navy focused, as it had before, on the Bremerton Navy Yard [89].

On the evening of April 20, Roosevelt spoke to the Washington State Democratic League. The talk was a partisan one, in the shadow of the Tampico affair and the congressional vote on Wilson's request for sanction to act. "President Wilson believes that what he is doing now is an act of averting war rather than an act of declaring war," said Roosevelt. At about this point, word of the House of Representatives' action arrived. The vote sustained the president, and FDR pointedly criticized congressmen who had put partisan politics ahead of national loyalty. Before closing he declared that the Tampico issue was not open to arbitration [90]. Wilson himself might at that point have agreed. Several days later, nevertheless, after the bloodshed at Veracruz, he gladly accepted the mediation of Argentina, Brazil and Chile [91]. Arbitration was one thing; mediation, a less constraining process, something else.

The next morning, Tuesday, April 21, Franklin and Eleanor took a navy tugboat across Puget Sound to the Bremerton Navy Yard, where they were guests of the yard commandant and his wife, Capt. and Mrs. DeWitt R. Blamer [92]. This was no social occasion, however. The government had $788,000 in ongoing or recently completed projects at the yard. FDR was significantly responsible for them, and he spent much of two days moving from site to site [93].

On April 22 a lunch with the Bremerton Commercial Club did interrupt the inspections. "I am going back to Washington and try to arrange to send you enough work to tide this yard over until next spring when the fleet will come through the canal," Roosevelt said. "Then there will be plenty of work to be done." Yard foremen had been asked to the occasion and must have responded positively to this prospect of continuing employment. Reportedly, FDR also said the next drydock to be built on the Pacific Coast would be at Bremerton; furthermore, he denied promising Mare Island the next one [94]. And in truth he had not "promised."

After the lunch Roosevelt cruised through the Strait of Juan de Fuca as far as Port Angeles, so he could get a sense of the strait and its fortifications. At day's end he and Mrs. Roosevelt were dinner guests aboard Admiral Doyle's flagship, *West Virginia* [95].

FDR had been indicating he was in charge on the Pacific Coast, and there were reports in the press of possible messages from Washington requiring changes of his itinerary [96]. But on April 22, ever so carefully, Daniels reined him in. Howe telegraphed, "Secretary says that as most of the vessels on the West Coast will be down in Mexico and in view of the great help you can be to him in Washington, he thinks the wise course is for you to return as originally planned" [97].

Recalled, in effect, how would Roosevelt behave?

## NOMINAL COMPLIANCE

Franklin and Eleanor started east on Thursday, April 23, scheduled this time to parallel the northern border [98]. If he was embarrassed or disheartened by what Daniels had done, Franklin was still vocal during stops.

The *New York Times,* heretofore silent about the tour, carried a very brief mention of Roosevelt at Minneapolis. "The people of the Pacific Coast want us to go through with our undertaking with President Huerta," he was quoted as saying. "If it means war, we are ready" [99]. Seeking peace, not war, the White House would scarcely have welcomed such rhetoric. Again, though, FDR was largely ignorant of the latest subtleties.

A Minneapolis paper was more detailed, saying FDR indicated that he had left for the West Coast with orders to do more than simply inspect; also, that he had provided Washington with intelligence about conditions along the southern border [100]. Yet there were two discrepancies. The crisis with Mexico had erupted after he left, not before. Also, if he had had confidential orders, he would have taken the most direct route to the coast and not diverted. When the reporters probed the first, FDR parried. He was already adroit at this. And of course they did not touch the second: the press release about the trip had not mentioned New Mexico. He could take advantage of being in the southern borderlands—without specifying why [101].

How much Daniels knew about Roosevelt's activities out west is uncertain. The eastern newspapers do not seem to have attended to them, and while he did keep a diary, whatever might have existed for 1914 (and 1916) has not been located [102]. Never mind, FDR's recommendation that the navy take Magdalena Bay and La Paz was itself enough to alert him.

Restrained he was, but no one's fool [103]. Thus he must have been somewhat relieved on April 27 when his eager assistant reached the capital [104].

Back in Washington, if less vocal, Roosevelt was not quiescent. The Argentine, Brazilian, and Chilean mediators began meeting at Niagara Falls, N.Y., on May 20 [105]. At this juncture FDR was the navy's acting secretary and as such said that *he* [emphasis added] would use force to prevent a blockade of Tampico. Just what information energized the statement is unclear [106].

Anyhow, quite probably in this very context, Franklin wrote Eleanor that he had his hands full, because Daniels was to leave for a day [107]. Indeed! Recalled from the West Coast not a full month earlier, the assistant was just as eager for action as ever.

## CONCLUSION

So what have we after scrutinizing Roosevelt's first trip to the West Coast? As asserted at the outset, we have what he was and what he was to be. That is, in many ways, the early personality prefigured the later, classic one. This was true of at least six qualities—love of the sea, a measure of deceptiveness, the will to act boldly, a talent with people, concern for social equity, and belief in national cohesion.

The first quality is among the easiest to demonstrate. Roosevelt was attracted to the sea from his earliest years. It had always seemed like home, he told Grace Tully, his last personal secretary [108]. And it is a challenge to identify a president equaling him as a mariner.

The Delanos—his mother's family—had been in the fabled China Trade, and as a boy he listened to seafaring anecdotes time after time. At age sixteen he received his own twenty-one-foot sailboat and became skillful at working her about the waters near the family's summer home on Campobello Island off the coast of Maine [109]. Skillful enough so that later, and of course more experienced, he conned a navy destroyer through the passage between the island and the coast [110].

Again during his early years, Roosevelt started collecting virtually anything nautical. The impulse did not wane as he grew older. At his death the trove included ship models, graphic art, and some 2400 books. Among the last were well-read volumes by navalist Alfred Thayer Mahan [111].

Although he might have had other places in Wilson's administration, asked by Josephus Daniels if he would like to be the navy's assistant secretary, Roosevelt answered that it would please him more than anything [112]. And on the job, he quite soon joined disciples of Mahan who were calling for a bigger fleet [113]. Unquestionably, then, the navalism he voiced while on the West Coast, if part of the job, was heartfelt.

Immediately he got to the White House, Roosevelt had to fight the Great Depression, and creating new jobs in naval construction became one of his ways of doing this. The process began as early as 1933, when significant National Industrial Recovery Act (NIRA) funds were allocated to building combat vessels. And it continued, so that by 1940 both the unemployment data had improved and the fleet was on the way to readiness for worldwide conflict [114].

How the navy conducted World War II in the Pacific—specifically, how it implemented War Plan Orange—drew from Alfred Thayer Mahan. Roosevelt guided Pacific strategy and was, early on, a Mahan enthusiast. Plausible linkage thus exists. But two caveats are important: FDR delegated significant responsibility for combat strategy; and the degree of Mahan's influence on Plan Orange is debatable. Even so, the admirals with top responsibility for the Pacific theater—Ernest J. King and Chester W. Nimitz—attended the Naval War College, and Mahanian ideas flourished there well after Mahan himself left. Plausible linkage hence remains [115].

After World War II began, while FDR's official priorities shifted, there was an interesting constant—his preferred mode of travel. During the 1930's, when such activity remained possible, he had taken lengthy vacations aboard warships. Voyages in 1934, 1935, and 1938, with fishing very much a part of them, are notable here because each entailed embarking or docking at a Pacific Coast port [116]. During the war, risk notwithstanding, Roosevelt used warships to attend three of the momentous conferences he had with Winston Churchill and Josef Stalin. That with Churchill at Plascentia Bay, Newfoundland, in 1940 was the first; those at Teheran in 1943 and Yalta in 1945, both of which included Stalin, were the other two. FDR did not like to fly, and the sea, with a chance to fish, refreshed him. Even so, he died just a few weeks after returning from Yalta [117]. An especially poignant note is that a watercolor, almost finished when he succumbed, depicted him in a navy boat cloak [118]. A mariner he was until the end.

A second facet of Roosevelt's personality was apparent on the West Coast. This was exaggeration at best or mendacity at worst—with deceptiveness, say, falling in between. "Never let your left hand know what your right hand is doing," he advised Treasury Secretary Henry Morgenthau Jr. [119]. While this was in 1935, he might have said substantially the same thing years earlier.

At Groton, his preparatory school, there was more than one episode wherein he masked reality [120]. At Harvard some classmates thought him two-faced. And he effectively let stand an untrue account about interviewing the university president for the *Harvard Crimson*, [121].

The announced purpose of the 1914 trip was inspecting West Coast naval facilities. At Albuquerque, however, the Roosevelts headed into southwestern New Mexico. The region had no naval facilities: it was simply a place where Bob and Isabella Ferguson had made a home. But passing through Minneapolis on the way back to Washington, in light of the crisis with Mexico, FDR sought to magnify what he had been doing.

Having reached California, Roosevelt soon said he was the advance agent of the fleet. Then, that Daniels had put him in charge of the navy's West Coast operations. In fact Daniels had done no more than instruct him to offer suggestions and keep in conference with West Coast officers.

Roosevelt said the government's main Pacific Coast radio station was to be on Yerba Buena Island, yet he had to have known about plans for Chollas Heights. Also, he said Mare Island was to build a dreadnought, yet he had to have known that the next dreadnought was intended for the New York Navy Yard—even if Mare Island eventually did get the job. Finally, he denied promising Mare Island would have a drydock, yet he had to have recalled at least leaving such a supposition.

It is noteworthy that deceptiveness was a widely perceived quality of Franklin Roosevelt's White House years [122]. For example Interior Secretary Harold L. Ickes more than once thought himself betrayed by his chief. And wrongly yet with good reason, "Assistant President" James F. Byrnes came to believe he was FDR's choice for vice president in 1944 [123]. Eleanor Roosevelt later said that her husband disliked being unpleasant and was given to evincing interest without intending agreement. [124]. Query as to how well this mollified people who felt taken in.

A third element of Roosevelt's personality was willingness to act boldly, though usually after careful thought. "I am like a cat," he once said. "I make a quick stroke and then relax" [125]. One can find the element during his very first days of public office.

Elected to New York's senate in 1910, taking his seat at the start of the next year, he soon became the leader of a group of insurgents challenging the legislature's leadership. At issue was the choice of the state's next U.S. senator. Even though FDR had proper advisers, plus TR's encouragement, the immediate result was at best a compromise. More important, however, was the wide attention gained by the young politician [126].

On the West Coast trip of 1914, heading north from San Francisco, Roosevelt suggested action in Lower California. Implemented, his idea would have entailed additional U.S. forces in Mexico. It was hardly fainthearted. What animated it?

A first possibility is that FDR simply read more into Daniels' telegrams—especially the second one—than Daniels intended. This would be enough to explain why he kept a navy tug at dockside in Seattle supposedly awaiting orders from Washington. But a second possibility is that, relying on Wilson's distaste for Huerta, he was trying to advance himself [127].

The trouble was the bloodshed at Veracruz: it appalled Wilson and prompted him to look for a way out—not for more involvement. Thus FDR's gambit, whatever the motive, achieved no result. Events prevailed.

During Roosevelt's White House years, bold strokes were surely evident. Episodes from his second term are illustrative.

In 1937 there was the attempt to expand the Supreme Court's membership. Roosevelt had been thinking about this for some time yet presented it so suddenly that even his friends in Congress were taken aback. The plan failed—not for want of audacity, but for lack of coordination with leadership on Capitol Hill [128]. It was a mistake from which to learn.

In 1938 when Mexican President Lázaro Cárdenas expropriated foreign oil properties and some U.S. oil men called for armed intervention, Roosevelt would have none of it [129]. He had announced the Good Neighbor Policy in 1933, of course, despite having suggested action in Lower California during 1914. Was he thus reversing himself? Was there, in psychological terms, discontinuity? [130] True, while the policy certainly curtailed armed intervention in Latin America, it scarcely halted other forms of meddling there [131]. The difference between what FDR sanctioned as president and what he suggested earlier was one of means, not ends. So boldness was arguably a continuous trait.

In 1940 came the agreement between the U.S. and the U.K. exchanging destroyers for bases. Although Roosevelt had had the matter in mind for months, especially because of Winston Churchill's urging, he delayed: public support was not universal and a third-term election was in the offing. But in August, after finding legal cover for bypassing Congress, he ventured a *coup d'audace*. And upheld he was by the election's outcome [132].

On reviewing some of FDR's most important words, it is hard to go away unimpressed by the number of times "bold" turns up—if not the word, then its spirit. "The only thing we have to fear is fear itself," he said at his first inauguration. "The only limit to our realization of tomorrow will be our doubts of today," he wrote on the day before he died [133].

A fourth Roosevelt characteristic pertinent to the 1914 trip was a talent with people. Said "brain trust" member Rexford G. Tugwell, "That he was likable, even lovable, everyone who knew him as a boy, as a youth, and as a man testifies" [134]. Not quite.

Certainly Louis Howe enlisted in his service shortly after interviewing him in 1911 [135]. But Frances Perkins thought him a snob during those same days and said charm would emerge later [136]. Yet often enough it never did: a blackball had kept him out of Harvard's Porcellian Club [137]. and in certain quarters he remained "that man."

Even so, by 1914 FDR did have friends aplenty. And for special tasks—some official, some not—he began to prevail on them, especially on those of long standing. George Sweet was one, Isabella Greenway another.

As noted, how Sweet and Roosevelt became acquainted is uncertain. Sweet was nevertheless on hand when the Roosevelts reached San Diego and present through the rest of the visit to the coast.

During World War I, Sweet had significant responsibilities for high-frequency radio transmitters at Annapolis, Md., and Bordeaux, France. The second (the Lafayette transmitter) was then the world's most powerful [138]. At the end of the war, FDR oversaw its sale to the French government. The transaction was successful, apparently not least because he had managed Sweet's posting to the Paris embassy [139].

Sweet remained Roosevelt's friend for life. Good enough that FDR took a personal interest in his 1940 navy assignment [140]. Good enough that during March 1945, in what turned out to be his last letter to the president, Sweet felt free to remark on FDR's obviously declining health [141].

Isabella Greenway had become a woman of consequence by the time of the 1932 Democratic Party convention in Chicago [142]. Chosen to second FDR's nomination for president, she did so as not anyone might. "In his personal life," she emphasized, "he has gallantly waged and triumphantly won a battle against fate such as few men are called upon to fight" [143]. She was clearly alluding to FDR's disability (the result of polio in 1921), about which he was always publicly guarded. That he trusted her to say just enough, and no more, is significant. But there is something else. Greenway appears to have had a role in persuading the California delegation to support Roosevelt on the convention's fourth ballot, the ballot which was crucial to his nomination [144].

Still, Isabella Greenway was her own person. She broke with FDR when he ran for president a third time, in 1940, and apropos of this said rather cutting things. She and Eleanor Roosevelt did continue to exchange letters; FDR, however, probably never forgave his erstwhile supporter [145].

In the White House, Roosevelt certainly tapped friends. Sumner Welles, a page at the Roosevelts' wedding, was his undersecretary of state; fellow Grotonian W. Averell Harriman served in various capacities at home and abroad, finally as ambassador to Russia [146]. Vincent Astor, for years close to the whole Roosevelt clan, undertook several quiet intelligence missions at FDR's behest; and Eleanor Roosevelt herself made trips domestic and foreign to places about which her husband needed astute reportage[147]. But FDR could drop friends, too, just as with Isabella Greenway. Eleanor Roosevelt once said that he discarded people when they no longer fulfilled his purposes [148]. And paradoxically, many of his circle, even his intimate circle, commented on how little they really knew him. Speechwriter Robert Sherwood's statement is a classic: "Being a writer by trade, I tried continually to study him, to try to look beyond his charming and amusing and warmly affectionate surface into his heavily forested interior. But I could never really understand what was going on in there" [149].

A fifth feature of Roosevelt's personality manifested itself on the 1914 trip. This was sympathy not only for labor, but also, if less clearly, for social equity. Never mind it was three decades later when he argued that needy people are not free [150]. the concept had been maturing. "What he cared about was improvement in people's lives," said Frances Perkins [151].

Before he went to Washington, Roosevelt had *seen* poverty—as a member of the Groton Missionary Society; as a visitor to a New York City settlement house [152]. And the impressions doubtless lingered. Yet he had neither really dirtied his hands nor met a payroll.

In Washington, through Louis Howe, FDR met working people. "This was Franklin's first close contact with labor . . . [and] it was one of the turning points in his development," ER stated [153]. On the West Coast in 1914, he certainly did attend to labor's paramount concern: that is, steady employment! This was obvious at both Mare Island and Bremerton.

In the White House, Roosevelt and the New Deal remained conspicuously sympathetic to America's workers [154]. More particularly the National Labor Relations Act (Wagner Act) of July 1935 assured them the right to organize unions and bargain collectively. The Social Security Act of August 1935 had a proviso for unemployment insurance. And the Fair Labor Standards Act (Wages and Hours Act) of 1938 was the nation's first significant minimum wage law [155].

Concrete results numbered at least two. Union memberships climbed from 2.9 million to 14.8 million between the years 1933 and 1945. And organized labor became one of FDR's reliable supports in national politics [156]. Something else was germinating, however.

In 1914 the Seattle Commercial Club had evoked FDR's praise: at its meetings, he had said, everyone sat side by side. The remark was probably little noted at the time. But as the years passed, going beyond sympathy for labor, he more and more openly espoused principles of social equity.

During the 1932 presidential campaign, Roosevelt popularized thinking about "the forgotten man"—the one the system had left out. He also mentioned an "economic declaration of rights" [157]. Generalization it might all have been, yet some of it found concrete realization in the Social Security Act of 1935 [158].

Moreover, the ideas saw continuing development. In his 1944 state of the union message, Roosevelt detailed an eight-point "second Bill of Rights," which would make for "equality in the pursuit of happiness." And the next year, in his last state of the union message, he returned to the same subject [159].

What might have eventuated had Roosevelt lived longer is simply an unknown, because he just kept unfolding. Nonetheless, it hardly seems that he would have been antipathetic to President Lyndon B. Johnson's attempts during the 1960's to achieve the Great Society. Johnson, in fact, was an FDR protégé [160].

A sixth quality evident on the West Coast was a belief that there was national cohesion either to be achieved—or just recognized. The idea recently drew the attention of British statesman and historian Roy Jenkins. Roosevelt, he said, "was peculiarly successful at transcending geography and uniting the continent" [161]. Allowing for hyperbole, Jenkins was onto a fact about which many Americans were becoming conscious even before FDR died. Indeed, the man had a kind of organic or holistic sense of what the nation should be.

The sense was taking shape as early as 1912, in Roosevelt's thinking about "liberty of the community" [162]. Eventually, it seems to have mixed with his view of social equity. Elements of both may have derived from Herbert Croly's *The Promise of American Life*, an influential book before World War I. Hypothesized Croly, "The individual becomes a nation in miniature, but devoted to the loyal realization of a purpose peculiar to himself. The nation becomes an enlarged individual whose special purpose is that of human amelioration and in whose life every individual should find some particular but essential function" [163].

Ascribing direct provenance to Croly is a temptation, especially because doing so signals a mix of equity and organicism—equity, after all, the thrust of the second bill of rights. The problem is that FDR drew broadly from the thought of his time as well as from individual thinkers [164]. The best approach, therefore, is to identify Croly as a source—perhaps direct, perhaps not [165].

As he moved along the coast in 1914, Roosevelt commented on the navy, on the two expositions, and on national unity. Now and then he put the items in the same context: this was true in Los Angeles; it was even more true in San Francisco. He viewed national cohesion as something which would be furthered not only by the navy, but also by the expositions. Then, too, in Seattle he disparaged the congressmen who put party before patriotism and did not back Wilson's request for authority to act in Mexico. Here, altogether, was a concept which would see development.

In 1933, at his first inauguration, the "interdependence of the various elements and parts of the United States" was on his mind. A decade later, in his 1944 state of the union message, he commented on "how interdependent upon each other are all groups and sections." But, he reflected, it took a second world war to teach the lesson [166].

At the same time, however, something else was afoot. Going beyond his compatriot Roy Jenkins, scholar Isaiah Berlin expressed this: Roosevelt did more than transcend U.S. continental geography; he appealed to people on every continent [167]. And part of the reason lay with giving organicism a global dimension.

In 1929, before he even reached the White House, Roosevelt said that "our civilization cannot endure unless we, as individuals, realize our personal responsibility to and dependence on the rest of the world" [168]. In his 1941 state of the union message, the one which set out the Four Freedoms, he declared that "the world order we seek is the cooperation of free countries, working together in a friendly, civilized society." And in 1945, during his fourth inaugural address, he maintained, "We have learned that we cannot live alone, at peace; that our well-being is dependent on the well-being of other Nations far away" [169]. What might have become of all this had FDR lived longer is simply another unknown—though today's globalization probably would not trouble him [170].

By way of summary, it might be useful to revisit Eleanor Roosevelt. Asked if FDR would have been president absent polio, she said yes, but a different kind of president [171]. Perhaps not so different: what he was in 1914 prefigured much of what he would be.

## NOTES

The documents cited in this paper come chiefly from the Franklin D. Roosevelt Library at Hyde Park, N.Y., together with the National Archives and the Library of Congress in

Washington, D.C. Also, while the people and terms involved are many, several appear constantly. For the sake of simplification, therefore, a certain number of special abbreviations have been used in the endnotes:

| | |
|---|---|
| ASN | Assistant Secretary of the Navy |
| ER | Eleanor Roosevelt |
| JD | Josephus Daniels |
| FDR | Franklin D. Roosevelt |
| FDRL | Franklin D. Roosevelt Library |
| LC | Library of Congress |
| LMH | Louis M. Howe |
| NA | National Archives |
| SDR | Sara Delano Roosevelt |
| TR | Theodore Roosevelt |

In several cases items from the same document or file appear often enough to warrant shortening after the first full citation. No individual notice of the shortening has been given.

## References

[1] The first visit was of course in 1914. The last (actually two, i.e., a departure from San Diego and a return to Seattle) came 30 years later. In between there were about a half-dozen, each with its own reason or reasons. Regrettably, for FDR there is nothing in print to match Earl Schenck Miers (ed.), *Lincoln Day by Day, A Chronology, 1809-1865*, 3 vols. (Washington, D.C.: Lincoln Sequicentennial Commission, 1960).

[2] Joseph W. Coady, *Franklin D. Roosevelt's Early Washington Years (1913-1920)*, Ph.D. diss., St. John's University, 1968 (Ann Arbor, Mich.: University Microfilms, 1968), seems to be the only monograph dealing just with FDR's service as assistant secretary. One of its themes, that the experience guided Roosevelt when he reached the White House, has suggested this study. But despite its value, Coady's work is significantly institutional. And at least three biographers have mentioned the capacity for growth latent in FDR's personality. These are James MacGregor Burns, *Roosevelt,* vol. 2, *The Soldier of Freedom, 1940-1945* (New York: Harcourt, 1970), 67; Arthur M. Schlesinger Jr., *The Age of Roosevelt*, vol. 1, *The Crisis of the Old Order, 1919-1933* (Boston: Houghton Mifflin, 1957), 406; Rexford G. Tugwell, *The Democratic Roosevelt, A Biography of Franklin D. Roosevelt* (Garden City, N.Y.: Doubleday, 1957), 73. Moreover, the supporting facts are at hand. Hence, the life-span approach to developmental psychology has been important also, and therein two questions—first, whether personality traits are the result of nature or nurture; second, whether such traits, having emerged, are continuous or discontinuous. For a review of the matter, see Richard M. Lerner, *Concepts and Theories of Human Development,* 3rd ed. (Mahway, N.J.: Erlbaum, 2002), esp. chaps. 4-5.

[3] For FDR as assistant secretary, aside from sources cited above, see Frank Freidel, *Franklin D. Roosevelt,* vol. 1, *The Apprenticeship* (Boston: Little, Brown, 1952), esp.

chap. 9. Also see James MacGregor Burns, *Roosevelt,* vol. 1, *The Lion and the Fox, 1882-1940* (New York: Harcourt, 1956), esp. chap. 3; Kenneth S. Davis, *FDR, The Beckoning of Destiny, 1882-1928, A History* (New York: Putnam's 1972), esp. chap. 11; Geoffrey C. Ward, *A First-Class Temperament, The Emergence of Franklin Roosevelt* (New York: Harper and Row, 1989), esp. chap. 6.

All the above reflect the fact that the navy's administration was not as tightly knit as today one might expect, nor were the assistant secretary's responsibilities as formally defined. Still, in the latter case, logistics had come to predominate. See Arthur W. Macmahon and John D. Millett, *Federal Administrators, A Biographical Approach to the Problem of Departmental Management* (New York: Columbia University Press, 1939), 246-51; Lloyd M. Short, *The Development of National Administrative Organization in the United States* (Baltimore: Johns Hopkins Press, 1923), 310-29.

For budget specifics see U.S. Navy, *Annual Reports of the Navy Department for the Fiscal Year 1914* (Washington, D.C.: GPO, 1915), esp. 289.

[4] Grenville Clark, in "Franklin Delano Roosevelt, 1882-1945, Five Harvard Men Pay Tribute to His Memory," *Harvard Alumni Bulletin*, 47 (28 Apr. 1945), 451-52; FDR to ER, 19 Jul. 1914, and FDR to SDR, 17 Mar. 1913, both in *F.D.R., His Personal Letters*, ed. Elliot Roosevelt, vol. 2, *1905-1928* (New York: Duell, Sloan and Pearce, 1948), 228-30, 199-200; *New York Times*, 7 Jul. 1920, 1; *San Francisco Chronicle,* 7 Jul. 1920, 1.

A subtext of FDR's early career is the example of his cousin, President Theodore Roosevelt. TR's record seems to have sparked at least some of FDR's intent to be president. Moreover, there is a striking similarity in the two men's paths to the White House. See for example James MacGregor Burns and Susan Dunn, *The Three Roosevelts, Patrician Leaders Who Transformed America* (New York: Atlantic Monthly Press, 2001), esp. 80. See also Nona Stinson Ferdon, *Franklin D. Roosevelt: A Psychological Interpretation of His Childhood and Youth*, Ph.D. diss., University of Hawaii, 1971 (Ann Arbor, Mich.: University Microfilms, 1971), esp. iv-v, 230-31.

[5] Memorandum for the Press, [1914], in FDR Papers as ASN, Personal Files, Correspondence, FDR (2), at FDRL.

[6] Blanche Wiesen Cook, *Eleanor Roosevelt*, vol. 1, *1884-1933* (New York: Viking, 1992), esp. chap. 9. See also ER, *This Is My Story* (New York: Harper and Bros., 1937), esp. chap. 10.

[7] Alfred B. Rollins Jr., *Roosevelt and Howe* (New York: Knopf, 1962), esp. chaps. 9-10; Lela Stiles, *The Man Behind Roosevelt, The Story of Louis McHenry Howe* (Cleveland: World, 1954), esp. chap. 3.

[8] Josephus Daniels, *The Wilson Era*, vol. 1, *Years of Peace—1910-1917* (Chapel Hill: University of North Carolina Press, 1944), esp. chap. 12; Carroll Kilpatrick (ed.), *Roosevelt and Daniels, A Friendship in Politics* (Chapel Hill: University of North Carolina Press, 1952), esp. intro.

[9] Freidel, *Apprenticeship*, chap. 8; Arthur S. Link, *Wilson*, vol. 1, *The Road to the White House* (Princeton: Princeton University Press, 1947), esp. chap. 14.

[10] David McCullough, *The Path between the Seas, The Creation of the Panama Canal, 1870-1914* (New York: Simon and Schuster, 1977), 608-10; Kevin Starr, *Americans and the California Dream, 1850-1915* (New York: Oxford University Press, 1973), 295-306, 402-13.

[11] Mexico's Great Revolution not only left tens of thousands of people dead or displaced, but also changed Mexican society fundamentally. It has been compared with upheavals occurring in Russia, China, and Iran at about the same time. (See for example John Mason Hart, *Revolutionary Mexico, The Coming and Process of the Mexican Revolution* [Berkeley: University of California Press, 1987], esp. 230-34.) Even in the U.S., its import has sometimes gone unrecognized.
For the Tampico incident and Veracruz intervention see P. Edward Haley, *Revolution and Intervention: The Diplomacy of Taft and Wilson with Mexico, 1910-1917* (Cambridge: MIT Press, 1970), esp. chap. 7; Arthur S. Link, *Wilson*, vol. 2, *The New Freedom* (Princeton: Princeton University Press, 1956), esp. chap. 12; Robert E. Quirk, *An Affair of Honor, Woodrow Wilson and the Occupation of Veracruz* ([Lexington]: University of Kentucky Press, 1962), esp. chap. 1.

[12] Itinerary of the Assistant Secretary of the Navy, Washington to Pacific Coast, [1914], in FDR Papers as ASN, Official Files, General Correspondence, Trip File: 1914, at FDRL outlines the whole trip. This was by rail, from city to city, and thus *The Official Guide of the Railways and Steam Navigation Lines of the United States* (New York: National Railway Publication Co., Apr. 1914) is useful for particular routes and schedules.
Inasmuch as there was money on both sides of the marriage, the Ferguson property was not the conventional "homestead." See John Higbee, *The Burro Mountain Homestead*, unpaginated pamphlet (Silver City, N.M.: Silver City Historical Society?), 1970.

[13] Kristie Miller, *Isabella Greenway, An Enterprising Woman* (Tucson: University of Arizona Press, 2004), esp. chaps. 1-4; Kristie Miller, "A Volume of Friendship, The Correspondence of Isabella Greenway and Eleanor Roosevelt, 1904-1953," *Journal of Arizona History*, 40 (1999): esp. 121-32; ER, *My Story,* esp. chaps. 4, 10, 11.

[14] Linda B. Hall and Don M. Coerver, *Revolution on the Border, The United States and Mexico, 1910-1920* (Albuquerque: University of New Mexico Press, 1988), esp. 53.

[15] See for examples *Santa Fe New Mexican*, 8 Apr. 1914, 1, 4; *Albuquerque Morning Journal*, 9 Apr. 1914, 1-2. Columbus, N.M., is only about sixty-five miles south-southeast of Tyrone. In 1916 revolutionary leader Francisco ("Pancho") Villa led a raid on Columbus, causing Woodrow Wilson to order a "punitive expedition" into northern Mexico. See Haley, *Revolution and Intervention*, chaps. 9-10.

[16] FDR to SDR, 29 Jul. 1913, in *Personal Letters,* 206-07.

[17] *American National Biography,* 9, s.vv. "Isabella Greenway"; *Who Was Who in America,* 3 (1951-60), s.vv. "Isabella Selmes Greenway"; *New York Times*, 19 Dec. 1953, 15.

[18] Itinerary of the Assistant Secretary, in Trip File: 1914, at FDRL; Gene Smith, *When the Cheering Stopped* (New York: Morrow, 1964), 76-78.

[19] U.S. 63$^{rd}$ Cong., 2$^{nd}$ Sess., 1 Dec. 1913, *Official Congressional Directory*, 1$^{st}$ ed. (Washington, D.C.: GPO, 1913), 10-11, 190; Royce Delmatier et al. (eds.), *The Rumble of California Politics, 1848-1970* (New York: Wiley, 1970), 174, 250-51.

[20] Lynn Bowman, *Los Angeles: Epic of a City* (Berkeley, Calif.: Howell-North, 1974), 216.

[21] Charles F. Queenan, *The Port of Los Angeles, From Wilderness to World Port* (Los Angeles: Los Angeles Harbor Dept., 1983), chap. 3.

[22] Ibid., chap. 4.

[23] *Los Angeles Examiner*, 12 Apr. 1914, sec. 1, p. 2. Pasadena may have been scheduled, but there is no evidence of anything more than that.

[24] *Los Angeles Examiner*, 12 Apr. 1914, sec. 1, p. 2. See also *Los Angeles Times*, 12 Apr. 1914, sec. 2, p. 12. Speaking here (and later) about an arriving fleet, FDR was not always specific. To celebrate completion of the Panama Canal, war vessels of some fifty nations—the U.S. included—were to transit the new waterway and sail up the Pacific Coast in 1915. And occasionally this may have been on his mind. But the outbreak of World War I in August 1914 thwarted the great pageant. Foreign commitment dwindled; the U.S. Atlantic Fleet stayed in the Atlantic; and in sum the storied though by then obsolete battleship *Oregon*, anchored in San Francisco Bay, drew the greatest public attention. See Daniels, *Wilson Era*, 213; McCullough, *Path between the Seas,* 608-10; Frank M. Todd, *The Story of the Exposition, Being the Official History of the International Celebration Held at San Francisco in 1915*, 5 vols. (New York: Putnam's, 1921), 2: 53-55, 398-400.

[25] *Los Angeles Examiner*, 11 Apr. 1914, sec. 1, p. 1; *Los Angeles Times*, 11 Apr. 1914, sec. 1, p. 1.

[26] *Los Angeles Examiner*, 12 Apr. 1914, sec. 1, p. 2. See also *Los Angeles Times*, 12 Apr. 1914, sec. 2, p. 12.

[27] *Los Angeles Times*, 12 Apr. 1914, sec. 2, p. 12. See also *Los Angeles Examiner*, 12 Apr. 1914, sec. 1, p. 2.

[28] *San Diego Union*, 12 Apr. 1914, sec. 1, p. 3; Clarence A. McGrew, *City of San Diego and San Diego County, The Birthplace of California*, 2 vols. (Chicago: American Historical Society, 1922), 2: 23-24.

[29] *San Diego Union*, 13 Apr. 1914, 1.

[30] L.S. Howeth, History of Communications-Electronics in the United States Navy (Washington, D.C.: GPO, 1963), 168-69; San Diego City and County Directory, 1914, s.vv. "Cleland Davis"; San Diego Union, 12 Apr. 1914, sec. 1, p. 3.

[31] Davis to FDR, 7 Apr. 1914, in Trip File: 1914, at FDRL.

[32] ER to SDR, 15 Apr. [1914], in Roosevelt Family Papers, Children, at FDRL; Lilian F. Rixey, *Bamie, Theodore Roosevelt's Remarkable Sister* (New York: McKay, 1963), 254. Anna ("Bamie") Roosevelt was the older of TR's sisters; she married Cowles in 1895.

[33] Howeth, *Communications-Electronics*, 169; *San Diego Union*, 13 Apr. 1914, 1. For the period 1913-15, Sweet's service record indicates simply a Washington, D.C., assignment to the navy's Bureau of Steam Engineering. (See Comdr. George Cook Sweet, Transcript of Naval Service, 20 Jun. 1961, in Military Personnel Records, National Personnel Records Center.) Thus his duty on the Pacific Coast in 1914 was probably temporary.

[34] Lillian C. White, Pioneer and Patriot, George Cook Sweet, Commander, U.S.N., 1877-1953 (Delray Beach, Fla.: Southern, 1963), chap. 6.

[35] Ibid., chaps. 12-13.

[36] *San Diego Union*, 13 Apr. 1914, 1.

[37] ER to SDR, 15 Apr. [1914], at FDRL.

[38] *San Diego Union*, 13 Apr. 1914, 1, 2. For background see John A. DeNovo, "Petroleum and the United States Navy before World War I," *Mississippi Valley Historical Review*, 41 (1955): 641-56.

[39] ER to SDR, 15 Apr. [1914], at FDRL; *San Diego Union*, 13 Apr. 1914, 1-2; Howeth, *Communications-Electronics*, 221-25.

[40] *San Diego Union*, 12 Apr. 1914, sec. 1, p. 3; 13 Apr. 1914, 2; 14 Apr. 1914, 3.

[41] *San Diego Union*, 14 Apr. 1914, 1.

[42] Ibid.

[43] Ibid., 1, 3. At this time the navy had Atlantic, Pacific, and Asiatic Fleets, plus two in reserve. But the Atlantic Fleet was the one in which the bulk of its strength, its battleship strength, was concentrated. Two premises co-existed here—first, that any major division invited effective defeat; second, that shifts of concentration could be accomplished soon enough to meet emergencies. Even so, the West began to agitate for what was really division. After World War I, the navy did shift its concentration to the Pacific. Yet the issue was not resolved until the "Two-Ocean Navy Act" (Naval Expansion Act) was approved in 1940. See George W. Baer, *One Hundred Years of Sea Power, The U.S. Navy, 1890-1990* (Stanford, Calif.: Stanford University Press, 1994), 134-35, 152; Harvey M. Beigel, "The Battle Fleet's Home Port: 1919-1940," *United States Naval Institute Proceedings*, 111 (Mar. 1985, hist. supp.): 54-63; William R. Braisted, *The United States Navy in the Pacific, 1909-1922* (Austin: University of Texas Press, 1971), 172-74; Julius A. Furer, *Administration of the Navy Department in World War II* (Washington, D.C.: GPO, 1959), 173-80; Alfred Thayer Mahan, "The Panama Canal and the Distribution of the Fleet," *North American Review*, 200 (1914): 406-17; U.S. Navy, *Annual Reports of the Navy Department for the Fiscal Year 1913* (Washington, D.C.: GPO, 1914), 36-37.

[44] Georgia D. Birchler, "Franklin D. Roosevelt as Godfather of San Diego," unpublished research paper, San Diego State University, 1976, esp. 1, 8-9, in Research Archives, vertical file, f. 497, Presidents, at San Diego Historical Society.

[45] ER to SDR, 15 Apr. [1914], at FDRL; *San Francisco Examiner*, 15 Apr. 1914, 5.

[46] *San Francisco Chronicle*, 15 Apr. 1914, 1; *Bulletin* (San Francisco), 15 Apr. 1914, 1.

[47] *Bulletin* (San Francisco), 15 Apr. 1914, 1. Actually, FDR had a little more immediate information than he indicated. Howe had written him that the State Department was unhappy about Mayo's ultimatum. "I am afraid Mayo is not a good 'watchful waiter'," he had said, referring to Wilson's early, cautious policy towards the Huerta regime. See LMH to FDR, 11 Apr. 1914, in LMH Papers, Correspondence, Jan.-June 1914, at FDRL.

[48] FDR to Aid for Operations, coded telegram and translation, 15 [April 1914], in RG 80, General Records of the Navy Dept., General Correspondence, f. 27824-32, at NA.

[49] San Francisco Chronicle, 15 Apr. 1914, 2.

[50] San Francisco Examiner, 16 Apr. 1914, 6.

[51] *San Francisco Chronicle*, 16 Apr. 1914, 12. See also *San Francisco Examiner*, 16 Apr. 1914, 1, 6.

[52] *San Francisco Examiner*, 16 Apr. 1914, 6. See also *San Francisco Chronicle*, 16 Apr. 1914, 12.

[53] *San Francisco Chronicle*, 16 Apr. 1914, 12. See also *San Francisco Examiner*, 16 Apr. 1914, 6. FDR gave no credit to the army's role in the acquisition of California—say to Stephen Watts Kearny or John Charles Frémont. Perhaps this reflected his fondness for the navy.

[54] San Francisco Chronicle, 16 Apr. 1914, 12; San Francisco Examiner, 17 Apr. 1914, 3.

[55] U.S. Navy, Annual Reports, 1914, 135.

[56] Vallejo Evening News, 16 Apr. 1914, 1; San Francisco Examiner, 17 Apr. 1914, 3.

[57] U.S. Navy, Annual Reports, 1914, 251; Vallejo Evening News, 17 Apr. 1914, 1.

[58] George F. Gruner, *Blue Water Beat: The Two Lives of the Battleship USS "California"* (Palo Alto, Calif.: Glencannon, 1996), chaps. 1-6.

[59] *Bulletin* (San Francisco), 17 Apr. 1914, 2.

[60] ER to SDR, 15 Apr. [1914], at FDRL; *San Francisco Chronicle*, 17 Apr. 1914, 9; *San Francisco Examiner*, 18 Apr. 1914, 3. Eleanor had spent the night of April 16 with "Mrs. Reid," and Franiklin was to join her there the next night. Mrs. Reid was in all probability Elisabeth Mills Reid, daughter of mining tycoon Darius O. Mills and widow of Whitelaw Reid, editor and publisher of the *New York Tribune.* She was a good friend of Bamie Roosevelt (see n. 32); her daughter, Jean, was close to Eleanor. For years the Mills family had had an estate at Millbrae, not far south of Hunters Pt. See ER to SDR, 15 Apr. [1914], at FDRL; Rixey, *Bamie,* 69, 195; ER, *My Story,* 107-08; also Joseph Dees, "History of D.O. Mills, Mills Estate," unpublished monograph, 1947, Student Monographs, 958/1, at San Mateo County History Museum Archive, Redwood City, Calif.

[61] LMH to FDR, telegram, 15 Apr. 1914, Trip File: 1914, at FDRL. LMH's draft is in RG 80, f. 27824-32, at NA.

[62] LMH to FDR, partly coded telegram, 15 Apr. 1914, in FDR Papers as ASN, Personal Files, Correspondence, LMH, at FDRL; JD to Flag Officer, *California*, translated telegram, 15 Apr. 1914, in JD Papers, reel 47, f. Mexico, 1913-1914 Apr., at LC.
Howe used the *Western Union Telegraphic Code (Universal Edition).* This was published in New York by the International Cable Directory Co. in 1900, and, without substantive change, saw later imprints. (One of these, measuring 5.5" x 6.5" was designed for travelers.) Howe and Roosevelt and Daniels employed it several times, in their own way, during the 1914 trip. It was probably the predecessor of the "dictionary code" the three used beginning about 1915. (See Ward, *First-Class Temperament*, 334: n. 31.) Imprints are in Western Union Telegraph Company Records, Series 13: Operating Records, 1868-1970, Subseries 4: Operator Code Books/Cipher Books, 1880-1917, at the Archives Center, National Museum of American History/Smithsonian Institution.
Credit for identifying the code is due Robert J. Hanyok of the Center for Cryptologic History, National Security Agency. Translations as needed are by the present author.

[63] Fiske to FDR, telegram, 16 Apr. 1914, in Trip File: 1914, at FDRL. Fiske's draft is in RG 80, General Records of the Navy Dept., General Correspondence, f. 27824-30, at NA.

[64] JD to FDR, telegram, 16 Apr. 1914, in FDR Papers as ASN, Personal Files, Correspondence, JD, 1913-1916, at FDRL.

[65] JD to FDR, coded telegram, 16 Apr. 1914, in FDR Papers as ASN, Personal Files, Correspondence, JD, 1913-1916, at FDRL.

[66] Quirk, Affair of Honor, 61.

[67] FDR to JD, telegram, 16 Apr. 1914, in RG 80, f. 27824-32, at NA; Doyle to FDR, telegram, 19 Apr. 1914, in Trip File: 1914, at FDRL.

[68] FDR to Davis, draft telegram, 16 Apr. 1914, and Davis to FDR, telegram, 16 Apr. 1914, both in Trip File: 1914, at FDRL.

[69] FDR to JD, telegram, 17 Apr. 1914, in RG 80, f. 27824-32, at NA. FDR's draft is in FDR Papers as ASN, Personal Files, Correspondence, JD, 1913-1916, at FDRL.

[70] *San Francisco Examiner*, 17 Apr. 1914, 3. See also *Bulletin* (San Francisco), 16 Apr. 1914, 1; *San Francisco Call and Post*, 17 Apr. 1914, 4.

[71] FDR to JD, coded telegram, 18 Apr. 1914, in RG 80, f. 27824-32, at NA.

[72] Eugene K. Chamberlain, "The Japanese Scare at Magdalena Bay," *Pacific Historical Review*, 24 (1955): 345-59; *New York Times,* 21 Dec. 1951, 7.
In the context of TR's influence on FDR (see n. 4), an earlier event requires mention. On 25 Feb. 1898, Navy Secretary John D. Long took the afternoon off. Returning the next day, he learned Assistant Secretary Theodore Roosevelt had instructed Commodore George Dewey to make ready for offensive operations in the Philippines should there be war with Spain. (See Nathan Miller, *Theodore Roosevelt, A Life* [New York: Morrow, 1992], 267-69.) FDR could well have had TR's activism in mind, loosely equating Magdalena Bay with Manila Bay.

[73] LMH to FDR, telegram, 18 Apr. 1914, in Trip File: 1914, at FDRL.

[74] LMH to FDR, coded telegram, 18 Apr. 1914, in Trip File: 1914, at FDRL. FDR wrote out a translation on the back of *Post-Intelligencer* to FDR, telegram, 16 Apr. 1914, in Trip File: 1914, at FDRL.

[75] Seattle Post-Intelligencer, 20 Apr. 1914, 1, 5.

[76] Proposed Schedule for Visit of Assistant Secretary of the Navy Franklin D. Roosevelt, [Apr. 1914], in Trip File: 1914, at FDRL; *Seattle Daily Times*, 21 Apr. 1914, 3; *Who Was Who in America*, 5 (1969-73), s.vv. "Milo F. Draemel."

[77] *Seattle Post-Intelligencer*, 20 Apr. 1914, 1; 21 Apr. 1914, 8.

[78] *New York Times*, 16 Dec. 1925, 25; 1 Jun. 1913, sec. 2, p. 5; 29 Jun. 1913, sec. 2, p. 1.

[79] Seattle Daily Times, 23 Apr. 1914, 1, 3; Seattle Post-Intelligencer, 24 Apr. 1914, 1.

[80] Seattle Daily Times, 16 Apr. 1914, 5; Seattle Post-Intelligencer, 20 Apr. 1914, 1.

[81] FDR to LMH, draft telegram and code worksheet, [19 Apr. 1914], in Trip File: 1914, at FDRL.

[82] LMH to FDR, partly coded telegram, 20 Apr. 1914, in Trip File: 1914, at FDRL.

[83] Quirk, *Affair of Honor*, 73-77, 103, 151.

[84] Seattle Sun, 20 Apr. 1914, 8; Seattle Post-Intelligencer, 21 Apr. 1914, 8.

[85] *Seattle Post-Intelligencer*, 27 Oct. 1905, 1; C.H. Hanford (ed.), *Seattle and Environs, 1852-1924*, 3 vols. (Chicago: Pioneer Historical Publishing, 1924), 1: 388, 391.

[86] *Seattle Sun*, 20 Apr. 1914, 8.

[87] Seattle Post-Intelligencer, 21 Apr. 1914, 8.

[88] Hanford, *Seattle and Environs*, 1: 415, 422; Neil H. Purvis, "History of the Lake Washington Canal," *Washington Historical Quarterly*, 25 (1934): 114-27, 210-13.

[89] FDR may not have made a written recommendation, but the visit did leave an impression. See esp. FDR to C.B. Yandell, 14 May 1914, in Trip File: 1914, at FDRL. Yandell was the secretary of the Seattle Chamber of Commerce.

[90] *Washington Democracy*, 24 Apr. 1914, 1, 5. See also *Seattle Daily Times*, 21 Apr. 1914, 4; *Seattle Post-Intelligencer*, 21 Apr. 1914, 8.

[91] Haley, Revolution and Intervention, 140-41; Quirk, Affair of Honor, 118.
The ABC mediation failed, but Huerta resigned soon after it did, and in Nov. 1914 the last U.S. forces left Veracruz. See Haley, esp. 150; Quirk, esp. 169-70.

There was a second intervention, however. In 1916 Pancho Villa raided Columbus, N.M. (see n. 15), and Wilson directed troops under Gen. John J. Pershing to hunt him down. But by early 1917, with Pershing over three hundred miles into northern Mexico, Villa still at large, and World War I a far greater problem, the operation was ended. See Haley, esp. 244.

[92] *Seattle Daily Times*, 21 Apr. 1914, 3; *Seattle Post-Intelligencer*, 22 Apr. 1914, 1, 7; Robert M. Doyle to FDR, 10 Apr. 1914 and DeWitt R. Blamer to FDR, 11 Apr. 1914, both in Trip File: 1914, at FDRL.

[93] U. S. Navy, Annual Reports, 1914, 139-40; Seattle Daily Times, 23 Apr. 1914, 3; Seattle Post-Intelligencer, 23 Apr. 1914, 5.

[94] *Bremerton News*, 18 Apr. 1914, 1; 22 Apr. 1914, 1; 25 Apr. 1914, 1. See also *Seattle Post-Intelligencer,* 23 Apr. 1914, 5.

[95] Seattle Daily Times, 21 Apr. 1914, 7; Seattle Post-Intelligencer, 23 Apr. 1914, 5.

[96] See, for example, *Bulletin* (San Francisco), 16 Apr. 1914, 2; *San Francisco Call and Post*, 17 Apr. 1914, 4; *Seattle Daily Times*, 21 Apr. 1914, 3; *Seattle Post-Intelligencer*, 21 Apr. 1914, 8. The last article said FDR actually kept a tug waiting at dockside through April 20, ready to take him to the Bremerton Navy Yard.

[97] LMH to FDR, telegram, 22 Apr. 1914, in Trip File: 1914, at FDRL; LHM's draft is in FDR Papers as ASN, Personal Files, Correspondence, FDR (1), at FDRL.

[98] Itinerary of the Assistant Secretary, in Trip File: 1914, at FDRL; *Seattle Daily Times*, 21 Apr. 1914, 4; *Seattle Post-Intelligencer*, 23 Apr. 1914, 5.

[99] *New York Times,* 27 Apr. 1914, 2.

[100] *Minneapolis Tribune*, 26 Apr. 1914, sec. 1, p. 3.

[101] The documents do not demonstrate intelligence gathering. Moreover, at this point Howe sent a two-page update in which Mexico is simply not mentioned (LMH to FDR, 4 Apr. 1914, in FDR, Papers as ASN, Personal Files, Correspondence, LMH, at FDRL).

[102] E. David Cronon (ed.), *The Cabinet Diaries of Josephus Daniels, 1913-1921* (Lincoln: University of Nebraska Press, 1963), viii-ix.

[103] JD was already prepared for activism. Early on, U.S. Senator Elihu Root had advised, "Whenever a Roosevelt rides, he wishes to ride in front." See Daniels, *Wilson Era,* esp. 127.

[104] Itinerary of the Assistant Secretary, in Trip File: 1914, at FDRL.

[105] New York Times, 21 May 1914, 1.

[106] Ibid.

[107] FDR to ER [19 May 1914], in *Personal Letters*, 219. There is an eerie similarity between this episode and the one in 1898 involving TR and Long (see n. 72).

[108] Grace Tully, *F.D.R., My Boss* (New York: Scribner's, 1949), 367.

[109] Robert F. Cross, Sailor in the White House, The Seafaring Life of FDR (Annapolis, Md.: Naval Institute Press, 2003), 25-34; Davis, Beckoning of Destiny, 71-72; Geoffrey C. Ward, Before the Trumpet, Young Franklin D. Roosevelt, 1882-1905 (New York: Harper and Row, 1985), 159-60.

How much of FDR's personality—here his love of the sea—was a result of nature as against nurture is a tantalizing question. Yet one would need much family history just to offer a conjecture. For the present purpose, it is probably best to join with developmental psychologists who argue that the two factors coexist in most people, even though one may be dominant in the case of a given trait. See Lerner, *Concepts and Theories,* chap. 4.

[110] William F. Halsey and J. Bryan III, *Admiral Halsey's Story* (New York: McGraw-Hill, 1947), 17-18.

[111] Cross, *Sailor*, 67-70; ER, *My Story*, 203-05; William J. Stewart and Charyl C. Pollard, "Franklin D. Roosevelt, Collector," *Prologue*, 1 (Winter 1969): 13-28.

[112] Burns, Lion and Fox, Daniels, Wilson Era, 124.

[113] Burns, *Lion and Fox*, 51-52; Freidel, *Apprenticeship*, 172-73.

[114] Cross, *Sailor*, 133-34; Thomas C. Hone, "The Evolution of the U.S. Fleet, 1933-1943: How the President Mattered," in Edward J. Marolda (ed.), *FDR and the Navy* (New York: St. Martin's 1998), 77-82, 99-101.

[115] William D. Leahy, *I Was There* (New York: McGraw-Hill, 1950), 103; Edward S. Miller, *War Plan Orange, The U.S. Strategy to Defeat Japan, 1897-1945* (Annapolis, Md.: Naval Institute Press, 1991), chaps. 1, 4, 30; Russell F. Weigley, *The American Way of War, A History of United States Military Strategy and Policy* (Bloomington: Indiana University Press, 1973), chaps. 9, 12, 13.

[116] Cross, *Sailor*, 81-82, 110-21; Kenneth S. Davis, *FDR, The New Deal Years, 1933-1937, A History* (New York: Random House, 1986), 330-35, 381-99, 580-88; Kenneth S. Davis, *FDR, Into the Storm, 1937-1940, A History* (New York: Random House, 1993), 260-65, 270-81.

[117] Cross, *Sailor*, 139-44, 168-74, 185-90; Burns, *Soldier of Freedom,* 125-31, 402-16, 564-80. See also K.C. Holm, "A Famous Old Sailor," *United States Naval Institute Proceedings*, 95 (Mar. 1969): 149-51.

[118] Bernard Asbell, *When F.D.R. Died* (New York: Holt, Rinehart, and Winston, 1961), 31-35. The watercolor by artist Elizabeth Shoumatoff is at the "Little White House" in Warm Springs, Geo.

[119] Quoted by John Morton Blum, *From the Morgenthau Diaries*, vol. 1, *Years of Crisis, 1928-1938* (Boston: Houghton Mifflin, 1959), 253-54. See also Arthur M. Schlesinger Jr., *The Age of Roosevelt*, vol. 2, *The Coming of the New Deal* (Boston: Houghton Mifflin, 1959), 583-84.

[120] Ward, Before the Trumpet, 204.

[121] Davis, *Beckoning of Destiny*, 146-47, 152; Freidel, *Apprenticeship*, 55-56.

[122] Burns, *Lion and Fox*, 472-77; Schlesinger, *Coming of New Deal*, 536-39.

[123] Harold L. Ickes, *The Secret Diary of Harold L. Ickes*, vol. 2, *The Inside Struggle, 1936-1939* (New York: Simon and Schuster, 1954), 345; James F. Byrnes, *All in One Lifetime* (New York: Harper and Bros., 1958), 216-31.

[124] ER, *This I Remember* (New York: Harper and Bros., 1949), 2-3, 5.

[125] FDR statement to Molly Dewson, quoted by Burns, *Lion and Fox*, 285. Mary W. ("Molly") Dewson was a Democratic Party leader and friend of both ER and FDR.

[126] Davis, Beckoning of Destiny, chap. 9; Freidel, Apprenticeship, chap 6; Ward, First-Class Temperament, chap. 4.

[127] See nn. 4, 72, 107. For FDR at least, while ambition was probably dominant as against navalism, uncertainty remains. Anyway, the latter would serve the former.

[128] Burns, *Lion and Fox*, chap. 15; Davis, *Into the Storm,* chaps. 2-3.

[129] Josephus Daniels, *Shirt-Sleeve Diplomat* (Chapel Hill: University of North Carolina Press, 1947), chap. 20.

[130] See Lerner, *Concepts and Theories*, chap. 5.

[131] Irwin F. Gellman, *Good Neighbor Diplomacy, United States Policies in Latin America, 1933-1945*, in Johns Hopkins University Studies in Historical and Political Science, ser. 97, no. 2 (Baltimore: Johns Hopkins University Press, 1979), 38.

[132] Burns, *Lion and Fox*, 437-42; Davis, *Into the Storm*, 603-11.

[133] FDR, First Inaugural Address, 4 Mar. 1933, and FDR, "Let Us Move Forward with Strong and Active Faith," [11] Apr. 1945, both in *The Public Papers and Addresses of Franklin D. Roosevelt*, comp. Samuel I. Rosenman, 13 vols. (New York: Random House et al., 1938-50), 2: 11; 13: 616.

[134] Tugwell, Democratic Roosevelt, 36-37.

[135] Rollins, Roosevelt and Howe, 27; Stiles, Man behind Roosevelt, 30-32.

[136] Frances Perkins, *The Roosevelt I Knew* (New York: Viking, 1946), 11-12.

[137] Davis, Beckoning of Destiny, 135-37; Ward, Before the Trumpet, 235-36.

[138] Howeth, Communications-Electronics, 237-45; White, Pioneer and Patriot, chap. 9.

[139] Frank Freidel, *Franklin D. Roosevelt*, vol. 2, *The Ordeal* (Boston: Little, Brown, 1954), 8-10; White *Pioneer and Patriot*, 99-102; [FDR], Memorandum for Secretary of the Navy, 8 Apr. 1919, and FDR to George C. Sweet, 9 Apr. 1919, both in RG 38, Office of Naval Intelligence, Confidential Correspondence, 1913-24, f. 21500:602, at NA. The assignment to France also appears in the transcript of Sweet's naval service.

[140] Sweet, Transcript of Naval Service; White, *Pioneer and Patriot*, 143-46.

[141] White, Pioneer and Patriot, 165-66.

[142] *New York Times*, 30 Jun. 1932, 17.

[143] Ewing Laporte (comp.), Official Report of the Proceedings of the Democratic National Convention Held at Chicago, Illinois, June $27^{th}$ to July $2^{nd}$, Inclusive, 1932 [Washington, D.C.: Democratic National Committee, 1932], 211.

[144] Thomas M. Storke, *I Write for Freedom* (Fresno, Calif.: McNally and Loftin, 1962), 108-18. A problem is that so many people were really or allegedly important to the fourth-ballot vote. (See Nathan Miller, *FDR, An Intimate History* [Garden City, N.Y.: Doubleday, 1983], 275-76.) For much detail see Russell M. Posner, "California's Role in the Nomination of Franklin D. Roosevelt," *California Historical Society Quarterly*, 39 (1960): 121-39.

[145] Duncan Aikman, "Mrs. Greenway Charts Her Own Course," *New York Times Magazine,* 21 Apr. 1935, 9, 11; Miller, *Isabella Greenway,* 244-45; Miller, "Volume of Friendship," 152.

[146] Irwin F. Gellman, *Secret Affairs, Franklin D. Roosevelt, Cordell Hull, and Sumner Welles* (Baltimore: Johns Hopkins University Press, 1955), esp. 59, 221; W. Averell Harriman and Elie Abel, *Special Envoy to Churchill and Stalin, 1941-1946* (New York: Random House, 1946), esp. 234-446.

[147] Christopher Andrew, For the President's Eyes Only, Secret Intelligence and the American Presidency from Washington to Bush (New York: HarperCollins, 1995), esp. 82-84, 92-94; Doris Kearns Goodwin, No Ordinary Time, Franklin and Eleanor Roosevelt: The Home Front in World War II (New York: Simon and Schuster, 1994), 27-29.

[148] Joseph P. Lash, Eleanor and Franklin, The Story of Their Relationship, Based on Eleanor Roosevelt's Private Papers (New York: Norton, 1971), 510.

[149] Kenneth S. Davis, *FDR, The War President, 1940-1943, A History* (New York: Random House, 2000), 7-8; Robert E. Sherwood, *Roosevelt and Hopkins*, rev. ed. (New York: Harper and Bros., 1950), 9.

[150] FDR, State of the Union Message, 11 Jan. 1944, in *Public Papers,* 13: 41.

[151] Perkins, Roosevelt I Knew, 333.

[152] FDR to [Parents], 26 Jan. 1899, in *F.D.R., His Personal Letters*, vol. 1, *Early Years*, ed. Elliott Roosevelt (New York: Duell, Sloan and Pearce, 1947), 253-55; Ward, *Before the Trumpet*, 319.

[153] ER, *This I Remember*, 23. See also Daniel R. Fusfeld, *The Economic Thought of Franklin D. Roosevelt and the Origins of the New Deal*, in Columbia Studies in the Social Sciences, no. 586 (New York: Columbia University Press, 1956), esp. 66-70.

[154] Foster Rhea Dulles and Melvyn Dubofsky, *Labor in America: A History*, 5th ed. (Arlington Heights, Ill.: Harlan Davidson, 1993), chap. 15.

[155] Ibid. See also T.H. Watkins, *The Great Depression, America in the 1930's* (Boston: Little, Brown, 1993), 266-67.

[156] U.S. Census Bureau, Historical Statistics of the United States, Colonial Times to 1970, 2 pts. (Washington, D.C.: GPO, 1975), 1: 177; Thomas H. Greer, What Roosevelt Thought, The Social and Political Ideas of Franklin D. Roosevelt (East Lansing: Michigan State University Press, 1958), 124-26; Tugwell, Democratic Roosevelt, 530-31.

[157] FDR, "The 'Forgotten Man' Speech," 7 Apr. 1932, and FDR, "New Conditions Impose New Requirements upon Government, and Those Who Conduct Government" [Commonwealth Club Speech], 23 Sep. 1932, both in *Public Papers*, 1: 624-27, 752-56.

[158] Watkins, *Great Depression*, 267-69.

[159] FDR, State of the Union Message, 11 Jan. 1944; FDR, State of the Union Message, 6 Jan. 1945, both in *Public Papers,* 13: 40-41, 503-05. For a monograph see Cass R. Sunstein, *The Second Bill of Rights, FDR's Unfinished Revolution and Why We Need It Now More than Ever* (New York: Basic Books, 2004), esp. intro.

[160] Robert Dallek, *Lone Star Rising, Lyndon Johnson and His Times, 1908-1960* (New York: Oxford University Press, 1991), 160-62.

[161] Roy Jenkins, *Franklin Delano Roosevelt*, ed. John Q. Barrett (New York: Holt, 2003), 3.

[162] Fusfeld, Economic Thought, 49-51; Greer, What Roosevelt Thought, 59-62.

[163] Herbert D. Croly, *The Promise of American Life* (New York: Macmillan, 1910), 414.

[164] Freidel, *Apprenticeship*, 132-33; Fusfeld, *Economic Thought*, 5-6, 51.

[165] This is not to scant any thread of ideas from Croly to TR, and from TR to FDR. See Burns and Dunn, *Three Roosevelts,* esp. 125, 277.

[166] FDR, First Inaugural Address, 4 Mar. 1933, 14; FDR, State of the Union Message, 11 Jan. 1944, 35.

[167] Isaiah Berlin, "Franklin D. Roosevelt," in *Personal Impressions*, ed. Henry Hardy (New York: Viking, 1981), esp. 28.

[168] FDR, First Inaugural Address as New York Governor, 1 Jan. 1929, in *Public Papers*, 1: 76.

[169] FDR, State of the Union Message, 6 Jan. 1941, and FDR, Fourth Inaugural Address, 20 Jan. 1945, both in *Public Papers*, 9: 672; 13: 524.

[170] Adviser Harry Hopkins thought that the Four Freedoms "everywhere in the world" might be a stretch; asked Roosevelt if Americans were concerned about, say, Java. FDR countered, "I'm afraid they'll have to be some day, Harry." See conversation as summarized by Samuel I. Rosenman, *Working with Roosevelt* (New York: Harper and Bros., 1952), 262-64.

[171] John Gunther, *Roosevelt in Retrospect, A Profile in History* (New York: Harper and Bros., 1950), 243.

In: Presidents and War
Editors: A. Eksterowicz and G. Hastedt, pp. 181-196
ISBN 978-1-61668-917-9


*Chapter 11*

# ABSORBING THE FIRST BLOW: TRUMAN AND THE COLD WAR

***John M. Schuessler***

*The views expressed in this academic research paper are those of the author and do not reflect the official policy or position of the US government or the Department of Defense.*

## INTRODUCTION

In the historiography on the Cold War, a common assertion is that the Truman administration had to use overheated rhetoric to shock the public into supporting its containment policy [1]. Ideological excess aside, however, what stands out about the Cold War is the relatively forthright way in which the Truman administration escalated the conflict. One finds few of the evasions and distortions that characterize American entry into World War II or Vietnam. The argument of this article is that the administration was able to be transparent about its intentions because, in contrast with the latter cases, it was not looking to provoke a fight with its adversary. However aggressive its containment strategy, it was the Soviet side that made the first overt move by giving the green light to the Korean War. Responding to what was widely seen as blatant aggression, Truman was able to deploy forces to Korea with little pushback from Congress or the public, even though he had failed to consult with them. Indeed, popular fears of a "garrison state" gave way to a massive military buildup and stronger commitments to NATO. If Truman had to contend with any opinion problem at the time, it was not isolationist sentiment but its opposite, as 1950 marked the high tide of preventive war agitation. In all these ways, the case attests to the political advantages of absorbing the first blow, advantages that Roosevelt and Johnson had to do largely without as they were mobilizing support for war.

The article unfolds in six sections. First, it briefly discusses the conditions under which one might expect leaders to deceive, using World War II and Vietnam as illustrations. It then takes up the Cold War case. It provides an overview of its origins; outlines the evolution of the containment policy; focuses on the events surrounding the outbreak of the Korean War; and discusses the escalation of the Cold War that Korea made possible. The final section concludes.

## EXPLAINING DECEPTION

Why do leaders resort to deception to sell wars to their publics? Elsewhere the author has argued that the need to generate public consent is itself to blame [2]. Specifically, leaders resort to deception when they anticipate domestic opposition to an open declaration of hostilities, and deception promises to blunt that opposition. Such dissent is especially likely in cases where the benefits of using force do not clearly outweigh the costs. As a general rule, the less substantial and imminent the threat and the less assured a quick and decisive victory, the more contentious a use of force is likely to be. Preventive war, for example, is usually contested on these grounds [3]. In such cases, leaders have incentives to preempt debate by escalating the use of force incrementally, taking pains to shift responsibility for hostilities onto the adversary. The process culminates in a manufactured crisis that justifies open warfare. Deception is entailed insofar as leaders conceal their designs, exploit pretexts to justify escalation, and oversell the use of force.

The American experiences in World War II and in Vietnam provide illustrations [4]. Starting with the former, Roosevelt feared that if Hitler were able to dominate Europe he would pose an intolerable threat to the Western Hemisphere. To stall the Nazi advance, the U.S. extended assistance to those powers resisting Hitler, first Great Britain and then the Soviet Union. Such assistance was limited to lend-lease aid and convoy protection, but by the fall of 1941 leading officials had concluded that the defeat of Germany would require American belligerency. The problem was that there was widespread opposition to expanded involvement in the war. A diverse anti-interventionist movement, with significant representation in Congress, had mobilized to challenge administration initiatives, and this movement fed off a deeply ambivalent public opinion, which supported aid to the allies but was strongly opposed to formal belligerency.

Roosevelt was sensitive to the domestic mood and believed that an effective policy abroad required a consensus at home. Given the persistence of anti-interventionism, such a consensus was bound to be elusive in the case of a declaration of war. The president thus maneuvered the country in the direction of open hostilities while assuring a wary public that the country would remain at peace. This strategy entailed three types of deception. First, Roosevelt went to some lengths to conceal his belligerent intentions, for example by pledging to keep the U.S. out of the fighting even when the thrust of official thinking suggested that full-scale intervention would be required. Second, when the Nazis threatened to overrun the Allies in 1941, he sought out pretexts that would justify escalation. He was less successful in the Atlantic, where naval "incidents" such as the *Greer* episode failed to excite popular opinion, than in the Pacific, where the Pearl Harbor attack finally united the country behind war with the Axis. FDR may not have deliberately allowed the Pearl Harbor attack to happen, but it does appear that he brought matters to a head with Japan in order to have some "back door" into the European war. Finally, he indulged in rhetorical overkill at critical junctures, amplifying the Nazi threat to the Western hemisphere and exaggerating the liberal credentials of allies to justify expanded American involvement on their behalf.

Turning to the Vietnam case, Johnson confronted the same dilemma as Roosevelt- how to take the country into a war that was sure to meet with considerable skepticism - and ended up resorting to the same tactics. The situation in South Vietnam had deteriorated rapidly since he had assumed office, and trusted advisers agreed that only American military power could turn the situation around. Like his predecessors, Johnson feared that if he did not contain communism in Indochina, then dominoes would fall both abroad and at home. The problem was that while there was certainly a vocal minority calling for stronger action, this did not amount to a groundswell of support for intervening in another land war in Asia. LBJ could not ignore the fact that powerful segments of elite opinion were opposed to intervention and that the public was ambivalent at best.

To avoid a divisive debate on the subject, Johnson chose to escalate incrementally, exploiting a series of pretexts to justify the bombing of North Vietnam and the deployment of ground forces. All the while, he denied that a major change in policy was in the offing. This strategy entailed three types of deception. First, it required that the administration conceal its ultimate intent. To this end, Johnson and his advisers made early promises that the U.S. would not take over the fighting, did their planning in secret, pressured Congress to limit debate once escalation got underway, and advanced half-hearted peace initiatives to appease liberal critics. Second, it required that they exploit a series of pretexts to justify progressively stronger military measures. Among these, the most notable were the Gulf of Tonkin "incident," which yielded a supportive Congressional resolution, and the Pleiku attack, which resulted in the Rolling Thunder bombing campaign. Rolling Thunder, in turn, provided the rationale for the introduction of ground forces, which were ostensibly needed to protect airbases but were soon taking the fight to the Viet Cong. Finally, it entailed engaging in rhetorical "oversell." Leading officials relied on crude versions of the domino theory to make the case that a communist takeover would be catastrophic and fostered the impression that victory was in sight, despite internal predictions of a long war with an indeterminate outcome. As in the World War II case, these deceptions were crucial for overcoming domestic aversion to a wider war.

As the behavior of Roosevelt and Johnson attests, leaders are most prone to deceive when they anticipate opposition to a declaration of war. The puzzle that remains is how Truman was able to overcome domestic resistance to a stronger containment policy without the evasions and distortions that characterize the latter two cases. I begin to unravel this puzzle by reviewing the origins of the Cold War.

## The Origins of the Cold War

As the end of World War II approached, the United States became increasingly wary of its Soviet ally. With the impending defeat of Germany and Japan, vacuums of power were opening up in Europe and Asia that American leaders feared Russia would fill. After all, Soviet armies had played the leading role in defeating the Nazis, now occupied much of Eastern Europe, and were poised to enter the war against Japan. Moreover, other key allies, such as Great Britain, had been gravely weakened, leaving the Soviet Union as the only great power in the region. As the Office of Strategic Services (OSS) warned in April 1945, "Russia will emerge from the present conflict as by far the strongest nation in Europe and Asia – strong enough, if the United States should stand aside, to dominate Europe and at the same time to establish her hegemony over Asia. Russia's natural resources and manpower are so great that within relatively few years she can be much more powerful than either Germany or Japan has ever been. In the easily foreseeable future Russia may well outrank even the United States in military potential" [5].

Having just fought to prevent the Axis powers from dominating Eurasia, American leaders were hardly keen to allow the Soviets to do so. Their primary concern was not military aggression. Top officials knew that the Soviet Union had suffered immensely at the hands of the Nazis and would focus on reconstruction for the time being. It would be the height of folly for them to provoke a war with the United States in their current state of weakness. As the OSS concluded in January 1945, "Russia will have neither the resources nor, so far as economic factors are governing, the inclination, to embark on adventurist foreign policies which, in the opinion of Soviet leaders, might involve the USSR in a conflict or a critical armament race with the great Western powers" [6]. Rather, the primary concern was that Communist parties would capitalize on political and economic instability in Europe and Asia to seize power, indirectly enlarging the Soviet sphere of influence. Through such a process of psychological conquest, the Kremlin could capture or co-opt the industrial infrastructure, natural resources, and skilled labor of Eurasia [7].

This development was anathema to the national security of the United States because if a totalitarian state like the Soviet Union became too powerful, it, like Nazi Germany, could stir up trouble in the Western Hemisphere and threaten the homeland with strangulation or attack. Recent advances in airpower, in combination with the atomic bomb, made the latter prospect especially frightening [8]. In the event that the United States found itself isolated in a totalitarian world, it was feared that a "garrison state" would be the result, as Americans would be forced to sacrifice political and economic liberties for the regimentation required for national defense [9]. The National Security Council summed up the dangers in March 1948, "Between the United States and the USSR there are in Europe and Asia areas of great potential power which if added to the existing strength of the Soviet world would enable the latter to become so superior in manpower, resources, and territory that the prospect for the survival of the United States as a free nation would be slight" [10].

As the end of World War II approached, these were still long-term concerns. At the time, leading officials held out hope that they could cooperate with the Soviet Union in the postwar world. Roosevelt, for example, had envisioned the United States and the Soviet Union working together to keep the peace as two of the Four Policemen [11]. Over the course of the war, a range of disagreements had come to sour relations between the two sides, however. First was the issue of a second front. From the time of Pearl Harbor, Stalin had pressed Roosevelt and Churchill to open a second front in Europe in order to relieve Nazi pressure on the Soviet Union. After leading Stalin to expect such a front in 1942, Roosevelt opted instead to endorse a British proposal to invade North Africa, delaying the Normandy invasion until 1944. It does not appear that it was Roosevelt's intent to exhaust the Russians by making them carry the main burden of the fighting [12]. He wanted to take the offensive against Hitler as quickly as possible, but also wanted to maximize the chances of success while minimizing casualties. All of these considerations pointed toward a landing in North Africa.

Stalin, however, suspected that the allies had deliberately let the Soviet Union bear the brunt of the fighting, exacerbating his distrust of them.

Second was the problem of Germany. Until the end of the war, the Roosevelt administration remained divided over how to deal with a defeated Germany. The Treasury Department, with Roosevelt's support, was inclined toward dismemberment, in order to prevent the resurgence of German power. The State Department, however, wanted to integrate a disarmed but united Germany into the world economy, in order to foster democracy there and promote the economic recovery of Europe. The Soviets, for their part, had suffered immensely at the hands of the Nazis and did not look kindly upon the prospect of a rehabilitated Germany. In particular, they were determined to exact reparations in order to facilitate reconstruction and circumscribe Germany's military potential. With the end of the war, the economic situation in Europe grew desperate, triggering fears that Communist parties would exploit the resulting instability to seize power. From that point on, the United States' top priority was to revive German coal production in order to spur European economic recovery. This meant that reparations shipments to the Soviet Union would have to take second place to German rehabilitation. Still reeling from the war, the Soviets could not help but look on these developments with bitterness [13].

The strong stand on reparations was part of a larger strategy on the part of the United States to withhold reconstruction assistance from the Soviet Union in the hopes of extracting political concessions [14]. Of particular concern to leading officials was the Soviets' heavy-handed behavior in Eastern Europe, especially in Poland. Because of its sensitive location, the Soviets wanted a Poland they could depend on after the war, which meant one ruled by Communists. Roosevelt had been prepared to concede to Stalin a sphere of influence in Eastern Europe, but wanted it to be a relatively open one. He accepted that the countries of the region would be closely aligned with Russia on matters of foreign policy, but hoped that they would enjoy a measure of domestic autonomy. By way of the Four Freedoms and the Atlantic Charter, he had certainly led the American people to expect as much. When the Soviet Union recognized the Communist-dominated Lublin Committee as the provisional government of Poland in early 1945, some measure of conflict was unavoidable. At Yalta, Roosevelt attempted to secure Stalin's agreement to reorganize the Polish government on a broader democratic basis, but the Soviet leader had no intention of following through on promises of free elections. Upon succeeding to the presidency, Truman fared little better. He wanted to remove the "Soviet blackout" in Eastern Europe, but understood that he had limited leverage while Russian armies occupied the region. He more or less gave up on trying to save democracy in Eastern Europe by the end of 1945. By that point, the damage had been done: Leading officials had prodded the Soviet Union to accept an open sphere in Eastern Europe as a litmus test of their intentions. By imposing police states in Poland, Rumania, and Bulgaria, the Kremlin had failed that test, triggering fears that they were intent on wider expansion [15].

Those fears were seemingly confirmed at the beginning of 1946 when the Russians tried to make inroads into the eastern Mediterranean and the Middle East, an area that was particularly sensitive to Great Britain. They were slow to withdraw their forces from northern Iran, abetting separatist movements there, and pressed Turkey for the right to build military bases in the Dardanelles area. The Soviets eventually backed down in both crises, but not before elements of the Truman administration had become convinced that they sought world domination. This assessment was articulated most forcefully by George Kennan, deputy head of the U.S. mission in Moscow, in the "Long Telegram" of February 22, 1946. The central thrust of Kennan's analysis was that the Soviet Union was a totalitarian regime which depended on the exploitation of external threats to justify its repressive rule at home. In the Kremlin, the United States confronted "a political force committed fanatically to the belief that with [the] US there can be no permanent *modus vivendi*, that it is desirable and necessary that the internal harmony of our society be disrupted, our traditional way of life destroyed, the international authority of our state broken, if Soviet power is to be secure" [16]. The "Long Telegram," together with the Kremlin's provocative behavior in the Near East, convinced leading officials that accommodation with them was futile and that it was time to "get tough with Russia."

Around this time, a new policy began to take shape which aimed to induce Russian restraint by impressing them with American "patience and firmness." Its first public expression came on February 28, 1946 in a speech delivered to the Overseas Press Club by Secretary of State James Byrnes. In the speech, Byrnes put the Soviets on notice, informing them that "we will not and we cannot stand aloof if force or the threat of force is used contrary to the purposes and principles of the [United Nations] Charter"[17]. From that point on, no major concessions were made, on issues ranging from the postwar treatment of Germany to the international control of atomic energy. This reorientation of American policy culminated in the Truman Doctrine of March 12, 1947. In that speech, Truman portrayed the Soviet-American conflict as a clash between two mutually irreconcilable ideologies and famously declared that "it must be the policy of the United States to support free peoples who are resisting attempted subjugation by armed minorities or by outside pressures" [18]. If there had been any ambiguity before, the Cold War was now officially underway [19].

## Containment

From the Truman Doctrine onward, the United States moved aggressively to contain Soviet influence in Europe and Asia. The essence of the strategy, as articulated by Kennan, was threefold: (1) to restore the balance of power by building up "strongpoints" in Western Europe and Japan; (2) to bring about fragmentation within the international communist movement by encouraging nationalism; and (3) to gradually moderate Soviet behavior by the steady exertion of "counterpressure" [20]. The aim, in the end, was "strength at the center; strength at the periphery; the retraction of Soviet power and a change in the Soviet system." [21]. In this way, leading officials hoped to perpetuate American preponderance.

However ambitious their goals, it is important to emphasize that the Truman administration did not expect a military confrontation with the Soviet Union when they moved to implement containment, nor was it their intent to provoke one. Intelligence assessments at the time repeatedly concluded that the Russians were too weak to risk war with the United States, their conventional superiority in Europe outweighed by American advantages in atomic weapons and industrial capacity [22]. Privy to this intelligence, leading officials saw the threat from the Kremlin as primarily political, rather than military, in character [23]. The fear was that demoralized populations in Europe and Asia would succumb to Communist rule in the face of economic dislocation and social unrest, enlarging the Soviet sphere of influence. As Kennan told a National War College audience in October 1947,

"Remember that...as things stand today, it is not Russian military power which is threatening us, it is Russian political power...If it is not entirely a military threat, I doubt that it can be effectively met entirely by military means" [24].

Accordingly, the first initiatives pursued by the Truman administration were in the political, economic, and diplomatic spheres. The Truman Doctrine, for example, was designed to mobilize domestic opinion behind aid to Greece and Turkey at a time when Great Britain was suspending assistance to those governments because of financial constraints. The situation was especially dire in Greece, where a communist-led insurgency threatened to topple the government and align Greece with the Soviet Union. Leading officials worried that if Greece fell to communism, then Turkey, Iran, and possibly even Italy and France would follow by way of a domino effect. The only alternative seemed to be a massive infusion of aid to prop up the Greek regime. The Truman Doctrine constituted a form of ideological "shock therapy" meant to bring a reluctant Congress and public on board [25].

Beyond immediate aid to Greece and Turkey, the Truman administration's top priority in spring 1947 was to promote Western Europe's economic reconstruction. At the time the situation looked dire. For example, on May 27, Undersecretary of State for Economic Affairs William L. Clayton reported, "It is now obvious that we grossly underestimated the destruction to the European economy by the war...Without further prompt and substantial aid from the United States, economic, social, and political disintegration will overwhelm Europe" [26]. Assessments such as these stirred the administration into action. On June 15, Secretary of State George C. Marshall launched the European Recovery Program. The Marshall Plan, as it was called, was motivated primarily by geopolitical and ideological factors [27]. Administration officials feared that local Communists would capitalize on the economic disarray to seize power, enlarging the Soviet sphere of influence. As Truman explained to Congress in his special message on the Marshall Plan:

> Our deepest concern with European recovery is that it is essential to the maintenance of the civilization in which the American way of life is rooted. It is the only assurance of the continued independence and integrity of a group of nations who constitute a bulwark for the principles of freedom, justice and the dignity of the individual. The economic plight in which Europe now finds itself has intensified a political struggle between those who wish to remain free men living under the rule of law and those who would use economic distress as a pretext for the establishment of a totalitarian state. The next few years can determine whether the free countries of Europe will be able to preserve their heritage of freedom. If Europe fails to recover, the peoples of these countries might be driven to the philosophy of despair – the philosophy which contends that their basic wants can be met only by the surrender of their basic rights to totalitarian control [28].

The Marshall Plan was intended to avert just such a deterioration in the balance of power by building up Western Europe as a bulwark against Soviet expansion.

It was widely understood among leading officials that the economy of Western Europe could not recover fully without a substantial German contribution. Ruhr coal was considered especially crucial [29]. By the spring of 1947, the Truman administration wanted to do more than revive German industry, however. Around this time, the "western strategy" began to take shape [30]. According to this strategy, the United States, Britain, and France would "organize" their zones of occupation into a West German state, which would be tied to the western powers in a variety of ways. The United States and Britain had already taken the first important steps in this direction when they had merged their zones of occupation the previous summer. The thinking behind the "western strategy" was that an occupied Germany could not contribute fully to European recovery, but that a divided Germany was to be preferred to a unified one that succumbed to Soviet control or grew powerful enough to play off East against West. As Secretary of State Dean Acheson later framed the issue, "We are concerned with the integration of Germany into a free and democratic Europe. We have made and are making progress to this end with the part of Germany which we control and we shall not jeopardize this progress by seeking a unified Germany as in itself good" [31]. In time, leading officials hoped, this west German state could be integrated into a European political community, a "Third Force" capable of balancing Soviet power and containing Germany without a permanent American military presence [32]. The United States and its allies had reached sufficient agreement on these points to move forward with the creation of a west German state in early 1948 [33].

Like the other major initiatives of the early Cold War period, the creation of a west German state was primarily a political, economic, and diplomatic exercise. It reflected the thinking among leading officials that the reconstruction of Western Europe had to come before rearmament [34]. This assessment was shared even at the Pentagon. Frustrated as he was by the widening gap between commitments and capabilities, Secretary of Defense James Forrestal agreed that the objectives of U.S. policy were "economic stability, political stability and military stability…in about that order."[35]. This is not to say that there was no military component to containment. By 1948, the Truman administration had secured an extensive system of overseas bases from which to project power in the event of war, enjoyed a monopoly over atomic weapons, and was considering extending alliance guarantees to Western Europe in the form of a North Atlantic Treaty [36]. Nor is it to suggest that leading officials were unaware that their initiatives were provocative, especially the creation of a west German state [37]. The important point, however, is that the Truman administration did not expect Soviet *military* aggression. It was for this reason that policymakers felt able to rebuild Western Europe while postponing rearmament.

In the meantime, the Truman administration was counting on its atomic monopoly to deter any residual threat of Soviet adventurism. The United States had demobilized rapidly after World War II, and by 1947 very little was left of the military machine that had been built up during the war [38]. This meant that the United States had to settle for a tripwire strategy in Western Europe [39]. According to this strategy, Russian armies would overrun the continent at the outset of any war, but the United States would ultimately prevail by way of a sustained campaign of atomic bombardment. The upside of the tripwire strategy was that the United States did not have to maintain a large military establishment or deploy ground forces in order to deter Soviet aggression in Europe. Limited resources could be devoted instead to the Marshall Plan. The downside, however, was that the United States would have to bomb her own allies in the event of a war, yielding at best a Pyrrhic victory. Administration officials were more than aware of the tripwire strategy's liabilities. Omar Bradley, then U.S. Army chief of staff, remarked in April 1949 that "It must be perfectly apparent to the people of the United States that we cannot count on friends in Western Europe if our strategy in the event of war dictates that we shall first abandon them to the enemy with a promise of later liberation." [40]. Around the same time, Truman reminded the NATO foreign ministers that "a Soviet attack today, while we could eventually defeat it, would involve an operation of incalculable magnitude in which, even if eventual victory is sure, the consequences to the U.S., and particularly to Western Europe itself, might well be disastrous" [41]. The prospect of such a war was sufficiently sobering that American leaders felt they could not pursue a firm policy of containment in the 1948-49 period. The Truman Doctrine notwithstanding, the administration decided against interventions in Italy and Greece to ward off Communist takeovers [42].

## NSC-68 and the Korean War

The tripwire strategy was by no means ideal, but it did promise to deter war at moderate cost as long as the United States retained its monopoly over atomic weapons. This explains why the test explosion conducted by the Soviet Union in September 1949 set off such alarm bells in Washington [43]. A Soviet atomic capability meant that victory in a third world war could no longer be taken for granted, compromising the American deterrent. Leading officials feared the diplomatic consequences. One concern was that if the Europeans concluded the United States would not risk atomic retaliation on their behalf, they would back away from provocative initiatives like the rehabilitation of Germany. Another was that atomic weapons would enhance the Kremlin's penchant for risk-taking. Surveying Soviet moves in February 1950, Paul Nitze, director of the State Department's Policy Planning Staff, reported:

> In the aggregate, recent Soviet moves reflect not only a mounting militancy but suggest a boldness that is essentially new – and borders on recklessness, particularly since in the present international situation great stakes are involved in any USSR move, and any move directly or indirectly affects the US and risks US counter action. Nothing about the moves indicates that Moscow is preparing to launch in the near future an all-out military attack on the West. They do, however, suggest a greater willingness than in the past to undertake a course of action, including a possible use of force in local areas, which might lead to an accidental outbreak of general military conflict. Thus the chance of war through miscalculation is increased [44].

Together with the "loss" of China, the breaking of the atomic monopoly contributed to a perception among leading officials that the Communist side was seizing the initiative in the Cold War.

In light of Soviet atomic capabilities, the Truman administration conducted a comprehensive review of its strategic posture in the spring of 1950. The culmination of this exercise was NSC-68, formally titled "United States Objectives and Programs for National Security" [45]. Authored by a State-Defense Policy Review Group under the direction of Nitze, NSC-68 reaffirmed the goals of the containment policy while calling for a "rapid build-up of political, economic, and military strength in the free world" to offset Soviet gains [46]. The fear was that U.S. credibility would erode with its military advantage, undermining deterrence. Sensing American weakness, key allies would be intimidated while the Soviets would be emboldened. In NSC-68's terms, "Without superior aggregate military strength, in being and readily mobilizeable, a policy of 'containment' – which is in effect a policy of calculated and gradual coercion – is no more than a policy of bluff" [47]. The point of maximum danger would come in the mid-1950's when it was estimated that the Soviets would have enough atomic bombs to launch a surprise attack. The arms buildup was intended to avert general war by restoring deterrence. This would require large nuclear and conventional forces, the first to launch a decisive attack on the Soviet homeland in the event of war and the second to allow the "forward defense" of Europe [48]. The problem was that while this buildup was underway, the country was going to have to cross a kind of danger zone in which the Soviets might be tempted to risk war while conditions were favorable. "The assumption," in Trachtenberg's words, "was that a 'window' favoring the Soviets had opened, and that the American attempt to close it might well lead to a war"[49].

Evidence of Soviet risk-taking was not long in coming. On June 25, 1950, North Korean armies poured across the 38th parallel into South Korea. It was taken for granted that the Soviets had authorized the invasion and could be planning for aggression in more vital areas, such as the Middle East and Europe [50.] When it became clear that Soviet action elsewhere was unlikely and that only U.S. troops could save South Korea, Truman approved the deployment of two divisions from Japan, reversing the prior policy of military disengagement from the peninsula.

The president, like his advisers, feared the consequences of inaction. He believed that "If we let Korea down, the Soviets will keep right on going and swallow up one piece of Asia after another...If we were to let Asia go, the Near East would collapse and no telling what would happen in Europe" [51]. Determined to draw the line, Truman was ready to assume the defense of South Korea [52].

The public, rallying around the flag, saw matters in much the same way [53]. They were shocked by the blatant nature of the North Korean attack and, convinced that the war would be a short one, strongly supported intervention. Assured of public backing, Truman was able to commit the country to a limited war in Korea with little pushback from Congress, even though he had failed to consult with them.

On July 19, 1950, the president explained his decision to the people: "The free nations have now made it clear that lawless aggression will be met with force. The free nations have learned the fateful lesson of the 1930's. That lesson is that aggression must be met firmly. Appeasement leads only to further aggression and ultimately to war" [54].

## Escalating the Cold War, to a Point

The consensus surrounding Truman's decision to intervene in Korea is surprising given the domestic constraints that had been placed on his prosecution of the Cold War thus far [55]. Deep-rooted strands of anti-statism and isolationism in American political culture meant that there were limits on how quickly the administration could build up a peacetime military establishment and take on new commitments worldwide. The common fear was that a "garrison state" would result, not from hemispheric isolation as Truman warned, but from the demands of the containment policy. A strategy that required military preparedness and "entangling alliances," after all, was bound to concentrate unprecedented power in the executive branch. As journalist Hanson Baldwin posed the dilemma, "How can we prepare for total war without becoming a 'garrison state' and destroying the very qualities and virtues and principles we originally set about to save?" [56].

Fears of a "garrison state" were articulated most forcefully by Republicans such as Senator Robert A. Taft. Like Baldwin, Taft feared that "an all-out war program in time of peace might mean the final and complete destruction of those liberties which it is the very purpose of the preparation to protect." [57]. It was for this reason that he and his conservative allies in Congress opposed the tax increases and budget deficits that would have been necessary to fund an expansion of the national security state. Partisan politics aside, Truman was every bit as determined to reconcile military and economic considerations as the Republican opposition. From 1945 on, the president had resisted demands from the Pentagon that he sanction larger defense budgets, mainly because he did not want to run deficits. Rather, he settled on a "tripwire strategy" that promised to deter war at a moderate cost by relying on air-atomic power. As Hogan argues, this strategy was closer to the "Fortress America" concept championed by conservatives than many realized at the time [58]. Even after the Soviet nuclear breakthrough, Truman wanted to hold the line on defense spending. His initial reaction to NSC-68 was to shelve it until its cost implications became clear, and he told a press conference in May 1950 that "the defense budget next year will be smaller than it is this year" [59].

With the onset of the Korean War, Truman's attitude quickly changed. The Soviets had demonstrated their penchant for risk-taking, and would only become more aggressive as their capabilities increased. The heightened risk of global war convinced him, along with many in the opposition, that rearmament could not be postponed any longer. The result was the massive military buildup that had been ruled out up to that point. Over the coming years, the armed forces would double in size, fueled by a staggering 262 percent increase in defense appropriations. Only a fraction of this increase was earmarked for the fighting in Korea. The rest was meant to restore deterrence by enabling victory in a general war. "The North Korean invasion," as Wells argues, "made the case for a rapid U.S. military buildup that Paul Nitze and his associates had not been able to do" with NSC-68 [60]. One of the primary objectives of the buildup was the "forward defense" of Europe. To shore up weaknesses in this area, the administration launched a series of initiatives to strengthen the NATO alliance [61]. These included a push for European rearmament, the appointment of Dwight Eisenhower as Supreme Commander to lead NATO forces, and the deployment of four divisions to serve under him. Truman made the latter move over strong Republican objections. They questioned the wisdom of stationing American troops in Europe at a time of continued fighting in Korea and challenged the president's right to deploy them without congressional approval [62]. The fact that Truman prevailed in this debate is another indicator that domestic opinion was ready to assume commitments that had been politically untenable prior to the Korean War. As Acheson confided to the British and French foreign ministers in September 1950, "The Government of the United States has searched its intentions deeply...and has come to decisions which I think can only be described as a complete revolution in American foreign policy and in the attitude of the American people." [63].

The problem that Truman had to contend with during the Korean War was not isolationist sentiment but its opposite, as 1950 marked the high tide of preventive war agitation [64]. In mid-August, a Congressional delegation warned Acheson, "There is a growing disposition on the part of the American people to support the concept of preventive war. This growing attitude is sired in fear and will continue to grow in volume unless some bold alternative course of action is presented by the Government" [65]. Fuel was added to the fire on August 25 when Francis P. Matthews, the secretary of the navy, gave a controversial speech calling on Americans to become the world's first "aggressors for peace" [66]. The administration immediately disowned the speech, with Truman reminding the public on September 1 that

"We do not believe in aggressive or preventive war. Such war is the weapon of dictators, not of free democratic countries like the United States" [67].

Official sanction of the preventive war option was so unwelcome because Truman was generally determined to say and do nothing that might provoke the Soviet Union at a time of relative weakness [68]. This was a sentiment shared throughout the administration. For example, General J. Lawton Collins, the Army Chief of Staff, recommended on January 12, 1951 that "Since the United States is not now prepared to engage in global war, and will not be ready before 1 July 1952, we should take all honorable means to avoid any action that is likely to bring Russia into open conflict with the United States prior to that date" [69]. It was agreed that this ruled out a major escalation of the Korean War, which had become a live issue when China intervened in late November 1950 and threatened to drive U.S. forces off the peninsula [70].General Douglas MacArthur, the local commander, wanted to retaliate against the Chinese mainland with air power and use Chiang Kai-shek's troops to offset the enemy's superior numbers. The Joint Chiefs, however, overruled him, with Omar Bradley famously testifying before Congress that such a strategy "would involve us in the wrong war, at the wrong place, at the wrong time, and with the wrong enemy" [71]. Having finally secured domestic support for a stronger containment policy in Europe, administration officials did not want to undermine it by way of a wider war in Asia.

## CONCLUSION

Truman's refusal to escalate the Korean War in the face of stalemate contributed to its growing unpopularity and provided a political opening for Republicans, who charged the administration with underestimating the Communist threat in Asia. Public support for the larger policy of containment, however, remained robust. In June 1951, an opinion survey of popular attitudes toward NSC-68 found that the public "appears by all reliable objective criteria to be favorably disposed," with 83 percent wanting to continue current levels of spending on rearmament, 52 percent supporting economic assistance to allies, and 57 percent favoring sending U.S. troops to Europe [72]. These numbers reflect the fact that, however unhappy they were with the situation in Korea, the public had largely come around to the administration position on the Cold War.

In this respect, the case attests to the political advantages of absorbing the first blow. Truman was able to escalate the Cold War because he waited for the Soviet Union to make the first overt move, which turned out to be in Korea. It was the Korean War, in turn, which overcame domestic resistance to a stronger containment policy [73]. It is a testament to Truman's political instincts that he did not press the issue earlier and jeopardize the Cold War consensus in the process. In contrast, Roosevelt and Johnson were intent on picking a fight before they had secured a domestic consensus for war. The result was that they had to resort to deception to preempt opposition to their designs. The enduring lesson is that, whatever disadvantages might accrue to a policy of restraint, the damage to the democratic process can be severe when a policy of preemption is pursued.

## References


[1] This is a point made in Steven Casey, "Selling NSC-68: The Truman Administration, Public Opinion, and the Politics of Mobilization, 1950-51," *Diplomatic History*, Vol. 29, No. 4 (September 2005), pp. 655-656. He cites John Lewis Gaddis, *The United States and the Origins of the Cold War, 1941-1947* (New York, NY: Columbia University Press, 2000), pp. 351-352; Gaddis, *Strategies of Containment: A Critical Appraisal of Postwar American National Security Policy* (Oxford, UK: Oxford University Press, 1982), pp. 107-109; and Thomas J. Christensen, *Useful Adversaries: Grand Strategy, Domestic Mobilization, and Sino-American Conflict, 1947-1958* (Princeton, NJ: Princeton University Press, 1996), pp. 49-58, 122-127, among others.

[2] John Schuessler, "Doing Good by Stealth? Democracy, Deception, and the Use of Force" (PH.D. dissertation, University of Chicago, 2007).

[3] Randall L. Schweller, "Domestic Structure and Preventive War: Are Democracies More Pacific?" *World Politics*, Vol. 44, No. 2 (January 1992), pp. 235-269.

[4] Chapter 2 of the dissertation deals with World War II while chapter 3 deals with Vietnam.

[5] Cited in Dale C. Copeland, *The Origins of Major War* (Ithaca, NY: Cornell University Press, 2000), p. 151.

[6] Cited in James McAllister, *No Exit: America and the German Problem, 1943-1954* (Ithaca, NY: Cornell University Press, 2002), p. 41.

[7] Melvyn P. Leffler, *A Preponderance of Power: National Security, the Truman Administration, and the Cold War* (Stanford, CA: Stanford University Press, 1992), Introduction.

[8] Aaron L. Friedberg, *In the Shadow of the Garrison State: America's Anti-Statism and its Cold War Grand Strategy* (Princeton, NJ: Princeton University Press, 2000), pp. 36-38.

[9] On postwar fears of a "garrison state," see Michael J. Hogan, *A Cross of Iron: Harry S. Truman and the Origins of the National Security State, 1945-1954* (Cambridge, UK: Cambridge University Press, 1998) and Friedberg, *In the Shadow of the Garrison State.*

[10] *Foreign Relations of the United States*, 1948, Vol. I, p. 546. Cited in Gaddis, *Strategies of Containment*, p. 57.

[11] The other two Policemen would be Great Britain and China. See Gaddis, *The United States and the Origins of the Cold War*, pp. 9-13.

[12] Gaddis argues that "Roosevelt generally resisted efforts to deploy forces for the dual purposes of defeating the Germans and containing the Russians." See Gaddis, *Strategies of Containment*, p. 6 and Gaddis, *The United States and the Origins of the Cold War*, chapter 3.

[13] On the German question, see Gaddis, *The United States and the Origins of the Cold War*, chapter 4; Leffler, *A Preponderance of Power*, pp. 63-71; Copeland, *The Origins of Major War*, pp. 153-155; and McAllister, *No Exit*, pp. 49-55. Trachtenberg argues that, by the summer of 1945, the United States and the Soviet Union had tacitly agreed to partition Germany, to let each side do what it wanted in its own occupation zone. See Marc Trachtenberg, *A Constructed Peace: The Making of the European Settlement, 1945-1963* (Princeton, NJ: Princeton University Press, 1999), pp. 15-33.

[14] Gaddis, *The United States and the Origins of the Cold War*, chapter 6 and Copeland, *The Origins of Major War*, pp. 155-156.

[15] On Eastern Europe, see Gaddis, *The United States and the Origins of the Cold War*, chapter 5; Leffler, *A Preponderance of Power*, chapter 1, esp. pp. 34-36 and 49-54; and McAllister, *No Exit*, pp. 56-66. Trachtenberg argues that by the end of 1945 the United States had come to accept Soviet predominance in Eastern Europe as the basis for a larger spheres of influence settlement. See Trachtenberg, *A Constructed Peace*, pp. 4-15.

[16] *Foreign Relations of the United States*, 1946, Vol. VI, p. 706. Cited in Gaddis, *The United States and the Origins of the Cold War*, p. 303.

[17] Cited in Gaddis, *The United States and the Origins of the Cold War*, p. 305.

[18] *Public Papers of the Presidents of the United States*: Harry S. Truman, 1947 (Washington, DC: United States Government Printing Office, 1963), pp. 178-179.

[19] On the reorientation of American policy in 1946, see Gaddis, *The United States and the Origins of the Cold War*, chapters 9-10; Gaddis, *Strategies of Containment*, pp. 19-24; Leffler, *A Preponderance of Power*, chapter 2, esp. pp. 77-81, chapter 3, esp. pp. 106-110, chapter 4, esp. pp. 142-146; and Trachtenberg, *A Constructed Peace*, chapter 2.

[20] Kennan, *Strategies of Containment*, chapters 2-3.

[21] Leffler, *A Preponderance of Power*, p. 18.

[22] Gaddis, *Strategies of Containment*, p. 62 and Leffler, *Preponderance of Power*, pp. 5-6, 149, 218-219, 261-262, and 306-308.

[23] Leffler, *A Preponderance of Power*, chapter 4, esp. p. 180.

[24] Cited in Gaddis, *Strategies of Containment*, p. 40.

[25] Christensen, *Useful Adversaries*, pp. 49-54; Gaddis, *The United States and the Origins of the Cold War*, pp. 346-352; and Leffler, *A Preponderance of Power*, pp. 142-146.

[26] *Foreign Relations of the United States*, 1947, Vol. III, pp. 230-232. Cited in Leffler, *A Preponderance of Power*, p. 159.

[27] Leffler, *A Preponderance of Power*, pp. 157-164. See also McAllister, *No Exit*, pp. 124-135.

[28] *PPPUS*: Truman, 1947, pp. 516-517. Cited in Leffler, *A Preponderance of Power*, p. 200.

[29] Leffler, *A Preponderance of Power*, pp. 151-157.

[30] Trachtenberg, *A Constructed Peace*, p. 55.

[31] *Foreign Relations of the United States*, 1949, Vol. III, pp. 872-873. Cited in Gaddis, *Strategies of Containment*, p. 76.

[32] On "third force" planning, see McAllister, *No Exit*, chapter 4 and Sebastian Rosato, "The Strategic Logic of European Integration," (Ph.D., The University of Chicago, 2006), chapter 3.

[33] Trachtenberg, *A Constructed Peace*, p. 78.

[34] Leffler, *A Preponderance of Power*, pp. 148-151.

[35] Cited in Gaddis, *Strategies of Containment*, p. 61. Forrestal elaborated elsewhere, "As long as we can outproduce the world, can control the sea and can strike inland with the atomic bomb, we can assume certain risks otherwise unacceptable in an effort to restore world trade, to restore the balance of power – military power – and to eliminate some of the conditions which breed war." Cited in McAllister, *No Exit*, p. 122.

[36] On overseas bases, see Leffler, *A Strategy of Preponderance*, pp. 56-59, 226-228 and Copeland, *The Origins of Major War*, pp. 152-153. On the atomic monopoly, see Leffler, *A Preponderance of Power*, pp. 94-96, 114-116 and Copeland, *The Origins of Major War*, pp. 162-164. On the origins of NATO, see Trachtenberg, *A Constructed Peace*, pp. 83-86 and McAllister, *No Exit*, pp. 141-156. Trachtenberg points out that the United States was pulled into the NATO system reluctantly.

[37] The Berlin blockade was a direct response to the policy of establishing a west German state. See Trachtenberg, *A Constructed Peace*, pp. 78-86.

[38] On the rapid pace of demobilization, see Gaddis, *The United States and the Origins of the Cold War*, pp. 161-163.

[39] Trachtenberg, *A Constructed Peace*, pp. 89-91, 96-97. On U.S. war planning, see also Marc Trachtenberg, *History and Strategy* (Princeton, NJ: Princeton University Press, 1991), pp. 119-121, 153-158 and Leffler, *A Preponderance of Power*, pp. 110-114, 221-226.

[40] Cited in Trachtenberg, *A Constructed Peace*, pp. 100-101.

[41] Cited in Trachtenberg, *A Constructed Peace*, p. 90.

[42] Trachtenberg, *A Constructed Peace*, pp. 86-89.

[43] On the implications of the end of the atomic monopoly, see Leffler, *A Preponderance of Power*, pp. 323-333 and Trachtenberg, *A Constructed Peace*, pp. 96-103.

[44] *Foreign Relations of the United States*, 1950, Vol. I, pp. 145-146. Cited in Leffler, *A Preponderance of Power*, p. 330.

[45] The full report can be found in *Foreign Relations of the United States*, 1950, Vol. I, pp. 235-292. On the context surrounding NSC-68, see Samuel F. Wells, Jr., "Sounding the Tocsin: NSC 68 and the Soviet Threat," *International Security*, Vol. 4, No. 2 (Autumn 1979), pp. 116-158; Trachtenberg, *History and Strategy*, pp. 107-115; Leffler, *A Preponderance of Power*, pp. 355-360; and Christensen, *Useful Adversaries*, pp. 122-127. For a strong critique, see Gaddis, *Strategies of Containment*, chapter 4.

[46] *Foreign Relations of the United States*, 1950, Vol. I, p. 282.

[47] *Foreign Relations of the United States*, 1950, Vol. I, p. 253. Cited in Leffler, *A Preponderance of Power*, p. 357.

[48] Trachtenberg, *A Constructed Peace*, p. 100.

[49] Trachtenberg, *History and Strategy*, p. 112.

[50] Kim Il-sung did, in fact, secure Soviet and Chinese approval before attacking. See William Stueck, *Rethinking the Korean War: A New Diplomatic and Strategic History* (Princeton, NJ: Princeton University Press, 2002), pp. 69-77.

[51] Cited in Leffler, *A Preponderance of Power*, p. 366.

[52] On the American decision to intervene, see Leffler, *A Preponderance of Power*, pp. 364-369 and Stueck, *Rethinking the Korean War*, pp. 78-82.

[53] On public opinion during the Korean War, see John E. Mueller, *War, Presidents, and Public Opinion* (New York, NY: Wiley, 1973), esp. chapter 3 and Benjamin I. Page and Robert Y. Shapiro, *The Rational Public: Fifty Years of Trends in Americans' Policy Preferences* (Chicago, IL: The University of Chicago Press, 1992), pp. 209-214.

[54] *Public Papers of the Presidents of the United States*: Harry S. Truman, 1950 (Washington, DC: United States Government Printing Office, 1965), p. 538.

[55] On these domestic constraints, see Christensen, *Useful Adversaries*, pp. 39-49; Hogan, *A Cross of Iron*; Friedberg, *In the Shadow of the Garrison State*, chapters 1-2.

[56] Cited in Aaron L. Friedberg, "Why Didn't the United States Become a Garrison State?" *International Security*, Vol. 16, No. 4 (Spring 1992), p. 112.

[57] Cited in Gaddis, *Strategies of Containment*, p. 120.

[58] Hogan, *A Cross of Iron*, pp. 335, 467.

[59] Cited in Gaddis, *Strategies of Containment*, p. 113. On Truman's reaction to NSC-68, see Wells, "Sounding the Tocsin," pp. 137-138 and Hogan, *A Cross if Iron*, pp. 302-304.

[60] Wells, "Sounding the Tocsin," p. 140. On the military buildup, see Gaddis, *Strategies of Containment*, p. 113; Leffler, *A Preponderance of Power*, pp. 369-374; and Hogan, *A Cross of Iron*, pp. 304-312.

[61] On the NATO initiatives, see Gaddis, *Strategies of Containment*, pp. 114-115; Leffler, *A Preponderance of Power*, pp. 383-390, 406-418; Trachtenberg, *A Constructed Peace*, pp. 96-103; and McAllister, *No Exit*, pp. 183-192. The latter two are primarily concerned with the question of German rearmament.

[62] On the so-called "Great Debate," see Hogan, *A Cross of Iron*, pp. 322-335.

[63] *Foreign Relations of the United States*, 1950, Vol. III, p. 316. Cited in Gaddis, *Strategies of Containment*, p. 114.

[64] Trachtenberg, *History and Strategy*, p. 122. See also Casey, "Selling NSC-68" and Casey, "White House Publicity Operations During the Korean War, June 1950-June 1951," *Presidential Studies Quarterly*, Vol. 35, No. 4 (December 2005), pp. 691-717.

[65] *Foreign Relations of the United States*, 1950, Vol. III, p. 199. Cited in Casey, "Selling NSC-68," p. 675.

[66] Trachtenberg, *History and Strategy*, p. 117 and Casey, "Selling NSC-68," p. 676.

[67] *PPPUS*: Truman, 1950, p. 613. Cited in Casey, "Selling NSC-68," p. 677.

[68] Casey, "White House Publicity Operations," p. 701.

[69] Cited in Trachtenberg, *History and Strategy*, p. 124.

[70] Trachtenberg, *History and Strategy*, pp. 118-126; Leffler, *A Preponderance of Power*, pp. 399-406; and Stueck, *Rethinking the Korean War*, chapter 5. American leaders became increasingly willing to escalate the Korean conflict as the military buildup bore fruit. See Trachtenberg, *History and Strategy*, pp. 126-130.

[71] Cited in Trachtenberg, *History and Strategy*, p. 125.

[72] Cited in Casey, "Selling NSC-68," p. 688 and Casey, "White House Publicity Operations," p. 708.

[73] Robert Jervis, "The Impact of the Korean War on the Cold War," *The Journal of Conflict Resolution*, Vol. 24, No. 4 (December 1980), pp. 563-592.

In: Presidents and War
Editors: A. Eksterowicz and G. Hastedt, pp. 197-210
ISBN 978-1-61668-917-9


*Chapter 12*

# *"It's Not Enough to Say We're in Viet-Nam Simply Because Ike Got Us There"*: Lyndon Johnson and the Constraints of Continuity in Vietnam Policymaking

*Nicole Anslover*

## Introduction

When Lyndon Johnson unpredictably became president in November 1963, he had an exceptionally perilous set of problems to face. He needed to calm a fearful nation, honor the memory of a slain leader, and cope with multiple foreign entanglements. When asked months later what his first priority was during the transition, Johnson stated, "I recognized that our first great problem was to assure the world that there would be continuity in transition…" [1]. This need for continuity would become a factor in many of Johnson's decisions, particularly in terms of the Vietnam War.

In the recent historiography of the Vietnam War, "blame" is one of the most common words historians use. In research and writing, trying to discern who is to blame for the escalation and mismanagement is often the primary goal. Lyndon Johnson is frequently the scapegoat. But we need a new perspective on how and why Vietnam-related decisions were made. Presidents feel the need to follow the examples of their predecessors in terms of foreign policy—in other words, a "compulsion for continuity". Regardless of whether or not continuity with previous administrations is the right choice, it is an important factor in presidential decision-making. LBJ was committed to continuity with JFK's policies; however, he was never part of Kennedy's inner circle and therefore had difficulty determining exactly what those policies were. To assure himself, and the nation, that he was following a plan already in motion, Johnson sought approval from Dwight Eisenhower and attempted to prove cohesion with his policies, too.

Johnson did not intend to make Vietnam his priority--he had grandiose plans for domestic reform. He wanted to be able to devote his time in office to building his Great Society, but feared (correctly) that he would have to focus on foreign policy. His days in the Senate and as vice president gave LBJ plenty of his own foreign policy experience to draw on. But his major concern was that the public expected him to carry forward Kennedy's policies. Johnson sought to appear outwardly confident that he could do this, and early on, repeatedly assured the public that he would not allow the conflict in Vietnam to spiral out of control. He promised his constituents: "The United States still seeks no wider war. We threaten no regime and covet no territory. We have worked and will continue to work for a reduction of tensions, on the great stage of the world. But the aggression from the North must be stopped "[2].

Despite assurances to the contrary, Lyndon Johnson dramatically escalated American involvement in Vietnam. That is an undeniable fact. After being presented with a "blank check" from Congress in the form of the Gulf of Tonkin Resolution, Johnson escalated involvement through initiatives such as Operation Rolling Thunder and the introduction of combat ground troops. However, what is still open to interpretation is *why* Johnson took the steps he did to advance American military intervention. Was it due to his ideology, some rigid anti-communist stance? Was it faulty advice from his military advisors? Or was he simply a power-hungry president afflicted with the curse of hubris? Certainly, when one studies the literature of the Johnson era, all of these possible explanations alone and in tandem are addressed at some point [3]. Johnson's strong, almost manic, personality marred by self-doubt must be taken into consideration, as well.

## Johnson Attempts to Ensure Continuity with Kennedy

However, scholars must heavily weigh another explanation. Because of his own insecurities, Lyndon Johnson had an almost obsessive need to ensure continuity with his predecessors [4]. One might assume that as vice president, Johnson had been privy to Kennedy's foreign policy plans—this assumption is incorrect. Indeed, Johnson considered the vice presidency to be the most "insignificant office" of any in government; this judgment was compounded when he was rarely asked for his opinion on foreign affairs.

However, Kennedy did want to keep Johnson relatively happy and realized that perhaps he could be of some assistance in foreign affairs. Shortly after the inauguration, Kennedy wrote to Johnson acknowledging the need to have a Vice President "who is fully informed and adequately prepared" in matters of national security, particularly foreign and military policies. Kennedy also assured his second in command that he wanted to form a "closer working relationship" than some previous executives enjoyed. In order to accomplish these goals, Kennedy authorized Johnson to preside over National Security Council meetings in his absence and granted him access to pertinent information from all agencies concerned with foreign policy [5].

Some historians and former Kennedy supporters argue that Kennedy was actively searching for a way out of Vietnam; his public and private statements well into 1963 demonstrate otherwise. Kennedy's own rigid anti-communism led him to consider plans to use a "significant number of United States forces to signify United States determination to defend South Vietnam" [6]. Because of Kennedy's offer to provide his VP with all pertinent information, Johnson would have been aware that Kennedy considered engaging U.S. troops.

Despite being aware of most policy decisions, Johnson was not an active participant in them. When he abruptly assumed command, he needed to reassess America's Vietnam policy due to Kennedy's sudden death; the murder of South Vietnam's President Diem further complicated the state of affairs . Paul Kattenburg, a senior member of the State Department, went to South Vietnam to assess the situation. Upon observing the political unrest in the country, he noted that "the time has come again for very careful stock-taking and analysis," and he stressed, "a great sense of urgency is unquestionably required." Kattenberg concluded that while there did not appear to be any new leadership firmly taking charge, the political climate was somewhat positive: "Generally, the country is breathing a deep sigh of relief after the elimination of the dictatorship and is feeling its way in the new freedom" [7]. The changing of the guard, as it was, in South Vietnam, required American officials to come up with new ideas on how to shape policy.

Kattenburg intended to offer concrete suggestions in his report, but this was difficult because he, and others, were confused as to what U.S. objectives actually were. He could not offer a clear definition of policy but stated optimistically: "I am assuming that our objective in the broadest sense continues to be to assist the Vietnamese in 'winning the war'." Unfortunately, according to Kattenburg, some of the South Vietnamese generals either did not understand that objective or simply interpreted it differently. If one did assume that the main objective was victory (however defined), Kattenburg cautioned that there would definitely be problems achieving this goal. He warned "nothing repeat nothing at all will really be achieved toward that objective until we manage to overcome the overwhelming feeling among the mass of Vietnamese population that the other side is winning and not ours." Therefore, Kattenburg suggested that the primary policy objective should be to "maximize our bargaining posture in the international arena vis-à-vis Viet-Nam," because that might be the arena where success could actually be measured [8]. From the beginning of his time in office, LBJ received vague reports such as Kattenburg's; unfortunately, many others within the administration seemed as confused about policy as he himself was, making it even more difficult to follow Kennedy's path.

## Johnson's Reliance on Kennedy's Aides

To help him gain his footing, it was logical for Johnson to retain the majority of Kennedy's advisors during his early days in office; he learned to rely on some of them and many stayed on to advise LBJ even after the 1964 election. Key voices on Vietnam that continued from the Kennedy years were Robert McNamara, Dean Rusk, and McGeorge Bundy. Many of these advisors emphasized the theme of continuity, thereby increasing it's importance to LBJ. Johnson's attention to continuity was probably heightened because it was a matter to which his senior advisors paid close attention. Dean Rusk, of whom Johnson had been very fond since his days as Vice President, emphasized past policies in several of his speeches. Shortly after the 1966 State of the Union, Rusk gave an address discussing the reasons for continued commitment in Southeast Asia. Not only was the security of Vietnam essential to the security of the U.S., according to Secretary Rusk, but it had deep reaching roots. In fact, "That determination was made first, before the Korean War, by President Truman, on the basis of protracted analysis in the highest councils of the government" [9]. Rusk and Johnson often respected one another's opinions; this issue is simply one more area where they found common ground.

Walt Rostow was another holdover from the Kennedy administration that Johnson worked well with. Johnson often relied on Rostow's optimism and dogged attitude regarding the military in Vietnam (until March 1968, that is). Rostow was emphatic that not only was escalation the right decision for Johnson, but that it was also what Kennedy would have done. Rostow took it upon himself to point out how closely Johnson was adhering to what Kennedy would have done. Frequently, Rostow and others made compilations of Kennedy quotes on the topic, marking the most significant passages for Johnson's attention. The quotes were worthwhile--Rostow remarked that he was surprised at how adamantly the Kennedy statements supported continued involvement in Vietnam. Rostow told Johnson that after re-reading these quotes, he realized the "basic elements in President Kennedy's position" were quite striking. For Rostow, the elements Kennedy highlighted were "his explicit linkage of the commitment in Viet Nam to the SEATO Treaty; his flat acceptance of the domino theory in Southeast Asia," and "his recurrent linkage of Viet Nam to Berlin, and the general theme that the fate of our own liberty was involved in Viet Nam." For Rostow, these themes were particularly important because this record of statements could possibly help Johnson refute detractors of his escalation policies. After all, Rostow remarked, "I don't believe any objective person can read this record without knowing that President Kennedy would have seen this through whatever the cost" [10]. With encouragement like this, it becomes more understandable that Johnson would feel so compelled to trod in Kennedy's path.

Johnson's National Security Advisor, McGeorge Bundy, advised Johnson to convince key legislators, as well as the public, of continuity. In the summer of 1964, Bundy encouraged him to make sure that Senator Mike Mansfield understood the essential need for heavy U.S. commitment to South Vietnam. Johnson should remind Mansfield, "…the whole history of our support to South Vietnam going back to 1954 makes it inevitable that the U.S. is deeply involved, and this would be true even if we had not made the decision to intervene on a substantial scale in the fall of 1961" [11].

From his first day in office until March 31, 1968, Lyndon Johnson sought to demonstrate continuity with the previous three presidents in terms of Vietnam policy. Johnson demonstrated this need by bringing it to the attention of his advisors, and by attempting to insert a testimony to other presidents' involvement in Vietnam into nearly all of his public addresses on the subject. Most Johnson speeches on foreign affairs referenced Kennedy, Eisenhower, or Truman, if not all three. This repetition emphasizes the importance that continuity played in Johnson's mind.

In preparation for his own speeches, Johnson thoroughly researched past presidential statements so that he might always sound informed (and keep his public reminded) of what his predecessors had to say on the subject. This habit began almost immediately after Johnson entered office; in February 1964, he requested a thorough compilation of Kennedy quotes on Vietnam. Bromley Smith compiled pertinent quotes beginning with the 1961 inaugural address and concluding in September 1963, with the promise of more applicable quotes available by the next morning. It is unclear exactly how aides made these particular selections; perhaps Johnson only requested those snippets that favored intervention in Vietnam. What is clear is that he received a compilation of statements that would have left absolutely no doubt as to what Kennedy intended to do in Vietnam. For example, Johnson read a quote in which Kennedy stated "that the United States is determined that the Republic of Viet Nam shall not be lost to the Communists for lack of any support which the United States Government can render." Kennedy made that statement in early August 1961.

Furthermore, the strong declarations Kennedy made in the months prior to his assassination would almost certainly have struck Johnson. In July 1963, Kennedy had informed the American people: "We are not going to withdraw that effort. In my opinion, for us to withdraw from that effort would mean a collapse not only of South Viet Nam, but also of Southeast Asia. So we are going to stay there." In September, Kennedy pointedly told CBS's Walter Cronkite "I don't agree with those who say we should withdraw [from Viet Nam]. That would be a great mistake" [12]. Based on this particular compilation of quotes, it is difficult to conceive that Kennedy would not have stayed the course in Vietnam. It is also important to note that public statements such as these were often the only information Johnson, as vice president, received from the Kennedy camp.

## Using the Media to Establish Continuity

Johnson's pursuit of a policy based on continuity is understandable, if not necessarily admirable. He did not always convey the proper tone when attempting to portray his feelings to the public. In an address before the members of the New Hampshire Weekly Newspaper Editors Association in the fall of 1964, Johnson attempted to describe a typical dialogue he might have about Vietnam. He related that someone would generally ask, why "are we in Viet-Nam, and how did you get us into Viet-Nam?" Johnson's reply, "Well, I didn't get you into Viet-Nam. You have been in Viet-Nam 10 years," was technically correct. At the same time, these editors might have viewed his response as terse and unnecessary. In typical fashion, Johnson then elaborated on the specific actions taken by Eisenhower and Kennedy (Truman was spared in this particular speech). The crux of his speech was essentially that President Eisenhower committed the U.S. to Diem and Kennedy followed through on that promise [13]. Who was Lyndon Baines Johnson to change course?

The theme of continuity was not one Johnson reserved for small speeches before particular groups of people. He also tended to reiterate it in his major addresses. His 1966 State of the Union Address was no exception; Vietnam was the first topic attended to and continuity was a large part of the explanation for the current policies. Johnson firmly told Americans that the nation would remain in Vietnam, and defended this plan, stating, "We will stay because a just nation cannot leave to the cruelties of its enemies a people who have staked their lives and independence on America's solemn pledge—a pledge which has grown through the commitments of three American Presidents" [14]. This time Truman was included, and LBJ emphasized this theme throughout his address.

By late 1967, Vietnam had become not just a major theme in LBJ speeches, but it was often the *only* theme. He began one speech, simply titled "Vietnam," by reiterating why America was still sinking in the quagmire. Again, he linked the situation to the three presidents before him, and he then focused on Eisenhower and Kennedy by reading very specific quotes from them. He followed a lengthy 1959 quote from Eisenhower with several Kennedy quotes, ending with his well-known 1963 statement: "we are going to stay there" [15]. Even at this late point in his administration, Johnson was still relying heavily on his predecessors' actions and trying to convince the public that he alone was not to blame for their problems in Vietnam.

Aside from senior members of his administration and the general public, Johnson also sought other sources of support for his efforts to affirm a policy of continuity. Like any modern president, he had a wide circle of unofficial advisors whose thoughts he sometimes solicited. His "outer circle" also tended to reiterate how closely his compared to Kennedy's Vietnam policy. One such advisor, Endicott Peabody, not only offered his own opinions but relayed those of another important figure at the time, John McCloy. Peabody composed a memo to Johnson relating a conversation that took place between himself and McCloy. He reported that Kennedy had solicited McCloy's advice when he was considering committing combat troops to Vietnam. Reportedly, Kennedy felt there were very few other options. Peabody told Johnson "In McCloy's mind, the die was cast at that point." He further reported that McCloy "blamed" Kennedy for making the initial decision to commit troops, and therefore, for all subsequent decisions made [16]. This statement would probably have been encouraging to Johnson, and was perhaps one contributing factor to his reluctance for fully developing his own foreign policy stance.

By late 1967, Johnson's Vietnam policies were under heavy attack. A large part of the criticism stemmed from the "credibility gap" that had emerged between his administration and the media, but another aspect was simply the increasingly crushing cost of waging the war and the shifting mood of the country. Johnson began to attempt some more aggressive public relations strategies; some of those strategies hinged on increasingly making the public aware of the continuity issue.

John Roche was a prominent attorney whom LBJ hired as a consultant to deal with the increasingly difficult credibility problem. Roche spent a significant amount of time studying the past actions of both Kennedy and Johnson and eventually arrived at a straightforward conclusion: Kennedy was wholly to blame. Interestingly, Roche opined that the problems stemmed not from Kennedy's aggressiveness, but from his inability to take proper action. He told Johnson, "Essentially I came to the conclusion that a great deal of our trouble on this has arisen from President Kennedy's virtually total concern with Europe and Cuba, a concentration which led him to ignore the danger signals in Southeast Asia…". However, Roche argued, Johnson, in his role as VP, had urged Kennedy to more carefully consider the situation. Therefore, any "blame" should be placed on Kennedy [17]. Johnson was merely following his example.

More significant than Roche's observations about JFK was the plan he suggested to Johnson to remedy the situation. Roche wanted to make the point that Kennedy was responsible but he acknowledged that this would be a "matter of incredible delicacy". If not done properly, any action that appeared to "blame" Kennedy could have two negative ramifications. First, Roche noted, "The Kennedy cultists would be up in arms." That, however, was "trivial" compared to what he viewed as the second complication: the involvement of both Rusk and McNamara in the actions of the Kennedy administration. Therefore, Roche offered the following suggestion: "I could prepare an article to be planted (under at least three levels of cover—and I am good at that) which would make the point with minimal reference to Secretaries Rusk and McNamara and with due deference to President Kennedy." He was willing to go to work on this if Johnson did not deem the plot too risky. Roche again reminded Johnson that Vietnam was not at all his fault. The way he saw it, "in large part we have a credibility problem because we are covering for him—we were eight months pregnant in Vietnam before we knew we had been laid" [18].

This memo, and increasing tensions with Robert Kennedy, may have been what led Johnson to request yet another report on consistency between himself and Kennedy. In November 1967, RFK charged that there had been a "switch" between his brother's policies and Johnson's recent actions in Vietnam. Johnson requested a report that would emphatically deny this accusation. He received a document that began with the basic SEATO commitment in 1955 and continued on to quotes from Kennedy that demonstrated how unwavering he was on Vietnam. The report concluded with a compilation of Johnson quotes that demonstrated his acknowledgement of "the deeper meaning of our involvement in Asia." In an accompanying memo, Walt Rostow offered Johnson staunch encouragement. He stated: "I doubt that any reasonable person could read this collection and still believe there had been any 'switch' whatsoever in our policy or our understanding of our commitment." Rostow further scoffed, "And it is hard to understand how a man could have been as close to all this as Bobby was and reach his stated conclusion" [19].

Johnson's pursuit of continuity is not just something evident in the historical record; it was noticed at the time, and was not always viewed as positive. Senator Mike Mansfield took care to warn the president early in his tenure that perhaps continuity was not desirable. Mansfield cautioned, "We are close to the point of no return in Vietnam…there ought to be less official talk of our responsibility in Viet Nam and more emphasis on the responsibilities of the Vietnamese themselves." In Mansfield's opinion, times had changed and peace through diplomacy was the proper course of action [20].

Mansfield's views were more of the exception, rather than the rule. Johnson was continuously reminded of what Kennedy might have done, and this greatly influenced his decision making on Vietnam. Shortly after Mansfield's warning, Henry Cabot Lodge presented Johnson with a different viewpoint. Lodge recalled the moment in Kennedy's inaugural address when he declared the challenge of the decade was, "not as a call to bear arms, though arms we need—not as a call to battle, though embattled we are—but the call to bear the burden of a long, twilight struggle year in and year out." Lodge wrote that the situation in Vietnam was precisely the type of struggle Kennedy referred to and noted that his words applied directly to the current situation. Lodge encouraged Johnson to stay the course—Kennedy's course [21].

## "Johnson Relying on Ike in Viet Debate"

The reasons for Johnson's desire to continue Kennedy's policies are clear. As not only a member of his party but his vice president, Johnson would have certainly felt pressured to try to accomplish Kennedy's goals. The tragic circumstances surrounding Kennedy's death only made this more necessary; it is doubtful that the American public would have reacted positively to any deviation from Kennedy's course after his assassination. It might have been seen as dishonorable to his memory. The continuity between the two is therefore understandable. It is perhaps more noteworthy that Johnson demonstrated the same obsessive need for continuity with Dwight Eisenhower. Whether or not Johnson truly desired Eisenhower's approval, or whether it was an attempt to benefit from Eisenhower's continued popularity is not entirely clear. In all probability, it was a combination of the two. What is clear is that Johnson spent a significant amount of time attempting to cultivate a positive political relationship with Eisenhower, and that he greatly wanted his support on Vietnam.

From the outset, Johnson's staff encouraged him to link his Vietnam policies to Ike's. In the spring of 1964, McGeorge Bundy advised him to answer questions on the importance of Vietnam by stating: "Ten years ago President Eisenhower rightly decided to support the new government of South Vietnam and we have continued that support ever since in good times and in bad." Bundy included a letter from Eisenhower to Diem, and pointed out that the language Ike used "reminds me very much of the language we still use." He urged Johnson to notice that Eisenhower spoke of the importance of reform and commitment and the need to respond to the Vietnamese people's aspirations. Bundy encouraged Johnson, saying, "In recent months the danger and difficulty in Vietnam have increased, but this is no time to quit, and it is no time for discouragement. [22].

Johnson's attempts to garner Ike's support began in earnest almost immediately after his 1965 inauguration. Presumably, he was working too hard in 1964 adjusting to his new role, and trying to determine his legacy from Kennedy to worry too much about Eisenhower. On the other hand, perhaps he still felt plenty of positive support from the public and did not feel a real need for further bolstering. Whatever the reason, 1965 ushered in a concerted Johnson effort to earn Eisenhower's public support. Johnson ordered his staff to compile Eisenhower quotes on Vietnam, exactly has they had been doing with Kennedy statements. He would have been pleased with the initial results; the first reports yielded quotes such as "Former President Dwight D. Eisenhower said today that President Johnson 'unquestionably has made the correct decision' in ordering a resumption of bombing in North Viet-Nam" [23].

In April, Eisenhower himself noted that the press often raised the continuity question. He wrote to Johnson personally, assuring him that he would not disparage him or his foreign policies publicly. When asked his views on Vietnam, Eisenhower told Johnson his reply had been (and would remain) to say simply that "under the circumstances as I now understand them I believe that you are employing a policy well calculated to serve the best interests of the United States." The closing line of the letter read, "With warm personal regard and great respect" [24]. Eisenhower also acknowledged that there had been "continuity of purpose and policy", despite an evolution of the situation and enemy actions [25]. Presumably, this would have at least been somewhat reassuring to Johnson. He used his correspondence with the former president to both thank and flatter Eisenhower. After addressing him as "My dear General," Johnson effused, "I cannot tell you adequately of my deep felt gratitude for the unhesitating support you give to the needs of your country." Johnson then went on to elaborate on how much he and the public needed Eisenhower's wisdom, and assured him that his legacy was now cemented. Johnson told Eisenhower, "But history will surely record that President Dwight D. Eisenhower, both in and out of office, never swerved from what he believed to be the truth nor from giving his courage and his energy to the people he serves as patriot, soldier, President, and now as wise counselor to the nation" [26]. It would be interesting to see what Johnson's response would have been if Eisenhower had not been willing publicly to support his policies at that time.

Although Eisenhower's political support was critical for Johnson's popularity, his advice was also considered important from a military perspective. Because of his own military and political experience, Johnson knew Eisenhower could offer a unique perspective on the Vietnam War. Johnson made certain to keep Eisenhower informed, and to gather his advice; of course, Johnson was not always available to brief Ike himself, but he did make certain that other members of his administration tended to the ex-president. For instance, he requested the Ambassador to South Vietnam, Henry Cabot Lodge, to have a personal meeting with Eisenhower. Lodge reported to Johnson that Eisenhower did indeed have specific views not only on how to wage the war, but also on what to tell the public about it. For instance, he suggested that Johnson should expend more effort on developing stronger points along the coast of Vietnam; conversely, he felt there should be "no formal announcements of total U.S. troop strength" [27]. Despite his retirement, Eisenhower still followed all aspects of U.S. involvement very carefully.

As Johnson was eager to keep close track of all of his interactions with Eisenhower, he ordered a thorough record of all meetings and conversations. Each notation included a record of how long the conversation lasted [28]. Conversations with Eisenhower totaled 21 during the early years of Johnson's tenure [29]. Johnson had dedicated a significant amount of time to cultivating a relationship with Eisenhower, but as president his schedule simply did not allow as much time as he would have perhaps wished to speak with the former president. The solution was to find a reliable person to be the go between himself and Eisenhower.

The role of intermediary fell to General Andrew Jackson Goodpaster, a soldier and scholar who had a long-time relationship with Eisenhower, most recently as a close adviser during his presidency. Johnson persuaded Goodpaster to meet regularly with Eisenhower with the goal of both briefing him on Vietnam and obtaining his opinions on the situation. As was typical of Johnson (further confirming his penchant for total control), Johnson requested regular updates as to how often Goodpaster was in contact with Eisenhower. Between February, 1965 and June, 1966, there had been 16 formal briefings, three phone conversations, and 30 informal discussions. Goodpaster noted that Vietnam had been discussed at every one of these encounters [30].

Despite Eisenhower's earlier statements about how successful Johnson's policies in Vietnam were the ex-president eventually began to display some doubts about the direction of the war. Initially, Goodpaster was able to offer him reassurances that positive things were still happening. In a 1967 report to Johnson, Goodpaster began by repeating several of Eisenhower's concerns, which seemed to stem mainly from rumors he was hearing. For instance, Eisenhower told Goodpaster that "many of the people who see him—neither 'Hawks' nor 'doves'—are talking in terms of discouragement about the course of the war in Vietnam. They say that nothing seems to going well and that, perhaps, it would be better to get out of it than to continue." Goodpaster assured Johnson that he had tried to dissuade Eisenhower from this opinion; he had promised Eisenhower that he would soon go over many details of the war with him, and, he had told the former president, "it differs considerably from their premise that nothing seems to be going well" [31].

This report might have been important to Johnson for other reasons. In it, Goodpaster noted that CBS wanted Eisenhower to do an hour-long television presentation on the state of the war in Vietnam. According to Goodpaster, Eisenhower was inclined to give the talk, but wanted to make sure that it remained factual and not opinionated. He would cover topics such as "how our interests are involved, why the area should not be let go to the Communists, why we put in advisers, and increased them, why we introduced our combat forces, why we are bombing the north, etc" [32]. For Johnson, this could have been an enormous opportunity to have someone else emphasize the theme of continuity on which he had been focusing so intensively.

Johnson's dependence on Eisenhower did not go unnoticed by the press. In the fall of 1967, *The Washington Post* ran a story headlined: "Johnson Relying on Ike in Viet Debate." According to the article, the purpose of utilizing the Republican war hero was to "help counter the growing opposition to the President's Vietnam policy." By enlisting Eisenhower's support, the administration was in effect attempting to launch a "counterattack against its Vietnam critics" [33]. This counterattack was not completely effective and neither did it last long. By early 1968, Eisenhower was becoming very vocal in expressing reservations about Johnson's Vietnam policy. During his meetings with Goodpaster, he consistently questioned him as to why Johnson was doing this or taking that step. He was no longer convinced that the war was being waged the way that it should be [34].

By that point, Johnson, too, no longer believed that the war was being waged properly, and the majority of Americans were extremely skeptical about Vietnam. The Tet Offensive was a major blow to LBJ's, and the American people's, confidence and is considered by many to be the turning point in the war. Despite the devastating psychological effects of Tet, shifts in Johnson's thinking, and important changes within the administration, continuity was still an important factor in Johnson's decisions. Shortly after taking on the post of Secretary of Defense, Clark Clifford requested a compilation of Kennedy quotes on Vietnam for LBJ's use. Clifford might have especially appreciated Kennedy's stance that, "while we would all like to lighten the burden, I don't see any real prospect of the burden being lightened" [35]. Kennedy's dogged determination was yet another way that Johnson could claim continuity.

On March 31, 1968, Lyndon Johnson dramatically announced in a nationally televised address: "I shall not seek, and I will not accept, the nomination of my party for another term as your President." Even knowing that his days in the Oval Office were numbered, the President could not restrain himself from referring once again to continuity as the guiding principle of the policy goals he had tried to achieve. In this address, Johnson chose the words of John F. Kennedy to remind Americans why he had continued to wage war in Vietnam. Johnson recalled that blustery Inauguration Day in 1961 when Kennedy proclaimed that America should "pay any price, bear any burden, meet any hardship, support any friend, oppose any foe to assure the survival and the success of liberty" [36]. According to a despondent Johnson, that had been his own primary goal throughout the painful journey of the years since.

## Conclusion: The Continued Constraints of Conformity

Perhaps continuity in American foreign relations is unavoidable and, arguably, in most circumstances desirable. The presumption is that a decision previously taken and widely accepted should be specially privileged. Perhaps even more important, presidents will strive to remind the public of their dedication to honoring and maintaining policies enunciated by their predecessors.

At times, this continuity is not sought, nor even desired by the incoming president. Jimmy Carter provides us with an excellent example of a candidate who based his platform largely on reforming foreign policy and getting rid of policies he felt were "highly secretive and partisan, immoral, and overly focused on relations with the Soviet Union." Despite several important successes (notably the Camp David Accords), some historians feel that

Carter actually did little other than to expand on policies already in place. For example, his ideas on limiting nuclear weapons had roots reaching back to Truman; his desire to build a constructive relationship with the PRC is easily traced to the Nixon administration. Eventually, Carter did not succeed in altering the structure of foreign policy, or in giving American foreign relations a focus other than the Soviet Union, and cold war tensions had actually escalated by the end of his term [37].

While in office, Carter was not able to escape the compulsion for continuity despite his good intentions. What makes his an interesting case is the path he chose as an elder statesman after leaving the White House. Carter made international relations his post-presidency priority and has been involved in important mediations in countries such as North Korea, Bosnia, and Somalia. Carter has also not hesitated to criticize his successors' policies when he disagrees with them, something he did not feel comfortable doing while in office [38]. Carter demonstrates that once released from the constraints of conformity, ex-presidents are able to focus on their own foreign policy ideology and goals.

Some contemporary presidents have gone in the opposite direction of Carter and attempted to cite continuity, even where there is none. In recent years, President George W. Bush has come under considerable fire for America's military intervention in Iraq. In attempts to defend his actions, Bush has more than once sought to draw a connection between himself and Harry S Truman. The February 12, 2007, issue of *Newsweek* featured a story about Bush's analysis of the circumstances that brought about the Iraq conflict. As the story reported, the President "compared his situation to the crisis Harry Truman faced in the early days of the cold war. Then, as now, Bush said, the United States confronted a dangerous ideological foe. Truman had answered with the Truman Doctrine, a vow to protect free peoples wherever they were threatened with communist domination." Bush then noted that, as with the situation he now faced, Truman's policies were unpopular at the time, but "history showed he was right."

Just as some questioned Johnson's claims of continuity trumping rationality, many do not see Bush's historical analysis as quite hitting the mark. *Newsweek*'s story offered as a counterweight the reaction of Senator Dick Durbin of Illinois, who pointed out to Bush, "Harry Truman had allies" [39]. There are of course, similarities being drawn between Iraq, the Cold War, and Vietnam that Bush would sooner not be addressed. For instance, some scholars compare the dishonesty of the Johnson administration regarding the Gulf of Tonkin Affair to the post-9/11 atmosphere surrounding the Bush administration. Both instances resulted in "the same manufactured atmosphere of crisis" [40]. Others have noted the correlation of "the decent interval", or the idea there should be a clear window between U.S. withdrawal and the collapse of South Vietnam—or Iraq, as the case may now be. Parallels drawn between a "disguised exit" in Vietnam and one in Iraq show the same motive—policy failure [41].

Tempting as it is (and useful as it may be) it is perhaps too soon to draw definitive parallels between Vietnam and Iraq. As it has done (and continues to do) for Vietnam, the historical record will continue to grow and shed light on the questions that need to be answered about Iraq. One of those questions will certainly be whether or not presidents still feel the compulsion for continuity, as Johnson demonstrated. And whether or not that is always a bad thing. Another question that must be considered is how much impact the cold war consensus played in the compulsion for continuity of recent presidents. Surely it was a large factor, but until historians gain complete access to the papers of the post-cold war presidents, we will not fully understand their foreign policy motivations, including their desire to seek (or avoid) continuity.

## References


[1] Transcript of Interview with the President Conducted by William H. Lawrence, 15 March 1964. File: "McGeorge Bundy March-4/14/65", Box 3, National Security File Memos to the President McGeorge Bundy, Papers of the President, Lyndon Baines Johnson Library, Austin, Texas. (Hereafter cited as LBJL).

[2] "Statement by the President", 25 March 1965. File: "Deployment of Major U.S. Forces to Vietnam, July 1965", Box 202, National Security File, Papers of the President, LBJL.

[3] See Robert Dallek, Flawed Giant: Lyndon Johnson and His Times, 1961-1973 (Oxford: New York, 1998), Fredrik Logevall, Choosing War: The Lost Chance for Peace and the Escalation of War in Vietnam (Berkeley: University of California Press, 1999), H.W. Brands,The Wages of Globalism: Lyndon Johnson and the Limits of American Power (New York: Oxford University Press, 1995), Michael Hunt Lyndon Johnson's War: America's Cold War Crusade in Vietnam, 1945-1968 (New York: Hill and Wang, 1996).

[4] See Paul R. Henggeler, *In His Steps: Lyndon Johnson and the Kennedy Mystique* (Chicago: I.R. Dee, 1991).

[5] John F. Kennedy to Lyndon Johnson, 28 January 1961. File: "National Security Council—Letter from Pres Kennedy re VP Johnson's Participation", Box 4, Vice Presidential Security File, LBJL

[6] Draft. National Security Action Memo. Undated. File: "National Security Council (II)", Box 4, Vice Presidential Security File, POP, LBJL.

[7] Paul M. Kattenburg, "Orientation Visit to Viet-Nam", 6 January 1964. File: "1963, Paul M. Kattenburg Trip, 11/22/63-12/19/63", Box 24, James C. Thompson Papers, John F. Kennedy Presidential Library, Boston, MA. (Hereafter cited as JFKL)

[8] Paul M. Kattenburg, "Orientation Visit to Viet-Nam", 6 January 1964. File: "1963, Paul M. Kattenburg Trip, 11/22/63-12/19/63", Box 24, James C. Thompson Papers, JFKL.

[9] Speech by Dean Rusk, 24 May 1966. File: "Quotations on Viet-Nam-Dean Rusk", Box 336, Ernest K. Lindley Papers, Spencer Research Library, University of Kansas, Lawrence, Kansas (hereafter cited as "Lindley Papers").

[10] Memo. Walt Rostow to Lyndon Johnson, 15 September 1967. File: "Past Presidential Statements", Box 97, Vietnam Country File, National Security File, POP, LBJL.

[11] Memo. McGeorge Bundy to Lyndon Johnson, 1 July 1964. File: "National Security File: Memos to the President", Box 1,,National Security File Memos to the President, POP, LBJL.

[12] Memo, with attachments. Bromley Smith to Lyndon Johnson, 22 February 1963. [Although this is dated 1963, the salutation "Mr. President" and the opening sentence "The quotations of President Kennedy which you requested are attached" make it clear that this memo was sent after Johnson took office, which means the date should almost certainly be 22 February 1964]. File: "Vietnam, Past Presidential Statements on USG

Commitment in SE Asia [1 of 2]", Box 97, Vietnam Country File, National Security File, POP, LBJL.

[13] Lyndon Johnson, "Remarks in Manchester to the Members of the New Hampshire Weekly Newspaper Editors Association", 28 September 1964. File: "Quotations on Viet-Nam Kennedy-Johnson", Box 336, Lindley Papers.

[14] "President's State of the Union Message", 2 January 1966. File: "Vietnam Speeches [2]", Box 17, Files of McGeorge Bundy, National Security File, POP, LBJL.

[15] Lyndon Johnson, "The President's Remarks in San Antonio Before the National Legislative Conference", 6 December 1967. File: "Past Presidential Statements", Box 98, Vietnam Country File, National Security File, POP, LBJL.

[16] Memo. Endicott Peabody to Lyndon Johnson, 6 November 1967. File: "Past Presidential Statements", Box 97, Vietnam Country File, National Security File, POP, LBJL. Endicott Peabody was a prominent political figure from Massachusetts from the early 1960s well into the 1990s. His personal papers are located at the Kennedy Library. John McCloy was a prominent banker who regularly advised Johnson during his tenure in office. McCloy was one of the "wise men" who would eventually recommend de-escalation to Johnson in mid-1968.

[17] Memo. John Roche to Lyndon Johnson, 15 November 1967. File: "Memos to the President", Box 8, Papers of John P. Roche, LBJL. .

[18] Memo. John Roche to Lyndon Johnson, 15 November 1967. File: "Memos to the President", Box 8, Papers of John P. Roche, LBJL. Johnson's response, if there indeed was a written response, has not yet been located at the Johnson Library. Despite his need to place blame elsewhere, there is no clear evidence that Johnson did actually approve a plan like this.

[19] Memo. Walt Rostow to Lyndon Johnson, 28 November 1967. File: "Past Presidential Statements", Box 97, Vietnam Country File, National Security File, POP, LBJL.

[20] Mike Mansfield to Lyndon Johnson, 6 January 1964. File: "National Security File: Memos to the President", Box 1, National Security File Memos to the President, POP, LBJL.

[21] Henry Cabot Lodge, 'Persistance in Viet-Nam" 2 March 1964, File: "McGeorge Bundy, Vol. 2, 3/1-31/64 [1 of 2], Box 1, National Security File Memos to the President, POP, LBJL.

[22] McGeorge Bundy to Lyndon Johnson, 14 March 1964. File: "McGeorge Bundy 3/1-31/64, Vol. 2 [1 of 2]", Box 1, National Security File, POP, LBJL.

[23] Dwight D. Eisenhower quoted in the *New York Times*, 1 February 1965. No page number given. Clipping located in file "Presidential Decisions-Gulf of Tonkin Attacks of Aug., 1964", Box 39, National Security Council Histories, National Security File, POP, LBJL.

[24] Dwight Eisenhower to Lyndon Johnson, 30 April 1965. File: "President Eisenhower [2 of 2]", Box 3, Name File, National Security File, POP, LBJL.

[25] Memo. McGeorge Bundy to Lyndon Johnson, 25 August 1965. File: "McGeorge Bundy, August 1965", Box 4, National Security File Memos to the President McGeorge Bundy, LBJL.

[26] Lyndon Johnson to Dwight Eisenhower, 19 August 1965. File: "Eisenhower, Dwight D., General [1954-1968] [2 of 2]", Box 2, Name File, National Security File, POP, LBJL.

[27] Memo. Henry Cabot Lodge to Lyndon Johnson, 11 August 1965. File: "Eisenhower, Dwight D., General [1954-1968] [2 of 2]", Box 2, Name File, National Security File, POP, LBJL.

[28] Report, "President Johnson's Contacts with President Eisenhower", File: "President Eisenhower [1965-1968] [1 of 2]", Box 3 Name File, National Security File, POP, LBJL.

[29] Memo. Unknown to Lyndon Johnson, 10 June 1966. File: "President Eisenhower [1965-1968] [1 of 2]", Box 3, Name File, National Security File, POP, LBJL.

[30] Memo. Bromley Smith to Lyndon Johnson, 11 June 1966. File: "President Eisenhower [1965-1968][1 of 2]", Box 3, Name File, National Security File, POP, LBJL.

[31] Andrew Goodpaster, Memorandum for the Record, 18 October 1967. File: "Eisenhower, Dwight D. General [1954-1968] [1 of 2]", Box 2, Name File, National Security File, POP, LBJL.

[32] Andrew Goodpaster, Memorandum for the Record, 18 October 1967. File: "Eisenhower, Dwight D.General [1954-1968] [1 of 2]", Box 2, Name File, National Security File, POP, LBJL.

[33] *The Washington Post*, "Johnson Relying on Ike in Viet Debate", 19 October 1967, p. A10.

[34] Andrew Goodpaster, Memorandum for the Record, 14 February 1968. File: "Eisenhower, Dwight D. General [1954-1968] [1 of 2]", Box 2, Name File, National Security File, POP, LBJL.

[35] Robert E. Pursley to Clark Clifford. 11 April 1968. File: "Kennedy on Southeast Asia, 1961-1963", Box 3, Papers of Clark Clifford, LBJL.

[36] Lyndon Johnson. "Address to the Nation Announcing Steps to Limit the War in Vietnam and Reporting His Decision Not to Seek Reelection". 31 March 1968. LBJL, On-line documents. http://www.lbjlib.utexas.edu /johnson/archives.hom/speeches.hom/ 680331.asp. Accessed 1 April 2007.

[37] William Stueck, "Placing Jimmy Carter's Foreign Policy" in Gary M. Fink and Hugh Davis Graham, ed., *The Carter Presidency: Policy Choices in the Post-New Deal Era* (The University Press of Kansas: Lawrence, 1998), 244-245.

[38] Douglas Brinkley, The Unfinished Presidency: Jimmy Carter's Journey Beyond the White House (Viking: New York, 1998), xvii.

[39] Holly Bailey, Richard Wolffe, and Evan Thomas. "Bush's Truman Show", *Newsweek,* 12 February 2007, p. 24.

[40] Eric Alterman, When Presidents Lie: A History of Official Deception and Its Consequences, (Viking: New York, 2004), 302.

[41] David Elliott in Lloyd C. Garner and Marilyn B. Young, ed., *Iraq and the Lessons of Vietnam: Or, How Not to Learn From the Past* (The New Press: New York, 2007), 32-37.

In: Presidents and War
Editors: A. Eksterowicz and G. Hastedt, pp. 211-231 ISBN 978-1-61668-917-9


*Chapter 13*

# LONESOME DOVE: THE POPE, THE PRESIDENT, THE CHURCH, AND VIETNAM, 1963-1969

***Lawrence J. McAndrews***

## INTRODUCTION

With his imposing stature and outsize arrogance, Lyndon Johnson seemed eager to take on the world as he ascended to the presidency in November 1963. And soon he would have to. Questions of war and peace, especially in Vietnam, would obsess and ultimately overwhelm the president and the nation, as American unilateralism earned international enmity and presaged national humiliation.

Nobody tried harder than Lyndon Johnson to achieve a durable peace in Vietnam and a meaningful respite from the Cold War. Nobody did, except perhaps Pope Paul VI. Just as Johnson often invoked John F. Kennedy in his determination to contain communism yet deepen détente, so too did Pope Paul build on the considerable foundations laid by Pope John XXIII. Pope Paul VI's tireless pursuit of peace prodded the American president, encouraged many American Catholics, and often embarrassed the American Catholic hierarchy, to whom the world remained, even in the wake of the historic Second Vatican Council, less modern than Manichean.

As a result, an American Catholic Church which so enthusiastically welcomed change in other areas seemed terribly frightened by it in this one. It is perhaps unsurprising, then, that when a president uncomfortable with nuance sought refuge from a world grown too complex, he would often find sanctuary in a Catholic church, where the uncertainties of his own faith would give way to the sturdy predictability of another. Yet ultimately neither Johnson nor the American Catholic bishops could escape the challenges to his foreign policy which undid his presidency and unsettled their Church [1].

## The Pope and the President

On the night of August 2, 1964, an American destroyer, the *U.S.S. Maddox*, conducting reconnaissance in the Gulf of Tonkin off the coast of North Vietnam, withstood an attack by North Vietnamese torpedo boats. Two nights later, the captains of the *Maddox* and another American ship, the *C. Turner Joy*, reported a second attack. Though the validity of the latter occurrence remained under question, President Johnson asked for, and overwhelmingly received, a Congressional resolution authorizing retaliation for the alleged two incidents. With a November election to win as a "peace" candidate, however, Johnson kept his "blank check" in his pocket while awaiting further provocation.

That moment arrived two months after his landslide victory over Arizona Republican Senator Barry Goldwater, when a Viet Cong assault on an American air force base in Pleiku, South Vietnam killed eight and wounded over one hundred. Over the lone dissent of Catholic Senate Majority Leader Mike Mansfield, Democrat of Montana, Johnson followed the advice of his National Security Council and Congressional leaders by ordering selective American bombing of North Vietnam [2].

Pope Paul VI responded to the American escalation of the Vietnam War first by endorsing a suggestion by French President Charles DeGaulle that the United Nations mediate the conflict. "May international institutions capable of preventing the attacks of force be reinforced," the pontiff pleaded in the week following the Pleiku incident. "May these be adapted, surrounded with general respect, to assure the honest execution, the honest observance of treaties." Two days later the Pope sent a letter to South Vietnam's Catholic bishops urging their efforts to prevent "the horrors of a prolonged and extensive commitment of arms"[3].

The Pope's pleas fell on deaf ears. Johnson showed no inclination to cease the bombing. "Much as I deplore the spread of communism in Asia," Trappist monk Rev. Thomas Merton wrote the president in February, "I hope that peace can be negotiated by an international group," leading to an end to the U.S. military presence. "As you have ignored appeals from Pope Paul, [U.N. Secretary General] U Thant, President DeGaulle, and so many others," Rev. Philip Berrigan, Martin Corbin, and James Forest of the Catholic Peace Fellowship telegraphed the White House in March, "we have little hope our protest will challenge your will to continue and even widen the war in Vietnam." Less than a week later, Johnson dispatched the first American combat troops to join the thousands of advisors already training South Vietnamese forces in the fight against the communists. "I thought you would like to see some of the support we are getting from some of the more level-headed clergy on Vietnam," White House press secretary Bill Moyers wrote Johnson in April, after receiving a copy of a pro-war column by the director of the American bishops' National Catholic Welfare Conference Social Action Department, Monsignor George Higgins, which was to appear in twenty-five diocesan newspapers throughout the country [4].

The Catholic bishops of South Vietnam similarly were more concerned about defeating the communists than accommodating them. White House aide Jack Valenti briefed Johnson on the president's February meeting with the Pope's Apostolic Delegate to the United States, Rev. Egidio Vagnozzi, by noting that "communists have infiltrated the Buddhist movement in South Vietnam," and that Rev. Patrick O'Connor of the National Catholic News Service "has been in Vietnam for over fifteen years [and]...could be useful" to the Administration.

Following a meeting with President Phan Huy Quat, the South Vietnamese bishops accused their government of failing to forestall a Buddhist-led purge of Catholic military commanders. Rev. Hoang Quynh, spokesman for the 900,000 Catholic refugees who had fled the communist North, was heading an effort in 116 parishes in the vicinity of Saigon, the Southern capital, to arm young Catholic men with knives and sticks to defend their communities. Not only were South Vietnam's Catholic leaders ignoring the Pope's entreaties for peace, but some of them had even intimated that the Johnson Administration was behind the purge as a step toward a negotiated settlement of the war [5].

Even a papal encyclical could not deter the South Vietnamese Church. In *Mense Maio* (In the Month of May), Paul VI implored the world's governments to "continue at all times to foster and encourage conversations and negotiations at all levels" and to "condemn acts of guerilla war and of terrorism, the practices of holding hostages and of taking repeated reprisals against unarmed civilians." The South Vietnamese hierarchy's reply was to tacitly approve the formation of the Greater Unity Force, a Catholic political organization devoted to "invading and holding" North Vietnam "to deliver our compatriots from the yoke of Communist dictatorship." A month later, the Quat regime fell to a military coup, with Catholic Major General Nguyen Van Thieu in charge of the new government [6].

The Pope did influence the president, however, as Johnson asserted his willingness to negotiate with the enemy in Vietnam. Then he prepared to sit down with Paul himself. "It is of great importance to impress the Pope with our passion for peace in Vietnam," Secretary of State Dean Rusk counselled Johnson, while conceding "faint indications that not all Vatican circles are persuaded on this point" [7].

After publicly urging the United Nations in October to commit itself to "never again war," Paul VI privately pressed Johnson toward that lofty goal. "The entire world is indebted to His Holiness, as I said to him in our private conversation," Johnson told the press, "for the sacrifices he has made in coming on this long trip across the water to provide leadership in the world's quest for peace. His Holiness and I discussed ways and means of advancing that cause" [8].

Yet Pope Paul and President Johnson did not engage in specifics about Vietnam, where the U.S. military presence continued to grow and American peace efforts continued to founder. Majority Leader Mansfield returned in December with four other Senators from a fact-finding mission in Vietnam with a report so pessimistic that Johnson ordered a bombing pause in hopes of igniting peace talks [9].

Without naming either side or even the conflict itself, the Pope's Christmas message deplored the "limits of self-interest or one's own ambitions" as "obstacles to peace," and called instead for "just and sincere negotiation to restore order and friendship." No sooner had the pontiff sent a message to the governments of North Vietnam, South Vietnam, and the United States praising a thirty-hour holiday truce, however, than the fighting resumed [10].

Pope Paul VI ushered in the new year with still another peace proposal, sent this time not only to the combatants in Vietnam but to two of their sponsors, China and the Soviet Union. Johnson began 1966 with an expression of regret – that he had not yet discovered a solution to the Vietnamese imbroglio. "The President believes that if he were to leave office tomorrow," the *New York Times*' John Pomfret wrote, "the judgment of history on him would probably be harsh because of his failure to deal successfully with the conflict" [11].

Having failed to reconcile the competing factions in Vietnam, the Pope turned to neutral parties, advocating an international peace conference convened by the United Nations and conducted by governments with no direct stake in the outcome. Johnson's U.N. Ambassador, Arthur Goldberg, also envisioned a role for the world body in defusing the Vietnam issue – by changing the subject. Goldberg recommended that Johnson travel to Geneva to jumpstart stagnant nuclear nonproliferation talks with the Soviet Union. "If we would get a nonproliferation treaty, the agitation on Vietnam would greatly soften," White House aide Jack Valenti conveyed Goldberg's argument to the president, "and Vietnam would be put in proper perspective." Johnson would reject Goldberg's advice, he would sign a nonproliferation treaty within two years, and the agitation on Vietnam would only harden [12].

After his latest endeavor produced only six months of inaction, Pope Paul VI not only acknowledged that "our sincere and disinterested efforts failed to come to fruition," but he warned of the "possible extension of the conflict" in Southeast Asia. Johnson conceded as much in a letter to Mansfield. "We can get out of Viet Nam. We can get out next week or next month," Johnson wrote the Catholic Senator. "But what happens then?...We know what would then happen to the Catholics, Buddhists, and every other non-Communist group, because we saw it happen in 1954-56." To Mansfield's contention that U.S. policy consisted largely of running in place, Johnson maintained that the enemy was deteriorating, and the end was near. "Once they become convinced that we are not weak; that we are not impatient; that we are not going to falter, that they cannot win; that the cost to them of their continued aggression is rising, that their bargaining position at a conference is getting weaker every day," the president concluded, "then peace will come, whether at the negotiating table or not" [13].

It would not come in 1966. In July Johnson's top commander in Vietnam, Gen. William Westmoreland, accepted the Honor et Veritas Award, the Catholic War Veterans U.S.A.'s highest honor, in appreciation of U.S. bombing of North Vietnamese military targets in Hanoi and Haiphong. In a letter to Johnson, the organization's leader, Martin Riley, expressed the wish for a "speedy and just victory in Viet Nam"[14].

In his strongest language yet, Pope Paul VI's September encyclical *Christi Matri* (To the Mother of Christ) urged "with piercing cry and with tears" an end to the "bloody and difficult war…in areas of East Asia." White House aide Tom Johnson informed the president that the Pope's pleas for peace were winning "considerable sympathy" among the American people. Ambassador to the United Nations Goldberg followed the encyclical with an offer that the world body mediate a settlement predicated upon a U.S. bombing halt, North Vietnamese and U.S. withdrawal from the South, and peace talks which would include the Viet Cong. Though Goldberg's "major policy speech to the [General] Assembly did not mention the Encyclical," the United States Catholic bishops' Office of United Nations Affairs observed, "the Encyclical assured discussion of the question [of Vietnam] within the context of international responsibility" [15].

Pope Paul VI sent a special envoy, Most Rev. Sergio Pignedoli, the Titular Archbishop of Iconio and Apostolic Delegate to Canada, on an October peace mission to Saigon. Then he commemorated the first anniversary of his U.N. speech by exhorting 150,000 Catholics in St. Peter's Square in Rome with words grown tragically ironic over the preceding twelve months: "Never again war." President Johnson also remembered the occasion by attending a special Washington Peace Mass at St. Matthew's Cathedral, where he heard Archbishop Patrick O'Boyle blame the enemy for failing to respond to the president's repeated peace overtures. As Christmas approached, Paul VI reiterated his previous year's hope that a holiday truce would unlock a lasting peace. From Austin President Johnson promised "sympathetic consideration" of the pontiff's latest plea, but from Saigon Secretary of State Rusk conveyed serious doubts [16].

Almost a year after greeting Foreign Minister Andrei Gromyko, the first Soviet official to enter Vatican City, Pope Paul VI hosted Soviet Premier Nikolai Podgorny in January 1967. A week later he appealed to Presidents Johnson, Ho Chi Minh of North Vietnam, and Nguyen Van Thieu of South Vietnam to extend their ninety-six-hour truce in observance of Tet, the lunar new year. Podgorny told Paul VI that his country would never abandon its North Vietnamese ally, and he rebuffed the pontiff's call for direct Soviet-U.S. negotiations on the war. Johnson reiterated his desire to negotiate "at any time and place, in any forum," while adding that surely the Pope "would not expect us to reduce military action unless the other side is willing to do likewise." Condemning the "U.S. imperialists [who] have sent to South Vietnam half a million U.S. and satellite troops and used more than 600,000 puppet troops to wage a war against our people," Ho Chi Minh encouraged Paul VI to "use his high influence to urge that the U.S. government respect the national rights of the Vietnamese people." Thieu joined the Catholic hierarchy in South Vietnam in implicitly supporting a Saigon street protest organized by a Catholic group, the Committee for a Just and Legitimate Peace, in opposition to any peace efforts which would "sell out" South Vietnam to the communists [17].

The Pope pressed on nonetheless. An April meeting with U Thant in Rome preceded the opening of the Pacem in Terris Institute in New York, where the Secretary General admiringly described the pontiff as "obsessed with peace." A month later, Paul VI observed the fiftieth anniversary of the appearance of the Virgin Mary to three shepherd children in Fatima, Portugal, with a call for a U.S. bombing halt and an end to North Vietnamese infiltration of the South. Yet in August, when celebrating the feast of the assumption of the Virgin Mary, the Pope lamented the absence of "the force and coherence and constancy" necessary to achieve them [18].

The Johnson Administration persisted in welcoming the Holy Father's peace efforts without changing its course in Vietnam. In 1967 alone the war would cost $25 billion and over nine thousand American lives. Noting that the Administration has "been getting rapped in many neighborhoods of the world over this Vietnam stuff," *Miami News* editor William Baggs urged Johnson to send another representative to a second Pacem in Terris meeting to be convened by the Center for Democratic Institutions in Geneva in May. While the Administration had no objection to such peace organizations and had been part of the previous gathering, Special Consultant to the President John Roche replied that it nonetheless had "no special obligation" to serve the group's interests, and would not be sending anyone this time. In a June meeting between Johnson and Soviet Premier Alexei Kosygin in Glassboro, New Jersey, the president extracted a pledge that another U.S. bombing pause would lead to negotiations. Then, Johnson would recall, "Kosygin slammed the door on us. We believe that he talked to North Vietnam, and they told him no"[19].

The president would also meet again with the Pope. This time, unlike in their meeting two years earlier, the two leaders were quite specific in their discussion of the Vietnam War. "You went to South Vietnam to protect your good intentions and your good hopes," Paul VI reassured Johnson in December in Rome. "But you must understand that I can never agree to war." The Pope then encouraged the president to end the bombing of the North.

"We have stopped bombing five times, but this only increases the murder," Johnson replied. "Archbishop [Patrick] Lucey [of San Antonio] went to South Vietnam as one of my observers during the [September] election. He told me that every time we quietened [sic] down they increase[d] their pressure. In the thirty-seven-day bombing pause [of 1965-66], they built up a seven-months' supply."

Charging that "Hanoi is ignoring and violating the Geneva Convention prisoner rules," Johnson urged the Pope to send a representative to visit the prisoners on both sides. He then proposed that the pontiff press South Vietnam and the National Liberation Front, the political wing of the Viet Cong, to engage in informal peace talks in Saigon, exclusive of their North Vietnamese and American sponsors. "Thieu is a good man – honest – and a Catholic," Johnson assured the Holy Father. "As you know, the Catholics are in a minority in South Vietnam. In the recent election, a new Senate was voted in, and a Catholic was elected as President of the Senate....I hope the Pope will encourage them to talk."

Johnson smiled broadly. "Just as the Pope encouraged me to pass my education bills. We are now spending nine billion dollars more on education. And the Pope can claim some responsibility for this."

Paul VI returned the smile, and, reaching out his hands toward the president, promised to try to investigate the treatment of POW's as well as attempt to bring the South Vietnamese government and the NLF together. "I will do whatever is possible. I will study the prisoner situation and see what contacts can be made. This is a cause which is close to my heart."

In return, the Pope inquired, "Is it possible that the truce at Christmas could be extended a day or two? Could you not show the world that on the day of peace January 1 you will also make this a day of truce?"

"My problem is this," Johnson responded. "My military leaders tell me that the North Vietnamese have trucks lined up bumper to bumper, and as soon as the truce begins they start them moving, and those supplies and those men kill our soldiers."

Having been refused yet again in his desperate quest for an end to the Vietnam War, the pontiff relented. "We shall pray for you," he told the president. "And we shall pray for your efforts for peace" [20 ].

Subsequent events would vindicate both Pope and president. For the first time, the Catholic hierarchy of South Vietnam criticized its government, not for being "soft" on communism, but for standing in the way of peace. The seventeen bishops, representing South Vietnam's two million Catholics, finally fell in line with the Holy Father in calling for an end to U.S. bombing and North Vietnamese aggression. "How can there be peace when those in responsible places mask their false promises behind rhetoric?" the bishops mocked the Thieu government. "How can there be peace if laziness, hypocrisy, and corruption prevail everywhere in society?" [21]

But for the umpteenth time, the North Vietnamese and Viet Cong violated a holiday truce, with a massive assault on some thirty major cities in South Vietnam, including Saigon, during the Tet cease-fire at the end of January. The ferocity of an enemy thought to be on its last legs horrified the millions of Americans witnessing the offensive on their television screens. "Eighty percent of the U.S. either follows the President or wants to do more," Johnson had told Paul VI only two months earlier. After Tet, however, an equal number of Americans wanted their country to leave Vietnam as wanted to win there. In February's New Hampshire Democratic presidential primary, Johnson barely defeated anti-war Catholic Senator Eugene McCarthy of Minnesota. So following two days of meetings with his foreign policy team, Johnson announced to the nation that he would virtually stop the bombing of the North, commence serious peace talks, and, to the amazement of even his closest aides, not seek reelection. The United States would not surrender to North Vietnam and the Viet Cong for another seven years. But on the last day of March in 1968, the president surrendered to the Pope [22].

## The Bishops and the President

But many American Catholic bishops kept fighting. Their staunch anti-communism and empathy for the Catholic minority in South Vietnam had long produced a sympathetic stance toward the war by most members of the hierarchy. Two weeks before the events in the Gulf of Tonkin, Harmon Burns of the bishops' National Catholic Welfare Conference Legal Department met with Michael Forrestal, Johnson's Assistant Secretary of State for Vietnamese Affairs, to demand that the South Vietnamese government release Major Dang Sy, a prominent Catholic prisoner. The bishops considered Dang Sy a victim of religious discrimination by a pro-Buddhist regime which blamed him for suppressing the Buddhist riots which helped insure President Ngo Dinh Diem's ouster in November 1963. Forrestal assured Burns that although the United States would not request the Major's release for fear of bloody protests by Buddhists in the northern part of South Vietnam, Johnson's Ambassador to South Vietnam Maxwell Taylor had secured from Prime Minister Nguyen Kahnh pledges of a reduction of his life sentence and eventual permission for him to leave the country [23].

The bishops' attention to the Dang Sy case stood in marked contrast to Pope Paul VI's view of the internal divisions within South Vietnam. At the end of August, *L'Osservatore Romano*, the Vatican newspaper, denied that South Vietnamese street clashes leading to the killing of a Catholic youth by a Buddhist mob were signs of a religious conflict [24].

The bishops' fear of communism also precluded a firm statement against nuclear war. Auxiliary Bishop Philip Hannan of Washington D.C. told the November meeting of the bishops' Catholic Association for International Peace that the proposed Schema 13 of the Second Vatican Council's *Constitution on the Church in the Modern World*, which would declare the use of nuclear weapons unjust in any case because their effects "cannot be imagined," fell outside the Church's "just war" tradition. A "just war," the Church had long taught, responds to an unwarranted violation of a legitimate nation's sovereignty only as a last resort and when greater evil would result in the absence of such hostilities. "Certainly we hold war in horror," said Hannan, "but we must state with precision what is prohibited in waging war to those who justly and laudably defend liberty" [25].

At Hannan's urging, a new draft would distinguish between unjust "wars of extermination" and "defensive wars." When Loyola University of Chicago sociologist Gordon Zahn assailed Hannan's dissent for undoubtedly bringing "cheer tonight in some Pentagon quarters as the votive martinis were raised," NCWC Social Action Department Director Msgr. George Higgins chided Zahn and his fellow pacifists for being "so infuriatingly holier than thou." Once and future CAIP president William O'Brien criticized the bishops for not speaking out against nuclear war, but he ultimately blamed the Pope.

"There has been no strong, blanket papal condemnation of nuclear war as immoral," O'Brien contended, calling for the Church to "study" the issue [26].

In May Higgins blasted an anti-war vigil at the Pentagon organized by national clergy which "almost inevitably took on the character of an anti-Administration gathering." Lyndon Johnson's favorite Catholic prelate, Archbishop Patrick Lucey of San Antonio, assured Catholic White House aide Jack Valenti that "the situation in Vietnam has...made a turn for the better." The CAIP's World Order Committee issued a July 1965 statement staunchly defending the new U.S. combat role in Vietnam. "We think the United States should be prepared to continue the use of military power as long as the Viet Cong with its supporters continue hostilities," wrote committee chairman Charles O'Donnell. O'Donnell nonetheless concluded his hawkish pronouncement with a nod toward those self-righteous pacifists. Quoting Pope John XXIII in *Pacem in Terris*, O'Donnell expressed the hope "that by meeting and negotiating, men may come to discover better the bonds that unite them" [27].

U.N. Ambassador Arthur Goldberg echoed this mixed message when he addressed the CAIP's annual convention in December. While recognizing the nation's "hard fight on the battlefields of Viet Nam calling for much courage and reserve," Goldberg nevertheless assured the group that "our peace effort is being waged with no less intensity." Though "the tragedy of our times may be that the Pontiff's cry of 'war never again' may be the one condition of survival in our atomic age," Goldberg cited Paul VI, he also lamented that quite possibly "men and nations are too wrapped up in the habits of the past to recognize it"[28].

So, perhaps, were the bishops themselves. A group of fifty college students picketed outside the chancery of New York's Archbishop Francis Cardinal Spellman in a December 1965 protest of Spellman's "silencing" of anti-war Jesuits Revs. Daniel Berrigan, Daniel Kilfoyle, and Frank Keating. Three weeks later Spellman arrived in Saigon for a Christmas visit with U.S. troops. When asked "What do you think about what America is doing in Vietnam?" the Cardinal replied, "I fully support everything it does." Then, paraphrasing the words of nineteenth-century American naval officer Stephen Decatur, Spellman proclaimed, "My country, may it always be right. Right or wrong, my country" [29].

Writing in the *New York Times* in February 1966, Edward Fiske related that the first major declaration of opposition to the Vietnam War by American clergy had emanated not from the pacifist fringe, but from the religious "establishment," in the form of a December 1965 critique by the General Board of the National Council of Churches, which Fiske called "the country's most conspicuous and easily mobilized Protestant institution." On the other hand, the nation's Catholic bishops remained either silent or supportive toward the war, a stance which "contrasts sharply with the peace efforts of Pope Paul," which even the bishops' Office for United Nations Affairs called "admittedly influential in the recent U.S. bombing pause and its world diplomatic initiative" [30].

A month later the *National Catholic Reporter* distributed a questionnaire on the war to the nation's 225 Catholic bishops. After five weeks, only six had replied, with half expressing support and the other half evading the issue. Rev. John Bennett, president of Union Theological Seminary and a leader of Protestant-Catholic ecumenical dialogue, marked the October anniversary of Pope Paul VI's United Nations speech by recalling that although "the Pope did all in his power...he had no leverage with the North Vietnamese, and apparently not much either with the Roman Catholic hierarchy of the United States on the question of peace." Bennett concluded, "If Pope Paul had been able to get a genuine response from even twenty members of the hierarchy, so that they really threw their weight on the side of peace, his visit might have been much more effective" [31].

Thus did the bishops strive to reconcile their own backing of the war with the Pope's search for peace. Baltimore Archbishop Lawrence Cardinal Shehan's June pastoral, "Peace and Patriotism," while stopping short of criticizing the Administration, nonetheless reminded Catholics of the wartime imperatives of the Second Vatican Council's *Constitution on the Church in the Modern World* to "exert whatever moral and civic influences seem dictated by...conscience." Without accusing the Administration of doing so, Shehan condemned "any act of war aimed indiscriminately at the destruction of entire cities or of extensive areas along with their populations." The bishops' November pastoral toed the same wobbly line. "It is reasonable to argue that our presence in Vietnam is justified," they wrote. "But we cannot stop here....It is the duty of everyone to keep looking for other alternatives" [32].

As evidence of how short a distance the bishops had travelled, the statement passed 169-5. "Your support for the war is accompanied by qualifications," a group of anti-war Catholics addressed the bishops from the nation's capital, "but you have so underemphasized these qualifications that they are being forgotten." The critics then cast their lot with Pope Paul VI, whose *Christi Matri* (Mother of Christ) had summoned both sides in the war to "stop – even at the expense of some inconvenience or loss," and against Cardinal Spellman, whose Christmas eve address to the American troops in Saigon calling for victory in Vietnam provoked unofficial angst in Vatican City, official repudiation in Moscow and Peking, and unusual vitriol from California Episcopal Bishop Kilmer Myers. "I can find no evidence that the Pope's stirring plea has ruffled the surface of American Catholic life," Rev. John Sheerin, editor of *Catholic World*, lamented. "Who speaks for the Church on Vietnam?" [33] .

Even when the hierarchy showed signs of straying from its endorsement of Administration policy, it did so haltingly and apologetically. The Christmas message of Boston's Archbishop Richard Cardinal Cushing, while approving of Pope Paul and Secretary General U Thant's peacemaking, refused to disapprove of President Johnson's warmaking. Eleven bishops conveyed some degree of sympathy for the January-February 1967 anti-war gathering in Washington convoked by the ecumenical Clergy and Laity Concerned About Vietnam, yet none accepted the organizers' invitations to attend. Rev. John Cronin, assistant director of the bishops' United States Catholic Conference Social Action Department, did attend, but only to scold the anti-war group for assuming that the Administration wasn't sincere in its quest for peace in Vietnam. Atlanta Archbishop Paul Hallinan spoke at a follow-up meeting of the group, where he called for a "second Selma" to organize for peace, but he would not commit himself to a particular method of attaining it [34].

Catholic Association for International Peace president William O'Brien criticized U.S. air raids around Hanoi and warned of escalation of the aerial war. Yet he refused to oppose the war itself, noting that many of CAIP's members "would agree substantially" with the bishops' peace pastoral. Though "I share your concern about Vietnam," the bishops' Social Action Department director Msgr. George Higgins, one of the authors of the pastoral, wrote John Twohey of the anti-war Catholic Committee on Vietnam in March 1967, he would not sign an open letter indicating such concern. "I respectfully express the earnest hope that the unwillingness of some of us (at the United States Catholic Conference) to sign your open letter will not be interpreted...as *prima facie* evidence that we are not in sympathy with Pope Paul's numerous statements on the crisis in Vietnam," Higgins added, only to take another step back. "This type of criticism, however well-intentioned, can easily degenerate into a crude form of blackmail" [35].

Later the same month Bishop James Shannon of Minneapolis-St. Paul joined ten presidents of Catholic colleges in denouncing the indiscriminate bombing of civilians in Vietnam but neglecting to address the overriding issue of the war itself. "Though the American people are divided on the Vietnamese War," Daniel Callahan wrote in the April *Atlantic Monthly*, for tactical or strategic reasons, "not one bishop has opposed it" [36].

The following year would expose a few cracks in the bishops' façade, however. In July Rochester Bishop Fulton Sheen became the first Catholic prelate to advocate immediate U.S. withdrawal from Vietnam. Though still refusing to break with the Administration, Atlanta's Archbishop Hallinan, Minneapolis-St. Paul's Bishop Shannon, Oklahoma City-Tulsa's Bishop Victor Reed, and Newark's Auxiliary Bishop John Dougherty lent their support in August to the "Negotiation Now" movement, which called for an end to U.S. bombing, a beginning of peace talks, and an enormous economic aid package under U.N. auspices as steps toward an end to the war. Without parting with the Administration, CAIP president William O'Brien decried the resumption of U.S. bombing near North Vietnamese cities, singling out an August 11 bombardment of Longbien bridge less than two miles from downtown Hanoi. "No one who takes seriously the social teaching of the Catholic Church on the moral limits of defensive warfare," O'Brien maintained, "can countenance counter-city warfare in North Vietnam" [37].

In November the bishops promulgated a new "Resolution on Peace," which continued to back "the repeated efforts of our government to negotiate a termination to conflict" while rejecting "peace at any price." The statement nevertheless recognized "considerable division among our people" over U.S. policy while espousing "more rational debate and greater solicitude for mutual understanding." It urged "even greater determination and action in the cause of negotiation" by the Johnson Administration. The following April, in the wake of the Tet Offensive, the bishops applauded Johnson's moves to restrict the bombing and pursue a diplomatic solution to the war, but confessed a "growing anxiety for peace." They formed a Secretariat for World Justice and Peace to better articulate their position on the war [38].

Yet the Administration did not feel threatened by these gathering clouds. "Not all churchmen are by any means opposed to what we are doing in Vietnam," press secretary Bill Moyers reacted to the World Council of Churches' December 1965 resolution. "Now I don't think the Church should abdicate its responsibility to hold men in public life to a very, very rigid standard," added the former Baptist minister. "I know that the President feels that the Church could do that more appropriately if it were more informed and impartial in its judgments"[39].

White House aide Joseph Califano shared with Johnson the September 1967 assessment of his fellow Catholic, Democratic Speaker of the House of Representatives John McCormack of Massachusetts, that "most Catholic clergy" were still "with you on Viet Nam." The president himself acknowledged Cardinal Spellman's death in December by foreshadowing "the first Christmas in many years when our men in uniform will not share the comfort of his presence." And three days before Johnson shocked the world by announcing that he would not seek re-election, Cardinal Cushing advised him that he should. "He said to look out for the Kennedys," Eugene Roscow relayed to fellow White House aide Marvin Watson. "He said he predicted to President Kennedy before he was killed that he would lose the election in 1964," Rostow recounted his conversation with the former president's favorite

Catholic prelate. "Bobby had made many enemies for President Kennedy, and the Cardinal didn't think those enemies had forgotten." Though Johnson would not run in 1968, Catholic New York Senator Robert Kennedy would, as an anti-war candidate whose campaign ended with an assassin's bullet in June [40].

## The Church and the President

"We must keep the world from being devoured by the Communists," *Commonweal* editor James O'Gera wrote in July 1965, "but we also must keep it from destroying itself." Such was the dilemma which American Catholics faced between the often conflicting aims of President Lyndon Johnson and Pope Paul VI on matters of war and peace. The result was an unsteady excursion between right and left, opposition and obedience [41].

To assist conscientious objectors and oppose the Vietnam War, Rev. Daniel Berrigan joined James Forest of the Catholic Worker Movement and James Douglass, a theology student in Rome, in forming the Catholic Peace Fellowship in the summer of 1964. When poet Daniel and professor Philip Berrigan joined five hundred others in signing a March 1965 "declaration of conscience" against U.S. policy in Vietnam, they became the first priests publicly to protest the war. The statement urged Americans to avoid the draft, refuse to participate in the manufacture or transportation of weapons, and obstruct the mobilization of U.S. troops [42].

But they were not the only Catholics. William Pfaff, formerly an associate editor of *Commonweal*, presciently surmised in April that "there is no evidence that the American public is prepared to sustain a major ground war in Vietnam." Associate editor Jay Neugeboren admonished as early as October 1965 that "there are few illusions left about the prospects of creating a democratic Vietnam out of the present chaos." In November Catholic Worker Roger LaPorte immolated himself in front of the United Nations building. After Rev. Daniel Berrigan eulogized LaPorte, his Jesuit superior exiled him to Mexico. In December, the Catholic Peace Fellowship placed two-page ads in the *National Catholic Reporter*, *Commonweal*, and *Ave Maria* urging Catholics to refuse service in the "unjust" Vietnam War. Rev. John Sheerin concluded in *Catholic World* in March 1966 "that the morality of our involvement in Vietnam is very doubtful." Sheerin marveled, "Is it not strange that so many of our clergy who have no hesitation about making positive moral judgments week after week in confession have no opinions on the great moral problem of our generation?" [43]

Catholic laypeople rushed to fill this void. Father Daniel Berrigan was among over one hundred clergy from many faiths who inaugurated the National Emergency Committee of Clergy Concerned About Vietnam (later Clergy and Laymen Concerned About Vietnam) in January 1966. By the end of the year, the group was advocating a negotiated peace in Vietnam and had grown to sixty-eight chapters. By mid-1966, James Forest, co-chairman of the Catholic Peace Fellowship, an anti-war organization with headquarters in New York, had published a booklet, "Catholics and Conscientious Objection," and his group was counselling up to fifty Catholics per week about how and whether to seek this option to military service. "It should not be left to a small, but happily growing, minority of Catholic priests and laymen to try to redeem the day for the Church in America," wrote war critic Gordon Zahn, author of *German Catholics and Hitler's Wars*. In the United States, unlike in Nazi Germany, where the Catholic Church had been largely silent toward Adolf Hitler's repression, "no Gestapo is likely to be pounding the doors or dragging their priests off to concentration camps. At least not yet." So there was no excuse for Catholic indifference to the horrors of Vietnam. *Commonweal* ended the year by advocating an immediate, unconditional withdrawal of U.S. forces from the "unjust" war in Southeast Asia [44].

"Why in the year 1966 are Catholics getting so involved in peacemaking?" asked Rev. Charles Palms, who answered that the seemingly unending advances in nuclear weapons, the no-holds-barred ambiguity of guerilla warfare, and the empowerment of Catholic clergy and laity by the Second Vatican Council helped explain such activism. "The Catholic Peace Fellowship and others who join in the quest for peace must know that they will not by themselves stop the war in Vietnam," Palms wrote. "But they are resolved to shock the national conscience into realizing the evils of war" [45].

And the newly energized Catholic Left would persist in doing so. Rev. Philip Berrigan of Baltimore was the only Catholic among twelve clergy who criticized the war in an open letter to President Johnson in December 1966. Rev. James Drane of Little Rock, Arkansas engaged in a shouting match in the Washington office of his state's pro-war Democratic Senator John McClellan, then returned home to lead a three-day fast by clergy and students which prompted Democratic State Senator Dan Sprick to label the young priest a "communist." Writing in *Catholic World* in May 1967, Gerhard Elston suggested that it was not too late for the Americans to learn from the French and extricate themselves from a civil war. "Could the United States be as greatminded as France under DeGaulle finally was in Algeria: admit an error, offer a settlement, and offer to help, not on our terms, but on those of the local boys?" [46].

But the Left remained largely left out of the American Catholic consensus on Vietnam. From the right, William Roberts, director of Catholic University's Institute of International Law and Relations, took on Rev. Philip Berrigan in a December 1965 debate in which Roberts declared Vietnam a "just war" in defense of "human rights." The *National Review*'s Anthony Bouscaren in March 1966 attacked the Berrigan brothers and *Catholic Worker* founder Dorothy Day for being soft on communism. *Catholic World*'s Rev. John Clifford asserted in September that it would not be immoral to stay in Vietnam, but rather to leave South Vietnam's sixteen million people helpless against the inexorable communist onslaught. *National Review* inveighed in January 1967 against *Commonweal*'s anti-war stance. "You will find nowhere in the *Commonweal* editorial," Catholic William F. Buckley's journal noted, "of the strategic implications, disastrous for the U.S. and for the world, of the Communist victory the editors announce themselves willing to concede" [47] .

Most American Catholics planted themselves firmly in the middle of the Vietnam debate. Rev. Andrew Greeley took issue in June 1965 with those "peaceniks" who equated the escalating resistance to the Vietnam War with the increasing mobilization against racial segregation. "If the peace movement members want to throw up picket lines, if they want to have 'teach-ins' (where mathematicians pontificate on foreign policy), if they want to sound like those who advised us that Mao and Castro were agrarian reformers," Greeley warned, "they are welcome to do their cause more harm than good." But he did not call upon them to cease and desist, for "we surely need a peace movement in this country if only as a counterbalance to the 'war hawks.'" [48].

Father Greeley thus could not have been happy with the tactics employed by a group of Protestant, Jewish, and Catholic seminarians who conducted a two-week peace vigil outside the White House in January 1966. But he would have approved of their message – encouraging more negotiations in Vietnam without attacking the Administration [49].

In July *America* applauded Cardinal Shehan's pastoral, which nimbly avoided criticizing Johnson while warning of any heightened conflict that would unnecessarily endanger civilians. "Has the President overstepped these bounds in Vietnam? We do not believe so," concluded *America*'s editors, while adding that the greater peril to civilians "comes not from the Administration but from those who would pressure the government into casting off the wraps of restraint under which we have been fighting....This the voice of Christian conscience must prevent." As for those disturbed by the other bishops' indifference to the war, Rev. Joseph Gallagher conceded in November 1966, the critics were right, but for the wrong reasons. The hierarchy should indeed speak out, if only to say that the war "is not clearly immoral," but that "the increasing suggestions that North Vietnam (with its fifteen million women and children) should be blasted off the map, turned into a desert, or bombed back to the Stone Age," clearly are [50].

Rev. James Schall similarly distinguished among three categories of "peace" advocates – pacifists represented by groups like the Catholic Worker movement, anti-nuclear organizations, and critics of the U.S. tactics of bombing civilians and the strategy of containing communism in an area outside the American sphere of influence. Father Schall attacked the second group for underestimating the evil of communism and the third for selective outrage not equally directed at violence in the American civil rights movement or the South African struggle against apartheid. But he was respectful, if unsympathetic, toward the first group's position for being "consistent," "religiously motivated," and "lived" [51].

*America* "has consistently supported the Administration policy in Southeast Asia on the grounds that we have been fighting a limited war for a limited objective – to guarantee the right of the people of South Vietnam to work out their own destiny free from the threat or use of outside force," the editors reiterated in January 1967. But amidst reports of accelerated U.S. bombing of urban areas, they excoriated the "civilian population be damned" attitude of Vietnam hawks. "It is perhaps not a simple matter to keep means proportionate to ends," the editorial concluded, "but the nation with a moral conscience can never cease trying" [52].

The next month the journal's editors rose to the defense of Father Cronin's impassioned dissent at the Clergy and Laity Concerned About Vietnam's anti-war demonstration in the nation's capital. Yet while lauding Cronin's support for the war, the editors again challenged all sides in the Vietnam conflict at home and abroad to press more vigilantly for peace. Cronin himself told the *National Catholic Reporter* that his remarks had intended not to reach either extreme but to ignite a rational dialogue. "Everybody wants peace. Nobody is in favor of napalming children," said Cronin. "But as long as the experts disagree about the facts, I would not join either the hawks or the doves in concrete recommendations with elements of political analysis or factual assumptions" [53].

In June's *Catholic World*, CAIP president William O'Brien offered his rebuttal to Gerhard Elston's Algerian analogy. Unlike a potentially precipitous American exit from Vietnam, O'Brien claimed, France's abandonment of its North African colony portended no deleterious international ripple effect. Yet O'Brien praised Elston's aversion to any significant escalation of the American war [54].

# Conclusions

An "argument without end" is how Lyndon Johnson's Secretary of Defense Robert McNamara would characterize the debate over the Vietnam War three decades after its conclusion. Since the United States was losing in Vietnam, the conventional wisdom has come to hold, the Johnson Administration was losing the argument which had put Americans there. To the communists, "we must say in Southeast Asia – as we did in Europe – in the words of the Bible, 'Hitherto shalt thou come but no further,'" the Commander-in-Chief explained the rationale for U.S. military involvement in Vietnam in April 1965. The American Catholic shepherds and much of their flock, who unabashedly or tacitly accepted this argument even at the risk of offending Pope Paul VI, therefore appeared complicit in this national tragedy [55].

After all, a Gallup Poll in late 1966 found far more Catholics than Protestants and Jews on Johnson's side in the Vietnam conflict. At the same time, a survey conducted by *World Campus*, a Maryknoll Fathers magazine, showed one-third of American Catholic college students in favor of U.S. policy in Vietnam, and over half supporting more bombing of North Vietnam while opposing demonstrations against the war. Two years later, American Catholics gave fifty-nine percent of their votes to Johnson's Vice President, Herbert Humphrey, who essentially vowed to continue the Administration's military and diplomatic initiatives in Vietnam [56].

In reassuring its president the American Catholic majority was largely rebuking its Pope. The pontiff himself seemed to recognize the limits of his effectiveness as the Church's and arguably the world's spiritual leader. In his September 1966 encyclical *Christi Matri*, Paul VI acknowledged that the acceleration of his petitions for peace had begotten only escalation on the battlefield. "What is the use of it?" he asked plaintively, answering that despite his many setbacks, he remained convinced that "to pray is not in vain" [57].

The Pope's seemingly hollow words were alienating many non-Catholics as well. *The New York Times*' Edward Fiske reported in December 1967 that many "high Protestant officials" in the United States considered Paul VI "naïve in believing that he can perform a mediator's function in the Vietnam War, in view of the fact that Catholics constitute one of the major political blocs in the country." One cleric was more blunt, contending that "this is too tough a world for activist gimmicks" like the Pope's Vietnam peace proposals [58].

But American Catholics were not always on the "wrong" side of the argument over Vietnam. *Commonweal*'s verdict that President Johnson's mantra of "we cannot just get out" was "not a suitable substitute for a war policy" arrived as early as August 1965, almost eight years before the remaining U.S. troops just got out. The same month, *Life* published a picture of Catholic Worker Christopher Kearns burning his draft card. By the end of August Congress had passed a law prohibiting such actions, and Catholic Worker David Miller would become the first person to go to prison for breaking it. In May 1968 the Berrigan brothers and six other Catholics raided the office of the Catonsville, Maryland draft board and burned the records with napalm [59].

Though most American Catholics repudiated such radical activities, a July 1967 Harris poll showed that they had become more dovish on the war than their Protestant counterparts, with one-quarter of American Catholics now in opposition. Even their bishops finally showed substantial movement in that direction. At their November 1968 annual meeting, the bishops issued a pastoral, "Human Life in our Day," in which they asserted that "one cannot accuse Catholics of either being partisans of any one point of view or of being unconcerned" about Vietnam. While expressing the hope that the Johnson Administration's bombing halt and peace negotiations would soon bear fruit, the bishops nonetheless wondered, "How much more of our resources in men and money should we commit to this struggle?" And they emerged from their anti-nuclear shell to advocate early Senate ratification of the Administration's August 1968 Nuclear Nonproliferation Treaty with the Soviet Union and sixty other nations, a fulfillment of Father Cronin's wish, virtually forgotten in the firestorm over his other remarks at the Clergy and Laity Concerned vigil, that Vietnam not derail nuclear détente [60].

Lest they be charged with undermining their Pope, the bishops voted 121-64 that their pastoral apply the principles of the Vatican II *Constitution on the Modern World* to the Vietnam War and 142-51 to the question of selective conscientious objection. They also voted 153-44 that the pastoral explicitly define the role of conscience during wartime. The results were the document's taut embrace of "Pope Paul's positive, dynamic concept of peace" and advocacy of a new law permitting conscientious objection to a particular war [61].

For his part Pope Paul VI offered American Catholics periodic reminders that in his feverish quest for peace he had not forsaken the Church's traditional anti-communism. On the seventy-fifth anniversary of Pope Leo XIII's *Rerum Novarum* (Of New Things) in May 1966, Paul VI repeated that encyclical's condemnation of Marxism, calling it an "erroneous and dangerous ideology." In October the pontiff refused to accept the resignation of New York's Francis Cardinal Spellman, even though the hawkish first Military Vicar of the United States Armed Forces was two years beyond the retirement age of seventy-five recommended by the Pope only three months earlier. Two years later the Holy Father denounced the Soviet invasion of Czechoslovakia as an affront to the Czechs' freedom and dignity [62].

More important than whether American Catholics were winning or losing the argument on Vietnam during the Johnson era, however, was the reality that the argument, like the war which it spawned, was not yet over. In this way the bishops' statements and their followers' responses to them reflected the extant mysteries of an arduous work in progress. "A careful reading" of the bishops' November 1966 pastoral, war critic Rev. John Sheerin opined in *Catholic World* in January 1967, "reveals that their assent to the policy is so provisioned as to be lacking in any enthusiasm." The fact that the bishops may not be "quite prepared to condemn Administration policy out of hand," *America* observed in March 1967, did not mean that they didn't "deplore war as much as the next Christian" [63].

And though the Vietnam War was fast becoming the paramount moral issue of the day, the question of how and whether American churches should address it remained as inconclusive as the war itself. Somewhere between President Lyndon Johnson's appeal to Americans' "Christian duty" to "help our neighbors" in Vietnam, and Rev. Martin Luther King, Jr.'s anti-war jeremiad from the pulpit of New York's Riverside Baptist Church, lay a religious "no-man's land" which only true believers on either side dared to enter. Despite historic fits and starts, the United States had never seen a Catholic Left before. Dr. Carl Henry, editor of *Christianity Today*, the world's most widely read interdenominational religious periodical, told the *New York Times* in March 1965 that his fellow clergy possessed "neither a divine mandate…nor special competence" to address the nation's burning political issues. "It's a terrible thing," Episcopal priest Rev. G. R. Wheatcroft of Houston told *Newsweek* in July 1967, but on the Vietnam War, "we don't know what to say." Methodist

Bishop J. O. Smith of Georgia concurred that on Vietnam, "the position of our church is that we live in a very imperfect world. The church kind of prays about it and hopes by faith we won't get involved next time." Rabbi Henry Siegman, vice president of the Synagogue Council of America, was even more explicit about organized religion's limited role: "I am prepared to accept the contention that Dean Rusk and Robert McNamara speak with no less moral authority than the heads of America's religious establishment." Even the civil disobedience of the civil rights movement, *Newsweek* concluded, had not adequately prepared the churches to confront the moral dilemmas posed by the military draft and conscientious objection [64] .

So civil rights champion Patrick Cardinal O'Boyle's instructions to the priests of the Archdiocese of Washington, D.C. that Vietnam not be a subject of their Sunday homilies or the admission by an official in civil rights opponent James Cardinal McIntyre's Archdiocese of Los Angeles that the war "is not a topic of debate in any of our churches" in many ways fell comfortably within the mainstream of American organized religion. And Auxiliary Bishop James Shannon of Minneapolis-St. Paul, himself growing more dovish by the day, could at once lament that his fellow bishops "obviously aren't getting the Pope's message" while at the same time attacking those non-bishops who said essentially the same thing. After Stanford University theologian Robert McAfee Brown deplored the bishops' absence at the January 1967 Clergy and Laity Concerned About Vietnam event, Shannon questioned Brown's authority to do so. "As a Christian he has a moral obligation to follow his conscience and to voice his reservations about American participation in the war in Vietnam," Shannon wrote of Brown in March 1967. "But he does not have the right to decide how his fellow Christians will voice their concern and current agony about this same problem." Thus did Shannon frame his dispute with Brown as not so much about Vietnam as about the hierarchical nature of his Church. "Dr. Brown's style of protest," Shannon succinctly summarized, "is simply not the style of the Catholic bishops" [65].

"We are having an argument within the family," an anti-war Chicago priest explained in December 1965. Many American Catholics would have preferred that it remain there. But a war which would fail to contain communism had shaken a Church which would fail to contain dissent. In this way the American Catholic bishops had more in common with Lyndon Johnson than even they realized [66].

## References

[1] Paul Conkin, *Big Daddy from the Pedernales: Lyndon Johnson* (Boston: Twayne, 1986), pp. 195-196.

[2] Bruce Schulman, *Lyndon B. Johnson and American Liberalism* (Boston: Bedford, 1995), p. 135; Robert Dallek, *Flawed Giant: Lyndon Johnson and His Times* (New York: Oxford University Press, 1998), pp. 247-248.

[3] Robert Doty, "Pontiff Appeals for Peace Effort," *New York Times*, 12 February 1965, sec. L, p. 1; "Peace in Vietnam is Sought by Pope," *New York Times*, 21 February 1965, sec. L, p. 24.

[4] Letter from Rev. Thomas Merton to President Lyndon Johnson, 20 February 1965, White House Central Files, Name File, Box 377, Lyndon Baines Johnson Presidential

Papers, Lyndon Baines Johnson Presidential Library, Austin, TX; Telegram from Rev. Philip Berrigan, Martin Corbin, and James Forest to President Lyndon Johnson, 2 March 1965, White House Central Files, Name File, Box 230, LBJPP, LBJPL; Memorandum from Bill Moyers to "Mr. President," 16 April 1965, White House Central Files, Name File – N, Box 24, LBJPP, LBJPL.

[5] Memorandum from Jack Valenti to President Lyndon Johnson, 26 February 1965, White House Central Files, Subject File – Religious Matters, Box 6, LBJPP, LBJPL, pp. 1-2; Jack Languuth, "Saigon Catholics Fearful of Buddhist Army Purge," *New York Times*, 13 April 1965, sec. L, pp. 1,4.

[6] "Text of Encyclical by Pope Paul Deploring Armed Conflicts," *New York Times*, 1 May 1965, sec. L, p.9; Jack Languuth, "Saigon Catholics Contend Regime is Easy on Reds," *New York Times*, 10 May 1965, sec. L, p.1; Jack Languuth, "Saigon Generals Striving to Form a Stable Regime," *New York Times*, 12 June 1965, sec. L, p.1.

[7] Robert Doty, "Papal Encyclical A Plea for Peace," *New York Times*, 1 May 1965, sec. L, p. 9; "Memorandum for the President: Talking Points for the Pope," n.d., Appointment File (Diary Back-up), Box 23, LBJPP, LBJPL, p.1.

[8] "Excerpts from Papal Address," *New York Times*, 4 October 1965, sec. L, p. 2; Tom Wicker, "Two Leaders Meet: Paul and President Confer Forty-Six Minutes on World Issues," *New York Times*, 4 October 1965, sec. L, p. 2.

[9] E. W. Kenworthy, "Masfield Report Seen as Urging U.S. to Get Peace Pact Quickly," *New York Times*, 9 January 1966, sec. L, p. 1.

[10] Transcript, Bill Moyers Press Conference, 4 October 1964, Appointment File (Diary Back-up), Box 23, LBJPP, LBJPL, p. 7; Robert Doty, "Pope's Christmas Plea: 'Sincere Negotiation,'" *New York Times*, 24 December 1965, sec. L, p. 1; Robert Doty, "Pope Sends Pleas: Pontiff Exhorts Hanoi, Saigon, Washington to Pursue Peace," *New York Times*, sec. L, p.1; Jack Raymond, "U.S. is Pessimistic as War is Resumed," *New York Times*, 26 December 1965, sec. L, p. 1.

[11] Robert Doty, "Pope Appeals to Peking and Moscow on Vietnam," *New York Times*, 2 January 1966, sec. L, p. 1; John Pomfret, "Vietnam 'Failure' Saddens Johnson," *New York Times*, 2 January 1966, sec. L, p. 1.

[12] Robert Doty, "Pontiff Suggests U.N. Arbitration in Vietnam War," *New York Times*, 30 January 1966, sec. L, p. 1; Memorandum from Jack Valenti to President Lyndon Johnson, 19 March 1966, White House Central Files, Subject File – Peace, Box 3, LBJPP, LBJPL.

[13] "Pope Regrets His Peace Bids' Failure," *New York Times*, 25 June 1966, sec. L, p. 5; Letter from President Lyndon Johnson to Senator Mike Mansfield, 22 June 1966, White House Central Files, Name File, Box 72, LBJPP, LBJPL, pp. 2-3.

[14] Letter from Martin Riley to President Lyndon Johnson, 1 July 1966, White House Central Files, Name File, Box 141, LBJPP, LBJPL.

[15] "Text of Pope's Encyclical on Peace," *New York Times*, 20 September 1966, sec. L, p. 18; Memorandum from Tom Johnson to President Lyndon Johnson, 3 October 1966, White House Central Files, Subject File – Peace, Box 1, LBJPP, LBJPL; "Report to the Bishops," United States Catholic Conference Office for United Nations Affairs, September 1966, General Administration Series, Subseries 3.3, Box 165, Folder: Report to Bishops, United States Catholic Conference Papers, Catholic University of America Archives, Washington, D.C., p. 1.

[16] "Papal Peace Vow Sent to Vietnam," *New York Times*, 1 October 1966, sec. L, p. 4; Robert Doty, "150,000 Join Pope in Plea for Peace by Negotiations," *New York Times*, 5 October 1966, sec. L, pp. 1,4; Robert Doty, "Pope Paul Urges Truce Extension, Then Peace Talk," *New York Times*, 9 December 1966, sec. L, pp. 1,17; "Rusk Pessimistic on Lengthy Truce," *New York Times*, 9 December 1966, sec. L, p. 17.

[17] "Pope to Receive Soviet President," *New York Times*, 4 January 1967, sec. L, p. 6; Robert Doty, "Podgorny Meets Pope at Vatican," *New York Times*, sec. L, pp. 1,16; "The Pope's Message," *New York Times*, 9 February 1967, sec. L, p. 2; "Meeting of the Pope and the President," 13 December 1967, Special Files – Meeting Notes File, Box 2, LBJPP, LBJPL, pp. 4-5; "The President's Reply," *New York Times*, 9 February 1967, sec. L, p. 2; "Ho Chi Minh Reply to Pope," *New York Times*, 14 February 1967, sec. L, p. 8; "Saigon Catholics Stage a Protest," *New York Times*, 25 February 1967, sec. L, p. 3.

[18] "Thant Hails Pope on Peace Efforts," *New York Times*, 27 April 1967, sec. L, p. 9; "Text of Sermon by Pope Paul and Shrine of Fatima," *New York Times*, 14 May 1967, sec. L, p. 47; "Pope Melancholy on Peace Outlook," *New York Times*, 17 August 1967, sec. L, p. 15.

[19] Schulman, p. 139; Letter from William Baggs to Walt Rostow, 27 March 1967, White House Central Files, Subject File – Peace, Box 3, LBJPP, LBJPL; "Meeting of the Pope and the President," p. 7.

[20] "Meeting of the Pope and the President," pp. 4,6,13,9,10,11,12,13,14.

[21] Bernard Weinraub, "Bishops of South Vietnam, Asking Peace, Score Thieu," *New York Times*, sec. L, p. 3.

[22] "Meeting of the Pope and the President," p. 2; Schulman, p. 148.

[23] "Poetic Justice in Vietnam?" *America*, 20 June 1964, p. 837; "Memorandum," National Catholic Welfare Conference Office for United Nations Affairs, 20 July 1964, General Administration Series, Subseries 3.5, Box 173, National Catholic Welfare Conference Papers, CUAA, p. 1; "Protest in Saigon," *America*, 27 June 1964, p. 862.

[24] "Vatican Appeals for Saigon Calm," *New York Times*, 30 August 1964, sec. L, p. 3.

[25] "Council Debates War and Peace," *CAIP News*, January 1965, General Administration Series, Subseries 3.6, Folder: CAIP – News, 1964-65, NCWCP, CUAA, p. 11; "Laymen Lay Low," *National Review*, 10 January 1967, p. 11.

[26] "Denies Schema Thirteen Now Approves Nuclear War," *CAIP News*, May 1965, General Administration Series, Subseries 3.6, Box 174, Folder: CAIP – News, 1964-65, NCWCP, CUAA, p. 9; Msgr. George Higgins, "Pacifist Attack," *CAIP News*, February 1965, General Administration Series, Series 3.6, Box 174, Folder: CAIP – News, 1964-65, NCWCP, CUAA, p. 9; "Church Criticized for Lack of Stand on Nuclear War," *CAIP News*, May 1965, General Administration Series, Subseries 3.6, Box 174, Folder: CAIP – News, 1964-65, NCWCP, CUAA, p. 10.

[27] Msgr. George Higgins, "National Policy and the Clergy," *CAIP News*, May 1965, General Administration Series, Subseries 3.6, Box 174, Folder: CAIP – News, 1964-65, NCWCP, CUAA, pp. 6-7; Letter from Rev. Patrick Lucey to Jack Valenti, 10 May 1965, White House Central Files, Subject File – Religious Matters, Box 6, LBJPP, LBJPL, p. 1; Charles O'Donnell, "Statement on the War in Vietnam by the CAIP World Order Committee," 17 July 1965, General Administration Series, Subseries 3.6, Box 174, Folder: CAIP – News, 1964-65, NCWCP, CUAA, pp. 6-7.

[28] Arthur Goldberg, "Efforts for Peace," 4 December 1965, in *Social Digest*, July-August 1966, General Administration Series, Subseries 3.6, Box 174, Folder: CAIP – Annual Convention, 1965, NCWCP, CUAA, pp. 219, 217-218.

[29] Douglas Robinson, "Catholics Picket Spellman Office," *New York Times*, 5 December 1965, sec. L, pp. 1, 10; "Spellman Arrives for Five Day Visit with Vietnam G.I.'s," *New York Times*, 24 December 1965, sec. L, p. 6.

[30] Edward Fiske, "War and the Clergy," *New York Times*, 15 February 1966, sec. L, p. 2; "Report to the Bishops," United States Catholic Conference Office for United Nations Affairs, February 1966, General Administration Series, Subseries 3.3, Box 165, Folder: Report to Bishops, 1966-1967, USCCP, CUAA, p. 1.

[31] "The Bishops and Vietnam," *Commonweal*, 15 April 1966, p. 93; John Cogley, "'Never Again War'," *New York Times*, 5 October 1966, sec. L, p. 4.

[32] "Peace and Patriotism," *America*, 16 July 1966, p. 50; "Peace and Vietnam," National Council of Catholic Bishops, United States Catholic Conference, 18 November 1966, in J. Brian Benestad and Francis Butler, ed. *Quest for Justice: A Compendium of Statements of the United States Bishops on the Political and Social Order 1966-1980* (Washington, D.C.: United States Catholic Conference, 1981), p. 53.

[33] "Statement on Peace," 18 November 1966, General Administration Series, Subseries 1.1, Box 70, Folder: NCWC Bishops General Meeting Minutes, 1963-66, NCWCP, CUAA, p. 192; "Open Letter to American Catholic Bishops," n.d., General Administration Series, Subseries 1.1, Box 7, Folder: Administration – Letters to Bishops, April-December 1966, NCWCP, CUAA, p. 2; "Text of Pope's Encyclical on Peace," p. 18; "Spellman's View Decried in Rome," *New York Times*, 28 December 1966, sec. L, p. 3; John Cogley, "The Spellman Dispute," *New York Times*, 29 December 1966, sec. L, p. 3; "Spellman's View on War Called Outrageous by Episcopal Bishop," *New York Times*, 4 February 1967, sec. L, p. 3; John Sheerin, "Who Speaks for the Church on Vietnam?" *Catholic World*, November 1966, p. 72.

[34] Cogley, "The Spellman Dispute," p. 3; Robert McAfee Brown, "An Open Letter to the U.S. Bishops," *Commonweal*, 17 February 1967, p. 547; "Challenge for the Churches," *America*, 18 February 1967, p. 234; "A Second Selma," *Christian Century*, 8 March 1967, p. 301.

[35] William O'Brien, "Appeal for Limitation of Vietnam War," *CAIP News*, 30 December 1966, General Administration Series, Subseries 3.6, Box 174, Folder: CAIP – News, 1966-67, USCCP, CUAA, pp. 3-4; Letter from Msgr. George Higgins to John Twohey, 2 March 1967, General Administration Series, Subseries 3.1, Box 172, Folder: USCC Division on Urban Life, 1964-1971, USCCP, CUAA, pp. 1-2.

[36] "Catholics Seek a Review on War," *New York Times*, 19 March 1967, sec. L, p. 3; Daniel Callahan, "America's Catholic Bishops," *Atlantic Monthly*, April 1967, p. 69.

[37] "In Recent Peace Plea Bishop Asks Withdrawal from Vietnam," *CAIP News*, October 1967, General Administration Series, Subseries 3.6, Box 174, Folder: CAIP – News, 1966-67, USCCP, CUAA, pp. 7-8; "Bishops Endorsing Negotiation Now," *CAIP News*, October 1967, General Administration Series, Subseries 3.6, Box 174, Folder: CAIP – News, 1966-67, USCCP, CUAA, pp. 6-7; William O'Brien, "Statement on Bombing Population Centers in North Vietnam," *CAIP News*, October 1967, General Administration Series, Subseries 3.6, Box 174, Folder: CAIP – News, 1966-67, USCCP, CUAA, p. 5.

[38] "On Peace," National Council of Catholic Bishops, United States Catholic Conference, 16 November 1967, in Benestad and Butler, pp. 56-57; "Resolution on Peace," National Council of Catholic Bishops, United States Catholic Conference, Fourth General Meeting, 23-24 April 1968, United States Catholic Conference Papers, United States Catholic Conference Archives, Washington, D.C., pp. 64-65; "Up Bishops' Sleeves," *Newsweek*, 24 April 1967, p. 88.

[39] "White House Rebuttal to Vietnam Critics," *Catholic World*, October 1966, p. 53.

[40] Memorandum from Joseph Califano to President Lyndon Johnson, 18 September 1967, White House Central Files, Subject File – Religious Matters, Box 6, LBJPP, LBJPL; Lyndon Johnson, "Statement by the President," 2 December 1967, White House Central Files, Subject File – Religious Matters, Box 6, LBJPP, LBJPL; Memorandum from Marvin Watson, 28 March 1968, White House Central Files, Subject File – Religious Matters, Box 6, LBJPP, LBJPL.

[41] James O'Gara, "Banning the Bomb," *Commonweal*, 23 July 1965, p. 522.

[42] Charles Meconis, *With Clumsy Grace: The American Catholic Left, 1961-1975* (New York: Seabury Press, 1979), p. 9; "Men of Peace," *Commonweal*, 19 March 1965, p. 779; Anthony Bouscaren, "The Catholic Peaceniks," *National Review*, 8 March 1966, p. 202.

[43] William Pfaff, "No Victory in Vietnam," *Commonweal*, 23 April 1965, p. 137; Jay Neugeboren, "Keeping the Consensus," *Commonweal*, 8 October 1965, p. 8; Meconis, p. 13; Bouscaren, p. 202; John Sheerin, "The Morality of the Vietnam War," *Catholic World*, March 1966, p. 330.

[44] Melvin Small, *Antiwarriors: The Vietnam War and the Battle for America's Hearts and Minds* (Wilmington, DE: Scholarly Resources, 2002), p. 51; Charles Palms, "Peace and the Catholic Conscience," *Catholic World*, June 1966, pp. 145-146; Gordon Zahn, "The Crime of Silence," *Commonweal*, 17 June 1966, p. 356; "Getting Out," *Commonweal*, 23 December 1966, p. 335.

[45] Palms, pp. 149,152.

[46] Emanuel Perlmulter, "Twelve Clerics Criticize Johnson on Hanoi Bombing," *New York Times*, 27 December 1966, sec. L, p. 6; "Arkansas Priest Leads Fight on War," *New York Times*, 26 February 1967, sec. L, p. 9; Gerhard Elston, "Vietnam: Some Basic Considerations," *Catholic World*, May 1967, p. 81.

[47] "Says Vietnam War Defends Christian Values," *CAIP News*, January 1966, General Administration Series, Subseries 3.6, Box 174, Folder: CAIP – News, 1966-67, USCCP, CUAA, p. 11; Bouscaren, p. 202; John Clifford, "Some Fallacies About the Vietnam War," *Catholic World*, September 1966, p. 364; "Laymen Lay Low," p. 12.

[48] Andrew Greeley, "Peaceniks Have a Lot to Learn," *CAIP News*, June 1965, General Administration Series, Subseries 3.6, Box 174, Folder: CAIP – News, 1964-65, NCWCP, CUAA, pp. 7-8.

[49] "Seminarians End Two-Week Vigil in Front of White House Today," *New York Times*, 30 January 1966, sec. L, p. 6.

[50] "Peace and Patriotism," p. 50; Joseph Gallagher, "The American Bishops on Modern War," *America*, 11 November 1966, pp. 548-549.

[51] James Schall, "Religion and War," *Commonweal*, 18 November 1966, p. 194.

[52] "Bombs in the North" and "The Moral Issue," *America*, 14 January 1967, p. 32.

[53] "Challenge to the Churches," p. 234; John Donavan, *Crusader in the Cold War* (New York: Peter Lang, 2005), p. 158.

[54] William O'Brien, "Comments on the Vietnam Debate," June 1967, p. 170.

[55] Robert McNamara, James Blight, Robert Brigham, Thomas Biersteker, Herbert Schandler, et al. *Argument Without End* (Washington, D.C.: Public Affairs, 2000); "President Lyndon Johnson Explains Why Americans Fight in Vietnam, 1965," in Dennis Merrill and Thomas Paterson, ed. *Major Problems in American Foreign Relations* (Boston: Houghton Mifflin), p. 450.

[56] James O'Gara, "Catholics and Peace," *Commonweal*, 11 November 1966, p. 158; "Campus Poll Shows Catholics Back War, Decry Draft Lottery," *New York Times*, 20 November 1966, p. 16; Jeffrey Jones, "The Protestant and Catholic Vote," available at http://www.gallup.com/poll/11911/Protestant-Catholic-Vote,aspx? INTERNET.

[57] "At a General Audience," *CAIP News*, October 1966, General Administration Series, Subseries 3.6, Box 174, Folder: CAIP – News, 1966-67, USCCP, CUAA, p. 6.

[58] Edward Fiske, "Papal Quest for Peace," *New York Times*, 25 December 1967, sec. L, p. 3.

[59] "Our War in Vietnam," *Commonweal*, 6 August 1965, p. 547; James Hennesey, *American Catholics* (New York: Oxford University Press, 1981), p. 319; Jay Dolan, *The American Catholic Experience* (Notre Dame, IN: University of Notre Dame Press, 1992), p. 451.

[60] "The Churches: What Should We Say?" *Newsweek*, 10 July 1967, p. 82; Dolan, p. 426; "Human Life in Our Day, Chapter II, 'The Family of Nations'," National Council of Catholic Bishops, 15 November 1968, in Benestad and Butler, ed., pp. 65,60; Donavan, p. 187.

[61] "Human Life in Our Day," pp. 59,67-68.

[62] "Pope Paul Warns of Marxist Peril," *New York Times*, 23 May 1966, sec. L, p. 9; Edward Fiske, "Pope Turns Down Cardinal Spellman's Offer to Resign," *New York Times*, 11 October 1966, sec. L, pp. 1,48; Henry ten Kortenar, "Does the Pope Realize?" *Commonweal*, 11 October 1968, p. 49.

[63] John Sheerin, "The Bishops and the Vietnam War," *Catholic World*, January 1967, p. 197; "The Bishops Taken to Task," *America*, 11 March 1967, p. 334.

[64] "Our War in Vietnam," *Commonweal*, 5 August 1965, p. 548; James Fraser, *Between Church and State* (New York: St. Martin's Press, 1999), p. 155; Small, pp. 6-7; Hennessey, p. 320; Dolan, p. 426; Meconis, p. ix; M. S. Handler, "Clergymen Clash on Role in Major National Issues," *New York Times*, 1 March 1965, sec. L, p. 78; "The Churches: What Should We Say?" pp. 81-82.

[65] "The Churches: What Should We Say?" p. 82; James Shannon, "Catholic Bishops and Vietnam," *Commonweal*, 17 March 1967, p. 671; "The Bishops Taken to Task," *America*, 11 March 1967, p. 337.

[66] John Corry, "The Catholic Student Protest: Priest Calls Support of Liberal Clergy 'Argument Within the Family'," *New York Times*, 26 December 1965, sec. L, p. 55.

In: Presidents and War
Editors: A. Eksterowicz and G. Hastedt, pp. 233-252
ISBN 978-1-61668-917-9


*Chapter 14*

# "NO WINNERS, NO LOSERS": REAGAN, THE IRAN-IRAQ WAR AND THE GULF'S PERPETUAL SECURITY DILEMMA

***Bernd Kaussler***

## INTRODUCTION

The Iran-Iraq war, which lasted from 1980 until 1988, was the longest conventional war in the 20th Century and claimed the lives of as many as half a million people on both sides. For Iran, the experiences on the battlefield do not only continue to inform current security and foreign policy, but marked the collective memory of an entire generation, fuelling mistrust and animosity vis-à-vis Europe in general and the United States in particular. The Reagan administration's policy during the Iran-Iraq war was as much defined by Cold War strategy and U.S. interests in the Levant and Persian Gulf as it was determined by Reagan himself, who entered office with a deep mistrust and hostility towards the new Iranian regime. By and large, Reagan's official position of neutrality during the war was a carefully guarded veneer of a war policy, which first supported Iraq in economic, diplomatic and military terms but then shifted to actual involvement by U.S. forces against Iran. The central argument of this paper is that Reagan's war policy during the conflict set the foundations for the Persian Gulf's ongoing balance of power politics, by introducing deterrence as the primary tenet of security in the region. Because of these policies and naval confrontations between Iranian and American forces, the major legacy of the war is that the fundamental Cold War concept of deterrence survives in the Persian Gulf, both in its military and diplomatic manifestation. As such, it is argued that a collective security framework is still elusive in that region, largely due to U.S. and Iranian experiences between 1980- 1988.

## Saddam's Motivations

Saddam Hussein's decision to invade neighboring Iran on 22 September 1980 reflected both historical tensions, his self-given role as pan-Arab leader and the Iraqi regime's disastrous assumption that it could bring about the fall of the new Islamic regime. Both Saddam Hussein's unease about new political realities in Iran and his bold, yet inept tactics vis-à-vis Tehran had already manifested themselves months before the invasion when an Iraqi terrorist group, funded by his regime, seized the Iranian Embassy in London in April, demanding the autonomy of the Arab-majority and oil-rich region of Khuzestan in Iran [1]. Whilst territorial and economic gain certainly were certainly vital for Iraq to advance into Iranian territory, Saddam Hussein's biggest grievance was with the Algiers Accord of 1975 in which he and the Shah settled a border dispute on the Shatt al-Arab waterway. With the new Islamic regime still in the early stages, Hussein saw an opportunity to reclaim the entire waterway [2]. Iran's volatile rhetoric coupled with its intent to export the revolution across the region also caused particular concern for regime stability, given Iraq's *Shi'a* majority. Following months of border skirmishes, Hussein eventually responded to Khomeini's open hostility to the Baathist regime, which in his own words "left him no choice but to fight" [3].

## Iraqi Advances and Iran's Counter Offensive

Anticipating an easy victory, without ever really stating specific war aims either to Iran or to his own generals, Hussein felt confident that the purge of Iran's military would favor Iraq's military campaign [4]. Catching Iran's leadership by surprise, the initial phase of the invasion allowed Iraqi forces to advance with three armored and two mechanized infantry divisions into Khuzestan with the aim of securing the major cities and infrastructure with little or no resistance. Failing to launch an extensive air attack against Iranian installations, the Iraqis failed to cripple the Iranian air force, allowing the Iranians to have enough aircrafts for retaliatory attacks. Lacking any real air or naval supremacy, Hussein prematurely declared a "glorious victory against the oppressor clique in Tehran" and stated his readiness to negotiate a ceasefire and negotiations to settle territorial disputes only a week after the invasion [5]. Misreading Iran's political map, the Iraqis failed to garner any support of Khuzestan's ethnic Arabs, who felt more alienated with the destruction and violence of the occupation than they had grievances vis-à-vis the Islamic Republic from which they had also no intention to secede from [6]. The anticipated two weeks campaign turned into a siege of strategically important cities of Abadan and Khorramshahr. Further north-west, the Iraqis occupied Mehran, advanced towards the Zagros Mountains and were able to cut off a supply corridor to Tehran by securing some territory forward of Qasr-e-Shirin. Overall, Iraq attacked only four targets along a 600 kilometers stretch of the border [7]. Even though the invasion temporarily halted Khomeini's purges of opponents and was under attack by President Bani-Sadr for having disintegrated a once powerful army, [8] the revolutionary regime soon managed to shift the military balance by recruiting thousands of volunteers (*Basij*) and putting them under the command of the Islamic Revolutionary Guards Corps (IRGC). Inspired by revolutionary ferocity as much as nationalism, Iranian forces managed to bring the Iraqi advance to a stall by March 1981. Since military planning in Tehran was still subject to domestic infighting, it was not until September 1981, that a major Iranian counter-offensive, launched by Iran's 16$^{th}$ and 92$^{nd}$ armored divisions, caused Iraqi units to retreat from desert positions and eventually forcing them to pull back its troops west of the Karun River, thus ending Baghdad's costly siege of Abadan [9]. The purging of the officer corps (the armed forces may have lost as much as 12,000 officers to the revolution) and the shortage of military hardware and their proper maintenance due to the US arms embargo severely impacted both Iranian maneuvering and firepower. However, Khomeini's use of so-called "human waves" substituted for this military imbalance. *Basij* and IRGC units broke through Iraqi lines with subsequent mobile army detachments exploiting breakthroughs. This new, and for Iraqi frightening form of asymmetrical warfare allowed the Iranian military to launch a series of successful campaigns, eventually allowing them to recapture Khorramanshar in May 1982 and forcing Iraqi forces out of Iranian territory by 20 June, 1982 [10]. Interpreting Iraq's retreat as a sign of God, Khomeini took the fateful decision to move the "Army of Islam" into Iraq. Contrary to the counsel of his generals, Khomeini launched a major offensive against the city of Basra on June 21, 1982 [11]. When Iran decided to take the war into Iraq, it was the beginning of a stalemate that would last another six years.

## POLICY DETERMINATS FOR THE WHITE HOUSE

When Reagan entered the White House, he regarded the loss of Iran in a rather "orientalist" fashion as the result of Carter's ineptitude and as such "absolved Iranians of their responsibility in the revolution. It was Carter and the Democrats who were responsible for losing Iran, and now a more robust foreign policy, realistic and which a clear idea of friend and foe, would reverse the mistakes of the preceding administration" [12]. Notwithstanding that Reagan's campaign staff had allegedly reached a deal with the Iranians to delay the release of the US hostages held in Iran until after the 1980 election [13], thus allowing Reagan to begin his term on a foreign policy success, the new administration showed nothing but public contempt for the Islamic Republic.

The main determinants for Reagan's policy towards Iran and Iraq were energy security in the Persian Gulf, fears that the Soviets may be able to exert influence in the region, particular exploit the loss of Iran as major U.S. ally, as well as the potential spread of Iran's revolution across the region [14]. Given its poor relations with either of the combatants, U.S. security concerns led immediately to reinforce air defenses by the deployment of AWACS to Saudi Arabia and to block the use of air bases in the Arabian Peninsula by Iraqi aircrafts to reduce the threat of expansion to the war. From the onset of his presidency, Reagan also turned Carter's Rapid Reaction Force into a Rapid Deployment and Joint Task Force, which became the U.S. Central Command (CENTCOM) in charge of the Persian Gulf region and the rest of the Middle East and Central Asia. Up until the reestablishment of diplomatic relations with Iraq, a 1983 U.S. State Department assessment of its position of strict neutrality served US objectives and interests as it: (1) avoided direct great power involvement (2) prevented spread of the war beyond the territory of the combatants to threaten Gulf oil supplies (3) contributed to the current stalemate (4) preserved the possibility of developing a future relationship with Iran while minimizing openings for expansion of Soviet influence [15].

As far as outside influence was concerned, Washington's two main regional allies Egypt and Israel had been instrumental in shaping President Reagan's shift toward Iraq. Even though the Israeli government supplied Iran with arms in the early war years for the purpose of income and in order to keep a stake in Iran, Israeli Defense Minister, Ariel Sharon warned the U.S. government, that Iran's conditions hardened following the success in its March 1982 offensive and may contribute to the demise of the Baathist regime, eventually putting neighboring Arab states, particularly Saudi Arabia, at risk of Iranian influence [16]. Mubarak's demands that the U.S. ought to help Iraq directly or indirectly were eventually heard as it became obvious to the Reagan administration that Iran was in the process of gaining the upper hand in the conflict [17]. As a prelude to the reestablishment of US-Iraqi relations in 1984, meetings between U.S. representatives and Saddam Hussein paved the way for a working relationship, causing the U.S. to gradually tilt towards Iraq in the conflict whilst pressuring the regime to adopt an evenhanded stand towards the Middle East peace process. Saddam Hussein, for his part, made it clear in February 1983, that the upgrade to full diplomatic relations was contingent on the resolution of the war and a cessation of US support for European and Israeli arms exports to Iran [18]. The final determinant causing the tilt towards Iraq was largely the result of Israel's invasion of Lebanon in 1982 and Iran's subsequent support for the country's *Shi'a* population. With *Hezbollah's* quick rise as a key militia in the Lebanese conflict, a fact which can mainly be attributed to Iran's material, financial and operational support, the Reagan administration began to largely frame its Iran policy within the context of Iran's support for international terrorism. The suicide attacks on the U.S. Embassy and the marine barracks in Lebanon in 1983 constituted not only Reagan's first foreign policy crisis but also influenced choices in the White House to eventually resort to military force against Iran [19].

## Reagan's War Policy

Before the U.S. committed itself militarily in the war, support for Iraq in the conflict manifested itself in financial, economic and diplomatic terms. A cornerstone for US policy was National Security Decision Directive (NSDD) 114, passed on November 26, 1983. Reflecting Reagan's priorities, it called for heightened regional military cooperation to defend oil facilities, and measures to improve U.S. military capabilities in the Persian Gulf, and directed the secretaries of State and Defense and the chairman of the Joint Chiefs of Staff to take appropriate measures to respond to tensions in the area. Concerning energy security, it stated "because of the real and psychological impact of a curtailment in the flow of oil from the Persian Gulf on the international economic system, we must assure our readiness to deal promptly with actions aimed at disrupting that traffic" [20]. Confident about U.S. naval supremacy, Reagan noted in his diary in March 1984 "if Iran should try to close the Strait of Hormuz, no real problem- they'll line up with us to keep it open" [21].

By December 1983, Reagan exerted pressure on its allies in Europe, Middle East and Asia to stop any military traffic to Iran, including arms sales by third countries [22]. Even though U.S. intelligence confirmed Iraq's "use of chemical weapons" [23] against Iran Presidential envoy, Donald Rumsfeld, was dispatched several times to Iraq in order to strengthen bilateral relations, discuss Iraqi military operations, mutual regional security concerns and the construction of an oil pipeline to Jordan and Saudi Arabia [24]. Overall, through Reagan's diplomatic initiatives, a total of $2 billion worth of US commodity credits were made to Iraq, bilateral trade was actively encouraged, including the sale of military hardware and sophisticated technology to Iraq [25] and Gulf states were pushed to extend financial support to Iraq. In fact, at one point the State Department expressed concern over President Reagan's public disclosure of the magnitude of Western European arms shipments to Iran and Iraq, as it would severely undermine the stated position of neutrality [26]. As far as U.S. reactions towards Iraq's use of chemical warfare were concerned, the government initially cautioned restraint, instructing the U.S. delegation at the UN Human Rights Commission not to support an Iranian sponsored resolution condemning Iraq's use of chemical weapons [27]. However, in the light of U.S. intelligence assessments that Iraq will continue to use all weapons in its arsenal including chemicals to dissuade any Iranian attack, [28] the U.S. government eventually condemned the use of WMDs publicly, [29] but avoided, as requested by the Iraqi government a UN Security Council Resolution against Iraq, in favor of a statement by the UNSC President without identifying any particular country for chemical weapons use. The U.S. government did, however, institute foreign policy controls on chemical exports to Iran Iraq, which could be used for chemical weapons manufacturing. It also exerted pressure on allies, in particular Germany, not to export any dual-use equipment to Iran and Iraq. In an effort not to alienate Iraqis, the U.S. Government quietly reiterated its intentions to remain in close dialogue and expanded commercial and eventual full diplomatic relations with Iraq [30]. Reagan's presidential directive, NSDD 139 in April 1984, paved the way for more assertive U.S. support for Iraq, including the sharing of intelligence and the actual entry of U.S. forces into the conflict. Emphasizing the U.S. objective of ensuring access to military facilities in the Gulf region, and upgrading U.S. intelligence gathering capabilities, Reagan set out policy guidelines "to avert an Iraqi collapse." Reagan's directive further demanded "unambiguous" condemnation of chemical warfare (without naming Iraq), while including the caveat that the U.S. should "place equal stress on the urgent need to dissuade Iran from continuing the ruthless and inhumane tactics which have characterized recent offensives." Deterrence and stepped up U.S. military presence in the Persian Gulf were the fundamental tenets of U.S. policy henceforth [31]. Even though NSDD 139 laid the policy foundations for the use of force against revolutionary Iran by the U.S and its future stake in Persian Gulf security, Reagan continued to be primarily concerned about Tehran's potential shift to Moscow, demanding in a draft NSDD in 1985 to "limit the scope and opportunity for Soviet actions in Iran" [32].

U.S. active involvement was eventually triggered with the "Tanker War" which had started in 1984 and seriously threatened international energy and maritime security. Between 1984 and 1986 Iranian mines and torpedoes damaged sixty-seven oil tankers, including eight registered in Kuwait, eventually forcing the Kuwaiti government in 1987 to ask the U.S. to reflag their vessels under the Stars and Stripes. During a NSC meeting in May 1987, Reagan made it clear that any attack on Kuwaiti ships sailing under American flag will be retaliated forcefully. Notwithstanding U.S. and Israeli arms sales to Iran in exchanges for hostages in Lebanon, Reagan's attitude towards the Iranians had increasingly been defined by contempt and impatience [33].

Reminding critics of Reagan's decision about perceived Cold War and economic realities, Caspar Weinberger stated that unless that the U.S. came to Kuwait's aid " we would be accepting Iran's right to close the international waters of the Gulf and, even worse, opening the door to the Kremlin, which would be more than happy to become the sole guarantor of the security of the small Gulf states." In the National Security Council, Weinberger also proposed to "drop the pretense of even-handedness [and] no longer talk about ending the war "with no winners or losers". Iran is the aggressor in this case and we should not only be supportive of Iraq, but should be seen supportive" [34]. By May 1987, Reagan had six American warships in the Gulf, in 1988 he had doubled the fleet to thirteen.

As far as Iranian tactics were concerned, IRGC and regular Iranian navy attacked Iraqi and international shipping, using F-4 fighters firing Maverick missile, helicopters firing French-made missiles, naval frigates firing Italian anti-ship missiles to the use of small-boat attacks by IRGC operating from islands or offshore oil platforms in the Strait of Hormuz. The Iranian navy also shifted to employing small boats operating in tandem with naval vessels. [35]. Notwithstanding the errant Iraqi missile, which had struck the *USS Stark* on 7 May 1987, killing thirty-seven sailors, and increased congressional criticism over his war policy, Reagan affirmed his support for Iraq's war effort in a personal letter to Saddam Hussein [36]. President Reagan had completely shifted to the Iraqi camp. By April 1988, the U.S. State Department concluded that given the Iraqi regime's heavily publicized use of chemical weapons on Iraqi civilians at Halabja, the basic nature of the war remained unchanged: "Iraq can't win but need not lose. Iran can win, but probably won't" [37]. In order to break this stalemate, the direct involvement of the U.S. navy and Air Force gradually shifted the military balance toward Iraq, which had been facing a series of large-scale Iranian offensives. "Operation Praying Mantis", which was launched by the Pentagon in April 1988, destroyed two Iranian frigates, six high-speed torpedo boats and an Iranian oil platform. The U.S. offensive, which coincided with Iraq's recapture of the strategic *al-Faw* peninsula, constituted a watershed event as it essentially ended the "Tanker War" and largely forced the Iranians to come to terms with UN initiatives for a ceasefire [38]. The shooting down of an unarmed Iranian airliner by the *USS Vincennes* in August 1988, largely the result of incompetence of the captain, killing all 290 passengers on board, was a tragic incident and the last straw for Khomeini to start talks at the United Nations in Geneva [39].

As far as military planers in the White House were concerned, confrontations with the Iranians not only secured the flow of oil through the Strait but also backed U.S. policy of deterrence, showing both superior military capabilities and political resolve. The fact that Reagan had been implementing an "arms-for-hostages" deal with Iran between 1985 and 1986 merely constituted what Weinberger an "aberration" of U.S. policy towards Iran [40]. Reagan later remarked at the Tower Commission that he "let [his] personal concern for the hostages spill over into the geopolitical strategy of reaching out to Iran" and that, by asking "so many questions about the hostages' welfare," he failed to see the implications of the arms transfer for the Iranian regime [41]. In fact, Washington's tilt towards Iraq after 1987 was as much a result of the above stated strategic determinants, as it was an effort to regain credibility in the eyes of its Arab allies in the region following the "Iran-Contra Affair". To that end, the confrontation with Iran was meant to reassure the Gulf monarchies of America's security umbrella in the region whilst at the same time intended to counter and deter Iranian naval attacks and eventually pressure Tehran to accept a ceasefire on U.S. terms.

Policies adopted by the Reagan administration significantly shifted the military balance towards Iraq, by providing vital intelligence on Iranian movements and diplomatic, financial and direct military support. This did not only prolong the war substantially but eventually forced the Iranian leadership (together with growing domestic dissension) to accept a ceasefire. In the long term, Iraq's import of sophisticated equipment facilitated by U.S. licenses, also proved fundamental for its WMD program. By and large, Reagan's policy of "neither winners nor loser" effectively was a policy of deterrence against Iran in an effort to secure energy security as well as to weaken the Iranian regime. In the immediate term, Reagan's gunboat diplomacy contributed to increased confrontations with Iran's armed forces. Even during the war, Gary Sick, the former principal White House aid for Persian Gulf affairs (1976-1981), criticized Reagan's policy for having deployed U.S. forces "aggressively and provocatively in the hottest parts of the Persian Gulf " which essentially laid the groundwork for the destruction of the Iranian airliner by the USS *Vincennes* [42]. In the long term, Reagan's policies during the war instilled a deep-grounded suspicion towards successive U.S. administrations amongst Iranian officials. However, it also brought about a newly found confidence about its military capabilities and strategic assets. As far as Iranian leaders were concerned, the end of the war neither brought about territorial loss nor military defeat. Against all odds, in terms of sophisticated weaponry, economic power and America's vast political clout, Ansari argues "this was the first Iranian state not to lose territory in nearly two hundred years." Much more than this, Iran's military planners had learned to adapt on their own terms, fighting a conventional war with unconventional means and limited resources. Far from limiting Iran's military procurement in the long-term, the embargo and diplomatic isolation of the country had encouraged the development of an indigenous arms industry [43]. By and large, Iran's sacrifices on the battlefield not only nurtured the cult of "martyrdom" but also continue to inform the country's basic defense doctrine: deterrence. Even though the end of the war and the death of Khomeini witnessed major changes in Iran's political arena, Iran's security policy remains a direct artifact of the Iran-Iraq war.

Essentially, U.S. policies and the use of force against Iran during the war created a reference point for future bilateral relations (or rather the lack thereof) and further consolidated an American security framework for the Persian Gulf. However, far from creating a sustainable peace after 1988, the Gulf Wars in 1990-91 and 2003 coupled with the policy of dual containment only reinforced the region's balance of power politics and the confrontational course Washington and Tehran had embarked on after 1979 [44]. As will be shown below, during the George W. Bush administration, this bilateral "Cold War mindset" reached new levels with both the U.S. and Iranian governments engaging in openly hostile rhetoric and confrontational actions. As far as the region's security environment is concerned, Reagan's Cold War lives on.

## Legacies of War: The Gulf's Perpetual Security Dilemma

Since the war, Iran's policy towards the Persian Gulf states and the U.S. has largely been determined by security concerns. Despite mutual strategic considerations, the Gulf States still seem unable to create and implement a multilateral regional security structure. With the Gulf Cooperation Council (GCC) member countries being strongly committed to their economic-strategic alliance with the U.S., Tehran's nuclear program and its recent behavior have been watched with increasing unease by the U.S. and its Gulf allies. Beyond the need to maintain popular acquiescence at home, a series of Iranian military maneuvers, actual operations in the region and involvement in Iraq, were meant to repel any possible threat from the U.S. or its GCC allies. Whilst this behavior is being interpreted by both the U.S. and the GCC members as yet another demonstration of hegemonic aspirations, Iran continued to frame these actions and policies in pure defensive terms. Conscious of U.S. capacities to deploy significant naval power in the region, Tehran has made it obvious that, following any U.S. attack on Iran, retaliation would inevitably also target Arab states.

Countering the impact of sanctions as well as defying demands by the UN, EU and U.S. with the above tactics has led to a quandary in the region, in which the GCC states continue to pledge allegiance to Washington's security umbrella in the Gulf, hosting U.S. military and naval bases and underwriting the U.S. economy for their defense. At the same time, they are also unwilling to become pawns in a U.S.-Iranian military show-down. Within this context, Iran's deterrence doctrine proved successful to the extent that GCC states maintain strong trading and diplomatic relations with both the U.S. and Iran whilst at the same time start to accommodate themselves with Iran's growing power [45].

Directly reflecting the realist mindset and defense strategy acquired on the battlefield during the Iran-Iraq war, since 2003, Iran's stepped up defense posture manifested itself on four levels: (1) Iran continued to consolidate its position as regional military power with the launch of new home grown military technology and procurement (2) Iran used a series of large-scale military maneuvers to demonstrate its armed forces' defense commitment and capabilities (3) The Revolutionary Guards took control over Iran's Persian Gulf defense command and were involved in a series of naval "renegade incidents". (4) Lastly, the establishment of an extensive security network in Iraq is as much an expression of Iran's political clout in Baghdad as it serves as a "2nd front" during a potential military confrontation with the US.

## Procurement

Since the U.S. imposed weapons embargo, Iran's deterrence doctrine has largely been based on its ability to consolidate indigenous technological military capabilities, which during the last three years predominantly included its nuclear program, various new domestically procured missile systems, the launch of Iranian-built jet fighters as well as a satellite carrier rocket. Reflecting its stepped up defense posture since the U.S.-led invasion of Iraq in 2003, Iran procured missiles from Russia, China and North Korea as well as developed missile systems and other military hardware on their own, which include: *Raad* Anti-Ship Cruise Missile (ASCM), Anti-Tank Guided Weapons (ATGW), various types of surface-to-surface and surface-to-air rockets, a new Russian-made air defense system ("TOR1"), the jet-fighters "*Azaraksh*" and "*Saeqeh*" as well as long-range artillery rockets designed and built in Iran, surface-to-air missiles and ballistic missiles, "Shahab-3" Medium-Range Ballistic Missile (MRBM). As far as major surface vessels are concerned, Iran's three destroyers are over 50 years old and non-operational, the remaining three frigates (Vosper Mark 5) and remaining two Corvettes (30 years old) lack sophisticated weapons [46]. Nonetheless, the launch of an Iranian-built submarine "Qadir" as well as missile-vessels "Jowshan" and "Peykan" all of which are equipped with 533mm torpedoes and mines, has provided Iran with a significant naval deterrent in the Persian Gulf [47]. Notwithstanding above-mentioned technological shortcomings and limits to Iran's defense, the regional military balance (excluding American forces) puts Iran in a dominant position. Quantity and commitment of Iran's armed forces, particularly the Revolutionary Guards Corps (IRGC), continue to be a bulwark and underwrite Iran's basic defense doctrine of total regional retaliation.

| Regional military balance in the Persian Gulf | Service personnel | Fighter aircrafts | Main battle tanks | Combat vessels |
|---|---|---|---|---|
| Bahrain | 11,000 | 29 | 140 | 1 |
| Iran | 663,000 | 332 | 1,710 | 201 |
| Iraq | 162,358 | 0 | 127 | 11 |
| Kuwait | 15,700 | 50 | 293 | 0 |
| Oman | 39,700 | 43 | 117 | 8 |
| Qatar | 12,400 | 9 | 30 | 7 |
| Saudi Arabia | 214,500 | 242 | 765 | 72 |
| UAE | 65,400 | 123 | 567 | 6 |

Source: Jane's Security Sentinel: Armed forces, 2008.

The Gulf states' concerns over this kind of procurement and potential Iranian encroachment, which was exacerbated since the election of the Arab world's first *Shi'a* government in Iraq in 2006, eventually culminated in numerous U.S. sponsored declarations condemning Iran's involvement in Iraq as well as demanding the government in Tehran to live up to its commitment under the IAEA and UN Security Council resolutions. American efforts to isolate Iran and rally its Arab allies against what the Bush administration labeled "murderous activities" in Iraq and "nuclear holocaust" initially seemed to be paying off when the U.S. President's proposal of selling defense systems and military aid packages, worth US$20 billion, to the Gulf was welcomed by governments in Saudi Arabia, UAE, Kuwait, Qatar, Bahrain and Oman in 2007 [48]. Far from creating a sustainable regional security regime, the deal, which aims to strengthen the maritime, air and missile defenses of these GCC members, seemed to have merely exacerbated the region's security dilemma. The Iranian Supreme Leader's Office was quick to condemn U.S. efforts to "exaggerate the Iranian threat" to the Gulf countries and considered it to yet another tactic to rally Arab countries against Iran. Reminding that Iran's military exercises were never targeted against its neighbors and recalling past Iranian security cooperation initiatives and memoranda of understanding with some Gulf countries, the Supreme Leader, Ayatollah Khamenei's representative in the National Security Council, Hasan Rowhani, called for an end of the arms race in the region and urged regional security cooperation [49]. President Ahmadinejad then presented the Supreme Leader's initiative at a first-ever appearance at the GCC summit in December 2007. However, the proposal of launching a security framework "without foreign influence" continues to be viewed skeptically by the Gulf monarchies, interpreting it as merely a legitimate way for Iran to replace the U.S. as the Gulf's dominant power [50].

## Sabre Rattling

Faced with this ongoing mistrust across the Gulf, and, again, in true realist fashion, Iran's leadership used numerous large-scale military maneuvers in Iran as well as in the Persian Gulf to parade both the commitment and capabilities of its armed forces. Massive mobilizations of Iran's IRGC, army, navy and air force not only showed off its indigenous defense systems but also, as a true expression of Iranian power, were meant to strengthen Iran's position during the nuclear negotiation [51]. Whilst such overconfidence certainly antagonized and alarmed the U.S. and EU more than it served as a bargaining chip, Iran's display of power largely catered to the US and its Arab allies in the region, demonstrating that Iran is too powerful a player to be provoked. Numerous military parades and exercises, most notably the "Great Prophet", maneuvers were meant, according to the military leadership, to display the armed forces' deterrence capabilities as well as to exercise new operational tactics and test new weaponry. This kind of projection of strength is, however, also catering to domestic constituents, showing critics of the government and public alike that should Iran enter negotiations again, it would do so from a position of strength [52]. A fundamental part of these deterrence maneuvers has always been the military's stress on its troops' unconditional commitment to defending the country. Official claims that suicide brigades of more than 10,000 trained military personnel can be easily mobilized continue to rank high amongst GCC members' security agendas and did little to defuse concerns over Iranian expansionism [53]. Lastly, a crucial part of Iran's deterrence strategy vis-à-vis the U.S. and the GCC has also always been a certain level of volatile rhetoric, aimed not at seeking military confrontation but questioning the very legitimacy of these pro-Western monarchies. As Iran's Deputy Foreign Minister, Manouchehr provocatively stated in August 2008 that "the next crisis [in] the Persian Gulf is the crisis of legitimacy of the monarchies and traditional systems, which considering current circumstances cannot go on living" [54].

Iran's highly publicized missile tests and military maneuvers served as much as an exercise in deterrence as they catered to domestic constituents. Determined to enter P5+1 negotiations only from a position of strength, Iran's government and military establishment followed a contradictory foreign policy course, combining détente with deterrence. Informed by the regime's inherent raison d'état to avoid appearing making concessions and fearing the impression of weakness, Iran's missile testing has largely overshadowed any diplomatic and conciliatory moves by Iranian diplomats and negotiators [55]. Thus, far from addressing own security perceptions in the Persian Gulf and constructively expressing such concerns [56] during nuclear negotiations, Iranian behavior only exacerbated the regional security dilemma.

## IRGC's "Controlled" Renegade Activities

More than ever before, the IRGC has taken on the dominant role in Iran's defense structures and readiness. Whilst naval encounters between IRGC vessels and British and U.S. forces may well be attributed to renegade behavior, it seems more conceivable that these incidents at sea were in fact carefully orchestrated moves. Following the US designation of the Guards as a "foreign terrorist organization", the Supreme Leader appointed Ali Jafari as new IRGC Commander in chief and brought in Mohammad Hosseinzadeh Hejazi as the chair of the Joint Chief of Staff and Ali Akbar Ahmadian as the head of the IRGC Strategic Studies Center, making the Guards' top leadership more homogenous and more answerable to Khamenei [57]. Like many of the country's top military officials, Jafari earned his stripes and combat experience on the battlefield of the Iran-Iraq war. Jafari, who reportedly developed a myriad of "asymmetrical warfare" defense strategies, [58] has already made a number of changes to the Guards' command structure and operational capabilities [59]. The cornerstone of the Guards' strategy remains in the words of a commander "to strike against the interests of any aggressor in any part of the world" through its own forces or proxies, like *Hezbollah* as well as to restrict "movement of enemies in the Persian Gulf."[60] Well aware that with 14 to 17 billion barrels of oil per day, 25 per cent of the world's oil supplies, passing through the Hormuz Strait, a naval blockade or mining of the strait would have severe economic implications for the entire world, Tehran continues to threaten with such naval retaliatory measures [61]. However, the assertion by the IRGC Navy's Rear Admiral Habibollah Sayyari that the Persian Gulf is entirely under Iranian control, [62] seems to be overconfident if not wrong. Even though the IRGC naval units proved themselves during the Iran-Iraq tanker war, targeting civilian oil-carrying maritime traffic as well as continue to display innovative and aggressive tactics and maneuvers, they are no match for U.S. naval power in the Persian Gulf, which would easily neutralize Iran's surface fleet in a matter of hours. At the same time, however, the IRGC could effectively employ tactics, which could limit the U.S. warships' counter-measures. Given the recent activities of small Iranian vessels and past experiences, Iran may well employ tactics used during the "Tanker War" and engage in a sort of "maritime insurgency" which would entail a campaign of mine warfare, missile and small craft attacks to harass and disrupt U.S. and coalition forces and civilian maritime traffic [63]. The arrest of 15 British Navy personnel in March 2007 as well as the encounter between five IRGC speedboats and five U.S. vessels in the Strait of Hormuz in January 2008 should be seen within this context. Both encounters occurred during heightened tensions between Iran and the US in which Tehran's leadership took the possibility of a military confrontation with the U.S. very seriously and as such seemed compelled to retaliate against perceived American belligerency [64]. Both incidents demonstrated in the eyes of hardliners Iran's defense readiness whilst at the same time purportedly uncovered U.S./UK scare tactics as being nothing more than empty bluff. Even though reformists criticized that such affairs would only raise the stakes in the nuclear negotiations and the opening of "new fronts" would only strengthen the consensus against Iran, hardliners in and around the government as well as the Supreme Leader's Office interpreted the "detention and release of the invading British as a mark of Iran's superiority" and a "decisive answer [to the US and UK] that Iran was militarily and politically alert" [65].Undoubtedly, both incidents were carefully orchestrated and served as much as a deterrent to the West and Israel as they catered to domestic audiences. For Iran's leadership this sort of propaganda coupled with actual military incidents seems to serve as a prelude to how a major international standoff in the Persian Gulf could look like. By and large, Iran's strong military presence as well as its controversial control over the three strategically located islands, Abu Mua and Greater and Lesser Tunbs, has largely been seen by the GCC, as a Saudi official put it, as "an hegemonic hold [to gain] control of international navigation routes and the flow of oil to international markets in case it faces a military attack" [66]. Iran's recent installation of additional offices on Abu Musa has been met with strong condemnation by the UAE and the GCC which described it as "flagrant violation of the 1971 memorandum governing the islands' status" [67]. Ongoing Iranian statements claiming sovereignty over the islands and dismissing any arbitration initiatives by the UAE as policies of "extremists in London and Washington" [68] seem to have convinced most Gulf Arab states that Iran's expansionism, fear-mongering and stepped up defense posture is directly targeted against them.

## Iranian Involvement in Iraq

Nowhere is this *Sunni-Shi'a* divide more evident than in Iraq where the Gulf states are too aware of an overbearing Iranian presence. The U.S.-led invasion of Iraq in 2003 not only removed one of Tehran's major foes, but in fact provided Iran in the words of Iran's Foreign Ministry with "an epochal shift in Iran's security position in the region", enabling Iran's "soft-power assets to exert considerable religions-political and cultural influence in Iraq [69]. Supporting both the *Shi'a* political-religious establishment in Iraq (the Supreme Council for the Islamic Revolution in Iraq) as well as emerging political heavyweights, Muqtada al-Sadr and his *Shi'a* insurgents, Iran seemed to be pursuing two goals: ensuring that the US occupation would not be used as a launch-pad against Iran, and helping Iraq's *Shi'a* majority to assume a dominant position in the country's new political landscape [70]. Six years after the invasion, Iran maintains very good relations with Prime Minister Nuri al-Maliki, who essentially represents Iraq's political *Shi'a* elite and which looks back on decades of exile in Iran. Iran's military and security establishment also continues to support *Shi'a* militias and has built an extensive religious-military infrastructure in that country, thus fuelling the insurgency and keeping a stake in radical factions should Iraq's transition to democracy fail [71]. Ironically, however, Iranian officials repeatedly stated during security talks with the U.S. that it too, favors Iraq to remain a single political entity, with central authority and without a sectarian civil war. Bearing in mind that like most foreign policy issues, Iran's agenda for Iraq continues to be subject to debate among Iranian factions, Tehran's recent behavior vis-à-vis Baghdad seems to indicate that even though diplomatic and trade links are probably better than with any other Gulf state, the course of U.S.-Iran relations is likely to shape Iran's tactics in Iraq – leaving all options on the table [72].

Essentially, Iran's stepped up defense posture kept the status quo in the region. By exacerbating the region's security dilemma, Arab states continue to remain committed to U.S. guardianship of the Gulf, whilst at the same time felt forced to accommodate themselves with Iran as the emerging regional hegemon.

Thus, despite America's overbearing naval supremacy in the Persian Gulf, Iranians perceive the balance of regional strategic power to be increasingly shifting in their favor: "Operation Iraqi Freedom" has lost support back home and struggles to maintain political and military momentum in Iraq, Israel's military prowess suffered significantly at the hands of Iran's Lebanese ally *Hezbollah* and it is evident that GCC governments are taking the Iranian threat (both conventional and nuclear) seriously. Overall, Iran's policy of deterrence has been somewhat successful. Since the political status quo of the Gulf monarchies fundamentally centers on their ability to distribute oil rents to their constituents, their rulers are not interested in becoming pawns in a US-Iranian conflict but rather seek to bandwagon in order not to jeopardize current and future business prospects. With GCC and individual member states clearly speaking out against any military option towards Iran, U.S. administration's efforts to contain and isolate Iran with help of its regional allies, largely appear to have fallen short of its goal [73]. At the same time, however, the GCC is far from discarding the U.S. as the central pillar of Persian Gulf security, dismissing Tehran's security initiatives as means to consolidate Iranian hegemony and continuing to treat their Persian neighbor with a certain extent of suspicion and ambiguous policies on their own [74].

## CONCLUSION

Reagan's policies during the Iran-Iraq war set the corner stone of contemporary Persian Gulf security, in which the U.S., Iran, the GCC member states and Israel continue to engage a high-stakes game of coercive diplomacy and deterrence. Over thirty years of containing Iran may have maintained security in the Persian Gulf, but has fallen short of creating any collective security framework in the region. Relics of the Cold War, both in their diplomatic and military manifestations continue to determine not only relations between the U.S. and Iran but also between Tehran and its Gulf neighbors. Experiences from the battlefield between 1980-1988 have inherently shaped Tehran's security conceptions vis-à-vis the United States and its Arab allies. Given this rather realist mindset amongst Iran's nomenclature, the leadership continues to embrace military deterrence as its fundamental security doctrine. Iran's rhetoric and demonstration of its striking capabilities in the Persian Gulf seem to have largely deterred GCC states from supporting an attack on Iran. At the same time, the hostile nature of U.S. – Iranian relations continues to prevent the creation of an indigenous regional security arrangement. Remaining committed to America's guardianship of the Gulf, Arab monarchies as well as Iraq are unlikely to engage in any multilateral agreement with Iran any time soon. Even though policies adopted by successive U.S. president towards Iran ranged from neglect and hostility under George H.W. Bush and Bill Clinton to outward belligerency under George W. Bush, it was Reagan's war policy, which determined the course and tenor of current bilateral relations. Hence, as far as international relations in the Gulf are concerned, Reagan's Cold War strategies and rhetoric live on.

Much hope had been placed on Iran's presidential elections in June 2009. Following President Barrack Obama's *Naw Ruz* address to Iran in March 2009, which opened the possibility of rapprochement, it was widely believed that the country's electorate would deny Mahmoud Ahmadinejad a second term due to economic hardship and international isolation, which were largely blamed by Iranians to be the direct results of their president's firebrand rhetoric and hostile foreign policy. Ahmadinejad's re-election was met with massive protests both in the streets and amongst the elite, calling the elections rigged and the new government illegitimate. Now, the alleged usurpation of the election by Ahmadinejad and his hardliner allies is heralding a new chapter in the Islamic Republic. Given its appalling human rights record, which appears to have culminated with massive state sponsored violence against protesters, the arrests of over four thousand and show trials of hundreds of Iranian citizens, including a former Vice-President under Khatami, Ahmadinejad's government seems close to perfecting the hardliners' vision of Iran: the militarization of politics and securitization of society. As much as the IRGC took over control of Iran's international security, so was deterrence and political violence used to stifle opposition domestically. Under Ahmadinejad the *Basij* and the IRG have gained tremendous momentum, creating new fault-lines in Iranian politics: an increasing rift between clergy and the Revolutionary Guards. During his first tenure, the clout of the IRGC network increased significantly, having been awarded by Ahmadinejad with numerous lucrative gas and oil contacts, and former and current officers having taken on cabinet positions and other high-profile government posts. On several occasions, IRGC commanders have openly challenged the clergy and called on them to leave governance to the military and politicians. Ahmadinejad's own interpretation of *Shi'a* eschatology and his claims to have personal contact with the Mahdi, the prophesized Messiah of Islam, infuriated the clergy in Qom as much as it revealed his disconnection from the majority of society. When, in November 2007, Major General Jafari, stated that "the main mission of the *Basij* and the IRG is to fight internal enemies" the new fault lines of Iranian politics were laid open. They would eventually manifest themselves on a large scale in the aftermath of the June 2009 elections [75].

Now the Islamic Republic finds itself in the greatest crisis of legitimacy since its foundation thirty years ago as the once revolutionaries are now transforming themselves to the very regime they once removed. Far from being able to form a cabinet and conduct government business, Ahmadinejad finds itself under fire from mainstream conservatives doubtful over his competency and wary of his domestic and foreign agendas as well as from reformists who largely fight for their political survival. A series of *fatwas* from senior clerics condemning the violence, mass arrests and show trials and calling the government illegitimate further lends support to the notion that the Islamic Republic finds itself at the crossroads. If Iran's nomenclature follows this current path of repression, republican elements of Iran's Islamic government may soon be replaced with a totalitarian interpretation of the *velayat-e faqih*. However, given the political maturity of Iranian society, existing democratic institutions and commitment of stakeholders for democracy, Iran's hardliners may well have started a fight they cannot win.

As far as Iran's foreign relations are concerned, the U.S. has rightly abstained from getting directly involved and taking sides but rather condemned human rights violations. Despite the time-sensitive nature of Iran's ongoing enrichment activities and conventional military procurement, direct U.S.-Iranian engagement seems still elusive. Contrary to his campaign manifesto on a change in foreign policy, President Obama continues the Iran policy of previous administrations. Even before the elections, Obama asked the Pentagon to rejuvenate contingency plans for possible strikes against Iran and maintains a strong U.S. naval presence in the Gulf. Further emphasizing the "deterrence card", U.S. Secretary of State, Hillary Clinton proposed to extend "a defense umbrella" to its allies in the Middle East in order to guard against a nuclear Iran. In her bid for an increased deterrent capability in the Gulf, Clinton stated "if the US extends a defense umbrella over the region, if we do even more to support the military capacity of those in the Gulf, it's unlikely that Iran will be any stronger or safer, because they won't be able to intimidate and dominate, as they apparently believe they can, once they have a nuclear weapon'' [76]. Yet again, these are realist deterrence strategies in what continues to be Reagan's Cold War between the United States and Iran.

## REFERENCES

[1] See *Washington Post*, May 8, 1990.

[2] FBI Interview with Saddam Hussein, US Department of Justice, Baghdad Operations Center February 8, 2004, Interview Session No.2 available on http://www.gwu.edu /~nsarchiv/NSAEBB/NSAEBB279/03.pdf

[3] ibid; In April, Iraq expelled 20,000 Iranians following border clashes whilst Iran put its armed forces on full alert, claiming it was a response to repeated Iraqi attack on border outposts and oil facilities. The Iranian government also accused Iraqi reconnaissance

planes of violating Iranian airspace. By April 1980, expulsions and withdrawals of diplomats ended any diplomatic relations between Baghdad and Tehran. *Washington Post*, Wednesday, April 9, 1980; *Washington Post,* April 11, 1980

[4] In his FBI interview, Saddam Hussein called the Iranian military in 1980 "weak and [lacking] leadership. It is also evident that he seriously underestimated Khomeini's grip of power in Iran. FBI Interview with Saddam Hussein, US Department of Justice, Baghdad Operations Center February 8, 2004, Interview Session No.2 available on http://www.gwu.edu/~nsarchiv/NSAEBB/NSAEBB279/03.pdf

[5] Kenneth M. Pollack, *The Persian Puzzle – The Conflict between America and Iran* (New York, Random House 2004), pp.185-186; Claudia Wright, "Religion and Strategy in the Iraq-Iran War", *Third World Quarterly*, Vol.7, No4, (Oct. 1985), p. 845; *Washington Post*, September 29, 1980

[6] Claudia Wright, "Religion and Strategy in the Iraq-Iran War", p. 846

[7] Efraim Karsh, *The Iran–Iraq War, 1980–1988.* Oxford, Osprey Publishing. p. 22; Claudia Wright, "Implications of the Iran-Iraq War", *Foreign Affairs*, Vol59, No2, (Winter, 1980), p. 287; Ghassan Salameh and Diane James, "Checkmate in the Gulf War" *MERIP Reports, No. 125/126*, The Strange War in the Gulf (Jul. - Sep., 1984), p. 20.

[8] See Said Amir Arjomand, *The Turban for the Crown*, (Bridgewater, Replica Books, 2000), p.144.

[9] Ghassan Salameh and Diane James, "Checkmate in the Gulf War", p.20.

[10] Kenneth M. Pollack, *The Persian Puzzle – The Conflict between America and Iran*, p.191; Lawrence G. Potter and Gary Sick, *Iran, Iraq, and the Legacies of War*, (New York, Palgrave McMillan, 2004), p.127.

[11] Kenneth M. Pollack, *The Persian Puzzle – The Conflict between America and Iran*, p. 193.

[12] Ali Ansari, *Confronting Iran – The Failure of American Foreign Policy and the Roots of Mistrust*, (London, Hurst, 2006), p. 100.

[13] According to Gary Sick, a White House aide for Persian Gulf affairs from 1976-1981, Reagan's campaign manager William Casey (later indicted for his role in the Iran-Contra scandal) met Iranian representatives in Europe in July, August and October of 1980. The agreed deal was to hand the hostages to the Republicans upon Reagan entering office in return for an immediate arms transfer via Israel and political benefits once the Reagan administration came to office. David Patrick Houghton, *US Foreign Policy and the Iran Hostage Crisis* (Cambridge, Cambridge University Press, 2001), pp. 141-142; Gary Sick, *October Surprise: America's Hostages in Iran and the Election of Ronald Reagan* (New York, Times Books/Random House, 1991), p.11.

[14] *Cover Memorandum from Peter Constable to Peter Tarnoff Dated November 10, 1980, US Department of State*, available at the Digital National Security Archive at George Washington University, Collection: Iraq-Gate, Item No. IG00034. See also Lawrence G. Potter and Gary Sick, *Iran, Iraq, and the Legacies of War*, pp.197-198

[15] *US Department of State, Secret Memorandum, October 7, 1983*, Iraq-Gate, Item No. IG00139.

[16] *Meeting with Israeli Defense Minister Ariel Sharon; US Department of State, Secret Briefing Memorandum, May 21, 1982*, Iraq Gate, Item No. IG00071.

[17] see *Congressional Delegation; White Meeting with Mubarak, Confidential Cable 08835, April 1982*, Iraq Gate, Item No.IG00069.

[18] See *Summary and Transcript of Meeting Between Representative Stephen Solarz and Saddam Hussein, August 25, 1982*, Iraq Gate, Item No. IG00075; By February 193, Hussein fundamentally shifted his position on the Arab-Israeli conflict by stating his willingness to accept any deal which is acceptable to the PLO. see *Letter to the Secretary of State From Tariz Aziz, February 7, 1983, Secret Briefing Memorandum, February 7, 198*3, Iraq-Gate, Item No. IG00103.

[19] See Brian M. Jenkins, "Defense Against Terrorism" in *Political Science Quarterly*, Vol. 101, No. 5, Reflections on Providing for "The Common Defense" (1986), pp. 773-786.

[20] GWU National Security Archive, http://www.gwu.edu/~nsarchiv/ NSAEBB/NSAEBB82/iraq26.pdf (accessed on 12 May 2009)

[21] Ronald Reagan, *The Reagan Diaries*, (New York, Harper Collins, 2007), p. 224.

[22] *Staunching Iran's Imports of Western Arms and Urging Restraint on Iraq, Secret Cable, 353843, December 14, 1983*, Iraq Gate, IG00152; for particular pressure on the British government on the export of arms and dual-use technology, see *US Department of State, Discussions Points for Visit of Prime Minister Thatcher, December 12, 1984*, Iraq-Gate, Item No. IG00232.

[23] *US Department of State, Iraq Use of Chemical Weapons, Information Memorandum November 1, 1983*, Iraq-Gate, Item No. IG00145.

[24] *US Department of State, Rumsfeld Mission: December 20, 1983 Meeting with Iraqi President Saddam Hussein, Secret Cable, 27572*, Iraq Gate, Item No. IG00156.

[25] In April 1984, the Baghdad interests section asked to be kept apprised of Bell Helicopter Textron's negotiations to sell helicopters to Iraq, which were not to be "in any way configured for military use" even though the order came from the Iraqi Ministry of Defense see GWU National Security Archive http://www.gwu.edu/~ nsarchiv/NSAEBB/NSAEBB82/iraq55.pdf (accessed 13 May 2009); Lawrence G. Potter and Gary Sick, *Iran, Iraq, and the Legacies of War*, p.198; for recommendations on increasing Iraq's Export-Import Bank and CCC credits, facilitating export licenses, and the pursuit of bilateral economic cooperation see *U.S. Department of State, Briefing Memorandum, July 23, 1986*, Iraq Gate, Item No. IG00346.

[26] *US Department of State, Arms Sales to Iran and Iraq, Memorandum, November 26 1985*, Iraq Gate, Item No. IG00289.

[27] *US Department of State, Confidential Cable, 074411, March 14, 1984*, Iraq Gate, Item No. IG00181.

[28] *US, Defense Intelligence Agency, Intelligence Report, DEB-85-84, September 25 1984*, Iraq Gate, Item No. IG00221.

[29] GWU National Security Archive http://www.gwu.edu/~nsarchiv/NSAEBB/NSAEBB82 /iraq43.pdf (accessed 13 May 2009).

[30] *US Department of State, Confidential Cable, 094420, April 6, 1984*, Iraq Gate, Item No. IG00197; *US Department of State, Cable 093714, March 31, 1984*, Iraq Gate, Item No. IG00192.

[31] GWU National Security Archive http://www.gwu.edu/~nsarchiv/NSAEBB/NSA EBB82/iraq53.pdf , (accessed 13 May 2009).

[32] The White House went so far as "to encourage Western allies [...] to help Iran meet its import requirements so as to reduce the attractiveness of Soviet assistance and trade

offers. [..] This includes provision of selected military equipment as determined on a case-by-case basis." *Routing Shhet and Draft NSDD Entitled U.S. Policy Towards Iran, Memorandum, June 11, 1985*, Iraq Gate, Item No. IG00254.

[33] Ronald Reagan, *The Reagan Diaries*, p. 470; p.496; p 472.

[34] Douglas Little, *American Orientalism – The United States and the Middle East Since 1945* (London, IB Tauris, 2003), p. 250; *U.S. National Security Council, Secret, PROFS, January 21, 1987*, Iraq Gate, Item No. IG00399

[35] *U.S. Department of State, Information Memorandum, May 18, 1987*, Iraq Gate, Item No. IG00436.

[36] *U.S. Executive Office of the President, Confidential Letter, JKune 24, 1987*, Iraq Gate, Item No. IG00447.

[37] *U.S. Department of State, Secret Briefing Paper, April 12, 1988*, Iraq Gate, Item No. IG00547.

[38] *U.S. Department of State, SPOT Intelligence Report, April 18, 1988*, Iraq Gate, Item No. IG00553.

[39] See Will Rogers, Gene Gregston, Storm Center: *The U.S.S. Vincennes and Iran Air Flight 655* (Annapolis, Naval Institute Press, 1992).

[40] Lawrence G. Potter and Gary Sick, *Iran, Iraq, and the Legacies of War*, p.198.

[41] Jeffrey D. Simon, "Misunderstanding Terrorism", *Foreign Policy*, No. 67 (Summer, 1987), p. 109.

[42] Gary Sick, "Failure and Danger in the Gulf", 6 July, 1988, *New York Times.*

[43] Ali Ansari, *Confronting Iran*, pp. 116-117.

[44] See Richard L. Russel, "The Persian Gulf's Collective -Security Mirage", *Middle East Policy*, Vol. XII, Winter 2005, Number 4, pp77-88.

[45] See *Jane's Iran Security Sentinel*, accessed 15 December 2008 on www.janes.com.

[46] *ibid*; Heinrich Böll Stiftung, *Iran Report*, (Nr.05/2006), p. 15; see statement by Defence Minister Mostafa Mohammad-Najjar, *Vision of the Islamic Republic of Iran West Azarbayjan Provincial TV,* (29 August 2008), BBC Monitoring; Heinrich Böll Stiftung, *Iran Report*, (Nr.0/2007), p.10

[47] see statement by Iran's Defense Ministry, *Fars News Agency website* (26 November 2008), BCC Monitoring; *Voice of the Islamic Republic of Iran,* (6 September2008)

[48] *Washington Post* (28 July, 2007); for congressional scrutiny over the arms deal see CRS Report for Congress, *The Gulf Security Dialogue and Related Arms Sale Proposals* (8 October, 2008) http://www.fas.org/sgp/crs/weapons/RL34322.pdf (website accessed 12 December 2008)

[49] *Al-Alam TV,* (28 April 2007) BCC Monitoring

[50] See "Iran and the Arabs", *The Economist* (19 December 2007)

[51] See comment by Deputy Defense Minister, Nasrollah Esatti, *ISNA*, (14 July 2008) BCC Monitoring

[52] Military officials claimed to have tested a new version of the Shahab 3, with a 2000 km range. *Hemayat,* (15 July 2008) BCC Monitoring; New anti-aircraft defense systems were used during three day long war games by IRGC and regular army, *ISNA*, (8 September, 2008) BCC Monitoring

[53] *Al-Alam TV* (5 November 2006); Iran's Former Ambassador to the UAE, Adel Al Assadi, claims that Tehran also assembled a widespread sleeper-cell network of IRGC infiltrators and collaborators across the Gulf, ready to destabilize the region when

needed. *Gulf News*, (15 September, 2008). Kuwait's Defense Secretary dismissed these allegations as "mere rumors" whilst Iranian officials denied them as "lies from enemy Western media." However, the government Dubai, which hosts over 450,000 Iranian expatriates, warned Iran not to drag its Arab neighbors into any conflict. *Kuwait Times*, (23 September 2008).

[54] The statement was immediately condemned by Gulf Cooperation Council Secretary General Abdurrahman al-Attiyah as another effort by Iran to create instability in the region. *Agence France Presse*, (7 August, 2008).

[55] This ambiguous dual track approach was particularly evident when Iran's Foreign Ministry increasingly sought to constructively respond to the 5+1 proposal whilst at the same time the IRGC tested a series of missiles, including the Shahab-3. IRGC Air fore Commander, Hossein Salami stated that the aim was to "demonstrate Iran's determination to respond to any attack" and that "our hands are always on the trigger." see *Iran Press TV*, (8 July, 2008) BCC Monitoring

[56] Such security initiative had been proposed under President Khatami in 2003 which essentially attempted to resolve most bilateral differences between the United States and Iran. In return for US security assurances and a "policy of mutual respect", the Iranians pledged their willingness and commitment to cease enrichment activities and transparency of their nuclear programm, end their military support for Hezbollah and Hamas and support for a democratic Iraq. The offer forwarded to the US by the Swiss Embassy in Tehran was declined by the Bush administration. For the original Iranian memo see http://www.nytimes.com/packages/pdf/opinion/20070429_iran-memo-expurgated.pdf

[57] MENAS, *Iran Strategic Focus*, (October, 2007), Vol.3, No. 10, p.5.

[58] Bernd Kaussler, "Khamenei's Move to Appoint Ali Jafari as Head of Revolutionary Guard" in *Terrorism Focus* Volume: 4 Issue: 31, 2007.

[59] Most important changes included the decision to put Iran's volunteer-militia, the *Basij*, under a single command system of the IRGC. *Basij* amount over 300,000 active volunteers and if mobilized constitute over 1,000,000 personnel, although *Basij* commanders continued to claim that there are over as much as 8 million *Basij*. Given Iran's basic defense doctrine to retaliate any "outside aggression" with outmost force and available manpower, Iran's leadership certainly seems to put much as faith in the *Basij*'s readiness as in their unconditional zeal. see *Vision of the Islamic Republic of Iran Network 2,* (25 November 2008); *Fars News Agency website*, (2 December 2008); *Vision of the Islamic Republic of Iran Ardabil Provincial TV*, (25 November 2008) BCC Monitoring

[60] *Keyhan website*, (23 April 2008); *Islamic Republic News Agency* (20 September 2008) BBC Monitoring.

[61] Tom Ripley, "Gulf of distrust - Naval stand-offs and the Persian Gulf", *Jane's Intelligence Review*, (March 01, 2008).

[62] *Aftab-e Yazd website,* (29 September 2008), BBC Monitoring.

[63] Tom Ripley, "Gulf of distrust - Naval stand-offs and the Persian Gulf"

[64] The detention of the British sailors coincided with the arrest of Iranian officials (allegedly IRGC Quds forces) in Iraq and with Iran's intelligence reports claiming that the US and Britain are fuelling ethnic tensions among Iranian Kurds, Arabs and Baluchis, see MENAS, *Iran Strategic Focus*, (April, 2007), Vol.3, No. 4, p.11.

[65] Statement by Ali Akbar Velayati who was instrumental during negotiations with British officials to get the sailors released. *Tehran-e Emrooz on* (9 April 2007); Criticizing the detention, spokesman of the Organization of the *Mojahedin*, Mohsen Armin, stated "that the opening of any new front will help to divert attentions away from the nuclear issue, and [..] create new arenas and fronts [..]. However, this diplomacy only leads to the creation of a more complete consensus against Iran, and to the worsening of the Iranian nuclear crisis as a whole. Once this happens, we will naturally face a more restricted arena for manoeuvres, and this by extension will be detrimental to the country's national interests." *E'temad website,* (11 April 2007) BCC Monitoring

[66] Statement by Mohammand Ali Zulfa, member of the Saudi Shua Council. *Gulf News*, (5 September, 2008).

[67] *AFP*, (17 August. 2008)

[68] In a speech Foreign Minister Manouchehr Mottaki criticized the UAE for its recent "anti-Iran claims" and called on the emirates "to disavow policies of 'bankrupt' extremists in Washington and London." *Iran Daily,* (6 December, 2008)

[69] Statement by Hamid Reza Dehghani,Garteh Porter, "Iran's Regional Power Rooted in *Shi'a* Ties" http://www.ipsnews.net/news.asp?idnews=45131 (website accessed 16 December, 2008)

[70] See Kamran Taremi, "Iranian Foreign Policy Toward Occupied Iraq, 2003-05' in *Middle East Policy*, Vol. XII, No.4, Winter 2005, p.30.

[71] On Iran's provision of weapons, logistics and training to *Shi'a* insurgents see testimonies by General David Petraeus who throughout his tenure continued to accuse Iran of providing advanced weaponry to Iraqi *Shi'a* insurgents and essentially charged Tehran with fighting a "proxy war" against the US. New York Times, (12 April, 2008); Report to Congress on the Situation in Iraq, General David H. Petraeus 11 September 2007 http://www.senate.gov/~foreign/testimony/2007/PetraeusTestimony070911a.pdf

[72] Iranian reactions to the Iraqi security of forces agreement (SOFA) reflect ongoing domestic tensions over tactics and agenda in Iraq. Whilst factions close to Iraq's SCIRI welcomed the agreement, the Supreme Leader's Office and parliament condemned it as "means of strengthening comprehensive US hegemony in Iraq". MENAS, Iran Strategic Focus, (December, 2009), Vol.4, No.12, p. 3.

[73] See GCC summit statement calling for a diplomatic solution to the nuclear stalemate. *AFP*, (8 December, 2007); see editorial by Saudi Foreign Minister Prince Saud Al-Faisa, "Peace Now" (15 January, 2008) on http://www.arabnews.com/?page=7andsection=0andarticle=105662andd=15andm=1andy=2008 (website accessed, 20 November, 2008); Statement by Jassem al-Kharafi, Speaker of the Kuwaiti parliament, calling US policy towards Iran "provocative" and "threatening" *Reuters*, (15 July, 2008)

[74] Iranian MPs decried the final communiqué of the GCC December summit in 2007 which reasserted UAE sovereignty over the disputed islands. Days later Bahrain hosted a US-sponsored security conference during which US Secretary of Defense, Robert Gates, urged GCC states to protect themselves form Iranian missile threat. MENAS, *Iran Strategic Focus,* (December, 2007), Vol.3, No. 12, p. 3.

[75] Bernd Kaussler, "Iran's Next Leadership", in Foreign Policy in Focus, http://www.fpif.org/fpiftxt/6131 (accessed 16 August, 2009); Bernd Kaussler, "The End

of the Republic?" http://english.aljazeera.net/focus/2009/08/20098171953790365.html (accessed 16 August, 2009).

[76] http://www.nytimes.com/2009/07/23/world/asia/23diplo.html (accessed 12 August, 2009).

In: Presidents and War
Editors: A. Eksterowicz and G. Hastedt, pp. 253-272
ISBN 978-1-61668-917-9


*Chapter 15*

# PRESIDENTIAL WAR POWERS AND THE WAR ON TERRORISM: ARE WE DESTINED TO REPEAT OUR MISTAKES?

*Martin S. Sheffer*

## INTRODUCTION

Can the President exercise "unconstitutional" authority in order to save the Constitution and constitutional democracy? The answer should be obvious, but scholars and jurists have made the issue (and answer) more complicated than it should be. Our myth about constitutional government refers to *Ex parte Milligan,* [1] *Duncan v. Kahanamoku,* [2] and *Youngstown Sheet & Tube v. Sawyer* ,[3] and the ideal that the Constitution is equally applicable in peace as well as war. The reality, on the other hand, demonstrates conclusively that war and peace are not the same thing, cannot coexist in the same place at the same time, and constitutional provisions applicable in time of peace may not be equally applicable in time of war. In other words, the Constitution does not function normally in abnormal times, and both the existence of a "wartime" constitution and the potential for "constitutional dictatorship" follow from that salient fact. Despite occasional rhetoric, statutes and decisions to the contrary, very little has really changed in two centuries from the way presidents have always acted during a dire emergency. In answering Lincoln's question, posed in 1861, constitutional democracy can be strong enough to maintain its own existence without destroying the liberties of the people it has been instituted to defend. But the nation's political leadership must be so inclined and simultaneously be willing to adhere to constitutional constraints.

Saying that, let me now specify the content and issues that follow for discussion: 1) the president must possess emergency powers capable of operating in abnormal times; 2) prerogative powers inherently belong to the president in his capacity as political head of the nation and ultimate protector of the Constitution; 3) the Bush administration is making many of the same mistakes in its war on terrorism as the Johnson and Nixon administrations made regarding the earlier Vietnam misadventure; 4) Congress, while regaining its capacity to exercise real legislative oversight over the presidential use of war powers in 1973-76, finds itself unwilling or unable to say *no* to the President since September 11, 2001; 5) legislation enacted since the terrorist attack in New York and elsewhere has enlarged not only the President's capacity to take the nation into war but has revolutionized the entire concept of separation of powers/checks and balances; and 6) emergency/prerogative power must be used in a dire emergency only, and when the initial emergency situation comes to an end so should the unfettered use of extraordinary presidential power.

In *Federalist* No. 23, Alexander Hamilton, writing about the concept of *crisis government* and the need for undefined power in the national government, declared that the war powers "ought to exist without limitation, because it is impossible to foresee or define the extent and variety of national emergencies, and the correspondent extent and variety of the means which may be necessary to satisfy them "[4]. The period of civil war permanently transformed our understanding of the war powers. Lincoln's imaginative combining of the commander-in-chief, take care, and executive power clauses into a notion of presidential war power independent of legislative authority — where ends justified means — laid to rest the earlier, limited meaning of commander-in-chief. Lincoln's assertion of this independent, virtually unlimited war power, held together by Locke's "prerogative" theory, [5] was legitimized and sanctioned by the Supreme Court within two years [6]. This transformation set the stage for the modern presidential office, applied the notion of constitutional dictatorship in the United States, and began the development of the "wartime" constitution.

Earlier in the development of the Republic, generally that period from Abraham Lincoln to Franklin Roosevelt, presidents would act illegally and then depend upon Congress to ratify their actions after the fact. Beginning with Harry Truman and Korea, and continuing through the Indochina war (embracing Vietnam, Laos, Thailand, and Cambodia), the claim was made that the president possessed the power to initiate war without the consent of Congress [7]. In facing two such potentially dangerous choices, the lesser of the two evils (at best) would always be for the president to act illegally and then to look to Congress for ratification of his actions. Should Congress refuse to ratify, then the President's actions stand before the public starkly for what they are — illegal actions forbidden by the Constitution. Such a course of action would be far more preferable than allowing the president to claim an emergency power to act contrary to the law for the good of the nation, or, even worse, to claim the exclusive right to determine what is good for the nation.

One could easily argue that a traceable developmental history exists in the United States regarding the use of military and paramilitary force [8]. Each step in the development contains several interconnected arguments which not only attempt to justify the presidential actions in question, but also reach a level of abstraction so extreme that even extra-constitutional actions are somehow clothed in the respectability of constitutional language. The first step posits that the power exercised by the president was actually delegated by Congress in the form of open-ended legislation — *i.e.,* the *posse comitatus* legislation enacted during the 1792 session of the first Congress, [9] or the Habeas Corpus Act of 1863 (enacted after Lincoln had already suspended the Great Writ) [10]. In effect, the presidential power specifically granted in the Constitution, such as the power contained in the take care and commander-in-chief clauses, justifies the presidential actions taken. Ultimately, the specific power granted the president by the Constitution is independent of any congressional authority and requires no prior congressional authorization. Moreover, the president may resort to the executive power clause in Article II, as a sort of presidential equivalent of Article I, Section 8,

Clause 18, thus allowing him to take any and all actions necessary and proper to achieve the national interest.

The second step, on the other hand, suggests an alternative argument, that the war powers of the United States exist in aggregate form and belong to the institution of government that most appropriately can use them during the required emergency [11]. Hamilton first suggested this argument in *Federalist* No. 23. Lincoln, of course, was the first to make use of this alternative argument when, by combining the executive power, duty to take care, and commander-in-chief clauses, he created a resulting power of dictatorial dimensions — *i.e.,* during a dire emergency all powers of government necessary to meet that emergency devolve upon the president in his capacity as chief executive and commander-in-chief [12]. Furthermore, as in step one, no prior congressional authorization was required before the president exercised this power [13]. This alternative argument, based on the notion of the war powers existing in aggregate form, switched the emphasis from *means* to *ends*, which in turn will usually justify the means [14].

The third step in this developmental argument allows presidential power to break free of the limitations imposed by the constitutional language itself [15]. This notion was first articulated by the Supreme Court in *Penhallow v. Doane,* [16] where the power to conduct war was treated as a matter of national sovereignty and not dependent upon the division of national powers contained in the Constitution. This notion was later expanded by Justice Sutherland's "sole organ theory" in his *United States v. Curtiss-Wright Export Corp.* decision [17]. In effect, this line of argument emphasizes the fact that since the president speaks for the United States in international matters, he must be the sovereign of the nation [18].

The last step in this developmental argument is the most dangerous, at least from the perspective of constitutional liberty. What is involved here is the resurrection of the Locke-Blackstone notion of prerogative power applied to presidential actions of an extra-constitutional nature. The effect is to justify the means of unconstitutional behavior in the name of ends labeled as a "higher good." This claim, of course, has taken several forms, "from the absolute prerogative of Stuart kings (based on the law of God), to the Locke-Jefferson theory of emergency powers (based on the hope of popular acceptance), to the Nixon theory of inherent national security powers (rooted in secrecy). In each of these instances, the end is said to justify the means" [19]. The end result is the development of a wartime constitution in the United States and the possibility of constitutional dictatorship.

## Emergency Power/Prerogative

When the Framers gave Congress the power to "declare" war rather than "make" war, [20] they believed, at the time, that they were giving the president the power to repel sudden attacks. There was no reason to consider whether the president could — while responding to an attack —declare the existence of *a state of war* and consequently change the legal rights of citizens and foreigners alike [21]. Nor was there any discussion among the Framers of the possibility that a president might provoke an attack, or manufacture an attack, and then recognize the existence of a state of war [22].

Not all hostile military actions against the United States are acts of war. The Constitution recognizes only war, rebellion, and invasion, [23] and implicitly acknowledges imperfect war by the clause governing letters of marque and reprisal [24]. Consequently, hostile military actions may, in the constitutional sense, be treated differently. Conversely, if the war powers are perceived in Hamiltonian terms as monolithic, then in times of dire emergency the war powers of the United States must be entrusted to the president in his capacity as commander-in-chief. By looking at a comprehensive war power, defenders of presidential prerogative shift the emphasis from the Constitution and its allocation of powers, to international law and its lack of concern for constitutional theories regarding the locus of sovereignty [25]. Lincoln [26] was the first president to completely accept this position; so did Franklin Roosevelt and all other prerogative exercising presidents during periods of dire emergency. It is, ultimately, the position taken whenever the United States has faced such an emergency and requires the leadership and direction of a potential constitutional dictator.

The remainder of this section — the actual development of presidential war powers and the periodic application of prerogative theory through the actions of presidents, [27] the delegations and legitimizations of Congress, [28] and the sometimes excessive justifications of the Supreme Court [29] — is reasonably familiar territory to everyone. Consequently, what follows is a generalized description and analysis only.

The purpose to be served by the use of emergency powers is to end the crisis and restore normal times. As Clinton Rossiter argued:

> The government assumes no power and abridges no right unless plainly indispensable to that end; it extends no further in time than the attainment of that end; and it makes no alteration in the political, social, and economic structure of the nation which cannot be eradicated with the restoration of normal times. In short, the aim of [emergency power] is the complete restoration of the *status quo ante bellum* [30].

It really makes no difference, at least in theory, whether we are talking about the president exercising simple emergency power delegated by Congress, using his own war powers as a result of combining the commander-in-chief, take care, and executive power clauses — and then taking them beyond constitutional and statutory limits, or his invoking vague and nebulous conceptions of inherent power suggested both by classic philosophers and far-ranging and very favorable court decisions. The fact of the matter is that the president alone is obligated to exercise *all necessary powers* (not just constitutional power) to save the nation in its moment of peril. The Congress expects it of him; and so do the American people. And if he is successful — as a prerogative president oftentimes is — the American people are likely to forgive and forget any unconstitutional means employed because of the ultimately successful ends achieved.

In addition to what presidents have done to aggrandize their war powers, aided more often than not by the Congress and the Supreme Court, a comment ought to be made about the work done by the White House and Justice and State Department lawyers, as well as the legion of law professors who come to the defense of sometimes questionable presidential behavior. A major difficulty faced by these defenders of presidential power is the rather cryptic language of Article II. Unlike Article I, where there are some "specifics" to work with, Article II presumes a great deal but says very little. How does one find specific constitutional authority in language like "executive powers," "take care," and "commander in chief?" How can specific constitutional authority be found for prerogative presidential actions? Generally, according to Arthur S. Miller, two techniques have been used: the vague and cryptic language of Article II has been read as generously and expansively as necessary to cover specific presidential actions [31]; or a theory of inherent power — the Locke-Blackstone-Hamilton approach — based on prior presidential successes is said to justify the means [32]. In other words, presidential duty has been transformed by lawyers' legerdemain into constitutional power [33].

And, finally, we come to prerogative theory generally, and presidential prerogative power specifically. Of the entire lexicon of power exercised by the president, this is the one critics of presidential power fear — and argue about — the most. It is potentially the most dangerous of presidential powers. The critics invariably stop there with their analysis, even though they cannot deny its existence, because they are unable to get beyond the notion of potential danger. They simply do not understand that oftentimes the risk of its exercise is the price that must be paid in order to save the nation. Granted that some presidents have abused the power in causes other than saving the nation — Richard Nixon comes immediately to mind — but on balance would there even be a United States if Lincoln, Wilson, and Franklin Roosevelt did not take virtually dictatorial actions during their respective periods of dire emergency?

Can the Constitution ever be sacrificed to the actions of the president? Of course it can, under appropriate circumstances, and only by the use of proper procedures. Even though the Constitution must be followed in the vast majority of instances, nevertheless a power does exist, inherent in the president, to nullify existing laws for the welfare of the United States. This power is what Locke (and later Blackstone) referred to as "prerogative," [34] and its use is justified by the principle *salus populi suprema lex* (the welfare of the people is the supreme law) [35].

In light of the fact that the preservation of the United States is our highest priority, it can be argued that during a dire emergency the demand for certain presidential actions may, and usually does, exceed the power granted him by Article II. It is therefore obvious that the president, free from the constraints imposed upon the legislature and judiciary, is most able to provide (as Hamilton initially argued in *Federalist* No. 23) the rapid and decisive actions which are the essence of prerogative. Precisely because the Framers of the Constitution left the powers of the presidency relatively vague, historical practice, precedent, and decisions of courts have contributed as much to the development of presidential prerogative power as the ambiguous and cryptic written Constitution. Yet, unlimited power, even if exercised because the president perceives it to be in the best interests of the nation, is dangerous to the healthy continuation of limited government. If the cure is to remain less harmful than the disease, prerogative must be narrowly and specifically circumscribed. The president must know that the exercise of prerogative is subject to strict review; that while he may have the power to perform acts which are *per se* unconstitutional, such acts may be taken only in response to a dire emergency and then only subject to certain limitations [36].

The existence of presidential prerogative powers is a recognition that the institutions of free government cannot operate normally in abnormal times. It is a recognition that war and peace are not the same thing and cannot coexist in the same place at the same time. It is a recognition that the president's use of prerogative power need not cause too great a dislocation to the principles of constitutional democracy. I believe, in spite of some of the scholarly criticism, that the doctrine of separation of powers/checks and balances, as well as the Constitution itself, are hardy and flexible enough to absorb the temporary shock which prerogative may deliver. In Rousseau's words: "In such a case there is no doubt about the general will, and it is clear that the people's first intention is that the State shall not perish

"[37]. In other words, even though constitutional democracy can be permanently changed, perhaps even destroyed, by the excessive use of prerogative powers over an extended period of time, that fact — in and of itself — should never be the controlling argument. The danger to our system of government is not lessened by prohibiting the exercise of presidential prerogative powers [38]. Wars and emergencies still happen; power must still be exercised; and constitutional liberties must sometimes be temporarily sacrificed. What is needed is not prohibition. Specific guidelines or democratic constraints are needed to "constitutionalize" the use of presidential power during an emergency.

## COMPARISON: 1964/2001

The Constitution is, as Charles Evans Hughes once said, a "fighting Constitution" [39]. There is a tacit understanding that virtually nothing, and certainly not legal niceties, will prevent the United States from successfully meeting the emergency or winning the war. National survival becomes the nation's first priority; and in the process the "law of necessity" supersedes the law of the Constitution. Whatever the president believes is necessary is done, constitutional constraints notwithstanding. Congress and the Supreme Court become willing partners in the enterprise of national survival. Congress delegates to the president its "war powers," virtually giving him unquestioned dictatorial powers [40]; while the Court permits a wide range of questionable presidential actions, which are then made legal by judicial decision. In effect, this is the "doctrine of necessity run riot" [41]. It is a reading into the wartime constitution of the doctrine of "constitutional reason of state." *Raison d'être* "is nothing but the doctrine that whatever is required to insure the survival of the state must be done by the individuals responsible for it, no matter how repugnant such an act may be to them in their private capacity as decent and moral men" [42].

The unchecked growth of presidential power after World War II occurred because of a combination of factors — *e.g.,* national security demands, the Cold War rivalry with the Soviet Union, a continued need for executive leadership of the legislature, the "new" television audience as a viable presidential constituency, and personal presidential ambition. In addition, even though the growth of presidential power continued with virtually no real constraints imposed by the legislature or the courts, many observers acknowledged that presidential leadership was both necessary and beneficial for the nation. Any attempts to burden presidential initiative and discretion with legislative restrictions, or "second-guessing" by the judiciary, was looked upon as potentially dangerous to the nation's security interests. Very few people seemed to understand that the United States was slowly, but surely, reverting back to a structure of government which the Framers categorically rejected in 1787: a system of Crown Prerogatives, where the monarch possessed not only the power to declare and make war, but the power to raise fleets and armies and demand funds to finance them [43].

Does the president, outside of a declared war, possess the independent authority to commit troops to combat? Are both Congress and the Supreme Court irrevocably bound by his perceived notion of what the national interest actually requires? When President Truman dispatched American combat troops into Korea in June 1950, these questions began to be asked; and they would continue to be asked for most of the next three decades. Our involvement in Korea not only was an act of independent presidential power, but the beginning of a new era in the exercise of presidential prerogative. Shortly after the beginning of our military involvement in Korea, the Department of State issued a "constitutional justification" of the president's action. Emphasizing the continued development of presidential war powers, the historical precedent of past presidential performance, and the Supreme Court's decision in *United States v. Sweeny,* [44] the memorandum argued that "the Presidents power to send the Armed Forces outside the country is not dependent on Congressional authority" [45]. Although reliance was properly acknowledged to both the U.N.'s Charter and the Security Council's Resolution authorizing "the United States to repel the armed aggression against the Republic of Korea," [46] independent, presidential power was the real reliance [47].

Scholars generally agree that several, contradictory precedents emerged from our involvement in the Korean Conflict. The Eisenhower administration showed far more caution, and far less initiative, in the use of combat troops. In addition, there was an increase in the use of "area resolutions," [48] as a form of prior congressional authorization. President Truman, however, had in fact already established, as firmly as had Lincoln almost a century earlier, a very clear precedent for all later presidential initiatives. When the United States became deeply involved in Vietnam in the 1960s, there existed very little precedent for the notion that Congress must authorize the presidential deployment of combat troops. Indeed, the presidential position here was that the independent war powers of the president, an argument that remained consistent from Lincoln through Nixon, was all that was required to dispatch American troops into a combat situation [49]. As an afterthought, the argument continued, Congress was free to offer support in the form of men, money and material — *i.e.,* anything from draft laws to appropriations, but its prior authorization for presidential activity was not required [50].

The Tonkin Gulf Resolution [51] was, in effect, the "functional equivalent" of a declaration of war [52]. While not specifically authorizing the increased commitment of United States combat troops for offensive operations, the resolution nevertheless supported such a commitment and more. In fact, the language was so open-ended that the president could interpret its meaning as though Congress had actually granted *carte blanche* authority. For example, Congress approved "the determination of the President, as Commander in Chief, to take all necessary measures to repel any armed attack against the forces of the United States and to prevent further aggresion" [53]. Congress then went on to say: "[T]he United States is prepared, as the President determines, to take all necessary steps, including the use of armed forces, to assist any member or protocol state of the [SEATO] Treaty requesting assistance in defense of its freedom" [54]. The two operative phrases contained in the resolution — "as the President determines" and "all necessary steps" — negated any presumed limitations on the power of the President to use military force and accomplished an apparent delegation of the putative war powers of the Congress without a clear understanding of the scope of their exercise [55]. In other words, was the United States preparing to prevent further aggression against American combat forces or prevent further aggression anywhere in Southeast Asia? Did the term "United States" as used in the resolution mean the United States government, Congress and the president together?, the United States as a whole?, or simply the President of the United States? From the perspective of the president, on the other hand, the resolution — whatever Congress initially believed it meant — gave the President authority to use force as he saw fit in vague future contingencies! And this type of exceedingly vague resolution was precisely the sort rejected as unacceptable in the early republic [56]. As far as the President was concerned, since he believed he had the inherent presidential power to do this on his own, [57] the role of Congress was not to sanction but to simply support the war. In fact, as far as President Johnson was concerned, Congress was to be ignored as long as possible, then to be humored, managed or circumvented, never to be sought out as a possible source of intelligent advice.

Let us now move ahead 37 years and see a great deal of history repeat itself. Three days after the terrorist attack on the United States, and President Bush's "declaration" of war against terrorism, Congress responded to the President's plea for statutory authorization by enacting a joint resolution entitled the "Authorization for Use of Military Force" [58]. Two interrelated problems begin immediately. First, the "use of force" legislation introduced into Congress and eventually enacted into law, has a "dark side." If applied expansively — as the Bush administration seems likely to do — it will permanently change both the historic and legal meaning of war powers under the Constitution. Powers intended to be exercised in time of war, or emergency short of war, will become available to the president at his sole discretion and usable in times of his choosing. The "imperial" presidency could become a common occurrence. Second, we have the problem of definitions. What is terrorism? How do we define it? How do we choose between competing definitions? Will any of the existing definitions suit our purposes? Put simply, if we cannot define it with enough precision to know exactly what is, how can we successfully make war against it? And if we cannot define it, how do we keep presidential power from once more becoming "imperial?"

By its very nature, the term "terrorism" is bound up in political controversy. It is a concept with a very negative connotation. Because terrorism implies the killing and maiming of innocent people, no country really wants to be accused of supporting terrorism or harboring terrorist groups. At the same time, of course, no country wants what it considers to be a legitimate use of force to be considered an act of terrorism. Because there is no universally accepted definition of terrorism, countries usually define the term according to their own beliefs and to support their own national interests; and international bodies, when they draft a definition, do so in the interests of their member states. The United States, and most European countries for that matter, tends to define terrorism narrowly, making sure that it applies to acts of nongovernmental organizations. For example, Title 22 of the U.S. Code defines terrorism as "premeditated, politically motivated violence" against "noncombatant targets by sub-national groups" usually with the goal to influence an audience [59]. The Department of Defense uses a definition that highlights another element of the Western concept of terrorism. Terrorism is "the calculated use of violence or the threat of violence to inculcate fear; intended to coerce or to intimidate governments or societies in the pursuit of goals that are generally political, religious, or ideological [60]. Here, terrorism is violence designed to advance some cause by getting a government to change its policies or political behavior. Now compare the two above definitions with a far broader, more encompassing, definition from an Iranian religious leader: "Terrorism is an act carried out to achieve an inhuman and corrupt objective and involving threat to security of any kind, and in violation of the rights acknowledged by religion and mankind" [61]. This is a far broader definition of terrorism, and under it nation states themselves could be guilty of terrorism. Any inhuman or corrupt objective coupled with an act that threatens security and rights regardless of motivation could be considered terrorism [62].

The "Authorization for Use of Military Force" statute, while specifically stating that nothing contained in this resolution supersedes any requirement of the War Powers Act — an act that Congress seems either unwilling or unable to enforce against presidential initiative, authorizes him to use all necessary force against those nations, organizations, or persons he determines planned, authorized, committed, or aided the terrorist attacks that occurred on September 11, 2001, or harbored such organizations or persons, in order to prevent any future acts of international terrorism against the United States by such nations, organizations, or persons. In effect, like the Tonkin Gulf Resolution of 1964, Congress has authorized the President to exercise the war powers of the nation at his sole discretion. Is there any real difference between the language acknowledging that the president "has authority under the Constitution to take action to deter and prevent acts of international terrorism against the United States"[63] and the 1964 statute that "approves and supports the determination of the President, as Commander in Chief, to take all necessary measures to repel any armed attack against the forces of the United States and to prevent further aggression" [64]. I think not! Although the language in the 2001 statute in far more guarded, Congress nevertheless accepts the notion that: 1) such acts of terrorism "render it both necessary and appropriate that the United States exercise its rights to self-defense and to protect United States citizens both at home and abroad" [65]; and 2) such acts continue to pose "an unusual and extraordinary threat to the national security and foreign policy of the United States" [66]. Remember, both self-defense and national security are exclusive domains of the chief executive. In each instance, both in 1964 and 2001, Congress recognizes that the president alone possesses the power to determine the existence of an emergency, may take whatever measures are necessary to meet the emergency, and ultimately determine when the emergency is over and the measures already taken no longer needed. This blank check to the president remains the continuing legacy of the Supreme Court and its decision regarding the use of presidential war powers.

## CONCLUSION

The president possesses the power to take this nation into war, without the need for prior congressional authorization. In order to keep the president from exercising power in an "imperial" manner, however, Congress must assume its constitutional authority to both oversee and (when necessary) check the exercise of presidential power. Power can corrupt and absolute, unchecked power can usually corrupt absolutely. Please remember, the exercise of arbitrary, excessive and oftentimes prerogative presidential war powers is not really the problem here. When the war is over the exercise of the questionable or extreme use of power comes to a halt. It is the long-range consequences of what was done during the emergency that should concern us. For invariably a precedent *has* been established. Earlier it was argued that presidential prerogative power should never be allowed to create a permanent precedent. And that is precisely what usually happens. The precedent created during a period of dire emergency seems available during a period of minor inconvenience as well [67]. The consequences of allowing history to repeat itself (and the United States to repeat its very costly mistakes) seems reasonably obvious. Instead of the quicksand of Vietnam, Cambodia, and Laos, we may very well have the quicksand of the Arabian peninsula, Pakistan, and several countries in Africa. And to what ultimate purpose? To end the threat of world-wide terrorism, particularly as directed against the United States? Nonsense. It is impossible to end the threat and/or destroy something that cannot be found, much less understood. One does not combat an idea by putting an army into the field; an idea can only be defeated by a superior idea. A nation should never sacrifice its treasure and a generation of its young manhood in fighting a war that may very well last for a generation or more and cannot possibly be won. Rather one must convince the supporters of the "invisible enemy" that the United States can offer them something far more beneficial and desirable than a martyr's death in exchange for Allah's grace. They must be offered — without strings attached — the two things they have never experienced: personal freedom and economic viability.

Of all the potential problems to come out of our war on terrorism, the most troublesome is the intended use of military tribunals to try those suspected of links to terrorism [68]. George W. Bush's executive order has aroused little public uproar. Why? Because, I am convinced, people do not understand the order's dangerous breadth. The order is described as if it is aimed only at Osama bin Laden and other terrorist leaders — the so-called "masterminds" of the September 11 attacks who (it is often argued) do not deserve constitutional protection. But the Bush order covers all non-citizens, and there are about 20 million of them in the United States — immigrants working towards citizenship, visitors, and the like. And the order is not directed only at those who mastermind or participate in acts of terrorism. In the vaguest terms, it covers such things as "harboring" anyone who has ever aided acts of terrorism that might have had "adverse effects" on the United States' economy or foreign policy. On a few occasions, acts of war have been treated as outside Sixth Amendment protection. Lincoln, Wilson, and Franklin Roosevelt all occasionally used military commissions to try combatants and non-combatants alike. The World War II occasion is the most pertinent; and, simultaneously, the most misunderstood of all precedents. Roosevelt set up a military tribunal to try Nazi saboteurs who landed on our shores in 1942. But that example — a tribunal for a particular occasion, limited in time and scope — shows the very danger of the Bush order. The current order is unlimited, in a fight against terrorism that could go on for years. And the Bush order could easily be extended to citizens, under this administration's legal theory. Because the 6th Amendment makes no distinction between citizens and aliens, the claim of war exigency could sweep its protections aside for anyone in this country who might fit the vague definitions of aiding terrorism. Up to this point the problem presented is clear enough. The nation faces an emergency and takes action to combat it. Whether the action taken is strictly constitutional (in the legal sense) or not matters little. Necessity — as it has done throughout our history — supersedes the law of the Constitution. And so long as the emergency continues, and the problems it presents persist at the same intensity level, the people and the courts will generally go along. Here, however, the situation changes. We have an obvious emergency with great loss of life; but all resemblance to the necessary precedents of the past begin and end at that point. Now the problem becomes much more complicated. Given the vagueness of the order, and the equally vague USA Patriot Act, [69] the potential to abuse both the presidential order and the congressional enactment does not seem so far fetched. But President Bush would never let his order be abused, said a recent defender of the Bush/Ashcroft position. And that comment is the crux of a very dangerous problem. *From the beginning of the Republic, Americans have refused to rely on the graciousness of our leaders. We rely on legal rules. We have, in the words of John Adams, "a government of laws, and not of men."* The Framers of the Constitution thought its great protection against tyranny was the separation of the federal government's powers into three departments. Each, they reasoned, would check abuse by the others. That is the greatest danger of the Bush order. It is an act of executive fiat, imposed without even consulting the Congress. And it seeks to exclude the courts entirely from a process that may fundamentally affect life and liberty.

The infamy of September 11 is over; and so is the immediacy of the emergency. Continued recourse to emergency rule flies in the face of reality. It flies in the face of all that is known about prerogative power. Remember, even the martial rule invoked after the bombing of Pearl Harbor — truly an emergency where an actual land invasion by the enemy was a distinct possibility — was eventually ruled unconstitutional [70] when it continued "too long" after the initial period of dire emergency. What the President attempts to do here, through his Attorney General, is establish a permanent condition of emergency so as to exercise prerogative power where the reality of the circumstances make it both unnecessary and potentially unconstitutional. There is nothing wrong with the exercise of presidential prerogative power. It belongs in the government's arsenal of powers to meet the emergency. But — and this is the big "but" that seems to escape the Bush administration and so many television commentators — the emergency must be real and continuing and the normal procedures of due process must either be inadequate or unavailable for the task at hand. Bush, Ashcroft, and their defenders in the media, simply have not made a convincing case for their questionable legal and political positions.

With the war on terrorism ongoing, but lacking the immediacy of September 11, 2001, President Bush has given us a new "villain" to occupy our thoughts — Saddam Hussein — and help justify his "imperial" presidency. Here, however, he has failed to make a strong enough case to warrant an enlargement of the war. His conjecture and somewhat faulty logic simply do not justify, at this point, starting a war in order to finish a war his father started in 1991 but failed to complete. Yet a majority of the American people support him here, even without real proof and certainly without any connective links between Iraq and the al Qaeda terrorists and Osama bin Laden. In a democratic republic we must demand more of our president than simply wagging the dog.

More important, however, is the dramatic change in American military strategy articulated by the Bush administration — the doctrine of striking foes first. This new military strategy towards pre-emptive action against hostile states and terrorist groups developing weapons of mass destruction is a basic (and potentially dangerous) shift in policy. The problems are numerous, but let me comment here on only one. Condoleezza Rice, the national security advisor, in explaining why pre-emption was replacing containment and deterrence as the foundation of American defense policy, interchanged very different concepts as though they were the same thing and then (to make matters more confusing) used the definitions incorrectly.

Pre-emption, preventive war, and anticipatory self-defense are not the same thing and their definitions are being twisted to fit the Iraq debate. While it is true that the United States does not have to wait to be attacked, *it does have to wait until it is about to be attacked.* Unfortunately, the only explanation that fits all the pieces together is that the confusion of language and misuse of concepts is deliberate. After all, it is hard to argue that Iraq is going to strike in hours or days when Saddam Hussein has possessed chemical and biological weapons for years, and the British argued that he is two to five years from having a nuclear device. Thus, attacking Iraq does not fit under the classic definition of pre-emptive self-defense. Yet, taking out his weapons, to say nothing of taking out Mr. Hussein himself to make sure they are not rebuilt, more closely resembles preventive war. And that is a problem for the administration because history and international law have frowned upon preventive war. It has oftentimes been used as an excuse for naked aggression [71]. Historically, preventive war has been regarded as illegitimate, because if countries act simply because rivals are getting relatively stronger, you end up with an increase of wars.

Not only do distinctions between preventive and pre-emption seem unimportant to President Bush, but he has argued time and again that the old definitions of war do not apply. Inevitably, what the White House seems to desire is a new category, something halfway between pre-emptive action and preventive war. With one caveat: In the case of Iraq they want to blend in a touch of regime change — the Bush administration's polite phrase for overthrowing a government — so that they only have to do this once. This is precisely why the action now being seriously contemplated by the President is neither pre-emptive nor preventive. At this moment one can only guess if the White House even knows what it is talking about.

## ACKNOWLEDGMENTS

A.B., A.M., Hunter College, CUNY; Ph.D., New School for Social Research. Senior Associate Professor (retired), Old Dominion University and Tuskegee University. I wish to thank my research assistant, and son, Andrew R. Sheffer for his invaluable help during the preparation of this article. Andrew, who holds a A.B. from the University of Virginia and a J.D. from Wake Forest University, is a trial attorney and partner in the law firm of Little & Sheffer, P.A., in Marion, NC.

## REFERENCES

[1] 71 U.S (4 Wall.) 2 (1866).

[2] 327 U.S 304 (1946).

[3] 343 U.S. 579 (1952).

[4] *Federalist,* No. 23, 153 (Hamilton) (Clinton Rossiter ed., New York: Penguin, 1961).

[5] Hamilton then continued: "The circumstances that endanger the safety of nations are infinite; and for this reason no constitutional shackles can wisely be imposed on the power to which the care of it is committed. This power ought to be coextensive with all the possible combinations of such circumstances; and ought to be under the direction of the same councils, which are appointed to preside over the common defense." *Ibid.*

[6] See John Locke, *Two Treatises of Government,* ch. XIV, §160 (Peter Laslett, ed., New York: New American Library, 1961). Locke defined prerogative as the "power to act according to discretion for the public good, without the prescription of the law and sometimes even against it." *Ibid.*

[7] *The Prize Cases,* 67 U.S. (2 Bl.) 635 (1863).

[8] See Francis D. Wormuth & Edwin D. Firmage, *To Chain the Dog of War: The War Powers in History and Law* (2nd ed., Urbana, IL: University of Illinois Press, 1989), 135-63. In effect, our armed forces have been used more than two hundred times

without declarations of war, and in many of these instances without congressional authorizations as well.

[9] See Christopher H. Pyle & Richard M. Pious, *The President, Congress, and the Constitution* (New York: The Free Press, 1984), 288.

[10] See Act of May 2, 1792, 1 Stat. 264. See also Act of Feb. 28, 1795, 1 Stat. 424; Act of Mar. 3, 1807, 2 Stat. 443; Act of July 31, 1861, 12 Stat. 282. In short, presidential power to use military force for enforcing the laws of the United States has undergone enlargement from the first, thanks to both presidential initiative and congressional legislation.

[11] See Act of Mar. 3, 1863, 12 Stat. 755. President Lincoln regarded the act, authorizing him to suspend the Great Writ, merely as declaratory.

[12] See Pyle & Pious, 289.

[13] See Horace Binney, *The Privilege of the Writ of Habeas Corpus Under the Constitution* (2nd ed., Philadelphia: Sherman & Son, 1862) and Martin S. Sheffer, "Presidential Power to Suspend Habeas Corpus," 11 *Okla.City U.L.Rev.* 1 (1986).

[14] Justice Grier's opinion spells out this point: "Without admitting that such an act [the recognition that a state of insurrection existed] was necessary under the circumstances, it is plain that if the President had in any manner assumed powers which it was necessary should have the authority or sanction of Congress, that on the well know principle of law, '*omnis ratihabitio retrotrahitur et mandato equiparatur,*' [the retroactive forgiveness for past actions at the express command of the sovereign power], this ratification has operated to perfectly cure the defect." *The Prize Cases,* 67 U.S. (2 Bl.) 635, 671 (1863). The Court is saying that the President is obligated to take whatever measures he deems necessary when reacting to a crisis; and his actions, in turn, need no prior authorization.

[15] See Pyle & Pious, 289.

[16] Ibid.

[17] 3 U.S. (3 Dall.) 54 (1795).

[18] The Supreme Court articulated the "sole organ theory" as follows: "It is important to bear in mind that we are here dealing not alone with an authority vested in the President by an exertion of legislative power, but with such an authority plus the very delicate, plenary and exclusive power of the President as the sole organ of the federal government in the field of international relations—a power which does not require as a basis for its exercise an act of Congress, but which,... like every other governmental power must be exercised in subordination to the applicable provisions of the Constitution." *United States v. Curtiss-Wright Export Corp.,* 299 U.S. 304, 319-20 (1936) (Sutherland, J.).

[19] Twentieth-century presidents have particularly invoked this notion—*i.e.,* Theodore Roosevelt, Woodrow Wilson, Franklin D. Roosevelt, Harry Truman, John Kennedy, Richard Nixon, Ronald Reagan, George Bush, and Bill Clinton. In spite of the events of Sept. 11, 2001, it is too early to categorize George W. Bush.

[20] Pyle & Pious, 289.

[21] Regarding the distinction between "declare" and "make," as well as the debate itself, see Max Farrand, ed., *Records of the Federal Convention of 1789* (2nd ed., vol. 2, New Haven, CN: Yale University Press, 1937), 318-19.

[22] Pyle & Pious, 321. "When the southern states declared their independence of the United States in April 1861, [President] Lincoln refused to treat them as a nation that other nations might recognize and supply. Nor could he treat them as a mere criminal conspiracy or minor uprising, which would require him to respect their property rights even as he used the military to suppress their violence. So he chose to treat them as nongovernmental belligerents, in the nature of, but not technically, foreign states." *Ibid.,* 322-23. Consequently, the President—during his so-called eleven-week dictatorship period—ignored laws and constitutional provisions by assembling the militia, enlarging the army and navy beyond their authorized strengths, calling for volunteers for three years' service (the logical conclusion to the notion of *posse comitatus*), spending public money without congressional appropriations, instituting new passport regulations, closing the post office to treasonable correspondence, suspending the privilege of the writ of habeas corpus, arresting people on mere suspicion of disloyalty, and instituting a naval blockade of southern ports. Eighty-one years later, FDR's Executive Order 9066 treated the west coast of the United States as "a theater of military operations," thus depriving the citizens of their civil liberties.

[23] By the deployment of troops near the disputed border with Mexico and positioning of reinforced naval units in the Pacific where they would be able to seize the Mexican province of upper California, President Polk sought to make the Mexicans feel militarily insecure. Secret agents encouraged American settlers in the coveted provinces to revolt, while at the same time diplomats offered to purchase California for as much as $40 million. Polk then ordered General Zachary Taylor and his troops into the disputed territory. Mexico then declared "defensive war" and some American troops were killed in the engagement. The President had already decided to ask for a congressional declaration of war when news of the incident enabled him to claim that Mexico had invaded Texas. Congress then voted to recognize the existence of a state of war and to reinforce Taylor's forces. See Louis Fisher, *Presidential War Power* (Lawrence, KS: University Press of Kansas, 1995), 30-34. In the same vain, and much more recently, there is Lyndon Johnson's 1964 message to Congress claiming North Vietnamese torpedo attacks on American naval warship in the Gulf of Tonkin.

[24] U.S. Const. art. I, §8, cl. 11; art. I, §9, cl. 2.

[25] U.S. Const. art. I, §8, cl. 11. The notion of imperfect war was legitimized by the Supreme Court, for example, in *Bas v. Tingy*, 4 U.S. (4 Dall.) 37 (1800); *Talbot v. Seeman*, 5 U.S. (1 Cr.) 1 (1801); *Little v. Barreme,* 6 U.S. (2 Cr.) 170 (1804).

[26] See, for example, the argument of John Bassett Moore: "In reality the word 'war' comprehends two meanings. It denotes (1) acts of war, and (2) the international conditions of things called a 'state of war.' Acts of war do not always or necessarily develop into the general international condition of things called a state of war, but they are nevertheless war and involve the 'making' of war in the legal sense." John Bassett Moore, *Collected Paper of John Bassett Moore* (Vol. 5, New Haven, CN: Yale University Press, 1944), 195-96.

[27] In a letter to J. G. Conkling on Aug. 26, 1863, Lincoln wrote: "I think the Constitution invests its commander-in-chief with the law of war, in time of war." Roy P. Basler, ed., *Collected Works of Abraham Lincoln* (Vol. 6, New Brunswick, NJ: Rutgers University Press, 1953), 406. In a letter to S. P. Chase on Sept. 2, 1863, he wrote: "As commander-in-chief ... I have a right to take any measure which may best subdue the enemy,...

including things ... which cannot constitutionally be done by Congress." *Ibid.,* 428. Earlier, on July 4, 1861, he told Congress: "[N]o choice was left to me but to call out the war power of the Government and so to resist force employed for its destruction by force for its preservation ... whether strictly legal or not, were ventured upon under what appeared to be a popular demand and a public necessity, trusting then, as now, that Congress would readily ratify them." James D. Richardson, *Messages and Papers of the Presidents* (Vol. 7, Washington, DC: Government Printing Office, 1897), 3224-25.

[28] Defenders of the Lincolnian view of presidential prerogative (who set the stage to defend all future acts of presidential prerogative) essentially argued that in time of war, presidential authority is not subject to any constitutional restrictions. For example, William Whiting (chief solicitor of the War Department) suggested that the "sovereign ... dictatorial military powers, existing only in actual war, ending when war ends, to be used in self-defense, to be laid down when no longer necessary, are, while they last, as lawful, as constitutional, as sacred, as the administration of justice by judicial courts in time of peace." William Whiting, *War Powers Under the Constitution of the United States* (43rd ed., Boston: Lee & Shepard, 1871), 52. See also, in the very same vain with essentially the same argument, Clarence A. Berdahl, *War Powers of the Executive of the United States* (Urbana, IL: University of Illinois Press, 1921). In response to a speech by Charles Sumner, critical of Lincoln's actions, Orville Browning denied "that Congress may decide upon the measures demanded by military necessities and order them to be enforced.... When the Constitution made the President 'Commander in Chief of the Army and Navy of the United States' it clothed him with all the incidental powers necessary to a full, faithful and efficient performance of the duties of that high office; and to decide what are military necessities, and to devise and execute the requisite measures to meet them, is one of these incidents. It is not a legislative, but an executive function, and Congress has nothing to do with it." *Cong. Globe,* 37th Cong., 2nd Sess., 2919 (June 27, 1862).

[29] See notes 9 & 10, *supra.* In addition to the congressional delegations and legitimizations listed, I offer the following as well: Alien Enemy Act, 1 Stat. 577 (1798); Confiscation Acts, 12 Stat. 319, 589 (1861); Legal Tender Acts, 12 Stat. 345, 370 (1862); Indemnity Acts, 14 Stat. 46, 432 (1866); Selective Service Act, 40 Stat. 76 (1917); Emergency Shipping Fund Act, 40 Stat. 182 (1917); Lever Act, 40 Stat. 276 (1917); Trading with the Enemy Act, 40 Stat. 411 (1917); Railway Control Act, 40 Stat. 451 (1918); Overman Act, 40 Stat. 556 (1918); Control of Communications Act, 40 Stat. 904 (1918); War-Time Prohibition Act, 40 Stat. 1046 (1918); Selective Service Act, 54 Stat. 885 (1940); Lend Lease Act, 55 Stat. 31 (1941); War Powers Acts, 55 Stat. 838 (1941), 56 Stat. 176 (1942); Emergency Price Constrol Act, 56 Stat. 23 (1942); War Labor Disputes Act, 57 Stat. 163 (1943). Comparable delegations can be found during the Korean and Vietnam periods as well. In essence, Congress has delegated its war powers, and much of its legislative powers as well, to the President.

[30] See, for example, *Martin v. Mott,* 25 U.S. (12 Wheat.) 19 (1827); *Durand v. Hollins,* 8 F. Cas. 111 (C.C.D.Pa. 1860) (No. 4186); *The Prize Cases,* 67 U.S. (2 Bl.) 635 (1863); *In re Neagle,* 135 U.S. 1 (1890); *In re Debs,* 158 U.S. 564 (1895); *United States v. Midwest Oil,* 236 U.S. 459 (1915); *United States v. Curtiss-Wright,* 299 U.S. 304 (1936); *United States v. Belmont,* 301 U.S. 324 (1937); *United States v. Pink,* 315 U.S.

203 (1942); *Ex parte Quirin,* 317 U.S. 1 (1942); *Hirabayashi v. United* States, 320 U.S. 81 (1943); *Korematsu v. United States,* 323 U.S. 214 (1944); *Woods v. Miller,* 333 U.S. 138 (1948); *Ludecke v. Watkins,* 335 U.S. 160 (1948); *Dames & Moore v. Regan,* 453 U.S. 654 (1981); *Crockett v. Reagan,* 558 F. Supp. 893 (D.D.C. 1982); *Beck v. Laird,* 429 F.2d 302 (2d Cir. 1970); *Mitchell v. Laird,* 488 F.2d 611 (D.C. Cir. 1973); *Holtzman v. Schlesinger,* 484 F.2d 1307 (2d Cir. 1973); *Dellums v. Bush,* 752 F. Supp. 1141 (D.D.C. 1990). The judicial attitude, more often than not, approximates the courts being an arm of the executive whenever an emergency erupts.

[31] Clinton Rossiter, *Constitutional Dictatorship* (Princeton, NJ: Princeton University Press, 1948), 7.

[32] Arthur S. Miller, *Presidential Power* (St. Paul, MN: West, 1977), 162.

[33] Ibid.

[34] Ibid.

[35] See note 5, *supra.*

[36] James R. Hurtgen, "The Case for Presidential Prerogative," 7 *U.Tol.L.Rev. 59* (1975).

[37] In order to remain compatible with republican government, the notion of prerogative must be understood as an extraordinary action by the President which does not set a precedent. It must always be understood that prerogative is not part of the President's usual constitutional powers. Prerogative is, and must always be, a temporary power to be used only during a dire emergency. It must be relinquished at the conclusion of the emergency, or when the legislature can sanction the President's actions. In other words, prerogative power should be invoked only when the demands of paramount necessity require—i.e., threat of invasion, dire impositions of war, or threat of civil breakdown exceeding the capacity of civil authorities to maintain order.

[38] Jean-Jacques Rousseau, *The Social Contract,* bk. IV, ch. 6 (Lester G. Crocker, ed., New York: Pocket Books, 1967), 131. Rousseau then went on to say: "But only the greatest dangers can outweigh that of changing the public order, and the sacred power of the laws should never be interfered with except when the safety of the country is at stake." *Ibid.*

[39] During the World War I period and Wilson's "constitutional dictatorship," Edward S. Corwin confronted this problem with the following argument: If democratic constraints are imposed upon presidential prerogative powers, the danger of carrying over wartime rule into peacetime ought to be minimized. What seems to be impossible to do, however, is finding a President willing to act within those democratic constraints during the emergency. Edward S. Corwin, *The President's Control of Foreign Relations* (Princeton, NJ: Princeton University Press, 1917), ch. 1. Regarding the constraints themselves, a small sampling of the list should suffice here: (1) The power of the presidency must be wielded by constitutional means. (2) The presidency must respect the capacity of the public to distinguish between good electoral candidates and bad, between wise men and fools. (3) The presidency must observe the rights of the opposition to criticize, to challenge, and possibly to overthrow its incumbency in a free election. (4) The ethical behavior on which democracy is predicated extends to the President himself. (5) Democracy and its public offices, including the presidency, require an ethical base in society. See Louis W. Koenig, *The Chief Executive* (5th ed., New York: Harcourt, Brace, Jovanovich, 1986), 13-14.

[40] *Home Bldg. & Loan Assoc. v. Blaisdell,* 290 U.S. 398, 426 (1934) (Hughes, C.J.). See also his "War Powers Under the Constitution," 42 A. B. A. Repts. 232 (1917).

[41] See the Lever Act, 40 Stat. 276 (1917) and the Lend Lease Act, 55 Stat. 31 (1941). In both instances Congress virtually delegated Article I to the President. The latter statute, in effect, was a qualified declaration of war. See Edward S. Corwin, *Total War and the Constitution* (New York: Alfred Knopf, 1947), 28-29.

[42] Miller, 178.

[43] Carl J. Friedrich, *Constitutional Reason of State* (Providence, RI: Brown University Press, 1957), 4-5.

[44] Louis Fisher & Neal Devins, *Political Dynamics of Constitutional Law* (St. Paul, MN: West, 1992), 189.

[45] 157 U.S. 281 (1895). According to the Court, the purpose of the commander-in-chief clause "is evidently to vest in the President the supreme command over all military forces,—such supreme and undivided command as would be necessary to the prosecution of a successful war." *Ibid.,* 284.

[46] "Authority of the President to Repel the Attack in Korea," 23 *Dep't St. Bull.* 173 (1950). Members of Congress were consulted informally and after the fact. The Memorandum then stated: "The President, as Commander in Chief of the Armed Forces of the United States, has full control over the use thereof. He also has authority to conduct the foreign relations of the United States. Since the beginning of United States history, he has, on numerous occasions, utilized these powers in sending armed forces abroad." *Ibid.*

[47] Ibid.

[48] Several months after our entry into the Korean Conflict, Secretary of State Dean Acheson testified before the Senate Committees on Foreign Relations and Armed Services. He said: "Not only has the President the authority to use the Armed Forces in carrying out the broad foreign policy of the United States and implementing treaties, but it is equally clear that this authority may not be interfered with by the Congress in the exercise of powers which it has under the Constitution." Quoted in *National Commitments,* S. Rep. No. 797, 90$^{th}$ Cong., 1$^{st}$ Sess., 17 (1967).

[49] During the Eisenhower years, Congress passed "area resolutions" covering Formosa, 69 Stat. 7 (1955), and the Middle East, 71 Stat. 5 (1957). Even President Kennedy initially sought, and secured, an area resolution on Cuba, 76 Stat. 697 (1962), before using independent presidential initiative in declaring a blockade. And since a blockade is tantamount to an act of war under international law, the presidential action can be considered an act of prerogative.

[50] Was this position, taken by the President in the 1960's, really any different from the one taken by Lincoln in the 1860's: the immediate basis of the Lincolnian dictatorship was the commander-in-chief clause and the insistence on a very strict interpretation of the separation of powers principle. In other words, according to Corwin, the constitutional basis for the war powers "has been shifted from the doctrine of delegated powers to the doctrine of inherent powers, thus guaranteeing that the full actual power of the nation is constitutionally available." Edward S. Corwin, *The President: Office and Powers* (4$^{th}$ ed., New York: New York University Press, 1957), 261.

[51] See Leonard C. Meeker, "The Legality of the United States Participation in the Defense of Viet Nam," 75 *Yale L.J.* 1085 (1966) [this article was a reprint of the official State

Department memorandum, 54 *Dep't St. Bull.* 474 (1966)]. After arguing that both the SEATO Treaty *and* the notion of inherent presidential power justified, without prior congressional authorization, the President's deployment of combat troops abroad, the State Department Legal Adviser stated rather uniquely that the changes that have occurred in the world between 1787 and 1966, changes that directly affected America's position in the world, have in effect amended the Constitution. He stated: "In 1787 the world was a far larger place, and the [F]ramers probably had in mind attacks upon the United States. In the 20th century, the world has grown much smaller. An attack on a country far from our shores can impinge directly on a nation's security. In the SEATO Treaty, for example, it is formally declared that an armed attack against Viet Nam would endanger the peace and safety of the United States." *Ibid.,* 1101. Meeker then continued: "Under our Constitution it is the President who must decide when an armed attack has occurred. He also has the constitutional responsibility for determining what measures of defense are required when the peace and safety of the United States are endangered. If he considers that deployment of U.S. forces to South Viet Nam is required, and that military measures against the source of Communist aggression in North Viet Nam are necessary, he is constitutionally empowered to take those measures." *Ibid.,* 1101-02. See also, in the very same vain, John Norton Moore, "The Lawfulness of Military Assistance to the Republic of Viet Nam," 61 *Am. J. Int'l L.* 1 (1967).

[52] Tonkin Gulf Resolution, Pub. L. No. 88-408, 78 Stat. 384 (1964).

[53] This was the basic position taken by the lower federal courts. See, for example, *Berk v. Laird,* 317 F. Supp. 715 (E.D.N.Y. 1970); *Orlando v. Laird,* 317 F. Supp. 1013 (S.D.N.Y. 1970), *aff.* 443 F.2d 1039 (2d Cir. 1971); *Massachusetts v. Laird,* 514 F.2d 26 (1st Cir. 1971); *Mitchell v. Laird,* 488 F. 2d 611 (D.C. Cir. 1973). In addition to the Tonkin Gulf Resolution, the courts also included, as part of the "functional equivalent" notion, continued appropriations and draft laws.

[54] 78 Stat. 384.

[55] *Ibid.* The measure was repealed in a one-sentence amendment to the Foreign Military Sales Act, 84 Stat. 2055 (1971).

[56] Clinton R. Rossiter, *The Supreme Court and the Commander in Chief* (Richard P. Longaker ed., Ithaca, NY: Cornell University Press, 1976), 138.

[57] Arthur M. Schlesinger, *The Imperial Presidency* (New York: Popular Library, 1974), 180. Whatever members of Congress actually thought the resolution meant—and how much power the President was able to use by invoking it—none really believed that they had authorized a large, costly, and protracted war on the Asian mainland. Congress would soon learn how wrong their assumptions were.

[58] President Nixon, on the other hand, abandoned reliance on the SEATO Treaty and, when the Tonkin Gulf Resolution was repealed by a one-sentence amendment to the Foreign Military Sales Act, 84 Stat. 2055 (1971), relied instead on the historical precedent of the numerous instances in which troops had been used abroad by previous Presidents without congressional authorization. In addition, Nixon argued (like Johnson before him) the "functional equivalence" theory; and when the validity of that argument came to an end, he once again relied on the inherent, independent powers of the President as commander-in-chief over armed forces in the field. According to Francis D. Wormuth, however, Nixon overstepped his hand here by adding a unique twist to the

argument: he now viewed his powers as a negotiating instrument to assure the independence of Vietnam and to protect American troops during the process of withdrawal from the war. For a full analysis of this argument see Francis D. Wormuth, "The Nixon Theory of the War Power: A Critique," 60 *Calif. L. Rev.* 623 (1972).

[59] Pub. L. No. 107-40, 115 Stat. 224 (2001).

[60] "America Responds to Terrorism: What Is Terrorism," *Constitutional Rights Foundation.* 11 Apr. 2002, http://www.crf-usa.org/terror/What_Is_Terrorism_rev.htm.

[61] Ibid.

[62] *Ibid.* The Iranian religious leader in question is Ayatulla Taskhiri and his arguments were delivered in a paper at a 1987 international terrorism conference called by the Organization of the Islamic Conference.

[63] Consider the following definitions of terrorism. (1) From the League of Nations, 1937: "All criminal acts directed against a State intended or calculated to create a state of terror in the minds of particular persons or persons in the general public." (2) From Alex P. Schmid of the United Nations Office for the Prevention of International Terrorism: "Acts of Terrorism =Peacetime Equivalent of War Crime." (3) From James M. Poland, professor of criminal justice at California State University: "Terrorism is the premeditated, deliberate, systematic murder, mayhem, and threatening of the innocent to create fear and intimidation in order to gain a political or tactical advantage, usually to influence an audience." See note 59, *supra.*

[64] 115 Stat. 224.

[65] 78 Stat. 384.

[66] 115 Stat. 225.

[67] Ibid.

[68] See, for example, Justice Jackson's dissenting opinion on this very point in *Korematsu v. United States*, 323 U.S. 214, 246 (1944): "A military order, however unconstitutional, is not apt to last longer than the military emergency....But once a judicial opinion rationalizes such an order to show that it conforms to the Constitution, or rather rationalizes the Constitution to show that the Constitution sanctions such an order, the Court for all time has validated the principle of racial discrimination in criminal procedure and of transplanting American citizens. The principle then lies about like a loaded weapon ready for the hand of any authority that can bring forward a plausible claim of an urgent need. Every repetition imbeds that principle more deeply in our law and thinking and expands it to new purposes....*A military commander may overstep the bounds of constitutionality, and it is an incident. But if we review and approve, that passing incident becomes the doctrine of the Constitution. There it has a generative power of its own, and all that it creates will be in its own image."* (Emphasis added).

[69] Unnumbered executive order of 13 Nov. 2001 entitled "Detention, Treatment and Trial of Certain Non-Citizens in the War Against Terrorism," 65 Fed. Reg. 57831 (11-16-01).

[70] See U.S. Cong., H.R. 3162, 107th Cong., 1st Sess. (2001).

[71] Duncan v. Kahanamoku (Hawaiian Martial Law Cases), 327 U.S. 304 (1946). See, also, Zimmerman v. Walker, 319 U.S. 755 (1943). Compare, Ex parte Quirin, 317 U.S. 1 (1942).

[72] In invoking Secretary of State Daniel Webster's ideas about self-defense, the Bush Administration has confused and incorrectly misstated his 1842 argument. Webster suggested that striking first against an enemy was acceptable only when the necessity of that self-defense is instant, overwhelming, and leaving no choice of means, and no moment for deliberation. What the President and his advisers seem unwilling to face, however, are the related questions of whether the Iraqi threat is instant?, is it overwhelming?, and is there really no moment for deliberation? In reality, Iraq looks less like a pre-emptive strike and more like a preventive war. "And there the classic example is one the White House is unlikely to cite with approval: December 7, 1941. Every schoolchild in Japan is taught that the United States-led embargo on Japan was slowly killing the country's economy and undermining its ability to defend itself. That is why Japan has kept a museum celebrating the heroes of Pearl Harbor." See David E. Sanger, "Beating Them to the Prewar," *New York Times,* 28 Sept. 2002, http://www.nytimes.com/2.../28PREE.html?

In: Presidents and War
Editors: A. Eksterowicz and G. Hastedt, pp. 273-293
ISBN 978-1-61668-917-9


*Chapter 16*

# PRESIDENTS AND WAR: NOTES ON THE END OF CONSTITUTIONALISM

***James K. Oliver***

## INTRODUCTION

James Madison's stature as a founding father is based on his seminal role as drafter of the Constitution and expositor of the institutional balance critical to constitutionalism; his presidency, notes one of his biographers, "is semi-forgotten" [1]. In foreign affairs he consistently over-estimated US economic power vis-à-vis England and persisted in his conviction that an embargo against Britain would ultimately force the British to recognize US commercial and maritime rights and stop the impressments of American sailors. The embargo failed and Madison sought and fought a war with England with insufficient land and naval forces, launched a disastrously failed invasion of Canada, and suffered the humiliation of British forces sacking Washington. A late run of western and naval victories and Andrew Jackson's spectacular rout of British forces attacking New Orleans saved Madison's and his Administration's popularity. Britain, preoccupied with reconstituting a conservative order in Europe, negotiated a peace that returned North America to the *status quo ante* – an outcome seemingly beyond the reach of the American negotiators at Ghent [2].

Madison wanted war with Britain so that he might advance his problematic "commercial strategy to its logical conclusion" [3]. Madison's strategic vision was seriously flawed. More important for the present study, however, was his conviction that war must be fought within the new constitutional framework. Madison, of course, was as sensitive as any of the founders to the dangers posed by war to the Constitutional framework [4]. In correspondence with Jefferson, he had emphasized that the Constitution presupposes "that the Executive is the branch of power most interested in war, and most prone to it. It [the Constitution] has accordingly with studied care, vested the question of war in the Legislature"[5]. Thus, as Madison approached war, there were, "constitutional doubts" for

> [T]his would be the first war undertaken after the ratification of the Constitution. The Constitution gives to the Congress alone the power of declaring war. There is no specific

mention of a presidential role at this stage. The president's power is to conduct the war once it has been declared. Should the president just wait for congressional action, or should he try to guide it? [6]

Madison, working with James Monroe and Henry Clay, "coordinated ways to choreograph congressional developments" [7]. He did so, however, within the strictures of the Constitution, that he, as much as any man, had conceived and embedded in the Constitution, especially the prerogatives of Congress. In the end, therefore, he got his declaration and congressional authorization without resort to any "inherent" or "plenary" powers or fabricated emergencies designed to create a fait accompli for the Congress. Moreover, and in bold contrast to his 20th and 21st successors,

> [H]e did not himself violate the civil rights of a citizenry at war. . . . He did stretch the Constitution at times; but the most notable examples of this occurred before the war, not because of the war. He seized West Florida by presidential fiat . . . [and reimposed] nonintercourse without congressional authorization. But during the war itself, as if to prove that the Constitution did not have to be jettisoned in a crisis, he was truer to its strictures than any subsequent war president [8].

The preponderance of contemporary analysis concerning the relationship of the president and war is that the exigencies imposed by world politics and the modalities of conflict in the late 20th and early 21st centuries ineluctably push the American political system away from Madison's example towards an expansion of presidential power at the expense of the Congress. That is, the exercise of world power and leadership require – or so a succession of President's asserted and, generally, Congress has acceded to – an enhancement of executive foreign and national security policy power at the expense of the balances of the late 18th century constitutional framework. By the end of George W. Bush's Administration an even more radical reading of the Constitution was advanced – one which elevated the President to a position of primacy and thereby displaced Madison's constrained definition and restrained exercise of the president's war powers.

In anticipation of a new presidency a conclave of notables – a National Warpowers Commission chaired by former Secretaries of State James Baker III and Warren Christopher – was convened by the Miller Center at the University of Virginia to consider the status and future of the war powers. The commission published a report in July of 2008 advancing a draft "National Powers Consultation Act" based on the principles of "pragmatism," and the hope that "our proposal maximize the likelihood that the President and Congress productively consult with each other on the exercise of war powers" [9].

This paper will review the contemporary war powers relationship between president and Congress including the recommendations of the National War Powers Commission. This review is not, however, primarily an historical reconstruction of the institutional relationship. Such histories are numerous and comprehensive [10]. Rather, the focus of this analysis is on the period since the end of the Cold War for it is during the last two decades that the theory and practice of presidential primacy or "presidentialism" has reached its zenith, surpassing even the "imperial presidency" [11] of the middle Cold War period, i.e. the 1960s and early 1970s. This presidentialism confronts the constitutionalism that Madison and his associates sought to codify at the turn of the 18th into the 19th century and invites analysis of the challenge to and whether the Madisonian vision retains relevance for the institutions and processes of US foreign and national security policy making.

## CONSTITUTIONAL TWILIGHT AND THE DAWN OF "PRESIDENTIALISM"

The course of post-World War II presidential primacy begins with President Harry Truman's assertion that his military response to the North Korean invasion across the 38th parallel in June 1950 did not require *any* Congressional authorization. The president's inherent power as commander in chief and chief executive as well as authority derived from US treaty obligations and permanent membership on the Security Council of the United Nations were deemed sufficient to initiate and prosecute war [12]. Truman's assertions of authority for the presidential commitment of military forces without Congressional authorization constitute the most common ground from which presidential authority has been justified for the succeeding fifty-eight years.

Truman's claimed ambit of presidential power was grounded in the 1936 Supreme Court decision in the case of *United States v. Curtiss-Wright,* [13] a case that stands as the foundation of all subsequent claims of inherent and unencumbered presidential powers in foreign and national security affairs. Chief Justice George Sutherland asserted the arguable notion that the national government was the recipient of sovereignty from Great Britain and as such, the "investment of the Federal government with the powers of external sovereignty did not depend upon the affirmative grants of the Constitution." More important for the war powers and foreign affairs,

> In this vast external realm, with its important, complicated, delicate and manifold problems, the President alone has the power to speak or listen as a representative of the nation. . . . As Marshall said in his great argument of March 7, 1800 in the House of Representatives, "The President is the sole organ of the nation in its external relations and its sole representative with foreign nations" [14].

Notwithstanding more than fifty years of scholarly attack, the "precedent" of *Curtiss-Wright* persists and is employed regularly by presidents and their advocates, to justify seemingly infinitely expandable presidential claims of foreign policy and war powers [15]. In Truman's case these extended to "emergency powers" which, the president argued, authorized seizing and managing vital domestic industries – in this instance, steel mills threatened by strikes. The case ultimately ended up before the Supreme Court and gave rise to a second construction of the executive-legislative war powers relationship; one in which the president must operate in a much more constrained constitutional environment.

The Court's 1952 ruling in *Youngstown Sheet and Tube v. Sawyer* [16], did not deny the existence of unenumerated powers but it rejected the *Curtiss-Wright* notion of broad inherent powers derived from some extra-constitutional reservoir of presidential power or an "emergency" [17]. Justice Robert Jackson in his oft referenced landmark concurring opinion, sought to illuminate the fundamental reality of the constitutional design: diffused institutional power which "enjoins upon its branches separateness but interdependence, autonomy but reciprocity. Presidential powers are not fixed but fluctuate, depending upon their disfunction or conjunction with those of Congress." Inevitably, he concluded, "there is a zone of twilight in which he and Congress have concurrent authority" [18].

During the Cold War, only Dwight Eisenhower occupied a position closer to Jackson's understanding of the Constitution. In the three instances in which Eisenhower deployed military forces – the Formosa Crisis of 1954-1955, in the Middle East in 1957, and the Lebanon Crisis of 1958 – he refused to resort to sweeping and pre-emptive claims of inherent presidential power. Even so, he successfully resisted attempts to limit what he understood to be his power as commander-in-chief to move US troops wherever and whenever he deemed it appropriate [19]. In each instance Eisenhower sought Congressional support in the form of permissively worded "Area Resolutions" authorizing and legitimizing his preferred course of action. Furthermore, when Eisenhower did not want to intervene or escalate a situation, such as in Vietnam, he set for Dulles – a proponent of intervention – a precondition of gaining Congressional support for the action calculating that Congress would be unlikely to provide such support in the immediate aftermath of the Korean Conflict. The critical element for Eisenhower was coordinated and mutually supportive inter-branch decision-making and stronger foreign policy he thought likely when such cooperation was operative [20].

John F. Kennedy's assertion of presidential initiative and denial that Congress was a constitutionally necessary partner in the management of the Cuban Missile Crisis was a decisive return to Truman's presidentialism. On September 13, 1962, Kennedy announced that he was prepared to engage Cuba and the Soviet Union on his own constitutional authority as Commander in Chief [21]. And when asked if there was any "virtue" in a Congressional authorizing resolution, Kennedy replied "No, I think it would be useful, if they desired to do so, for them to express their view. I'd be very glad to have those resolutions passed if that should be the desire of the Congress" [22]. But, when Kennedy proclaimed a quarantine of Cuba in order to interdict the shipment of missiles and military supplies, he did so under "the authority entrusted to me by the Constitution as *endorsed* by the resolution of the Congress." He continued in his proclamation that he was "acting under and by virtue of the authority conferred upon me by the Constitution and statutes of the United States, in accordance with the aforementioned resolution of the United States Congress and of the Organ of Consultation of the American Republics" [23].

That is, nothing was authorized by Congress which the president did not already possess though there was no specification of what authority found in the Constitution and/or statutes Kennedy was referring to in this claim. Finally, reference to the Organ of Consultation of the American Republics (Organization of American States) as an "organ" of international engagement and commitment was no more legally compelling than Truman's specious claim that US membership in the UN and the existence of UNSC resolutions satisfied compliance with U.S. constitutional procedures authorizing the use of U.S. military forces.

Lyndon Johnson's response to purported attacks on US warships in the Tonkin Gulf, August 3, 1964, bore some superficial resemblance to Eisenhower's approach to the war powers. The immediate retaliation against North Vietnam was followed by consultation with the congressional leadership and a request by Johnson for a joint resolution from Congress, the model for which would be Eisenhower's Formosa and Middle East area resolutions and Kennedy's Cuba Resolution. However, the language of the Tonkin Gulf Resolution had been prepared by the Administration three months earlier and in the interim the United States Navy undertook operations along the North Vietnamese coast designed to provoke a North Vietnamese response [24]. The resolution itself was rushed through the Congress with limited hearings and debate and provided "That the Congress approves and supports the determination of the President, as Commander in Chief, to take all necessary measures to repel any armed attack against the forces of the United States and to prevent further aggression" [25].

Putting a constitutional gloss on the executive-legislative interaction in his signing statement, Johnson said the military response stemmed from his authority as Commander in Chief and "was mine – and mine alone." He conceded that he also had a responsibility "of submitting our course to the representatives of the people, for them to verify it or veto it" [26]. The language of the Resolution is clear, however, and notwithstanding subsequent efforts by members of Congress to deny it, [27] they approved and supported – by 88-2 and 416-0 votes in the Senate and House respectively – what the President had already initiated under his authority as Commander in Chief.

## After Vietnam: Congressional Government Truncated and Presidentialism Redux

Richard Nixon's constitutionally dubious expansion of the Vietnam conflict to include Cambodia led to Congress reasserting itself as a co-participant in the exercise of the war powers. This ultimately took the form of the War Power Resolution passed over Nixon's veto in 1973, the operational core of which centers on two mechanisms. The first involves a set of 60-90 day deadlines on presidentially initiated military action without Congressional approval. Congressional inaction would be sufficient to end the use of force. However, the countdown to closure is not triggered unless the president reports under Section 4(a) (1) of the Resolution that US forces have been introduced into circumstances in which "hostilities" are imminent. As Fisher notes: "For fairly obvious reasons, Presidents do not submit reports under that section. Instead they report more generally" [28]. Thus in more than 120 instances since the passage of the Resolution, presidents have filed general informational reports that are deemed *by them* "consistent" with the War Powers Resolution. In only two instances – the *Mayaguez* incident during the Ford Administration and Reagan's Lebanese intervention in 1983– did the reports fall under Section 4(a)(1) . In the former case the report did not reach Congress until hostilities had ended, and in the latter, Congress passed a resolution authorizing Reagan to maintain the US presence for up to eighteen months [29].

The mechanism whereby Congress could terminate the use of US military forces at any time would be the passage of a concurrent resolution directing the president to remove US forces from hostilities. However, such "legislative vetoes" were declared unconstitutional by the Supreme Court in the case of *I.N.S. v. Chadha* because concurrent resolutions do not meet the "presentment" requirements of the Constitution. Because the powers ostensibly constrained by Congress are constitutionally granted in part to the president, the president must be presented with a bill or joint resolution for signature or veto [30].

With, therefore, its operational mechanisms presumptively unconstitutional and/or circumvented by every president who has operated under the War Powers Resolution, the Resolution has remained essentially inoperative. Ford, Carter, Reagan, and George H.W. Bush all employed force unilaterally either asserting that they were undertaking limited force to effect rescues, repel attacks on US forces, protect US nationals or property, or under cover of international treaty obligations. In other instances where major military involvements seemed more likely, presidents followed the pattern set by Kennedy and Johnson and undertook consultation with the leadership of Congress and solicited Congressional resolutions of support. Nonetheless, no president unambiguously acknowledged that they did not possess the authority as Commander in Chief and Chief Executive to act without Congressional affirmation however politically useful the latter might be.

Immediately following the Vietnam War and Watergate, the resort to force declined with Ford and Carter using military force in only three cases, all of which involved to some degree a rescue operation. Ford and Carter may have felt restricted by the events of the immediate past and their likely effect on domestic and Congressional support. Perhaps, also, the presence and lack of experience with the newly passed War Powers Resolution introduced greater caution [31]. However, under Reagan and the first Bush, a decidedly more robust inclination towards the use of force ensued. Along with eight major commitments of US forces, Reagan and Bush filed fourteen and seven reports respectively under the War Powers Resolution though none of them were submitted under the strictures of Section 4(a)(1). At every turn, the prerogatives of the Commander in Chief were asserted and deemed sufficient to initiate the use of force.

The major military action taken during the period was Bush's response to Saddam Hussein's invasion of Kuwait in August of 1990. Bush immediately sent American troops to the region, proclaimed the action defensive and fully within his powers as commander in chief, and explicitly denied that any Congressional authorization was necessary [32]. Simultaneously, the Administration worked assiduously to establish global support and legitimacy for its actions via construction of a coalition of financial and/or military support in the Arab world and among US allies and in the United Nations Security Council securing a Resolution on November 29, 1990 authorizing "all means necessary" to force the Iraqi's from Kuwait [33].

With the hours before launching war counting down, Bush sought a resolution of support for his actions, and both houses passed authorization for the president to take offensive actions against Iraq. Nonetheless, in a signing statement Bush again rejected the notion that such authorization was necessary:

> As I made clear to congressional leaders at the outset, my request for congressional support did not, and my signing this resolution does not, constitute any change in the long-standing positions of the executive branch on either the President's constitutional authority to use the Armed Forces to defend vital U.S. interests or the constitutionality of the War Powers Resolution [34].

Or, as Bush stated more pungently during the 1992 presidential campaign, "I didn't have to get permission from some old goat in the United States Congress to kick Saddam Hussein out of Kuwait" [35].

## The Apotheosis of Presidentialism

Even as the tensions and foreboding atmosphere of the Cold War evaporated, the claims for presidential supremacy grew more bold and preemptory, peaking during the administrations of Bill Clinton and George W. Bush. Clinton used military force more frequently than any president since the Second World War and like his predecessors claimed in every instance the power to do so as commander in chief and chief executive without Congressional authorization. But it was Clinton's successor, George W. Bush through the initiative of his Vice President Richard Cheney, who formulated an expansive "New Paradigm" of war powers proceeding from an institutional foundation of presidentialism and a neutered Congress.

## Bill Clinton and the Practise of Preemptory Presidentialism

During his eight years in office, Bill Clinton forwarded 60 reports to Congress under the War Powers Resolution, none of them under Section 4(a) (1) [36]. Ten of Clinton's uses of military force entailed "imminent" or actual hostilities. Four involved missile or air strikes and in a fifth case, deployment of American combat forces in anticipation of an invasion of Haiti to remove the military leader General Raoul Cedras (1994). Clinton abjured Congressional authorization, arguing that he possessed authority as commander in chief to respond to threats against American citizens abroad (Iraq, 1993), attacks against American embassies (Sudan/Afghanistan, 1998) or in response to UN Security Council Resolutions authorizing member state use of force (Haiti and air strikes against Iraq in 1998).

With the 1996 strikes against Iraq following Saddam's attacks on Irbil, however, Clinton advanced a justification different from those employed by his predecessors: the missiles "sent the following message to Saddam Hussein: When you abuse your own people or threaten your neighbors, you must pay a price" [37]. The argument was and remains disconcerting for it justified preemptory attacks solely on the authority of the president whenever the commander in chief determined that *any* state posed an imminent threat, not just to the United States, but to the targeted state's own population or its neighbors. This justification for war is "both novel and startling" [38] but also an harbinger of the pre-emptive war powers concept advanced by George W. Bush in response to the 9/11 attacks and as the centerpiece of his global war on terrorism.

Finally, combat operations in Somalia in 1993 were justified in terms of protection of US nationals and their property and as a continuation of the humanitarian and peacekeeping intervention begun under Security Council authority during the Bush Administration. Congress sought to constrain the Administration, but failed to pass binding resolutions.

The most sustained and potentially dangerous engagement of US military forces during the Clinton years occurred in the Balkans. The first round of actions in Bosnia entailed the 1993 deployment of US combat aircraft in support of humanitarian flights and the enforcement of a no-fly zone. Subsequently, US forces were ordered by Clinton to undertake airstrikes against Serbian militias in Bosnia (1994), and, finally, the introduction of US ground troops in support of the Dayton Accords ending the fighting in Bosnia in 1995.

Throughout this escalation, Clinton never conceded that Congressional authorization was necessary. He reported his actions to Congress, sought support for them, but never explicitly requested authorization though he averred that he would "welcome and encourage congressional authorization of any military involvement in Bosnia" [39]. When, however,

Congress approached restrictions on his actions, he invariably asserted that these constituted encroachments on his powers as commander in chief and chief executive [40]. When in 1994 and 1995 US engagement escalated to airstrikes and then the introduction of ground troops, Clinton asserted that he had sufficient authorization from the United Nations Security Council and NATO.

Congressional reaction was fragmented, inconsistent, and incoherent [41]. Clinton's initiatives provoked debate and much rhetoric concerning the prerogatives of Congress to limit the President via a priori limitations on the introduction of US troops into Bosnia, appropriations restrictions, but also "respect" for the President's authority as ". . . Commander in Chief to conduct foreign policy . . . [T]here is no greater threat to American lives than a Congress that attempts to micro-manage foreign policy" [42]. In the end, the Congress failed to pass anything stronger than non-binding measures supporting US forces deployed in the Balkans while dissociating the Congress from the President and his policies.

Three years later in Kosovo, Clinton again asserted a unilateral prerogative to place American forces in harm's way – in this instance an attack on a sovereign state – without congressional authorization. The scope and implications of Clinton's decision are as expansive as his earlier justification for the punishment of Saddam for the attack on Irbil: "Yesterday I decided that the United States would vote to give NATO the authority to carry out military strikes against Serbia if President Milosevic continues to defy the international community" [43]. Louis Fisher summarizes the scope and gravity of Clinton's action:

> Note the language: "*I* decided that the United States . . . ." Clinton alone would decide America's policy. The decision to go to war against another country rested in the hands of one person, exactly what the framers thought they had avoided. Moreover, Clinton would be giving *NATO* authority, instead of the Congress giving the *President* authority [44].

Congress subsequently passed confused and inconsistent concurrent resolutions authorizing, in the House version, peacekeeping, and in the Senate, support for military operations. Even if the substance of the resolutions had been synchronized, however, neither constituted legal authorization for Clinton's actions because concurrent resolutions are not legally binding [45].

## The New Paradigm of Presidentialism

If Bill Clinton succeeded in asserting, elaborating, and using unilateral presidential war power more extensively than any of his predecessors, he never really grounded his activism in an explicitly articulated constitutional argument or doctrine. George W. Bush's Administration on the other hand, synthesized the historical strands of a presidentially centered construct of foreign affairs. The driving force behind this effort was Vice President Richard Cheney. Before examining this doctrinal framework and justification for presidentialism, it is important to address a seeming paradox of the administration's use of the war powers.

The Administration is defined by two applications of force: [46] the "war on terrorism" commenced in Afghanistan after the 9/11 attacks and the invasion of Iraq in March 2003 followed by a war stretching beyond the Bush Administration into that of his successor. Both the Afghanistan and Iraq wars were formally covered by broadly permissive Congressional resolutions authorizing the use of force [47]. Bush and Congress seemed, therefore, to act in concert and within the framework established in the Constitution and the War Powers Resolution. While not declaring war, the Congress nonetheless authorized the use of force.

However, Bush and his Administration understood the two "authorizing" resolutions as supplementary and not antecedent to the inherent powers of the President acting as commander in chief and chief executive. In neither case did the President accede to or act pursuant to Congress's authorization powers. Indeed, in signing statements, Bush informed Congress, first, regarding Afghanistan: he acted "pursuant to my constitutional authority to conduct U.S. foreign relations as Commander in Chief and Chief Executive." Further,

> I am providing this report as part of my efforts to keep the Congress informed, consistent with the War Powers Resolution and Public Law 107-40 . . . . I appreciate the continuing support of the Congress, including its enactment of Public Law 107-40, in these actions to protect the security of the United States of America and its citizens, civilian and military, here and abroad [48].

Then, with respect to the Iraq resolution, Bush characterized the "authorization" as a "resolution of support" and that, he did not regard it as "constitut[ing] any change in the long-standing positions of the executive branch on either the president's constitutional authority to use force to deter, prevent, or respond to aggression or other threats to U.S. interests or on the constitutionality of the War Powers Resolution" [49].

Some have wondered why, given the sweeping authority extended to the president in Public Law 107-40, Bush did not utilize the statute as his source of authority rather than the claim of inherent constitutional powers [50]. The answer would seem to lie in the argument advanced by the Administration, primarily through Vice President Cheney, that the president's authority as the sole and essential agent of US relations with the international system is not dependent upon statutory definitions of authority.

From the beginning of his government career Cheney maintained, as he stated in the Minority Report on the Iran-Contra Affair in 1987, that a proper reading of the Constitution and constitutional history must acknowledge that

> . . . Presidents exercised a broad range of foreign policy powers for which they neither sought nor received Congressional sanction through statute.
>
> This history . . . leaves little, if any, doubt that the President was expected to have the primary role of conducting the foreign policy of the United States. Congressional action to limit the President in this area therefore should be reviewed with a considerable degree of skepticism. If they interfere with the core presidential foreign policy function, they should be struck down. Moreover, the lesson of our constitutional history is that doubtful cases should be decided in favor of the President [51].

Obviously, Cheney is paraphrasing the "plenary powers/sole organ" argument advanced in the *Curtiss-Wright* decision and reiterated by every president since World War II. What is distinctive here is that George W. Bush's declaration exploited the 9/11 terrorist attacks to not only initiate an open-ended "Global War on Terrorism" and an invasion of Iraq, but also expanded the argument justifying presidential primacy beyond that articulated by Sutherland into a far more comprehensive doctrine of presidential plenary foreign policy and war powers extending beyond conventional distinctions between foreign and domestic affairs [52].

The central element in the effort to solidify a coherent doctrine of presidentialism was the summary codification of the several dimensions of the presumptive exclusive plenary foreign affairs and war powers of the president after 9/11. Two weeks after the 9/11 attacks, Deputy Assistant Attorney General John C. Yoo from his position in the Justice Department's Office of Legal Counsel submitted the first of many memoranda to the White House, the Department of Defense, Central Intelligence Agency, senior officials in the Office of Legal Counsel and Justice Department. "The President's Constitutional Authority to Conduct Military Operations against Terrorists and Nations Supporting Them," provided the basic reading of the Constitution from which subsequent specific interpretations would be derived.

Quoting liberally from Hamilton's numbers in the *Federalist Papers*, Yoo sought to elevate to legal readings and interpretations, repeated post-World War II Presidential assertions and practice including: (1) "The *centralization of authority* in the President *alone* is particularly crucial in matters of national defense, war, and foreign policy, where a *unitary executive* can evaluate threats, consider policy choices, and mobilize national resources with a *speed and energy that is far superior to any other branch*." [53]. (2) "[T]he *process* used for conducting military hostilities is different from other government decisionmaking" in that it requires the speed and centralization that distinguishes the presidency. (3) The *powers* allocated to the Congress and the President are qualitatively and substantively different because Congress's powers are restricted to those enumerated in the Constitution whereas the President possesses unenumerated foreign affairs powers unique and *exclusively* available to the president. Yoo insists, therefore, that the *Curtiss-Wright* Court's reading of presidential power is correct: "This foreign affairs power is *exclusive*: it is "the very delicate, plenary and exclusive power of the President as sole organ of the federal government in the field of international relations - a power which does not require as a basis for its exercise an act of Congress."

Finally, Yoo undertakes a crucial conceptual move by conflating foreign affairs and war powers uniquely available to the president and not the Congress. Specifically, the conduct of military hostilities is characterized as "a central tool for the exercise of the President's plenary control over the conduct of foreign policy." Thus, "the President's broad constitutional power to use military force to defend the Nation, recognized by the Joint Resolution itself, would allow the President to take whatever actions he deems appropriate to pre-empt or respond to terrorist threats from new quarters." Moreover, and crucial for the entire presidentialist paradigm:

> In both the War Powers Resolution and the Joint Resolution, Congress has recognized the President's authority to use force in circumstances such as those created by the September 11 incidents. *Neither statute, however, can place any limits on the President's determinations as to any terrorist threat, the amount of military force to be used in response, or the method, timing, and nature of the response. These decisions, under our Constitution, are for the President alone to make* [54].

Subsequently, the OLC issued numerous memoranda affirming the legality of Administration initiatives regarding: seizure, incarceration, and rights (Guantanamo and military tribunals) of belligerents including moving prisoners to other countries for interrogation ("rendition"); the detention of U.S. citizens; and several rulings on methods of interrogation understood to violate international agreements on torture, [55] but opining that such agreements might be suspended and did not bind the president. In addition, the OLC extended opinions authorizing warrantless surveillance under the Foreign Intelligence Surveillance Act (FISA). Perhaps the most expansive and broadly implicative of these opinions was an October 23, 2001 memorandum concluding: ". . . the President has the independent, non-statutory power to take military actions, domestic as well as foreign, if he determines such actions to be necessary to respond to the terrorist attacks upon the United States on September 11, 2001 and before." Yoo, having asserted that the use of military force domestically falls within the president's plenary powers as commander in chief, went on to suggest that, "First Amendment speech and press rights may also be subordinated to the overriding need to wage war successfully," and "the current campaign against terrorism may require even broader exercises of federal power domestically" [56].

With this last opinion, Yoo and his associates crossed a bright redline drawn by Justice Jackson in his *Youngstown* opinion.

> . . . [N]o doctrine that the Court could promulgate would seem to me more sinister and alarming than that a President whose conduct of foreign affairs is so largely uncontrolled, and often is unknown, can vastly enlarge his mastery over the internal affairs of the country by his own commitment of the Nation's armed forces to some foreign venture.
>
> . . . [T]the Constitution did not contemplate that the title Commander in Chief *of the Army and Navy* will constitute him also Commander in Chief of the country, its industries and its inhabitants. He has no monopoly of "war powers," whatever they are. . . No penance would ever expiate the sin against free government of holding that a President can escape control of executive powers by law through assuming his military role. . . .
>
> Loose and irresponsible use of adjectives colors all non-legal and much legal discussion of presidential powers. "Inherant" powers, "implied" powers, "incidental" powers, "plenary" powers, "war" powers and "emergency" powers are used, often interchangeably and without fixed or ascertainable meanings.
>
> . . . The claim of inherent and unrestricted presidential powers has long been a persuasive dialectical weapon in political controversy. . . . But prudence has counseled that reliance on such nebulous claims stop short of provoking a judicial test" [57].

Unfortunately for the Bush Adminsitration and advocates of the extraordinary presidentialist claims outlined by the OCL, these claims provoked a judicial test – *Hamdan v. Rumsfeld* [58] -- and failed. Most important, the Court "refused to accept the government's core premise that a new 'crisis paradigm' required that ordinary legal rules be jettisoned"[59] and that in these extraordinary circumstances, the president's prerogatives as commander in chief constituted a sufficient and constitutional warrant not only for foreign affairs, but domestic affairs – including judicial process – as well. The Court rejected Bush's claim that the president's inherant or plenary powers authorized acting without Congressional authorization in establishing military tribunals for dealing with alien detainees including diminution of their rights established in the Uniform Code of Military Justice and the Geneva Conventions.

More broadly, *Hamdan*, in reasserting presidential deference to legislative authorization, judicial prerogatives, and treaty obligations

> . . . not only gives broad direction on how a war on terror may be constitutionally conducted but also disproves exorbitant claims already made during that war regarding the President's supposed freedom to authorize torture and cruel treatment ant to carry out widesprread warrantless domestic wiretapping in the face of contrary statutes [60].

The Administration immediately secured from Congress the Military Commissions Act of 2006 which authorized the President to establish and convene military commissions quite similar to those previously declared unconstitutional "because they did not comport with the UCMJ and the Geneva Conventions" [61]. Nonetheless, the Bush Administration acceeded to the Court's ruling.

Moreover, even as the implications of Hamdan reverberated through Administration, Congress and the judicial system, the political ground was cut from under the administration as popular and Congressional skepticism coallesced. The decisive moment came with the 2006 election and Republican loss of control of the Congress. Details of the OLC materials emerged and investigative reporters belatedly began working in earnest. Cheney's closest aid, Lewis Libby, was indicted and convicted of illegaly leaking the name of a CIA analyst, Valerie Plame whose husband, Joseph C. Wilson, a former ambassador, had publically challenged and discredited the veracity of Bush's claims of Iraq's acquisition of nuclear raw materials from Niger. Finally, in October of 2008 and again on January 15, 2009, the OLC itself repudiated Yoo's previous analysis [62].

Though Yoo et al's memos have been withdrawn in most cases, the central claim of presidential primacy has not. Bush's successor has not rejected the notion of inherant consititutional powers possessed by the President. In addition, the War Powers Resolution has not been redeemed and remains in a state of limbo. Indeed, the only recent attempt to assess the Resolution, The Warpowers Commission, rendered a negative verdict concerning its utility. More important, the Commission advanced a set of procedural recommenadations which if adopted, would leave presidentialism still very much in control of the institutional initiative [63].

## "Something That Would Work"

The War Powers Commission deals with the conflicted history of the war powers by simply summarizing the post Cold War positions taken by Presidents and Congress. However, the positions taken and claims made by Presidents and/or proponents of Congressional prerogatives are not subjected to any analysis or critique. Thus, for example the Commission simply observes: "Advocates of congressional power cite Truman's decision as a turning point in the war powers debate, when Presidents began asserting more and more power. Advocates of presidential power dispute that the Korean War represented a sea change"[64].

The Commission concludes from this cataloging of "President says"/"Congress says" tit-for-tat that because for every claim there is an opposite and no less intensely held counter-claim, the war powers are ambiguous and there can be no resolution of the constitutional questions until the courts decide. And "Because the courts have not ruled on the merits in these cases, the questions of which branch may exercise which war powers remain open" [65]. Thus, "We take no position on the underlying constitutional questions. Nor do we judge the actions of any President or Congress. We merely note the persistence and intensity of the debate, as it informs any recommendations we can reasonably and practically make" [66].

It is clear, however, that they do in fact judge negatively the actions taken by the Congress, i.e. the constitutionality of the War Powers Resolution of 1973 [67]. And when they turn to "recommendations we can reasonably and practically make", there is little doubt where the Commission's sentiments lie.

On each point of their summary of criticisms of the 1973 Resolution, the President's complaints are privileged. Moreover, in their exegesis of the *Chadha* case the Commission reveals that it *does* believe that the Supreme Court has ruled negatively on the most fundamental operational principle of the Resolution: the practice of using one-house "legislative vetoes" of administrative actions. Furthermore, "The general view is that if the War Powers Resolution were put to the same test in *Chadha*, Section 5(c) of the Resolution, and perhaps other provisions, would fail" [68]. Finally, Mr. Baker asserted in July of 2008, "[The 1973 Resolution] is not effective, at best. It's unconstitutional at worst. It's a bad law that ought to be replaced with a good law, something that would work" [69].

## The "War Powers Consultation Act"

The proposed War Powers Consultation Act encompasses: (1) a mandatory executive-legislative consultation process in the event of "significant military actions" and (2) a process whereby Congress would be required to vote approval or disapproval of military actions taken by the president. In the event both houses of Congress pass a joint resolution of disapproval, the resolution would be presented to the president who could exercise a veto which could, in turn, be overridden by a two-thirds vote in both houses. Failure to override would mean the president's war would proceed.

## Required Consultation

The proposed consultation process requires that the president meet with a newly constituted Joint Congressional Committee consisting of: the Speaker of the House and the Senate Majority Leader and the Minority Leaders of the House and the Senate as well as the bipartisanship leadership of the House and Senate Committees on Foreign Relations/Affairs, Armed Services, Intelligence, and Appropriations [70]. The president is required to consult with, not merely notify, the Joint Committee before armed forces are deployed in any "significant armed conflict." The only exception to this requirement is in the event of covert operations in which case, the president must consult with the Joint Committee within three calendar days of the deployment of forces.

The notion of "significant armed conflict" is obviously pivotal in this process and is understood as meaning: "(i) any conflict expressly authorized by Congress, or (ii) any combat operation by U.S. armed forces lasting more than a week or expected by the President to last more than a week" [71]. Significant armed conflict does not extend to: (i) repelling attacks, or preventing imminent attacks; (ii) limited reprisals against terrorists or states that sponsor terrorism; (iii) humanitarian missions in response to natural disasters; (iv) investigations or acts to prevent criminal activity abroad;(v) covert operations; (vi) training exercises; or (vii) missions to protect or rescue American citizens or personnel abroad [72]. Should any of these actions escalate into a significant military action, the President is required to undertake consultation with the Joint Committee.

Several of these exceptions constitute exclusions from Congressional authorization of the use of force heretofore within the province of Congress. With the possible exception (i), (vii) and perhaps (iii) [73], the effect is, therefore, to replace the presumption that *all* uses of force must be *authorized* by Congress with the constitutionally problematic notion of "consultation." As Fisher notes,

> The Constitution is not designed to ensure that Congress will be "consulted" before the president initiates war. It is written to place singularly in the hands of Congress the decision to take the country from a state of peace to a state of war. The president needs authorization or a declaration from Congress, in *advance*, and not simply "consult" with a few senior lawmakers before committing U.S. forces to an offensive war [74].

Moreover, "consultation" entails no obligation to act on the advice rendered, nor does the requirement of consultation and the admonition that it be serious necessitate anything more substantive than "consultation" with the leadership of the Congress than in the past.

In addition, presidentially initiated covert operations and "limited" reprisals against terrorists and/or states supporting terrorists provide the president substantial and statutorily covered range of opportunities for initiating wars. For example, presumably any state placed on the State Department's list of sponsors of international terrorism would be "pre-approved" for a presidentially initiated use of force. And if the operations were covert, the President would be free to delay "consultation" [75].

## Congressional Approval or Disapproval of Presidential Actions

The process whereby Congress approves or disapproves a president's actions is designed to force the Congress to act and present the president with a joint resolution requiring presidential signature before it can become law. If no authorization of declaration of war has been passed by Congress within 30 days of the president initiating significant military action, the Chair and Co-chairs of the Joint Committee must introduce identical joint resolutions approving the action in their respective houses of Congress which must be voted on within twelve calendar days. If the resolution is disapproved, any member of the House and Senate may introduce a joint resolution of disapproval of the military action which must be voted on within five calendar days. However, "The effect of the passage of this joint resolution shall not have the force of law unless presented to the President and either signed by the President or subsequently approved by Congress over the President's veto" [76].

This procedure retains one of the most heavily criticized elements of the War Powers Resolution, i.e. providing at least two months time during which a Congressionally unauthorized war might be initiated and fought. In addition, the process whereby Congress registers its support or disapproval, is decidedly tilted against Congress. Thus, either a Congressional resolution of disapproval or one introduced by any member is likely to elicit a presidential veto leading to the necessary two-thirds override vote in both houses. "In other words, the president could initiate a war and continue it as long as he has one-third plus one in a single chamber. The procedure is flatly unconstitutional" [77].

In sum, the Commission, under the self-imposed requirement that it produce, "something that would work," is constitutional, and perceived as fair and balanced by all parties, fails its own test. It fails because their paradigm of what "works" is the constitutionally dubious presidentialism asserted by Truman, practiced by all his successors with the possible exception of Eisenhower, and tendentiously codified during George W. Bush's presidency. "The Baker-Christopher Commission fails to offer a solution for war powers disputes," Fisher concludes

> Because it never addressed the central tenets of the Constitution, including the principle of popular government and the explicit text that places the war power with Congress. The commission's draft bill weakens Congress, plays to executive strengths, and undercuts the rule of law. It does great damage to the core structural safeguard of separation of powers and checks and balances. . . .[78].

## Moving Beyond Presidentialism?

The post-Cold War expansion and elaboration of presidentialism has been, slowed as it was in the 1950s and again in the 1970s by the erosion of military, political, and popular support for a divisive, presidentially initiated war as well as in the case of the Korean War, a crucial judicial decision. Harold Hongju Koh has suggested that "In *Hamdan*, the Supreme Court has given us a *Youngstown* for the twenty-first century," [79] for ". . . *Hamdan* goes a long way toward restoring the constitutional vision that the [Bush Administration] had turned upside down. It marks a major step toward reestablishing what Justice Jackson termed in his *Youngstown* concurrence the "equilibrium established by our constitutional system" [80].

The analysis undertaken in this paper suggests that however major and necessary a step has been taken, it is far from sufficient. However, elegant and compelling Jackson's concurrence in *Youngstown*, it was overwhelmed in less than a decade by the terrifying exigencies of the nuclear duel at the brink of Armageddon off Cuba. It was deemed necessary to set aside Madison's equilibrated constitionalism for the presidentialism required to prosecute first, global containment and then a global war on terrorism. Moreover, what the Court gave, it could take away as *Chadha* cast a pall over the War Powers Resolution and the flawed reassertion of "Congressional government" in the decade after Vietnam.

Madison's constitutional equilibrium assumes that presidential aggrandizement is a near inevitable concomitant of war, his restraint in the War of 1812 notwithstanding to the contrary. However, Madison and the framers also theorized that the Congress would jealously guard its war power prerogatives and "push back" a too assertive president. The Tonkin Gulf Resolution experience led Senator J. William Fulbright to conclude the contrary:

> In adopting a resolution with such sweeping language, however, Congress committed the error of making a *personal* judgment as to how President Johnson would implement the resolution when it had a responsibility to make an institutional judgment, first as what *any* President would do with so great an acknowledgment of power, and,

second, as to whether, under the Constitution, Congress had the right to grant or concede the authority in question [81].

The subsequent behavior of Congress suggests, however, that the problem is deeper than a situational "error" of judgment; that it reflects a fundamental structural weakness; a conceptual flaw in the Madisonian design. Is the contemporary Congress – a collective body comprised of self-interested politicians preoccupied with their short-term electoral needs – any longer capable of the far-seeing "institutional judgments" necessary to the constitutionlist paradigm of 1787? By the time Clinton undertook his sustained campaign of unilateral uses of force, and presidentialism approached its apogee under George W. Bush, Congress's "institutional judgment" continued to be rendered through resolutions of "support," eleventh hour "authorizations," and often incoherent but politically expedient legislation encompassing "support for the troops" but not the president's policy. None of this conforms to the institutional role envisioned by Madison and his associates, an institution whose constitutional prerogatives and authority a President Madison respected and engaged with care.

Jackson observed that in a Constitution of concurrent authority, ". . . congressional inertia, indifference or quiescence may sometimes, at least as a practical matter, enable, if not invite, measures on independent presidential responsibility" [82]. Within eight years of his landmark opinion, congressional quiescence; indeed, deference – the operational corollary of presidentialism – had become thoroughly instantiated in the executive-legislative relationship culminating in the second Bush Administration's extraordinary "New Paradigm" of presidential primacy. The more extreme formulations of presidentialism advanced by the George W. Bush's Administration have been set aside. Nonetheless, the Warpowers Commission has rendered a report recommending a presidentialism in which Congress is to play a ritualistic and, arguably unconstitutional "consultative" role.

President-Elect Barrack Obama entered office at least rhetorically committed to a presidency consultatively engaged with Congress on foreign and national security policy and during the transitional period, met with the National Warpowers Commission [83]. Though Obama has not explicitly endorsed the Commission's recommendations, during his campaign, he outlined a more open and cooperative relationship with the Congress including the strengthening of traditional and the fashioning of new institutional and consultative linkages between executive and legislative branches [84].

It remains to be seen if the "traditional and . . . new institutional and consultative linkages between executive and legislative branches" will challenge presidentialism's status as the default executive-legislative relationship.

## References

[1] Garry Wills, James Madison (New York: Times Books/Henry Holt and Company, 2002): 1.

[2] Wills' history of Madison's presidency along with Robert Allen Rutland's The Presidency of James Madison (Lawrence, Kansas: University Press of Kansas, 1990) and J.C.A. Stagg's Mr. Madison's War: Politics, Diplomacy, and Warfare in the Early

American Republic, 1783-1830 (Princeton: Princeton University Press, 1983) are essential sources.

[3] Wills: 94 and Rutland: 188.

[4] See Louis Fisher, "Studies on Presidential Power in Foreign Relations, Study No. 1: "The 'Sole Organ' Doctrine," (The Law Library of Congress, August 2006): 6 and the shorter, "*The Law*: Presidential Inherent Power: The 'Sole Organ' Doctrine," Presidential Studies Quarterly 37 (March 2007): 139-152.

[5] Quoted by Fisher, "The 'Sole Organ' Doctrine": 6.

[6] Wills: 94.

[7] Ibid.

[8] Wills: 154. See also, Rutland: 189.

[9] National Warpowers Commission Report: 9 http://millercenter.org/dev/ci/system/application/views/_newwebsite/policy/commissions/warpowers/report.pdf ; (Hereafter, WCR).

[10] Among the best of these are: John Hart Ely, War and Responsibility: Constitutional Lessons of Vietnam and Its Aftermath, (Princeton, NJ: Princeton University Press, 1993); Louis Fisher, Presidential War Power, second edition revised (Lawrence, Kansas: University Press of Kansas, 2004); Michael J. Glennon, Constitutional Diplomacy, (Princeton, NJ: Princeton University Press, 1990); Louis Henkin, Foreign Affairs and the US Constitution, 2d edition, (New York: Oxford University Press, 1996) and Henkin, Consitutionalism, Democracy, and Foreign Affairs, (New York: Columbia University Press, 1990), and Harold Hongju Koh, The National Security Constitution: Sharing Power after the Iran-Contra Affair, (New Haven: Yale University Press, 1990). A comprehensive casebook of foreign affairs and national security law is Thomas M. Franck, Michael J. Glennon, and Sean D. Murphy eds., Foreign Relations and National Security Law: Cases, Materials, and Simulations, 3d edition, (St. Paul, Minnesota: West Publishing, 2007).

[11] The term is that of Arthur Schlesinger, Jr., The Imperial Presidency, (Boston: Houghton Mifflin Company, 2004).

[12] Subsequently, Truman restated the argument for the Administration's decision to send US troops to Europe, again claiming that the President possessed the inherent power to do so as commander in chief as well as authority under the then new North Atlantic Treaty.

[13] United States v. Curtiss-Wright (1936).

[14] U.S. v. Curtiss Wright.

[15] Perhaps the most thorough critique of Sutherland's opinion has been that provided by Louis Fisher. See in addition to Presidential War Powers, "The 'Sole Organ' Doctrine," and "*The Law*: Presidential Inherent Power: The 'Sole Organ' Doctrine": 139-152.

[16] Youngstown Sheet and Tube Co. v. Sawyer, 343 U.S. 579 *(*1952).

[17] Thus Associate Justice Hugo Black stated unequivocally in his majority opinion: "The President's power, if any, to issue the order [to seize the steel mills] must stem either from an act of Congress or from the Constitution itself." Ibid.

[18] Ibid.

[19] Fisher notes, for example, Eisenhower's successful opposition to Senator Wayne Morse's attempt to amend the Middle East Resolution to restrict the President's armed forces deployment prerogatives. Presidential War Power: 122-123.

[20] Presidential War Power: 124-125.
[21] Public Papers of the Presidents, 1962: 674.
[22] Ibid: 679.
[23] Ibid: 807 and 810; emphasis added.
[24] See Stanley Karnow, Vietnam: A History, (1991): 373ff, William Conrad Gibbons, The U.S. Government and the Vietnam War: Executive and Legislative Roles and Relationships, Part II: 1961-1964, (1986): 228-235 and 291-292, and Joseph C. Goulden, Truth Is the First Casualty: The Gulf of Tonkin Affairs – Illusion and Reality, 1969.
[25] The Southeast Asia (Tonkin Gulf) Resolution, August 7, 1964. 78 Stat. 384 (1964).
[26] Public Papers of the Presidents, 1963-1964, II: 946.
[27] Ely systematically obliterates Fulbright's claims of Johnsonian duplicity; see War and Responsibility: 19-30.
[28] Fisher, Presidential War Powers: 150.
[29] See Fisher's discussion at ibid as well as Richard F. Grimmett, "Congressional Research Service, War Powers Resolution: Presidential Compliance", CRS Report RL33532, 12-14 (June 12, 2007) and Michael J. Glennon, "The War Powers Resolution: Sad Record, Dismal Promise," (excerpts from 17 Loy. L.A. L. Rev. 657, 658-70 (1984), in Foreign Relations and National Security Law: Cases, Materials, and Simulations: 717-720 and 721-723.
[30] I.N.S. v. Chadha, 462 U.S. 919 (1983).
[31] Apparently, it also produced great resentment among the foreign policy staffers in the Ford Administration and no one felt it more intensely than Ford's Chief of Staff, Richard Cheney. See Charlie Savage's "Takeover: The Return of the Imperial Presidency," at The Rule of Law and the Global War on Terrorism: Detainees, Interrogations, and Military Commissions Symposium at the Washburn University School of Law, November 13, 2008: 310.
[32] "Crisis in the Persian Gulf Region: U.S. Policy Options and Implications," hearings before the Senate Committee on Armed Services, 101st Cong., 2d Sess, 1990: 701-702.
[33] United Nations Security Council Resolution 678, November 29, 1990. Reprinted in part in Foreign Relations and National Security Law: 657-658.
[34] Public Papers of the Presidents, 1991, I: 20.
[35] Cited by Fisher, Presidential War Power: 172.
[36] In contrast, the five other Presidents who have served under the War Powers Resolution of 1973 filed 61 reports.
[37] Public Papers of the Presidents, 1996, II: 1469.
[38] Fisher, Presidential War Powers: 192.
[39] Public Papers of the President, 1993, I: 1455.
[40] Ibid: 1768.
[41] The latter term is Fisher's characterization of a compromise bill passed by the Senate in response to Clinton's dispatch of 20,000 troops to Bosnia in a peacekeeping mission. Fisher, Presidential War Power: 190 and 183-192 for Bosnia.
[42] Statement of Representative James B. Longley Jr. (R-Maine) among the twelve Republicans who ultimately voted against a measure designed to restrict Clinton's capacity to introduce American troops into Bosnia. Quoted by Fisher, Presidential War Power: 188.

[43] Public Papers of the Presidents, 1998, II: 1765.

[44] Fisher, Presidential War Power: 198.

[45] See Fisher's discussion of this critical point at ibid: 199.

[46] Though Bush filed more than 35 reports to Congress under the War Powers Resolution. This total was exceeded only by Bill Clinton who filed 60 or almost half of all the reports filed under the War Powers Resolution. See Grimmett, in Foreign Relations and National Security Law: 717-719.

[47] "Authorization for Use of Military Force Against Perpetrators of 9/11," S.J. Res. 23, Pub. L. No. 107-40, 115 Stat. 224 (Sept. 18, 2001) and "Authorization for Use of Military Force against Iraq Resolution of 2002," H.J. Res. 114, Pub. L. No. 107-243, 116 Stat. 1498 (Oct. 16, 2002). Both excerpted in Foreign Relations and National Security Law: 671-672 and 680-684 respectively.

[48] 37 Weekly Compilation of Presidential Documents: 1447 and 1448.

[49] 38 Weekly Compilation of Presidential Documents: 1778 .

[50] Fisher: 210.

[51] Report of the Congressional Committees Investigating the Iran-Contra Affair with Supplemental, Minority, and Additional Views. S. Rpt. No. 100-216 and H. Rpt. No. 100-433, 100th Cong., 1st Sess., November 17, 1987. Michael Malbin drafted the Minority Report, but Cheney, as the ranking minority member of the Committee, was the intellectual source of the arguments therein. See Paul Starobin, "Imperial Presidency Has Long History," National Journal (February 22, 2006) at http://www.govexec.com/story_page_pf.cfm?articleid=33442.

[52] Crucial elements of the Cheney operation included Louis "Scooter" Libby a long time Cheney associate and David Addington, who had served as a staffer for the Minority at the time of the Iran-Contra congressional hearings. Addington served as Cheney's Legal Counsel and Chief of Staff during the second term and was the pivotal operative in a network of "presidentialists" including John C. Yoo, Deputy Assistant Attorney General in the Office of Legal Council in the Justice Department, between 2001 and 2003, Jay S. Bybee, director of the OLC during the first Bush Administration (and now a federal appellate court judge), and Steven G. Bradbury, the director during the second Bush Administration. The legal opinions crafted in the OLC by this group, apparently under Addington's oversight, Cheney and Bush's "New Paradigm" of Presidential power. See Jane Mayer, "The Hidden Power: The legal mind behind the White House's war on terror, The New Yorker (July 3, 2006), www.newyorker.com/archive/2006/07/03/060703fa_fact1.

[53] All quotes in the next two paragraphs are from John C. Yoo, ""The President's Constitutional Authority to Conduct Military Operations Against Terrorists and Nations Supporting Them," Memorandum of Opinion for the Deputy Counsel to the President, September 15, 2001; emphasis added.

[54] The following OCL memoranda are relevant: John C. Yoo, "Constitutionality of Amending Foreign Intelligence Surveillance Act to Change the "Purpose" Standard for Searches," OCL, September 25, 2001; John C. Yoo and Robert J. Delahunty, "Authority for Use of Miliatary Force to Combat Terrorist Activities Within the United States, OCL, October 23, 2001; John C. Yoo and Delahunty, "Authority of the President to Suspend Certain Provisions of the ABM Treaty," OLC, November 15, 2001; Yoo, "The President's power as Commander in Chief to Transfer Captured

Terrorists to the Control and Custody of Foreign Nations," OLC, March 13, 2002; Patirck Philbin, "Swift Justice Act," OLC, April 8, 2002; Jay S. Bybee, "Determination of Enemy Belligerency and Military Detention," OLC, June 8, 2002; Memorandum to Daniel J. Bryant, Assistant Attorney General, Office of Legal Affairs, Applicability of 18 U.S.C. 4001(a) to Military Detention of United States Citizens," OLC, June 27, 2002.

[55] OLC Memorandum for John Rizzo, Acting General Counsel of the Central Intelligence Agency, "Interrogation of al Qaeda Operative [Abu Zubaydah], OLC, August 1, 2002; Memorandum for John A. Rizzo, Senior Deputy General Counsel, Central Intelligence Agency, Application of 18 U.S.C. 2340-2340A to the Combined Use of Certain Techniques in the Interrogation of High Value al Qaeda Detainees," OLC, May 10, 2005; Memorandum for John A. Rizzo, Senior Deputy General Counsel, Central Intelligence Agency, "Application of 18 U.S.C. 2340-2340A to the Combined Use of Certain Techniques in the Interrogation of a High Value al Qaeda Detainee," OLC, May 10, 2005; and Memorandum for John A. Rizzo, Senior Deputy General Counsel, Central Intelligence Agency, "Application of United States Obligations Against Torture to Certain Techniques that May Be Used in the Interrogation of High Value al Qaeda Detainees," OLC, May 30, 2005.

[56] See Yoo and Delahunty, Re: Authority for the Use of Military Force to Combat Terrorist Activities Within the United States," Department of Justice, Office of Legal Counsel, October 23, 2001: 14, 24-25 and Neil A. Lewis, "Memos Reveal the Scope of Power Bush Sought in Fighting Terror," The New York Times, March 3, 2009 at www.nytimes.com/2009/0303legal.html.

[57] Jackson's concurring opinion in Youngstown Sheet and Tube Co. v. Sawyer in Foreign Relations and National Security Law,

[58] 126 S.Ct. 2749-2825, 165 L.Ed.2d 723 (2006).

[59] Harold Hongju Koh, "Setting the World Right," 115 Yale L.J., 2350-2367 (2006) excerpted in Foreign Relations and National Security Law: 93-97; quotation is at 94.

[60] Ibid: 96. Legal challenges to the constitutionality of the MCA are now working their way through the judicial system.

[61] Thomas Frank, "U.S. Presidential Power in 'Wartime'," 5 International Journal of Constitutional Law, 7 (2007) quoted in Koh, "Setting the World Right," Foreign Relations and National Security Law: 98.

[62] Steven A. Bradbury, Principal Deputy Assistant Attorney General, "Memorandum for the Files, Re: October 23, 2001 OLC Opinion Addressing the Domestic Use of Military Force to Combat Terrorist Activities," October 6, 2008 and Bradbury, "Memorandum for the Files Re: Status of Certain OLC Opinions Issued in the Aftermath of the Terrorist Attacks of September 11, 2001, "January 15, 2009.

[63] James Baker quoted in Peter Baker, "Obama to Hear Panel on Changes to War Powers Act." For another of Louis Fisher's critiques – to which this summary is indebted – see his, "*The Law:* The Baker-Christopher War Powers Commission," Presidential Studies Quarterly, 39 (March 2009): 128-140.

[64] WCR: 19.

[65] Ibid.

[66] Ibid: 17.

[67] Ibid: 25.

[68] Ibid: 23.
[69] Peter Baker, "Obama to Hear Panel on Changes to War Powers Act," The New York Times, December 12, 2008. http://www.nytimes.com/2008/12/12us/politics/11web-baker.html?
[70] WCR: 45-46. The Chairmanship and Vice Chairmanship of the committee would alternate between the Speaker of the House and the Majority Leader of the Senate.
[71] Ibid: 45, Section 3(A). Definitions.
[72] Ibid: Section 3(B).
[73] Repelling imminent attacks and rescues have, been understood as the only exceptions to a priori Congressional authorization of the use of force since the drafting of the Constitution.
[74] Fisher, "The Baker-Christopher War Powers Commission": 137.
[75] Ibid: 137-138.
[76] Ibid: Section 5(C): 48.
[77] Fisher, "The Baker-Christopher War Powers Commission": 139.
[78] Ibid.
[79] Koh, "Setting the World Right," in Foreign Relations and National Security Law": 95.
[80] Ibid: 97.
[81] "U.S. Commitments to Foreign Powers," Hearings before the Senate Foreign Relations Committee, 90th Congress, 1st Sess. 3 (1967). Language from S. Rept. No. 129, 91st Cong., 1st Sess. 8 (1969): 23. Emphasis in the original.
[82] Jackson in *Youngstown*, excerpted in Foreign Relations and National Security Law: 28.
[83] "Obama to Hear Panel on Changes to War Powers Act."
[84] http://www.barackobama.com/issues/foreign_policy/index.php. See also Charlie Savage, "Barack Obama's Q and A," The Boston Globe, December 20, 2007, http://www.boston.com/news /politics/2008/specials/Candidate QA/Obama QA. Transcript.

In: Presidents and War
Editors: A. Eksterowicz and G. Hastedt, pp. 295-298
ISBN 978-1-61668-917-9


*Chapter 17*

# Speech on the Implementation of the GI Bill Extending Educational Benefits to Veterans

***Barack Obama***

PRESIDENT OBAMA:
Hello. Thank you. Thank you. Thank you.

(APPLAUSE)

Please have a seat. Please have a seat.
Good morning, everybody.

AUDIENCE: Good morning.

OBAMA: It is wonderful to see all of you and wonderful to have one of the best partners that anybody could have in elected office, our vice president, Joe Biden. Thrilled to have him here.

(APPLAUSE)

I want to thank Staff Sergeant Miller (ph) for the gracious introduction. I want to thank President Merten for his hospitality.

There are a couple of people here who deserve all the credit, because they got a very tough bill done. And part of the reason they were able to get it done was just because of their extraordinary personal credibility. These are -- one is new to the Senate and one had been there a while, and yet together they formed an incredibly formidable team. They're both class acts.

Please give a big round of applause to Virginia's own John Warner and Jim Webb.

(APPLAUSE)

I know that we've got a number of member of Congress who are here, and I want to thank them all for their outstanding work.

I want to point out that Senator Mark Warner could not be here, but we appreciate him.

We've got the secretary of veterans affairs, a hero in his own right, General Eric Shinseki. And I want everybody to please acknowledge him.

(APPLAUSE)

And of the original bill sponsors who could not be here today, we've got Senator Chuck Hagel, Senator Frank Lautenberg, Representative Harry Mitchell, Representative Bobby Scott, Representative Ginny Brown-Waite and Representative Peter King. All of them worked hard, along with the delegation that is present.

OBAMA: And so, we are very grateful to all of them.

I want to join all of today's speakers in thanking those of you who worked so hard to make this occasion possible. But above all, I want to pay tribute to the veterans who are now advancing their dreams by pursuing an education.

Obviously, I'm honored to be here and to renew our commitment to ensure that the men and women who wear the uniform of the United States of America get the opportunities that they have earned.

I was a proud cosponsor of the post-9/11 G.I. Bill as senator. I'm committed to working with Secretary Shinseki to see that it is successfully implemented as president.

And we do this not just to meet our moral obligation to those who've sacrificed greatly on our behalf and on behalf of the country. We do it because these men and women must now be prepared to lead our nation in the peaceful pursuit of economic leadership in the 21st century.

This generation of servicemen and -women has already earned a place of honor in American history. Each of them signed up to serve, many after they knew that they would be sent into harm's way.

Over the last eight years, they have endured tour after tour of duty in dangerous and distant places. They've experienced grueling combat, from the streets of Fallujah to the harsh terrain of Helmand province.

They've adapted to complex insurgencies, protected local populations and trained foreign security forces.

So by any measure, they are the authors of one of the most extraordinary chapters of military service in the history of our nation. And I don't make that statement lightly, for we know that anyone who puts on the uniform joins an unbroken line of selfless patriots that stretches back to Lexington and Concord.

The freedom and prosperity that we enjoy would not exist without the service of generations of Americans who were willing to bear the heaviest and most dangerous burden.

OBAMA: But we also know this: The contributions that our servicemen and -women can make to this nation do not end when they take off that uniform.

We owe a debt to all who serve. And when we repay that debt to those bravest Americans among us, then we are investing in our future -- not just their future, but also the future of our own country.

Now, this was the lesson that America was sometimes too slow to learn. After the Civil War and World War I, we saw far too many veterans who were denied the chance to live their dreams; men who were unable to find in peace the hope that they had fought for in war.

And FDR knew this. In 1943, before the beaches of Normandy were stormed and the treacherous terrain of Iwo Jima was taken, he told the nation that the veterans of World War II would be treated differently.

He said that they must not be demobilized, and I quote, "to a place on a bread line" -- "demobilized to a place on a bread line or on a corner selling apples."

"Instead," Roosevelt said, "the American people will insist on fulfilling this American obligation to the men and women in the armed forces who are winning this war for us."

That is precisely what the American people did. The G.I. Bill was approved just weeks after D-Day, and carried with it a simple promise to all who had served: You pick the school, we'll help pick up the bill.

And what followed was not simply an opportunity for our veterans. It was a transformation for our country. By 1947, half of all Americans enrolled in college were veterans.

OBAMA: Ultimately, this would lead to three presidents, three Supreme Court justices, 14 Nobel Prize winners and two dozen Pulitzer Prize winners.

But, more importantly, it produced hundreds of thousands of scientists and engineers, doctors and nurses, the backbone of the largest middle class in history.

All told, nearly 8 million Americans were educated under the original G.I. Bill, including my grandfather.

No number can sum up this sea change in our society.

Reginald Wilson, a fighter pilot from Detroit, said, "I didn't know anyone who went to college. I never would have gone to college had it not been for the G.I. Bill."

H.G. Jones, a Navy man from North Carolina, said, "What happened in my rural Caswell County community happened all over the country. Going to college was no longer a novelty."

Indeed, one of the men who went to college on the G.I. Bill, as I mentioned, was my grandfather. And I would not be standing here today if that opportunity had not led him west in search of opportunity.

So we owe the same obligations to this generation of service men and women as was afforded that previous generation. That is the promise of the post-1911 (sic) G.I. Bill. It's driven by the same simple logic that drove the first G.I. Bill: You pick the school; we'll help pick up the bill.

And looking out at the audience today, I'm proud to see so many veterans who will be able to pursue their education with this new support from the American people.

And this is even more important than it was in 1944. The first G.I. Bill helped build a post-war economy that has been transformed by revolutions in communication and technology. And that's why the post- 1911 -- 9/11 G.I. Bill must give today's veterans the skills and training they need to fill the jobs of tomorrow.

Education is the currency that can purchase success in the 21st century. And this is the opportunity that our troops have earned.

I'm also proud that all who have borne the burden of service these last several years will have access to this opportunity.

OBAMA: We are including reservists and National Guard members because they have carried out unprecedented deployments in Afghanistan and Iraq. We are including the military families who have sacrificed so much by allowing the transfer of unused benefits to family members. And we are including those who pay the ultimate price by making this benefit available to the children of those who lost their life in service to their country.

This is not simply a debt that we are repaying to the remarkable men and women who have served. It is an investment in our own country. The first G.I. Bill paid for itself many times over through the increased revenue that came from a generation of men and women who received the skills and education that they needed to create their own wealth.

The veterans who are here today, like the young post-9/11 veterans around the country, can lead the way to a lasting economic recovery and become the glue that holds our communities together. They too can become the backbone of a growing American middle class.

And even as we help our veterans learn the skills they need to succeed, I know that all of us can learn something from the men and women who serve our country.

We've lived through an age when many people and institutions acted irresponsibly, when service often took a backseat to short-term profits, when hard choices were put aside for somebody else, for some other time. It is a time when easy distractions became the norm and the trivial has been taken too seriously.

The men and women who have served since 9/11 tell us a different story. While so many were reaching for the quick buck, they were heading out on patrol. While our discourse often produced more heat than light, especially here in Washington, they have put their very lives on the line for America. They've have borne the responsibility of war.

And now, with this policy, we are making it clear that the United States of America must reward responsibility and not irresponsibility. Now, with this policy, we are letting those who have borne the heaviest burden lead us in to the 21st century.

And so today we honor the service of an extraordinary generation and look to an America that they will help build tomorrow. With the post-9/11 G.I. Bill, we can give our veterans the chance to live their dreams, and we can help unleash their talents and tap their creativity, and be guided by their sense of responsibility to their fellow citizens and to this country that we all love so much.

May God bless our troops and our veterans, and may God bless the United States of America.

Thank you very much, everybody.

(APPLAUSE)

END

# About the Contributors

*Nicole L. Anslover* earned her PhD from the University of Kansas and is currently Assistant Professor of History at Indiana University Northwest, where she teaches classes on Cold War America. She is working on a book addressing the compulsion for continuity from Presidents Truman to Johnson.

*Jeff Bloodworth* is an assistant professor of history at Gannon University. In addition to articles in the *Pacific Northwest Quarterly* and *Wisconsin Magazine of History*, he is working on a history of American liberalism during the 1970s.

*Anthony J. Eksterowicz* is Professor of Political Science at James Madison University where he teaches courses on the Presidency, Congress, American Government, First Ladies, Health Care and Political Reform. He has published over forty articles and five books on various subjects such as, Foreign Policy and the Presidency, First Ladies, Politics and Pain Care, Political Parties, Stem Cell Research, the Presidential Pardoning Power and Citizen Participation. His two latest books are; *The President and Foreign Policy: Chief Architect or General Contractor*, NOVA Press 2005 and *The Presidential Companion: Readings on First Ladies*, Second Edition, University of South Carolina Press, 2006.

*Glenn Hastedt* is Professor and chair of the Justice Studies Department at James Madison University. His areas of specialization are United States foreign policy and strategic intelligence with an emphasis on questions of intelligence failure and the politics of intelligence. His recent publications *include American Foreign Policy: Past, Present, Future*, 7the d (Pearson, 2008), *American Foreign Policy 09/10* (McGraw Hill, 2008) and articles on intelligence in *Intelligence and National Security*.

*Bernd Kaussler* received his PhD from the School of International Relations at the University of St Andrews in Scotland and is currently Assistant Professor of Political science at James Madison University where he teaches U.S. Foreign Policy, Middle East Security and Political Islam. His research interests include Iranian and US foreign policies, political violence and human rights in Iran as well as Persian Gulf security. ‘

*Tom Lansford* is the Academic Dean of the Gulf Coast, and a Professor of Political Science, at the University of Southern Mississippi. Dr. Lansford is a member of the governing board of the National Social Science Association, an associate editor for the journal *White House Studies*. He has published articles in journals such as *Defense Analysis*, *The Journal of Conflict Studies*, *European Security*, *International Studies*, *Security Dialogue* and *Strategic Studies*. Dr. Lansford is the author, coauthor, editor or coeditor of 31 books. His books include, most recently, *All for One: NATO, Terrorism and the United States* (2002), A *Bitter*

*Harvest: U.S. Foreign Policy and Afghanistan* (2003), *Strategic Preemption: US Foreign Policy and the Second War in Iraq* (2004), *To Protect and Defend: US Homeland Security Policy* (2006) and the *Historical Dictionary of U.S. Diplomacy Since the Cold War* (2007). His more recent edited collections include: *America's War on Terror* (2003), *George W. Bush: A Political and Ethical Assessment at Midterm* (2004), *Transatlantic Security Dilemmas: Old Europe, New Europe and the US* (2005), and *Judging Bush* (2009). Dr. Lansford is the author of more than one hundred essays, book chapters, and reviews.

*David Leary* is a California native who received his A.B. from Stanford University and Ph.D. from the University of Southern California. He taught history at Pasadena City College for a number of years and is now professor emeritus. Remaining active in scholarship and given to travel, he often visits places of historical significance.

*Lawrence J. McAndrews* is Professor of History at St. Norbert College in DePere, WI. He is the author of *Broken Ground: John F. Kennedy and the Politics of Education* and *The Era of Education: The President and the Schools, 1965-2001.*

*James K. Oliver* is Emma S. Morris Professor Emeritus at the University of Delaware where he completed 35 years of service in 2003. He is the recipient of the University's Excellence in teaching, Excellence in Graduate Advisement, and the College of Arts and science Distinguished Lifetime Service Award. He has published five books and more than twenty papers on American foreign policy and defense policy, international organization and governance, and international relations theory.

*George H. Quester*, Ph.D. was the John M. Olin Professor at the U.S. Naval Academy from 1991-1993 and is currently Professor of Government at the University of Maryland at College Park. His publications include *American Foreign Policy: The Lost Consensus* and *Nuclear Monopoly.*

*John Schuessler* is an Assistant Professor of Strategy and International Security at the Air War College. He received his PhD in 2007 from the Department of Political Science at the University of Chicago, specializing in international relations. Before coming to the Air War College, he was a Lecturer and Post-Doctoral Fellow with the Committee on International Relations, also at the University of Chicago, as well as a Research Fellow with the International Security Program at the Belfer Center for Science and International Affairs at Harvard University. He thanks the Belfer Center for their support, as well as the Eisenhower Institute. He also thanks Robert McMahon and Sebastian Rosato for helpful comments on previous drafts. He can be contacted at john.schuessler@maxwell.af.mil.

*Martin S. Sheffer*, A.B. and A.A.M., Hunter College, CUNY, Ph.D., New School for Social Research, is a senior professor (retired) from Old Dominion University and Tuskegee University. He has taught part time with the Junior Statesman Program at George University and has published on the presidency.

*Ryan Staude* is a Ph.D candidate at the University at Albany, SUNY. His dissertation explores George Washington's political philosophy and its effect on nationalism and national identity in the 1790s. Additionally, he is active in film studies and has presented several papers examining film's relationship to history, and how filmmakers treat the past cinematically. He is currently finishing his dissertation, and working on a study analyzing the depiction of colonial and Revolutionary America on film.

*Brent A. Strathman* is a Visiting Assistant Professor of Government at Dartmouth College, and the Editorial Assistant for Security Studies.

Dr. *Craig L. Symonds* is Professor Emeritus at the United States Naval Academy from which he retired in 2005. The first person ever to win both the Naval Academy's "Excellence in Teaching" award (1988) and its "Excellence in Research" award (1998), he also served as History Department chair from 1988 to 1992, and received the Department of the Navy's Superior Civilian Service medal three times. He served as Professor of Strategy at the U.S. Naval War College in Newport, Rhode Island (1971-74) and at the Britannia Royal Naval College in Dartmouth, England (1994-95).

Symonds is the author or editor of twenty-three books, including prize-winning biographies of *Joseph E. Johnston* (1992), *Patrick Cleburne* (1997), and *Franklin Buchanan* (1999), as well as *The American Heritage History of the Battle of Gettysburg* (2001). *Decision at Sea: Five Naval Battles that Shaped American History* (2005), won the Theodore and Franklin D. Roosevelt Prize for Naval History. His 2008 book, *Lincoln and His Admirals: Abraham Lincoln, the U.S. Navy, and the Civil War*, won the Barondess Prize, the Laney Prize, the Lyman Prize, and the Lincoln Prize for 2009. He also won the Nevins-Freeman Prize in 2009.

He and his wife Marylou live in Annapolis, Maryland. They have one son and one grandson.

*Joseph R. Thysell*, Jr. is Associate Professor of Government at Nicholls State University. He is the author of many articles on judicial issues.

*Frank J. Williams* is a retired Chief Justice of the Supreme Court of Rhode Island and is the founding chair of The Lincoln Forum - an organization devoted to the study of Abraham Lincoln and the Civil War. In 2000, he was appointed to the U.S. Abraham Lincoln Bicentennial Commission created by the Congress to plan events to commemorate the 200th birthday of Abraham Lincoln in 1909. His essay is a revised version of the paper he delivered at Lincoln Memorial University on April 27, 2001.

# INDEX

## D

## E

## F



## G



## H

## I



## J

## N

## Q



## R

## S